THE CATHOLIC CRUSADE AGAINST THE MOVIES, 1940–1975

For more than three decades the Catholic church, through its Legion of Decency, had a power that modern politicians can only dream about: the power to control the content of Hollywood films. From the mid-1930s to the late 1960s the Catholic Legion served as a moral guardian for the American public. Hollywood studios submitted their films to the Legion for a rating, which varied from general approval for all age groups to outright condemnation – the mere threat of which could spur Hollywood executives to remove offending material.

The Catholic Crusade against the Movies, 1940–1975, details how a religious organization got control of Hollywood and how films like *The Outlaw, Duel in the Sun, A Streetcar Named Desire, Lolita*, and *Tea and Sympathy* were altered by the Legion to make them morally acceptable. Documenting the inner workings of the Legion, this book also examines how the changes in the movie industry, the Catholic church, and American society at large in the post–World War II era eventually conspired against that institution's power and led to its demise.

Gregory D. Black is Professor of Communication Studies at the University of Missouri, Kansas City. He is the author of *Hollywood Censored: Morality Codes, Catholics, and the Movies* and coauthor of *Hollywood Goes to War: How Politics, Profits, and Propaganda Shaped World War II Movies.*

To
Robert Dale Black
for a lifetime of support, encouragement, and friendship

CONTENTS

ILLUSTRATIONS

The following photographs appear on unfolioed pages in the middle of the book:

ACKNOWLEDGMENTS

I am extremely grateful for all the help and support I have received in writing this book. It would not have been possible without the full cooperation of the Catholic church, which has graciously made its various archives open to me. I wish to also thank the University of Missouri Research Board for its generous support of my research, and the National Endowment of the Humanities for a Fellowship that gave me the opportunity to write the manuscript.

Historians could not function without the help of archivists, who preserve the written records from which we interpret the past. I am especially indebted to the following people for all their help:

Sam Gill and the staff at the Margaret Herrick Library of the Academy of Motion Picture Arts and Sciences in Beverly Hills, California, for help with the Production Code Administration files;

Msgr. Francis J. Weber of the Archives of the Archdiocese of Los Angeles;

Mr. Henry Herx, Director of the Office of Film and Broadcast of the Archdiocese of New York, who has control of the Legion of Decency archives and who generously allowed me to interrupt his working environment;

Nicholas B. Scheetz, Manuscripts Librarian of Georgetown University;

Charles Bell, Archivist at the Harry Ransom Humanities Research Center at the University of Texas at Austin;

James D'Arc of the Harold B. Lee Library at Brigham Young University;

Mary Corliss and Terry Geesken of the Museum of Modern Art; and the staff at the Archives of Catholic University.

My colleagues at the University of Missouri–Kansas City gave generously of their time. I thank Thomas Poe for his reading of the manuscript, and especially Gaylord Marr for his considerable contributions as historian, editor, and friend.

My editor at Cambridge, Beatrice Rehl, has been extremely supportive during our working relationship over the past several years. I am grateful to her and to my production editor, Michael Gnat, whose ability to spot inconsistency is amazing.

Finally, my wife, Carol, herself an excellent editor, saved me from countless messy sentences. I thank her for her support and for watching all those old movies with me.

THE CATHOLIC CRUSADE AGAINST THE MOVIES, 1940–1975

INTRODUCTION

For more than three decades, from 1934 to the late 1960s, the Catholic church, through its Legion of Decency, had the power that modern Christian conservatives like Pat Robinson, Jerry Falwell, and Ralph Reed, political conservatives like William Bennett and Bob Dole, media personalities like Rush Limbaugh, and countless politicians of all stripes can only dream about – the power to control the content of Hollywood films. The Catholic church's Legion of Decency could, and did, dictate to Hollywood producers the amount of sex and violence that was allowable on the screen. The producers meekly removed any scene that offended the church.

For more than three decades the Legion served as moral guardian for the American public. The Catholic church was able to force Hollywood to submit every film it produced to a small group of Legion reviewers in New York before its release. The Legion then issued a rating for the film, which could vary from approval for all age groups to the most feared rating, "C" (condemned) – forbidden viewing for all Catholics.

Hollywood producers could avoid a condemned rating by entering into negotiation with the Legion. If they were willing to remove the offending material, the Legion would reclassify the film, which would allow Catholics to attend. This scenario was repeated countless times between 1934 and the end of the censorship system in the late 1960s. *Duel in the Sun, Forever Amber, A Streetcar Named Desire, Lolita, Baby Doll, Tea and Sympathy,* and *Suddenly Last Summer* represent just a few examples of films discussed in this book that were heavily censored by the Legion before the public was allowed to see them.

The Catholic church, the Legion of Decency, and many modern advocates of tighter control of the mass media have always maintained that the Legion did not censor movies but only classified them. A Catholic publication, *Ave Maria,* editorialized that familiar stance in 1949. When critics complained of Legion censorship the magazine told readers that "the Legion of Decency is not a censorship body. It simply grades pictures on moral values. It advises but does not command."[1] Russell Whelan, writing in the

American Mercury, repeated that theme when he wrote that "the Legion technically is a pressure group, and not a censor. . . . It applies mundane pressure on Hollywood to prevent certain subjects and modes of treatment from reaching the screen."[2] Nothing could be further from the truth than the myth that the Legion did not censor movies.

It did much more than just rate films for Catholic audiences. As this book shows, the Legion demanded that offending films be altered to Catholic tastes before the Legion would bless them. They further demanded that Hollywood not exhibit any print of the film anywhere in the world other than that approved by the Catholic Legion of Decency. In addition to this type of censorship, the Legion called for a nationwide boycott of all condemned films and demanded that all Catholics stay away from any theater that dared exhibit a condemned film for six months to a year. It is important to note that the films discussed in this book were not obscene or pornographic in any sense. They were the products of the Hollywood studio system and most had been approved by the Hollywood Production Code Administration (PCA) and/or the state and municipal censorship boards that functioned during this era.

A Legion condemnation also brought a fury of attacks against the offending film, and the theaters that played it, from the Catholic press and pulpits. The mere threat that the more than twenty million Catholics would join in unison against a single film made the Hollywood executives quake with fear.

The process, however, did not start with a public condemnation. Most of the time when the Legion first threatened to condemn a film they did so privately. They did not officially review scripts – that was the job of the PCA; rather, the Legion reviewed the final print of the film when it was sent to New York for duplication and then distribution to the nation's theaters. This reviewing process included an opportunity to change the film. If the Legion did not like what it saw, word was sent to the producing studio that negotiations were in order. A letter or a telephone conservation would detail Legion objections, and the process of censorship would begin. If the offending film was altered to suit Catholic tastes, the condemned rating would be changed to a classification that would not ban Catholics from attending. Here the Legion moved away from its role of moral judge to that of censors: Legion priests negotiated with studios to eliminate certain scenes, reshoot or recut others, change dialogue, or add a prologue or epilogue to a film to make it acceptable to the Catholic church. This action turned the Legion into a national board of censorship.

The Legion often worked hand in hand with the industry's censorship board, the Production Code Administration, to keep the movies from exploring social, political, and economic issues that it believed were either immoral or a danger to the Catholic church. For twenty years, from 1934 until the retirement of PCA director Joseph I. Breen, the PCA and the Legion were linked so closely that it is next to impossible to separate them. The PCA sent the Legion scripts and asked for an "unofficial" opinion on the overall theme or a particular scene. That opinion was often sent back to the studio with a warning that it needed to be altered to avoid Legion wrath. The files of both organizations, which are open without restrictions to scholars, are full of correspondence from representatives of each agency; they were in constant contact with each other.

This is not to say that they always agreed on what was immoral – they did not; but the working relationship was extremely close. The Legion was, however, also quite capable of independent action. It was not adverse to slapping Breen's hands in the belief that he had allowed some moral infraction to slip into a movie. After Breen's retirement in 1954, the relationship between the Legion and the PCA under the directorship of Geoffrey Shurlock was not as close as it had once been, but neither was it an adversarial relationship.

How this religious organization got this power, used it, and finally lost it is the subject of this book. *The Catholic Crusade against the Movies* is a continuation of my work on censorship and film. In 1994 my book *Hollywood Censored* concentrated on the decade of the 1930s, when this dual system of censorship was established. After a brief recap of these events in Chapter 1, the present book picks up the story where *Hollywood Censored* left off and covers roughly the period 1940–75, when the full impact of the movie ratings system was clearly established.

A CATHOLIC COUP AGAINST HOLLYWOOD

My eyes nearly popped out when I read it. This was the very thing
I had been looking for.
– Will Hays after reading Father Daniel Lord's movie code.

Late in 1995, the Pontifical Council for Social Communication identified
forty-five films produced in the United States, Europe, and Asia that, it said,
possessed special artistic or religious merit. The list was prepared as part of
the Vatican's contribution to the hundredth anniversary of the cinema. For
the average moviegoer there were many recognizable films: The Vatican
council cited, among others, Fred Zinnemann's *A Man for All Seasons,*
William Wyler's *Ben Hur,* Gabriel Axel's *Babette's Feast,* Frank Capra's *It's
a Wonderful Life,* Louis Malle's *Au Revoir les Enfants,* Victor Fleming's *The
Wizard of Oz,* and Steven Spielberg's *Schindler's List.* The purpose of the
council's list, said Henry Herx, director of the United States Catholic Conference Office for Film and Broadcasting, was to recognize films that all critics "would agree were major works of international significance."[1]

Nevertheless, those familiar with the history of the relationship between
the movie industry and the Catholic church in America know that only recently has the church taken such an enlightened view of the movies. For example, the council cited *Open City,* Roberto Rossellini's classic account of
Rome under Fascist rule, under the values category. Upon the film's release
fifty years earlier, however, the Catholic Legion of Decency had issued *Open
City* a "B" classification (objectionable in part), objecting to its "suggestive"
costumes and its portraying narcotics use; such a classification was interpreted by many priests and bishops as meaning a film was off limits for all
Catholics. Two other films that won a place on the select list, Federico Fellini's *La Strada* and Vittorio De Sica's *The Bicycle Thief,* had also been branded by the Catholic Legion of Decency in the late 1940s and mid-1950s as
"morally objectionable in part for all."

The Pontifical Council's evaluation of films represents a truly remarkable
change of attitude by the Catholic church toward the movies. It is especially

remarkable when compared to the stance taken by the church from the early 1930s until the late 1960s. During that era Catholic prelates and priests played a dominant role in determining what was seen on the screen. A Catholic priest, Father Daniel Lord, wrote the Production Code that defined what was acceptable movie content for Hollywood. From 1934 until the early 1950s a staunch lay Catholic, Joseph I. Breen, rigorously enforced Lord's code at the Production Code Administration (PCA), often over the protests of studio executives, producers, directors, and screenwriters.

The PCA, however, represented only the first step in the process of purification that all Hollywood films underwent during the Legion's reign. After receiving a Production Code seal of approval, films were shipped to New York for duplication and distribution; but before that process could begin each film was submitted to the Catholic Legion of Decency for a final review. The PCA and the Legion worked closely together and often combined forces to prevent studios from offending Catholic sensibilities, but the Legion always stood ready to condemn any film it believed immoral. A Legion condemnation shook Hollywood to its core because Catholics, some twenty million strong, were theoretically forbidden, under the penalty of mortal sin, to attend the condemned film. Any theater that exhibited a condemned film was targeted for boycott by Catholic organizations such as the Knights of Columbus. The industry believed that the combination of negative publicity and Catholic boycott would make it impossible for any Legion-condemned film to make a profit. Rather than risk a loss of income or challenge the Legion's authority to censor their product, producers bowed to the pressure and cut the offending material from all prints exhibited worldwide. In reality, then, the Legion's view of sex and politics reached an international market.

The story of the Legion is inextricably entwined with the history of Hollywood filmmaking. The Legion had a direct, overt effect on the content of Hollywood films; it also had a "chilling" effect on studio executives, producers, directors, and writers, who realized that certain subjects were either banned from the screen or could be presented only within a certain framework because of Catholic opposition. The history of the relationship between the Legion and Hollywood, of a religious organization's censorship of a mass medium, is the subject of this book. It entailed a cultural war between the Legion, which believed it spoke for the moral values of the American public, and the the movie industry, which fought – often rather meekly – for freedom of the screen.

From the mid-1930s until Otto Preminger's release of *The Moon Is Blue* in 1953, no Hollywood studio seriously challenged the right of the priests to censor their films. From 1953 until the establishment of the current ratings system, only a handful of independent producers, foreign and domestic, refused to submit their films to Legion censors.

It would be wrong, however, to imply that only the Catholic church wanted movies censored. Moral guardians of all religious and political stripes had long feared that movies, more than any other form of communication or entertainment, had the ability to change radically the moral and political beliefs of their audience. The problem was that movies graphically visualized topics of sex and politics that many people did not want discussed in public. From the very beginning, filmmakers had turned to popular literature, drama, and contemporary issues for story lines. Historians Kevin Brownlow, Kay Sloan, and Janet Staiger have shown that the content of early silent films was contemporary, wide-ranging, and frank. Brownlow chronicled a silent cinema that revealed "the corruption of city politics, the scandal of white slave rackets, the exploitation of immigrants" and had gangsters, pimps, loan sharks, and drug addicts sharing the screen with Mary Pickford.[2] Sloan noted that "the cinema championed the cause of labor, lobbied against political 'bosses,' and often gave dignity to the struggles of the urban poor."[3] Staiger's analysis revealed a frank discussion of sexuality and desire in pre–World War I cinema.[4] All three historians found that silent films not only upheld traditional standards but debunked and challenged them as well.

The movies were born during the height of the Progressive reform movement in the United States. Progressive reformers exposed corruption in government and shocked the American public with lurid exposés about child labor, urban living conditions, prostitution, and alcoholism. As remedies they sponsored legislation to regulate the use of child labor, used the licensing power of the state to enforce safety and sanitary codes, passed compulsory education laws, regulated the production of consumer products with "pure food and drug" acts, and reformed the electoral process on the local, state, and federal levels.

The movies, of course, were an especially troublesome recreation form for Progressive reformers. For one thing, the environment was all wrong: Rather than staying in the open, with clean air and exercise, children were flocking to dirty, dingy movie theaters. Jane Addams, the consummate reformer whose Hull House in Chicago brought her international recognition, wrote that the movies were a "veritable house of dreams" for the children of America. Addams was convinced, like so many of her day, that films were a more powerful influence on the minds of children than any other form of communication or education. She believed that what children saw on the screen directly and immediately was transformed into action.[5]

Nonetheless, Addams and the Progressives recognized that, conversely, if films could preach positive values, their potential to educate, to play a positive role in socializing the citizenry, was unlimited. Convinced that movies were "making over the minds of our urban population," Addams thought they ought to advocate good citizenship, the superiority of Anglo–Saxon ideals, and the value of hard work. If films could be turned into morality lessons for workers, they could become an ally in the Progressive fight to protect the masses against the combined forces of poverty, corruption, and injustice.

Ministers, social workers, civic reformers, police, politicians, women's clubs, and civic organizations joined with Progressive reformers in accusing the movies of inciting young boys to crime by glorifying criminals, and of corrupting young women by romanticizing "illicit" love affairs. These "moral guardians" – a loose-knit confederation of reformers who ranged from thoughtful and sometimes perceptive critics like Jane Addams to religious reactionaries like New York's Canon William Shaefe Chase – claimed that movies were changing traditional values, not reflecting them, and demanded that government use its licensing and regulatory powers to censor this new form of entertainment.

Chicago enacted the first film censorship law in 1907 when it required exhibitors to secure a permit from the Superintendent of Police before exhibiting films. In 1909, in response to growing demands for strict censorship, Progressive reformer Charles Sprague Smith formed the New York Board of Motion Picture Censorship. The industry, which was then located in New York City, quickly agreed to submit films for review to this board, which comprised volunteers from a variety of New York civic and social organizations. Despite its name, however, the board was reluctant to censor. The result was that the movies continued to provoke controversy.

The Pennsylvania legislature reacted to continued complaints from moral guardians when, in 1911, it declared the board "ineffective" and passed a law that created its own board to screen films before exhibition in the state. Kansas and Ohio followed suit in 1913. By 1915 – by which time the New York censorship board had been renamed the National Board of Review of Motion Pictures (NBR)[6] – a host of municipal and state censorship boards had been created to impose local community standards of morality on films.

The common denominator was that all the censorship boards were committed to eliminating depictions of changing moral standards, limiting scenes of crime (which they believed to be responsible for an increase in juvenile delinquency), and avoiding as much as possible any screen portrayal of civil strife, labor–management discord, or government corruption and injustice. The screen, these moral guardians held, was not a proper forum for discussing delicate sexual issues or for social or political commentary.[7]

The movie industry disagreed, arguing that movies had the same constitutional protections of free speech that other forms of communication were afforded. The constitutional challenge to film censorship came in Ohio, where the state board was especially restrictive. All films required prior approval by the board, which held that only "such films as are in the judgment and discretion of the board of censors of a moral, educational or amusing and harmless character" could be exhibited in the state.[8] Ohio, as with most of the censorship boards, charged a fee to film distributors to have their films licensed for exhibition.

Perhaps overly confident that the courts would extend to movies the same free-speech rights enjoyed by the press, Harry E. Aitken's Mutual Film Corporation, an interstate film exchange, sought an injunction against the state. The Ohio law, Mutual claimed, restrained trade by forcing Mutual to pay a license fee for each film exhibited. Mutual further maintained the law was a clear violation of the free-speech provisions of the federal and Ohio constitutions. When the District Court denied their injunction, Mutual appealed to the United States Supreme Court. It would prove to be a calamitous decision.[9]

Before the U.S. Supreme Court, William B. Saunders, Mutual's lawyer, argued that movies were no different from other forms of communication protected under the provisions of "free speech"; therefore, movies were "part of the press" and were "increasingly important . . . in the spreading of knowledge and the molding of public opinion upon every kind of political, educational, religious, economic and social question."[10]

The film industry was stunned when the Supreme Court unanimously rejected Saunders's arguments. Justice Joseph McKenna, who wrote the opinion, stated: "We feel the argument is wrong or strained which extends the guaranties of free opinion and speech" to theater, the circus, or movies because "they may be used for evil." McKenna concluded that movies were "a business pure and simple," and not "regarded by the Ohio constitution . . . as part of the press . . . or as organs of public opinion."[11]

The Supreme Court's description of the movies as "evil" was music to the ears of moral guardians everywhere. The judges had recognized that movies communicated ideas more effectively and more seductively than any of the traditional forms of communication or education. Moreover, the ideas they disseminated were potentially "evil."

This logic, strange as it may seem today, was not outside the American judicial mainstream. In upholding the Ohio law, the Court affirmed the power of local communities to protect themselves from outside "evil" through licensing, whether of the physical theater or of the content of the product offered the public.

No matter how ill-informed or unfair the *Mutual* decision might have been, the hard reality was that it was the rule of law for the next four decades. Government censorship of movies prior to their exhibition was legal. The very thing the industry feared most – an explosion of municipal and state censorship laws, each one conflicting with the other – now seemed probable.

The demand for action against the movies accelerated when a series of sensational sex scandals about the private lives of the stars rocked the industry. The most famous centered around rotund comedian Roscoe "Fatty" Arbuckle. Second only to Charlie Chaplin in popularity, Arbuckle was at the peak of his career when an actress, Virginia Rappe, died after a wild Hollywood party hosted by Arbuckle at San Francisco's St. Francis Hotel. The press had a field day with Arbuckle, insinuating that the combination of his weight and perverse sexual appetite had killed the woman. After three sensational trials (the first two were hung juries) Arbuckle was exonerated. The third jury felt so strongly of his innocence that they issued him an apology. Public opinion, however, judged him guilty.

Nor did the scandals stop with Arbuckle. Director William Desmond Taylor was found murdered, and a series of front-page stories revealed a life-style of drugs and sex. America was shocked when matinee idol Wallace Reid died from drug complications. Even America's sweetheart, Mary Pickford, was caught in the web of sexual impropriety: Her divorce from actor Owen Moore and almost immediate marriage to Douglas Fairbanks shocked the nation. The conduct of the stars and the content of the movies confirmed for critics that Hollywood was the modern Babylon.

The embattled movie industry united in January 1922 to create a trade association, the Motion Picture Producers and Distributors of America (MPPDA). Movies, the studio owners believed, needed a squeaky clean image and an astute politician who could organize effective political campaigns to combat censorship bills at the federal and state level. They chose as their new "czar" the Hoosier William Harrison (Will) Hays, Postmaster General in President Warren Harding's cabinet and chairman of the Republican National Committee.

Hays was a perfect choice. His roots were solidly midwestern, his politics conservatively Republican, his religion mainstream Presbyterian, and he was "passionately opposed to state interference with business."[12] During his first eight years as head of the trade association he used his political base in the Republican Party to fend off censorship bills in the states, most notably Massachusetts, and to kill proposals for federal regulation that cropped up on a yearly basis in Congress. He worked hard at sanitizing the offscreen image of the industry and established a cooperative spirit among the fiercely competitive movie companies. Under his stewardship Hollywood became the unquestioned leader in the production of worldwide popular entertainment. In 1922 Hollywood averaged forty million paid admissions per week; by 1928 the figure stood at sixty-five million; and in 1930 it hit a record ninety million! Foreign revenues reflected a similar growth.[13]

Hays first attempted to achieve self-regulation for the MPPDA in 1924 when he presented its Board of Directors with "The Formula." This requested that each studio forward to the Hays Office a synopsis of every play, novel, or story under consideration for a future film; the office would then judge the suitability of the material for the screen. In most ways, this voluntary scheme failed. Even though 125 proposals were rejected, "The Formula" did little to quiet protests.[14]

In a continuing effort to gain control over the studios and the content of films, Hays next created a Studio Relations Department (SRD) and appointed Jason Joy, a former executive secretary of the American Red Cross, as its director. Headquartered in Los Angeles, Joy worked closely with the studios trying to delete material that would offend censors. The SRD drew up a code of the most common demands of the municipal and state censorship boards. The working document became known as the "Don'ts and Be Carefuls" and prohibited, among other things, profanity, nudity, drug trafficking, and white slavery; it also urged producers to exercise good taste in presenting such adult themes as criminal behavior, sexual relations, and violence. Even so, each studio interpreted these guidelines according to its own inclination, and criticism continued.

The advent of sound films late in the decade simply complicated the situation. Now, instead of exaggerated pantomime, films stars used dialogue. Men and women openly discussed their love affairs on the screen, criminals bragged about their crimes, and politicians spoke cynically about the important issues facing the government. This new openness delighted movie fans and infuriated the moral guardians, who intensified their demand that government regulate this powerful medium of communication. What Hays needed was some mechanism that would allow the movies to continue to attract huge numbers of paying customers while muting the protests of a very vocal, influential minority.

Ironically, it was a religious institution, the Catholic church, that offered Hays a solution. Since the inception of the movies at the turn of the century the Catholic church had adopted no official policy toward films. Catholics were free to choose which films they saw and when they saw them. Although an occasional priest might conduct a local campaign against "evil" films, the hierarchy of the church refused to condemn the film industry or join the Protestant demands for federal regulation. Catholic organizations such as the International Federation of Catholic Alumnae (IFCA), a Catholic women's organization, cooperated with the Hays Office by publicizing "good films" and ignoring the rest. By 1929, however, a small group of Catholic laymen and priests were becoming more and more uncomfortable with what they perceived as the declining moral quality of films.

Martin Quigley, a staunch lay Catholic and owner and publisher of the industry trade journal *Exhibitors Herald*, published in Chicago, took the first steps toward Catholic involvement. Quigley, a native of Cleveland, had attended Niagara University and Catholic University of America before embarking on a career in journalism. His journal would soon merge with *Moving Picture World* to form the *Motion Picture Herald*, which became an important industry trade publication. While not as well known outside the industry as *Variety,* this new *Herald* gave Quigley a pulpit for promoting film morality. An advocate for theater owners, he opposed government censorship as ineffective.

Quigley argued instead that if censurable material could be eliminated during production, political censorship boards would be unnecessary. In turn this would also undercut the demands of the Protestant lobby for an elimination of block booking, the industry practice whereby theater owners had to rent films not individually by title (which would allow exhibitors to take local community standards into consideration), but in a block. Quigley thus advocated stricter self-regulation by the industry as a means of reducing criticism and ensuring continued popularity of the movies.

While he opposed Protestants' methods, Quigley shared their conviction that movies were increasingly immoral. He was further convinced that movies ought to avoid social, political, and economic subjects: Moving pictures, in his view, should be simple entertainment, not social commentary. In Chicago during the summer of 1929, he and a local parish priest, Father Fitz-George Dinneen, S.J., began to formulate a new code of behavior for the film industry. Both men hoped it would force moviemakers to consider the moral issues in their films as well as the entertainment values.

Father Dinneen arranged for Quigley to meet privately with George W. Cardinal Mundelein to discuss his concept of a Catholic code for the movies. Mundelein had long favored police censorship of the new medium. Quigley countered that a new code of behavior written by Catholics and backed by the hierarchy of the church would eliminate the need for police or political censorship. He stressed to Mundelein that the Catholic church – twenty million strong, heavily concentrated in urban centers, and boasting its own national press with a circulation of more than six million readers a week – was in a unique position to exert influence on the industry. Being more centralized than the Protestant denominations the mere threat of united Catholic action, Quigley argued, would force the industry to reform.[15]

Mundelein supported Quigley's idea that the Church draft a moral code for the movies.[16] When Father Dinneen suggested bringing in Father Daniel Lord, S.J., to write the document, the cardinal gave his blessing.[17]

No reclusive cleric, Lord was professor of dramatics at St. Louis University and editor of the widely read *Queen's Work,* which preached morality and ethics to Catholic youth. Lord, like so many Catholic intellectuals, deplored the modern trend in drama and literature, which dealt with sexual and social issues in increasingly realistic terms.[18]

He began a prolific publishing career in 1915 with an attack on George Bernard Shaw in *Catholic World*. In editorials in *Queen's Work*, in pamphlets, in Catholic newspapers and journals, Lord attacked the ultrasophistication of modern living as reflected in literature and drama. Other topics like evolution, birth control, abortion, secular education, and the growth of communism also drew his wrath. As Lord later recalled, he and Dinneen "often groaned together over the horrible stuff that came pouring out of Hollywood."[19]

Joseph I. Breen was another key figure in this small group of provoked Catholics. An active Irish Catholic, Breen graduated from St. Joseph's College in Philadelphia and began a career in journalism as a reporter for the *Philadelphia North American*. After four years in the United States consular service, he went to Washington as the Overseas Commissioner of the National Catholic Welfare Conference. He continued his involvement in Catholic affairs when he was appointed the press relations chief for the 1926 Eucharistic Congress in Chicago, where, by that time, he had also become public relations director of the Peabody Coal Company.[20]

Breen combined political conservatism with deep religious conviction. He blamed "radical teaching in our great colleges and universities" for undermining American youth. He wrote a series of articles on the threat of communism in the United States for the Jesuit publication *America,* under the pseudonym of "Eugene Ware."[21] He was strongly opposed to public discussion of such moral issues as divorce, birth control, and abortion. This was especially true in movies – because Breen believed that average moviegoers were "youngsters between 16 and 26," most of them "nit-wits, dolts and imbeciles."[22] An extreme anti-Semite, Breen held the Jewish moguls responsible for the decadence on the screen.

Breen and Quigley met through their Catholic connections. From the beginning Breen saw himself as a potential censor. His first suggestion was that he head a Chicago "Board of Examination" to censor film scripts before production. Although this proposal was rejected, Breen would eventually emerge in 1934 as the director of the PCA.[23]

For several months Quigley, Breen, Lord, Father Dinneen, and Father Wilfrid Parsons, editor of *America,* discussed a new and more stringent code of behavior for the movies. After studying various state and municipal censorship codes, the Hays Office's "Dont's and Be Carefuls," and the objections of Protestant reformers, Daniel Lord drafted a Catholic movie code. What emerged was a fascinating combination of Catholic theology, conservative politics, and pop psychology – an amalgam that would control the content of Hollywood films for the next three decades.[24] (A copy of this document is included as the Appendix to this volume.)

Although this code is most often discussed as a document that prohibited nudity, required married couples to sleep in twin beds, and effectively ruined the movie career of that saucy favorite, Mae West, its authors intended it to control much more. Lord and his colleagues shared a common objective with Protestant film reformers: They all wanted entertainment films to emphasize that the church, the government, and the family were the cornerstones of an orderly society; that success and happiness resulted from respecting and working within this system. Entertainment films should reinforce religious teachings that deviant behavior, whether criminal or sexual, cost violators the love and comforts of home, the intimacy of family, the solace of religion, and the protection of law. Films should be twentieth-century morality plays that illustrated proper behavior to the masses.

As Lord explained, Hollywood films were first and foremost "entertainment for the multitudes" and as such carried a "special Moral Responsibility" required of no other medium of entertainment or communication. Their universal popularity – cutting across social, political, and economic classes and penetrating local communities, from the most sophisticated to the most remote – meant that filmmakers could not, Lord argued, be permitted the same freedom of expression allowed producers of legitimate theater, authors of books, or even editors of newspapers.[25]

Movies had to be more restricted, Lord believed, because they were persuasively and indiscriminately seductive. Whereas audiences of books, plays, and even newspapers were self-selective, the movies had universal appeal. Hollywood's films, its picture palaces, and its beautiful and glamorous stars combined to create an irresistible fantasy.

Therefore, the basic premise behind the code was that "no picture should lower the moral standards of those who see it." Recognizing that evil and sin were legitimately part of drama, the code stressed that no film should create a feeling of "sympathy" for the criminal, the adulterer, the immoralist, or the corrupter. No film should be so constructed as to "leave the question of right or wrong in doubt." Films must uphold, not question or challenge, the basic values of society. The sanctity of the home and marriage must be upheld. The concept of basic law must not be "belittled or ridiculed." Courts must be shown as just and fair, police as honest and efficient, and government as protective of all people. If corruption was a necessary part of any plot, it had to be restricted: A judge could be corrupt but not the court system; a policeman could be brutal, but not the police force. Interestingly, Lord's code stated that "crime *need not always be punished, as long as the audience is made to know that it is wrong.*" What Lord wanted films to do was to illustrate clearly to audiences that "evil is wrong" and that "good is right."[26]

"I received this morning your final draft of our code," Quigley wrote Lord in November 1929. Quigley was excited by Lord's blending of Catholic attitudes toward entertainment with traditional movie taboos.[27] With the power of the church behind him, Quigley took Lord's draft to Hays and began agitating for industry adoption. According to Hays, "My eyes nearly popped out when I read it. This was the very thing I had been looking for."[28]

With the dramatic stock market crash only a few weeks behind them, film corporation heads in New York were jittery, and Hays convinced them that the code would be good for business: It could quiet demands for federal censorship and undercut the campaign to eliminate block booking. It remained for Hays to convince Hollywood producers that the code made good sense from an entertainment, as well as an economic, point of view. With the full support of the corporate offices in New York and the backing of Cardinal Mundelein in Chicago, Hays and Quigley set off for Los Angeles to "peddle a script" for movie behavior.[29]

Not surprisingly, Hays found the producers less than enthusiastic over the tone and content of Lord's code. In fact, the code was, as one scholar of modern Catholicism has written, "hopelessly out of sympathy with the creative artistic mind of the twentieth century." Taken literally, it forbade movies even to question the veracity of contemporary moral and social standards.[30]

A small group of producers – MGM's head of production Irving Thalberg, studio boss Jack Warner of Warner Bros., production head B. P. Schulberg of Paramount, and Sol Wurtzel of Fox – recognized this and offered a counterproposal.[31] The producers rejected Lord's basic contention that the movies had to be more restrictive in presenting material than did other art forms. They maintained that films were simply "one vast reflection of every image in the stream of contemporary life." In their view, audiences supported movies they liked and stayed away from those they did not. No other guidelines were needed.[32]

The two positions could not have been further apart. From the producers' perspective Lord's code, representing reformers of all sorts, asked them to present a utopian view of life that denied reality and, frankly, lacked box-office appeal as they understood it. Daniel Lord, however, convinced that the screen was undermining church teachings and destroying family life, wanted a partnership among the movie industry, church, and state that would portray a moral society that uniformly condemned sin, crime, and corruption.

Lord admitted that the world's imperfections were the stuff of good drama, but he saw no reason why films should not show simple and direct solutions to complex moral, political, economic, and philosophical issues. The producers countered that the American people were the real censors and the box office was their ballot box.

The fascinating aspect of this conflict was that despite strong opposition in Hollywood, Lord's position, backed by Hays and the Catholic church, was accepted with barely a whimper. Hays liked the new code because it gave him more control over the studios; Lord and Quigley liked it because they believed it would force producers to infuse movies with morality; and from the producer's point of view, filmmakers had lived and even prospered with local codes since 1911. Furthermore, few people in Hollywood believed the code meant exactly what it said. Even if it did, the producers insisted on one concession that gave them, not Hays, the final say over film content: If any studio felt the Hays office interpreted the code too stringently, a "jury" of producers, not MPPDA officials, would decide whether or not the offending scene should be cut. With that understanding, the code was accepted by the Hollywood producers.[33]

While a facade of harmony appeared on the surface, it is clear that from the very beginning there was fundamental misunderstanding over what had been negotiated in Los Angeles. Lord, for example, informed Mundelein that Jason Joy, who was to be the enforcer of the code for Hays, had authority to reject scripts, which meant "that the picture will not be filmed"; further, that finished films rejected or questioned by Joy would be submitted to a committee or jury of producers who could prevent the film from being shown. Lord left Los Angeles with the impression that his code would be rigidly enforced by Joy and that the producers were in full agreement. Nothing could have been further from the truth. As it will soon be made clear, the producers fought Joy from the beginning and saw the code as at best a general guideline for movie morality.

The years between the adoption of the movie code in 1930 and the creation of the Legion of Decency and the PCA during 1933–4 are one of the most misunderstood periods in film history. Scholars and movie fans alike often refer to films produced during this time frame as "precode" films, implying that they were made before the censorship system was imposed on the industry. The fact is that the code was indeed enforced during these important four years – just not as severely as it would be after Joseph Breen was appointed Hollywood censor and the Catholic church created the Legion, both to support him and to take him to task if he failed to purge from films material to which the church objected.

This period is confusing because it was one of the most dynamic and creative in Hollywood history. The talkies opened up Hollywood movies to deal with subjects in a more direct fashion than was possible in the silent cinema. Now sexy starlets could rationalize their immoral behavior; criminals using hip slang could brag about flouting law and order; and politicians could talk about bribery and corruption. Film dialogue could and did challenge conventional norms, and the censors and the studios fought over the movie image of gangsters, fallen women, and filmed versions of modern literature. The cultural battle that raged on the Hollywood front would eventually bring about a new crisis with the formation of the Catholic Legion of Decency.

Hays gave the task of enforcing the code to Jason Joy and the SRD in Hollywood. Producers voluntarily submitted scripts to Joy, who served as chief censor until 1932; his replacement, Dr. James Wingate, served until the Legion of Decency crisis in 1934. Both men attempted to alter films to make them consistent with the code, but both experienced major problems.

With some ninety million fans packing its theaters every week, industry leaders in 1930 gloated that the movies were "depression proof." Soon after the code's adoption in March, however, a serious box-office downturn began, and within a year weekly attendance had plunged to sixty million. The studios responded in typical fashion: They tried to lure fans back into the theater with sensationalism.

Early sound gangster movies illustrate the problems Hollywood faced in its cultural war with censors. The dangerous but fascinating urban underworld epitomized life in the fast lane: Movie gangsters spoke a colorful argot, their guns barked out their own form of law, their cars squealed around corners at breathtaking speed. In the era of the Depression, their reward was money, fast cars, admiring friends, fancy clothes, and even fancier women. They flouted the traditions of hard work, sacrifice, and respect for institutions of authority. That these gangland hoods lost all that they had gained either by death or arrest in the last reel of the film did not, claimed the critics, undo the harm they caused to impressionable moviegoers.

The movie screens were flooded with gangster films in the early 1930s. *Doorway to Hell* was a "swell . . . trigger opera," said *Variety*, which "bumps off plenty of the boys" and introduced James Cagney as a tough guy.[34] Within months *The Finger Points, City Streets, The Secret Six,* and *Star Witness* were all released. They featured tough, exciting guys willing to kill, boring, incompetent cops, and beautiful, sexy women. Edward G. Robinson in *Little Caesar,* James Cagney in *The Public Enemy,* and Paul Muni in *Scarface* murdered their way to the top of the gang world and caused delight and outrage among moviegoers, critics, and law-enforcement officials. In 1930 nine gangster films were released; 1931 saw twenty-six; 1932 had twenty-eight; and 1933 had fifteen.[35]

Joy found the gangster films violent, to be sure, but anticrime in their overall tone and infused with the strong moral lesson that the criminal was the enemy of society and always paid for his crimes in the end. It was important, in his view, that censors not be "small, narrow, picayunish" individuals who remove the details and fail to see the overall impact of the film. If this happened, the code would destroy the industry or the industry the code, because producers would have no room to create serious drama. "We are sure," he wrote, "that it was never intended that censorship should be destructive . . . but rather that its duty should be a constructive one of influencing the quality of the final impression left on the minds of audiences by the whole."[36]

Thus, despite the code, in the early 1930s movies with themes not only of crime but also of politics appeared with increasing frankness. So too did movies with frank sexual themes. Mae West delighted audiences with a barrage of one-liners loaded with sexual innuendo in her smash hits *She Done Him Wrong* and *I'm No Angel*. Marlene Dietrich seduced an aging professor in *The Blue Angel* and bedded a gangster in *Blonde Venus*. Greta Garbo, rejected by her lover, turned openly to prostitution in *Susan Lenox: Her Fall and Rise*. In *Possessed*, Joan Crawford rose from a poor factory worker to a life of luxury as the mistress of an ambitious politician. Joy challenged MGM producer Irving Thalberg over this production, but Thalberg argued that because there was no nudity in the film and the subject was handled in "good taste," there was no violation of the code. Joy admitted to Hays there was little he could do to force Thalberg to make changes because, in his view, a jury would most certainly rule for Thalberg.[37]

The Mae West films illustrated the censors' dilemma. James Wingate, Joy's replacement as chief censor, found little to object to in either film. After seeing *She Done Him Wrong* at an audience preview, he told Hays he found nothing really offensive in the film and that "the audience loved" it. While he realized that some people would object to the "general low tone," Wingate accepted the movie on its own terms, as a comedy. When Paramount submitted the script of *I'm No Angel* Wingate made no objection, and he later told studio authorities that he "enjoyed the picture as a piece of entertainment."[38]

The critics agreed. West was, observed the *New Republic*, "the most honest and outrageous and lovable vulgarity that ever was seen on the screen." To the *New Orleans Tribune* West was a performer who "has caught the trick of satirizing the flamboyant creatures she impersonates. That imperils the morals of nobody but the humorless."[39]

Wingate, fully realizing that Mae West made any attempt at censorship look foolish, and quite aware that she could turn the most innocent sounding dialogue in a script into blatant sexual innuendo, took her for what she was: A comic, a satirist poking fun at, in Joy's terms, the "small, narrow and picayunish." Although both Joy and Wingate did fight with producers to eliminate violence, cut overt sexuality, and tame views critical of American life, neither believed that films had to be so restrictive as to eliminate the gangster, the adulterer, or the comic from the screen.[40]

Others did, however. Lord, invited to Los Angeles to evaluate the effectiveness of the code after one year of operation, praised Joy's efforts but condemned the industry for drifting into subject areas that were "fundamentally dangerous" no matter "how delicate or clean the treatment." When the priest saw *She Done Him Wrong,* he was horrified. He wrote to Hays that he had drafted the code to prevent just such films. When Hays responded that fans and critics alike had praised the film, Lord demanded that Catholic youth boycott it. He urged the industry to move away from stories of "degenerates" and instead to fill the silver screen with uplifting stories of "business, industry, and commerce." Lord wanted Hays to replace gangsters and kept women with movie biographies of American heroes like Lindbergh, sports figures like Babe Ruth or Bobby Jones, or political leaders like Al Smith. The code he had written in 1930, he told Hays, was not a document open to liberal interpretation. Unlike Jason Joy, Lord found no moral lessons in thugs or floozies, and he was appalled by the sexual humor of a Mae West.[41]

Complaints against the content of films encompassed not only the ribald comedies of Mae West and gangster films but also works of recognized literary merit. A basic premise of the code was that Hollywood did not have the same freedom accorded books and Broadway plays to produce artistic works.

In the early 1930s, just as the Catholic campaign against the movies was beginning, the church also began to intensify its attack on "obscene" and dangerous literature. At the annual meeting of Catholic bishops in Washington in 1932, just one year before the Legion of Decency campaign against the movies was launched, the hierarchy adopted a resolution deploring the lack of "uplifting" literature and called on Catholics to avoid "immoral" books.[42] Father Lord joined the battle. In a speech to the New York chapter of the IFCA he condemned the writings of such authors as Theodore Dreiser, James Joyce, and Eugene O'Neill because they were fraught with the "sordid things of life."[43]

Lord was joined by the Rev. Francis X. Talbot, S.J., who on radio and in the pages of *America* demanded federal censorship of novels with "literary pretensions," novels that, he said, were hiding behind the protection of the First Amendment. Talbot called Sinclair Lewis, William Faulkner, and Ernest Hemingway "crawling vermin."[44] The priest would later become a major force in the Legion of Decency.

Still, it was only natural that Hollywood would attempt to bring the works of popular American authors to the screen. Best-sellers brought name recognition and proven public appeal; but filming these books brought incongruous cultures into collison. Moral guardians believed them to be obscene or, at best, vulgar, and were determined either to keep them off the screen or to change their message radically in the films. Hollywood was equally determined to bring reasonably accurate filmed versions of Faulkner, Hemingway, and Lewis to the public.

When Paramount announced that it had purchased the screen rights to Ernest Hemingway's powerful antiwar novel *A Farewell to Arms,* the Hays Office censors warned that it contained "profanity, illicit love, illegitimate birth, desertion from the army and a not very flattering picture of Italy during the war."[45] Paramount worked closely with the Italian government to remove Hemingway's anti-Italian sentiments, infused the script with a strong voice for morality, and toned down the illicit love angle of the two main characters. When Hemingway saw the film he called it "preposterous." Father Dinneen, however, was outraged by the immorality and fought its exhibition in Chicago.[46]

The reaction to a filmed version of Sinclair Lewis's novel *Ann Vickers* further illustrated the depths of the cultural war being fought over the movies. *Ann Vickers* is the story of a young woman of solid middle-class credentials. After college she becomes a social worker. On the eve of the American entry into World War I she meets a handsome young army officer with whom she has an affair. Pregnant, she discovers he does not love her, and has an abortion.

On the rebound from a broken heart and the abortion, Ann marries a nice but very dull man. Their marriage is torn apart by Ann's rising fame as a reformer and by her attraction to a distinguished New York judge, Barney Dolphin. Vickers carries on a torrid love affair with him while she lives with her husband; but tragedy strikes when Dolphin is sent to prison for corruption, and Ann is again pregnant. She decides to leave her husband and have Dolphin's baby. When he is freed from prison, the lovers are reunited and carry on their lives. The point of the novel was, said Lewis, that "women have almost caught up with men" as complete human beings with "ideas, reasons, ambitions . . . with virtues and faults."[47]

RKO bought the screen rights to the novel and submitted a script of *Ann Vickers* to the SRD in May 1933. James Wingate asked Joseph Breen, who had been hired by Hays in a public relations capacity, for his opinion. "This script simply will not do," he screamed after reading it. Breen told Wingate that he had not "read anything quite so vulgarly offensive" in years.[48]

Wingate agreed totally with Breen and informed RKO that the script was unacceptable. The studio was furious; RKO vice-president in charge of production, Merian Cooper (who coproduced and codirected *King Kong*), fired back a stinging reply. The script was based on a best-selling novel by a Nobel Prize–winning author. Although the story, admitted Cooper, included some controversial material, "it does not pander to cheap sex, nor to cheap and vulgar emotions." RKO planned for the film to be a major production, and Cooper assured Wingate that the story of *Ann Vickers* would bring acclaim to the motion picture industry.[49]

Wingate refused to budge, and after months of bickering RKO agreed to make a few additional cuts in *Ann Vickers;* this pacified Wingate, who told Hays that the "subject has been handled as well as it could be."[50] RKO's investment had been protected, and the film was released in the fall just as the

Catholics began the Legion of Decency crusade. Despite the howls from film reformers, the sanitized version of *Ann Vickers* suffered only a few cuts from the state and municipal censorship boards.

During the negotiations over *Ann Vickers* Hays had written to all the studios informing them that films dealing with "illicit sex relationships" are "never justified," no matter how well they are treated. He told RKO that he considered *Of Human Bondage* and *Ann Vickers* a "very grave danger" to the industry. MGM was scolded for Jean Harlow's *Bombshell* and Joan Crawford's *Dancing Lady*. Paramount was warned about Noël Coward's *Design for Living* and the Marx Bros.' political satire *Duck Soup*. Hays again threatened that if these films did not conform to the code, he would personally intervene.[51]

The studios, however, paid little attention to the threats from Hays. In desperate need of revenues they turned to popular novels, gangsters, and bedroom farces as needed box-office tonic. Movie fans enjoyed and supported these films, which, for the vast majority of Americans, were little more than frivolous entertainment.

From his position in Los Angeles, Joseph Breen confirmed what many already felt: that "nobody out here cares a damn for the Code or any of its provisions." In frustration he wrote Father Wilfrid Parsons that, in his opinion, Hays had sold them all "a first class bill of goods when he put over the Code on us." It may be that Hays thought "these lousy Jews out here would abide by the Code's provisions but if he did he should be censured for his lack of proper knowledge of the breed." The code would never work in Hollywood, Breen lamented, because the Jews who controlled the industry were, in his words, "dirty lice," "the scum of the earth."[52]

The entire nation, Breen told Parsons, was being "debauched by the Jews" and their movies; the only standard of ethics understood in Hollywood was the box office. Breen was convinced that if Catholics were going to reform the industry successfully it would have to be through box-office pressure.[53] To Breen, a rabid anti-Semitic, the problem was simple: The Jews who controlled were immoral and had to be forced to make movies moral. It was a job he believed he was destined to fill.

Quigley's views were slightly more sophisticated. He agreed with Breen that effective reform required economic pressure, but he did not place all the blame on the Jewish owners, producers, and writers. In his view the code failed because the Catholic church had failed to maintain pressure on the industry to force them to uphold it.[54]

By the beginning of 1933 Lord, Quigley, and Breen conceded that, for a variety of reasons, the code was not working as they had envisioned it. At the same time over forty national organizations passed resolutions condemning the film industry and demanded federal control and the elimination of block booking. To make matters worse, in the spring a sensational book published by Henry James Forman, *Our Movie Made Children,* openly accused movies of corrupting the nation's youth. Forman's book was a summary of nine other publications, each written by respected academics under the sponsorship of the Payne Fund. Whereas the academics had been careful to avoid sweeping generalizations and stressed that films influenced individuals on different levels, Forman boldly charged that 72 percent of all movies were unfit for children and were "helping to shape a race of criminals." He toured the country denouncing the movies. The Payne Studies, but especially Forman's summary, provided movie reformers with seemingly irrefutable evidence that the content of films was damaging and had to be controlled.[55]

Sensing that Hays and the industry were now vulnerable to outside pressure, Quigley lobbied for increased Catholic involvement. The publisher saw an opportunity when he learned that the newly appointed apostolic delegate to the United States, Monsignor Amleto Giovanni Cicognani, would deliver a speech to the Catholic charities meeting in New York. Archbishop John T. McNicholas of Cincinnati arranged for Quigley and Breen to meet with Cicognani. After listening to their presentation, Cicognani agreed to incorporate into his speech a draft statement prepared by Quigley calling for Catholic action against the movies. "What a massacre of innocence of youth is taking place hour by hour," Cicognani told the assembly. "Catholics are called by God, the Pope, the Bishops, and the priests to a united and vigorous campaign for the purification of the cinema, which has become a deadly menace to morals."[56]

The strategy was clever and pointed. Cicognani was the Pope's representative in America; his speech was a papal directive. It was no longer a question of whether the bishops would take up the cause of "immoral" movies, it was when and how. When the bishops gathered in Washington several weeks later the film industry was an important agenda item.

At this conclave, held in November at Catholic University in Washington, D.C., Bishop John Cantwell of Los Angeles spoke at length about Hollywood. The movies had always been vulgar, Cantwell began; but now with the addition of sound they were no longer just entertainment but had become an educational system that preached a "sinister and insidious" philosophy of life. A strong and faithful marriage, purity, and the sanctity of home were "out-moded sentimentalities" in movies. Cantwell bemoaned the presentation of "social problems," such as divorce, race suicide (mixed marriages), and "free love," on the contemporary screen, which "condoned" sin and "lowered the public and private standards of conduct of all who see them." He cited *Ann Vickers* as a specific example of a "vile and nauseating" film.[57]

Cantwell ended with a plea for forceful action. It would not be enough for the bishops to simply issue a statement condemning the industry. The church had to wound Hollywood at the box office to stop the production of offensive films. After a lengthy discussion the bishops appointed an Episcopal Committee on Motion Pictures (ECMP). Archbishop McNicholas of Cincinnati, who had placed the movie question on the agenda, was elected chairman, and Cantwell, along with Bishops John Noll of Fort Wayne and Hugh Boyle of Pittsburgh, were asked to coordinate a Catholic Legion of Decency.[58] Under guidance from Quigley, the bishops quickly adopted a three-part plan for the Legion to (1) create a pressure group, (2) boycott offensive films, and (3) support self-regulation and conformity with the Production Code.[59]

This Legion of Decency, which would soon capture the attention of millions of Americans, was to spearhead a national Catholic attack against the movie industry. The bishops agreed to call for boycotts against films they judged to be immoral, to use the Catholic media as a weapon in the campaign, and to lash out against the evil of the movies from the pulpit.

"The pest hole that infects the entire country with its obscene and lascivious moving pictures must be cleaned and disinfected," said the Episcopal Committee, launching the Catholic campaign.[60] Although Hays had expected a Catholic declaration of war against the movies, the final reality of the appointment of a committee of bishops to "disinfect" his business was upsetting to say the least. Catholics comprised only one-fifth of the population, but they were heavily concentrated in cities east of the Mississippi River. Chicago was one-half Catholic, as was Boston. New York, Buffalo, Philadelphia, Pittsburgh, Cleveland, and Detroit had sizable Catholic populations. These cities were also important to the movie industry because they were home to huge studio-owned, first-run theaters, which exhibited their films before they were released in general run. An effective Catholic boycott in a few selected cities could thus seriously hurt the industry, which was already reeling from financial losses suffered during America's deepening economic depression.

The Catholic church had national media already in place. Clerical publications included the *Catholic World, America, Sign,* and *Thought;* the *Ecclesiastical Review,* a journal directed at priests; and *Catholic Digest,* for those who wanted their theology in condensed form. Catholic lay organizations published their own journals: The Knights of Columbus informed its members through its publication *Columbia,* and lay Catholics controlled *Commonweal,* an urbane, sophisticated journal edited by George Schuster.

Most of the 103 American dioceses had a local newspaper, and the church operated a national Catholic news bureau in Washington that supplied local papers with a Catholic slant to international and domestic news as well as with syndicated opinion columns. Catholic opinion was also broadcast over the airwaves on *The Catholic Hour,* a national radio program. The "radio priest," Father Charles Coughlin, broadcasting from WJR in Detroit, held millions of Americans spellbound with his angry denunciation of Jewish bankers, socialists, communists, and eventually New Dealers. Detroit was a hotbed of Legion activity. Would Coughlin add the movies and their Jewish owners to his growing list of conspirators?

The Legion movement spread across America with a vengeance. Individual Legion campaigns were formed in each Catholic diocese. Enthusiastic priests began to draw up lists of forbidden films, which were given to the faithful. Theaters showing these films were boycotted. Unfortunately, these local Legion committees often disagreed on what was moral entertainment and what was not. *Of Human Bondage,* for example, was condemned as indecent by Legion officials in Detroit, Pittsburgh, Omaha, and Chicago, but Catholics in the rest of the country were free to attend the movie.

With Legionaries attacking Hollywood on all fronts Hays moved quickly to pacify Catholics. As a first step, in December 1933, only weeks after the official Catholic announcement of a Legion of Decency campaign, Hays named Joe Breen as chief censor in Hollywood.

It was a shrewd move on the part of Hays. He was well aware that Breen had been informing Quigley, Lord, and Cantwell of his every move; but from Hays's perspective, it was better to have Breen as an employee inside the firm, with some authority over him, than to have him totally allied with church forces.

In Hollywood Breen immediately launched his war with producers for control of film content. One of his first actions as head of the PCA was to write a new definition of "moral compensating values" for the movies – a document that is vital to an understanding of his stewardship of the PCA. He went further than even Daniel Lord in advocating film as a vehicle to promote proper social and political behavior. Every film, according to Breen, must now contain "sufficient good" to compensate for any evil that might be depicted. Films that include crime or sin as a major part of the plot must contain "compensating moral value" to justify the subject matter. To Breen this meant these films must have a good character who speaks as a voice for morality, who clearly tells the criminal/sinner that he or she was wrong. Each film must contain a stern moral lesson: regeneration, suffering, and punishment. He urged that whenever possible stars, not stringers, play the characters that represent good. In building respect for the law, Breen held that the existing code was a "full mandate to enforce respect for all *law* and all *lawful* authority." Nothing "subversive of the fundamental law of the land" could be shown in a movie. "Communistic propaganda is banned from the screen," said Breen. The screen was to promote "social spirit" and "patriotism" and not confuse audiences with a "cynical contempt for conventions" nor too vivid a recreation of the "realism of problems" encountered in life.[61]

Breen and his staff looked at each script with an eye toward its impact on this new "industry policy." This was particularly the case for those films that, while technically within the code, were judged by Breen or Hays to be "dangerous" to the well-being of the industry. Undefined to allow as much latitude as possible, "industry policy" was invoked by Breen and the PCA on scripts that touched on social or political themes. This limited the studios, who feared loss of valuable markets, both domestic and international, in their selection and presentation of social criticism.

The new censor went to work on scripts with a finely sharpened red pencil. He slashed all the sexual innuendo out of Mae West's *Belle of the Nineties* and purged a filmed version of Tolstoy's *Anna Karenina* so severely that the *Nation* found it "lifeless."[62] When Sam Goldwyn attempted to film Herbert Asbury's best-seller, *The Barbary Coast,* an account of sin, sex, gambling, crime, and corruption on San Francisco's waterfront, Breen attacked the script with a vengeance, turning hardened prostitutes into innocent dance-hall girls. He proudly told Hays he had transformed the novel into a film about "a fine, clean girl" and a sentimental young man. There was "no sex," he bragged, and no "unpleasant details of prostitution" in the film.[63]

Breen's success in purging overt sexuality from most films and infusing a sense of moral compensation, however shallow, into them convinced Archbishop McNicholas that Legion activities should be centralized in New York. He believed that if Catholic Legions in the various dioceses continued to denounce different movies, the Catholic campaign would suffer. When the bishops assembled in Washington, D.C., for their annual meeting in 1935, the movies were once again on their agenda.

Archbishop McNicholas opened the discussion. The church had, he told the conclave, improved the content of Hollywood films during the past year. The Production Code Administration, in his opinion, had been a success. McNicholas urged the bishops to concentrate Legion activities in New York and produce a single Catholic list of films to serve as a viewing guide for all Catholics. It was essential, McNicholas stressed, that such a list include "black" or condemned films. Cantwell agreed but spoke at length of his displeasure over the number of films that had been condemned in one diocese and approved in others. It was important, he emphasized, that the church have unified standards as well as a unified list.[64]

McNicholas and Cantwell urged that an official Legion office be opened in New York and that all Catholic reviewing be done from that office. It was vital, they argued, for that city to serve as the locus because it was where most movies first played: Films could be seen there and have their ratings published before going into general release. After a lengthy discussion, the bishops agreed to establish a National Legion of Decency office in New York under the guidance of Patrick Cardinal Hayes; they further agreed that the ratings produced by this new agency would be the "official" list printed in all Catholic publications.[65] As evidence of their continuing commitment to purification of the movies, the conclave approved an appropriation of $35,000 to fund the national office. The first list issued from New York would be dated February 1936.

Administratively the National Legion office operated out of the Catholic Charities Office in New York under the direction of Father Edward Robert Moore and the preying eyes of Martin Quigley, who had moved his publishing empire from Chicago to New York. Cardinal Hayes appointed Father Joseph Daly, both a priest from St. Gregory's Church in New York and a professor of psychology at the College of St. Vincent, as executive secretary.

The task of determining the moral values of the movies was given to the Catholic women's organization, the IFCA. In 1922, under the direction of Rita C. McGoldrick, the IFCA had created a Motion Picture Bureau, which adopted the philosophy advocated by Will Hays: "praise the best and ignore the rest." For twelve years the women published reviews of films that they felt were good and deserved Catholic support. Movies they considered vulgar, tasteless, or immoral were simply ignored.

In 1930 Mrs. Mary Looram – widow and mother of three, a native of Brooklyn who had attended Barnard College – was named head of the Motion Picture Bureau of the IFCA, a post she would hold for over three decades. Under her guidance more than a hundred women, divided into an East Coast group under the spiritual direction of Rev. Francis X. Talbot, S.J., and a West Coast group under the direction of Rev. John Devlin, worked as film reviewers. Looram compiled the reviewers' comments and published in the *Brooklyn Tablet* a regular column of film reviews that was reprinted in most Catholic publications. The IFCA reviews were also broadcast over a twenty-four-station radio network.

With the creation of the Legion, the ladies of the IFCA were shunted aside; in typical fashion, the priests took over. The IFCA was labeled by some in the hierarchy as a "puppet of the Hays Office"; its refusal to issue "black lists" of condemned films was seen as allowing the industry to continue to produce "immoral" films. By 1936, however, the bishops had come full circle: Father Devlin lobbied Cantwell and McNicholas for IFCA reinstatement as the official reviewing body for the National Legion of Decency, and the bishops voted agreement at the November 1935 conclave. The women were back in grace after they agreed to add a "condemned" category to their reviews.[66]

The National Legion of Decency and the IFCA constructed a four-tiered rating system that would be used to classify movies:

A1   Unobjectionable for general patronage;
A2   Unobjectionable for adults;
B   Objectionable in part;
C   Condemned.[67]

This division into four categories was important. First, it recognized that not all films had to be made for children. By dividing the approved (A) category into two levels, the National Legion could sanction films like *Anna Karenina* for adults without necessarily approving them for children; whether or not children could attend A2 films would be a parental decision. This was significant because the vast majority of films produced by the Hollywood studios and approved by Breen would fall under these two classifications. The third category was left purposely vague: B films were defined as those that contained a scene, scenes, or themes that reviewers believed objectionable. This category was confusing, however, because some bishops and priests considered B films to be unfit viewing for all Catholics, whereas others thought them acceptable for adults. By the mid-1950s the B category would become a major controversy within the Legion; but in 1936 most Catholics considered a B rating an approval from the Legion. Catholic wrath was reserved for the C, or condemned, classification: All Catholics were forbidden to see films classified as condemned, as these were considered dangerously "immoral."[68] Meanwhile, at masses all across the nation, Catholics were given no choice by their priests but to stand and take the Legion pledge, written by Bishop McNicholas. Movies were "a grave menace to youth, to home life, to country and to religion," the priests intoned, and all Catholics must pledge to God that they would not attend a film judged by the church to be "vile and unwholesome." Supplementing oral pledges during Mass, many Catholic churches asked their members to sign a formal document.[69]

In February 1936, Father Daly and the National Legion of Decency issued the first New York list of films. Charlie Chaplin's *Modern Times* was placed in the "A" grouping despite "a few vulgarities." Marlene Dietrich's *Desire* was approved for adults in spite of "a few long, drawn out kisses and suggestive remarks." Even Jean Harlow's *Wife versus Secretary* was approved by the Catholic women. No films were condemned, but several were placed in the B category. Father Daly and the IFCA reviewers restricted Boris Karloff's *The Walking Dead* because this *Frankenstein* spin-off implied that the mad doctor created life in his laboratory. *Mr. Cohen Takes a Walk* was given a B because a Jewish boy and an Irish girl are married "by a priest and then by a rabbi."[70] Mixed marriages were discouraged by the Catholic church.

Father Daly, however, soon came under a blistering attack from Martin Quigley for being too liberal and too complimentary to Hollywood. There is little doubt that Quigley was determined to control the Legion, a matter that came to a head over Mae West's *Klondike Annie:* Daly and the IFCA reviewers thought it harmless and recommended a B; Quigley branded it "unfit" for Catholic consumption and demanded it be condemned.[71]

Quigley lost the battle and the Legion rating stood; but he won the war. Quigley complained bitterly to Archbishop McNicholas that Daly was undermining the Legion. When Father Daly began praising some Hollywood productions for their artistic merits, Quigley complained to Archbishop Mc-

Nicholas that the new director was "hopeless." The Legion, he argued, could maintain its credibility only if it restricted evaluation of movies to moral issues. McNicholas agreed, and Daly was sacked.

In New York Cardinal Hayes acted quickly to avoid the impression that the Legion was a continuing source of disagreement among the hierarchy. On the recommendation of Father Edward Moore, he picked a 30-year-old priest, Father John J. McClafferty, as the new Legion director. A trained social worker, McClafferty had been working for the Catholic Charities of New York when he was tapped to help maintain the purity of the movies. He knew nothing about movies and, as one scholar has noted, his best attribute was his ability to take advice.[72] Martin Quigley stood ready to advise.

Although the Legion of Decency is often envisioned as a huge bureaucratic arm of the Catholic church, in fact it was minuscule. McClafferty's support staff comprised a secretary and Mrs. Mary Looram, head of the IFCA's Motion Picture Bureau. Looram coordinated the volunteer IFCA reviewers, who usually numbered between ten and fifty for each film. After seeing a film, the reviewers would submit written evaluations and recommendations for classification to Looram; she and McClafferty would tabulate these and make the final decision. Their ratings were then sent to Catholic publications and local Legion directors for distribution to Catholics nationwide.

Headquartered in New York City, the National Legion of Decency was in fact little more than a loose confederation of local organizations. Each diocese appointed a local Legion director, usually a parish priest, who was responsible for Legion activities in that diocese. It is important to remember, however, that in the Catholic hierarchy each bishop was a prince onto himself. The level of enthusiasm for the Legion depended on the commitment of the bishop. For the most part, local directors did little more than maintain contact with local theater owners and managers to kept them informed of Legion concerns, speak to local Catholic organizations and schools about the Legion, distribute Legion literature, answer questions about controversial films, and submit a yearly report.

The most active local Legion director was Father John Devlin of Los Angeles. Devlin had a close working relationship with the studios and with Joe Breen. Anxious to avoid problems with the Legion, Hollywood producers sent Devlin scripts long before they went into production. Also, when a particularly troublesome script reached Breen, he would forward it to Devlin for an opinion, which he would then use to convince the studio to remove the offending line or scene. Although they sometimes disagreed, the PCA and the Legion maintained a close working relationship, which solidified their control over the content of films.

Devlin's level of involvement was unusual, however. A majority of the bishops paid very little attention to the Legion and gave nothing more than lip service to its activities. Churches gave members the Legion pledge once a year in early December, and posted the Legion's classifications.

By mid-1937 there were only occasional differences of opinion between Breen's PCA and the Legion. In 1938, for example, only a small fraction – 32 out of 535 PCA-approved films – were given a B classification, and no film from a major studio was condemned. In fact, no PCA-approved film was condemned by the Legion for the rest of the decade. Catholic control over Hollywood was complete: A Catholic censor, Joe Breen, rode roughshod over Hollywood and, in New York, the Catholic Legion quietly approved his moral judgments. In the early 1940s, however, a maverick independent producer and one of Hollywood's most respected executives would upset the comfortable relationship the PCA and the Legion had reached. Two unusual westerns and a sex-charged courtesan challenged conventional morality.

CHAPTER 2

COWBOYS AND COURTESANS
CHALLENGE CENSORS

As the film stands [*The Outlaw*] it is a gross libel on you and your
public reputation. Its influence is evil and reflects on your enviable
reputation as citizen, industralist, financier and notable contribu-
tor to aviation.

— Martin Quigley to Howard Hughes

Even for Hollywood, Howard Hughes was unusual. In the 1990s Hughes is
remembered as a reclusive, billionaire hypochondriac who shunned all public contact. But it wasn't always so. In his youth, and indeed until a near fatal air crash in 1938, Hughes was a dashing public figure who thrilled the
American public with his daring transcontinental aviation speed records; as
a celebrity he was often photographed with beautiful Hollywood starlets
draped around him. Tragically, Hughes retreated into a world only he knew,
but not before he left his mark on the Hollywood film industry.[1]

In many ways his entry into Hollywood was amazingly typical. In 1925,
at the tender age of 19, he and his young bride, Ella, moved from Houston,
Texas, to Hollywood with the same dream that millions of other young
Americans had: success in the movies. Unlike those other youthful dream-
ers, however, Hughes did not envision stardom; his dream was to make movies, not star in them.

Not that this was unrealistic: Hughes was not a penniless actor but a teenage millionaire who ran his own business, Hughes Tool Corporation, which
he had inherited a year earlier when his father died unexpectedly. In 1925,
the film industry was still fluid enough to allow a young man with millions
to make movies. Within three years Hughes used surplus cash from his lucra-
tive oil-drilling business to produce four films: *Everybody's Acting, Two Arabian Knights* (for which Lewis Milestone won an Academy Award for direction), *The Mating Call,* and *The Racket* (also directed by Milestone). These
films attracted respectable box office and established Hughes as a legitimate,
if minor, player in Hollywood.[2]

In 1930 he broke into the big time with his spectacular World War I drama *Hell's Angels.* Hughes spent millions on the film. He hired World War I

flying aces to recreate their aerial exploits, bought a fleet of vintage airplanes, hired a hundred mechanics to keep them flying, and spent close to half a million dollars to create a Zeppelin raid on London. The results were astounding.

The critics raved over the aerial scenes but panned the film as mediocre. Hughes was undeterred, however, and his persistence paid huge dividends when his next two films – *The Front Page,* a fast-paced, witty, urbane look at modern journalism, and *Scarface,* a bloody, violent portrayal of urban gangsters – were huge hits with critics and fans.

A key element in the success of both films was that Hughes was no longer behind the camera. After paying Ben Hecht and Charles MacArthur $125,000 for the screen rights to their Broadway smash hit *The Front Page,* he paid them an additional $80,000 to adapt it for the screen. He then hired Lewis Milestone, who had just completed his powerful antiwar *All Quiet on the Western Front,* to direct, and actually left Milestone alone. Starring Edward Everett Horton, Adolphe Menjou, and Pat O'Brien, *The Front Page* infuriated journalists and delighted everyone else.

For *Scarface* Hughes wanted a hard-hitting drama that would portray gangsters as they were in real life: cold-blooded killers. Screenwriter Ben Hecht promised twenty-five killings, but he and director Howard Hawks delivered many more than that. By the end of the film, every major male character is dead, with the exception of the Police Inspector who breaks up the gang. The film was completed in 1931, but Hays refused to approve it until Hughes added a prologue that stated the film was "an indictment of gang rule," shot new scenes that removed any implication that corrupt municipal governments and police were responsible for America's crime wave, and added a new ending in which Tony is gunned down by the police in the final scene. With these additions, Hays finally allowed Hughes to release *Scarface* in the spring of 1932.[3]

Hughes was furious over the interference of Hays and threatened to sue the MPPDA and every political censorship board in the country. He issued a public statement condemning censorship:

> It has become a serious threat to the freedom of honest expression in America when self-styled guardians of the public welfare, as personified by our censor boards, lend their aid and their influence to the abortive efforts of selfish and vicious interests to suppress a motion picture simply because it depicts the truth about conditions in the United States which have been front page news since the advent of Prohibition.[4]

As an independent producer, Hughes bristled at the restrictions of industry censorship. He refused to play by the rules of the Hays Office and released unaltered prints in areas without censorship. While Hughes had many critics, he was praised by the *New York Herald Tribune* as the only "producer who has the courage to come out and fight this censorship menace in the open. We wish him a smashing success."[5]

Even Hughes, however, could not win the fight with the Hollywood system that tightly controlled the product put on the screen through its censorship office and even more rigidly refused to screen films that did not meet code guidelines in industry-owned theaters. Joseph I. Breen, head of the Production Code Administration as of 1934, refused numerous requests by Hughes to rerelease *Scarface* after its initial run, despite the film's popularity. Hughes was incensed when it was denied a seal in 1935. He argued that the film already had code approval and again threatened to sue, but Breen refused to budge.[6] *Scarface* remained locked in the vaults.

Perhaps it was his frustration with the very restrictive censorship system that caused Hughes to withdraw from active film production after *Scarface*. Whatever the reason, eight years were to pass before the industrialist would again challenge Will Hays, industry and political censors, and religious organizations with a new film. For his next film Hughes moved from urban outlaws and sultry molls to the Old West of coldhearted gunslingers, fearless sheriffs, and powerful women. *The Outlaw,* yet another Hollywood version of the exploits of William Bonney, alias Billy the Kid, was as controversial as *Scarface* and generated more publicity for an unknown actress (Jane Russell) than any other film in history. Completed in 1941, the film was not released to the general public until 1946. It was condemned by the Catholic Legion of Decency for almost a decade, denounced in pulpits from coast to coast, and banned by state and municipal censorship boards – and it broke box-office records wherever it was allowed to play.

Rumors flew fast and furious in Hollywood in late 1939 that Hughes was going to make another movie. Confirmation came when director Howard Hawks discussed the project with Geoffrey Shurlock and Joe Breen at the PCA offices in April 1940. Hawks told the censors he and Hughes wanted to make "a serious western" but did not want to have to arrest or kill his hero, Billy the Kid, at the end of the movie. Would the PCA allow this to happen if no criminal acts were committed by Billy during the movie? Breen and Shurlock were uncomfortable, but suggested it might be permissible if Hawks made it clear that Billy "was going to die."[7]

Given some encouragement from the PCA, Hughes assembled a first-rate production team. Hawks and Hecht were reunited as director and screenwriter; Gregg Toland, one of the finest cinema photographers in Hollywood, whose credits included *We Live Again, Dead End,* and *The Grapes of Wrath,* was signed to shoot the western. Adding luster to the team were veteran actors Thomas Mitchell, penned in as Sheriff Pat Garrett, and Walter Huston, who agreed to play the flamboyant Doc Holliday. Hughes, ever the show-man, wanted two unknowns to play Billy and the female romantic lead, Rio, a hot-blooded half-breed who loves Doc but marries Billy.

To create a national search for his two leads, Hughes turned to Russell Birdwell, who had just created an international frenzy with his publicity campaign to cast Scarlet O'Hara in *Gone with the Wind.* For $1,500 a week Birdwell signed on with Hughes to discover a beautiful starlet and a hand-some, young Billy. From the thousands of photographs submitted, Hughes selected Jack Buetel, a 23-three-year-old Texan who had come to Hollywood to make it in the movies. Buetel, who had no acting experience, looked like the teenager Billy the Kid was in real life. For Rio Hughes picked the photo of a 19-year-old Los Angeles receptionist, Ernestine Jane Geraldine Russell, whose had done some local theater and modeling. Russell became a star and a Hollywood legend; Buetel soon faded from the screen and the public gaze.

Had Hawks and Hecht remained with the production, *The Outlaw* might have been the "serious" western Hawks envisioned; but both men battled with Hughes and left. Hughes then hired Jules Furthman to write the script. Furthman, a screenwriter whose first credit had come in 1915, had penned such sexually charged films of the 1930s as *Morocco, Shanghai Express,* and *Blonde Venus* for Marlene Dietrich and Jean Harlow's wonderful satire on Hollywood sex stars, *Bombshell.* He and Hawks had collaborated in 1939 on the adventure drama *Only Angels Have Wings.* However, it was soon ob-vious that Furthman was no Hecht, and Jane Russell no Dietrich or Harlow; and when Hughes decided to direct, it was very clear he was no Hawks.

Furthman's script was submitted to the PCA in December 1940. The plot, such as it was, bore no relationship to history and revolved around the ten-sion among Sheriff Garrett, Doc Holliday, and Billy. Garrett and Doc are best friends until Billy rides into town on Doc's horse, Red. Garrett wants to arrest Billy, but Doc is taken with the young outlaw and refuses to help. Throughout the movie Doc and Billy bicker over who owns Red, a very smart horse, and Rio, a very attractive woman. They share both. In the end Doc is killed by Garrett, and Rio, after bouncing back and forth between Doc and Billy, rides off into the sunset with Billy.

There were several issues of controversy for the PCA: an implied rape of Rio by Billy; the open sexual relationships between Rio and Doc and then Rio and Billy with no "voice of morality" declaring such actions wrong; and, most important, the scenes of Jane Russell in a scoop-necked peasant blouse. Throughout the film Billy and Doc are extremely cavalier about their rela-tionship with Rio, constantly comparing her with the horse, Red. Both re-spect and covet Red for his intelligence and work habits; Rio, on the other hand, is little more than a plaything that these gunslingers use for temporary entertainment.

In 1941 any movie that dealt with rape or implied that casual sex was acceptable was automatically rejected by the PCA. With or without Jane Russell, then, *The Outlaw* was destined for censorship problems. When the PCA's Geoffrey Shurlock, Al Lynch, and Joe Breen read the script they immediately decided it violated the Production Code with scenes of illicit sex, the killing of a sheriff, and the "glorification" of a criminal who was allowed to go unpunished. The PCA told Hughes to correct these problems and warned that there must "be no exposure of Rio's person."[8]

At any Hollywood studio this letter would have forced a major rewrite of the script to bring it in compliance with the code and to ensure access to industry theaters. Hughes, however, ignored Breen's letter and forged ahead with the film, as he had done with *Scarface.*

The set was total chaos. After Hawks quit, Hughes brought the entire crew back from location in Arizona to Los Angeles. Hughes was rarely on the set: His days were consumed with his developing aircraft industry as America geared up for war; it was only late at night that he turned into a director. Furthman worked as writer-director-producer but with no authority to make decisions. The crew often sat around for days with little to do. Huston and Mitchell seethed as Hughes demanded retake after retake. Buetel and Russell did as they were told. The end result was one of the "shabbiest, contrived, and cornball westerns every made."[9]

When the censors at the PCA reviewed the completed film in March 1941 they were shocked: not because it was corny, but because of the "inescapable suggestion of illicit relationship between Doc, Rio and Billy" and the countless shots of Rio "in which her breasts are not fully covered."[10] There would be no seal of approval from the PCA until these issues were corrected.

Breen realized that Hughes was unlikely to take his demands seriously and warned his boss, Will Hays, that an appeal of his ruling was brewing. In recent months, Breen wrote, "we have noticed a marked tendency on the part of the studios to more and more undrape women's breasts." Breen had lately denied a code to Universal for a "shocking display of women's breasts" and had refused Columbia a seal for a film that featured "sweater shots," which "emphasized women's breasts by way of tight, close-fitting garments"; but *The Outlaw,* Breen claimed, "outdoes anything we have ever seen on the screen."[11]

To stop this trend Breen fired off a letter to every studio demanding that all cleavage shots be eliminated and threatening to reject any film featuring women in tight angora sweaters "in which the breasts are clearly outlined."[12] The sweater industry immediately protested to Hays, as angora sweaters were the current fashion rage. Even *Newsweek* chuckled that movie censors were preventing the studios from showing onscreen what was commonly seen on the streets of America. In fact, the issue was not just cleavage: Breen would not approve scenes in which women were dressed in any clothing that emphasized their bodies, especially their breasts or hips.

Much has been written about Jane Russell and the amount of flesh exposed in *The Outlaw*. Most of the accounts are as tasteless as the advertising campaigns that accompanied the film (to be recounted later in this chapter). Popular accounts, as well as more recent academic writing, fall into an adolescent tittering that use boyish puns to describe Russell's anatomy. There is no doubt that Russell was selected to play the role for her looks, and that Hughes and Birdwell exploited her shamelessly; but it is also important to note that for at least two-thirds of the film Russell wears a print blouse that goes no more than an inch or two below her neck and exposes no cleavage at all. The blouse is not tight and could be described, even for 1941 dress styles, as modest.

The controversy over Russell is centered on the last third of the film, during which she wears a white, low-cut peasant blouse. There are numerous scenes in which she bends over to pick something up, with the camera lingering on her; these do, in fact, expose some cleavage. There is also a scene in which Russell is tied to two stakes with her arms extended. While she is struggling to get free, there are additional glimpses of cleavage.

Several meetings between Hughes and the PCA failed to resolve their differences over Russell's presentation, and the producer demanded a hearing from the MPPDA Board of Directors in New York. At the hearing the questions of sexual impropriety among the major characters, to which the PCA had objected, seemed forgotten. The debate instead focused on whether or not the shots of Jane Russell violated the code and decency. Russell Birdwell represented Hughes and Neil McCarthy the PCA. It must have been a strange meeting: Birdwell came armed with stacks of "cheesecake" photos of Hollywood starlets. He used hundreds of publicity stills from countless movies as exhibits, and argued that women in slinky evening gowns, satiny lingerie, and low-cut blouses were a Hollywood tradition.[13] The moguls must have squirmed a bit as they examined stills and publicity shots from their own movies.

McCarthy had his own version of Hollywood history. He countered that the PCA had consistently rejected films since 1934 for excessive exposure, and gave board members stills of scenes and costumes from films that had been refused a seal. After some consideration the board reached a diplomatic solution: They upheld the PCA ruling but agreed to give Hughes a seal (no. 7440) if he deleted some twenty-five feet of film (about a minute) in which Russell was bending over, peasant blouse agape.[14]

With a clear victory and approval to open the film nationwide, Hughes inexplicably withdrew the film. He offered no explanation, but it was obvious that as America armed for war Hughes was more interested in his aircraft company than in the movies.

Breen undoubtedly was disappointed in the board's ruling, but he had been planning a new career move for months. He felt pressure from all sides: The industry wanted more freedom, and the Catholic Legion wanted movies to be even more restrictive. He wrote to Father Daniel Lord that he was completely frustrated with the Legion of Decency. The Catholics, he complained, "would have us make only stories of Pollyanna and The Rover Boys." He lashed out at the Legion for assigning B classifications to *Tobacco Road* and *Back Street,* and for condemning with a C rating *This Thing Called Love,* which he believed had been completely purged of the original "vile" material. Breen characterized Legion ratings in general as "mistaken."[15]

It came as no surprise that a couple of months later, on May 1, 1941 – two weeks before the board's decision on *The Outlaw* – Breen announced he was "punch drunk" from work as the Hollywood censor and resigned. *Newsweek* speculated that he may have resigned because of the "barrage of nationwide laughter and criticism that followed the now famous injunction against the 'sweater girl' on the screen."[16] It seems more likely that Breen was simply tired of the constant criticism.

In a bizarre twist, Breen announced the following day that he was moving to RKO – the studio through which Howard Hughes would soon distribute *The Outlaw* – as general manager. Breen was going to make movies! He stated confidently that there was no subject that could not be treated under the code, and criticized the industry for what he saw as a lack of entertainment value in films. Breen promised that RKO films would be both code pure and entertaining; but he quickly discovered that it was harder to create than to criticize, and within a year he was summarily fired.[17]

Breen was not to be unemployed for long: Just one year after his move to RKO he would return to his job as Hollywood censor in May 1942. Despite an intensive search for a replacement, the industry was unable to find a person on which Martin Quigley, the producers, the Catholic church, and Will Hays could agree. The Legion pressured Hays to agree that any replacement must be a Catholic;[18] but which Catholic? Martin Quigley, Breen's old mentor, lobbied hard for Judge Stephen S. Jackson, a New York State judge, to replace Breen, and Jackson did have some support from the National Legion office. Quigley believed that the PCA had become a one-man operation under Breen; moreover, Breen had often ignored his advice.[19]

In February 1942 J. Robert Ruskin, vice-president and general counsel of Loew's Inc., formed an informal selection committee to appoint a new PCA director. Ruskin met with his counterparts from Paramount, Columbia, Warner Bros., and RKO. To a man they favored moving Breen back into his old position. The studios wanted Breen for his contacts with the Catholic church and his ability to anticipate censorship problems with private and government boards; they also worried that the war would bring increased government scrutiny to their industry. The studios worked quietly with George J. Schaefer at RKO to avoid the appearance that Breen was being "dumped," and when the Legion gave its approval, returned Breen to what he did best: censor films.[20]

Although Breen was back in his old haunt, his power base had been seriously eroded. Hollywood was, and still is, a very small, tight community. Success is immediately rewarded with recognition, massive amounts of money, invitations to the best parties, and access to the inner sanctums of power; but an industry in which one is only as good as one's last film can also be cruel to those who fail to produce. The Hollywood party circuit was certainly agog with stories of Breen's inefficacy at RKO. After bragging that he knew how to produce clean entertainment, he had failed miserably.

The film community was also too small not to have heard the rumors of Quigley's refusal to support Breen, and of the dissatisfaction in the Legion office. Nevertheless, Breen had survived, had regained his $100,000-a-year salary, and would again do battle with producers until his retirement in 1954. More often than not, Breen would win; but everyone in Hollywood knew he had been publicly humiliated by his venture into the studios.

Breen returned to the PCA offices just as America was building a war machine of incredible proportions. Millions of Americans volunteered for or were drafted into military service, and millions more, mostly women and African-Americans, moved in huge numbers to replace them in the war factories. America had been reluctant to go to war, however, and the administration of Franklin D. Roosevelt quickly recognized the power of film to propagandize as well as entertain. The war made Hollywood a boom town much as the factories for war made Detroit, Seattle, and other cities boom. Within a month after Breen's return to the PCA, the federal government announced the creation of the Office of War Information (OWI), whose goal was to enhance public understanding of the war through the press, radio, and motion pictures.[21]

To the newly appointed director of OWI, radio journalist Elmer Davis, the "easiest way to inject a propaganda idea into most people's minds is to let it go in through the medium of an entertainment picture when they do not realize that they are being propagandized." Breen, of course, had long fought against this type of "propaganda" in films. During the 1930s he had successfully muted the political content of films like *Fury, Dead End, They Won't Forget,* and *Idiot's Delight.* The PCA had prevented the filming of Sinclair

Lewis's *It Can't Happen Here* and wanted "good Germans" to balance the "bad Germans" presented in prewar films like *Confessions of a Nazi Spy*.

To challenge this conservative view of the world, OWI opened a Hollywood office and recruited a group of liberal New Dealers who were determined to sharpen the political content of Hollywood films. The Hollywood branch was headed by Nelson Poynter, an avid interventionist and owner-publisher of the *St. Petersburg Times*. Poynter and his staff drafted a manual for filmmakers. The central question OWI asked of Hollywood was, "Will This Picture Help Win the War?" The manual asked filmmakers to present the war as a "people's war"; to show America unified in its support of democracy and its hatred of fascism; to illustrate the common bonds between Americans and their allies, the Russians, British, and Chinese; and to portray the enemy not in racial stereotypes but in ideological terms. OWI emphasized that fascism, not race, was the enemy.[22]

The OWI manual was a second Hollywood code for the war years. The government canon functioned in the same manner as the PCA code: It explained to filmmakers how to interpret and portray political doctrine. Filmmakers were requested to submit scripts to OWI for preproduction evaluation, and most did. If OWI and the PCA clashed on ideological issues, OWI usually won out. For example, when Breen read the script for the Warner Bros. paean to Stalin and the Soviet Union, *Mission to Moscow,* he objected to what he saw as a glorification of communism, and alerted Jack Warner that "considerable protest" would greet the picture; but OWI brushed his opinions aside, and Breen admitted that, "In the face of all this, it seems to me that . . . we can do little but approve the material."[23] For the duration, Breen and the PCA were restricted to moral issues – the OWI determined the political stance of American movies.

When Howard Hughes suddenly decided to release *The Outlaw* in San Francisco in February 1943, there was little doubt that the issue was morality not politics. While the film had been on the shelf for two years, Birdwell had launched a massive publicity campaign to make Russell a star. Photographic spreads in *Life* and *Look* brought national attention. *Pic* and *Click,* two magazines that were on the condemned list of the Catholic National Office of Decent Literature (the print equivalent of the Legion of Decency), carried photographs of censored scenes, and *Esquire* ran a two-page spread that was a national sensation.[24] Russell was a household name before she was seen on the screen.

When Hughes finally decided on San Francisco for his premiere, Birdwell littered the Bay Area with provocative billboards of Russell that exposed far more flesh than the movie. Appealing to a wartime audience, the billboards proclaimed: SEX HAS NOT BEEN RATIONED! In newspaper ads Russell was pictured in a sultry "come and get me" pose in a hayloft, her gaping blouse falling off her shoulders with the ads inquiring, "How would you like to tussle with Russell?" To lure fans to the theater Hughes and Birdwell created a vignette featuring Russell and Buetel on stage acting out a scene that was "too hot for the movies." The promise, unkept, implied that patrons would see what had been cut from the film.[25]

When the critics finally saw the film they were quick to pan it. The *Hollywood Reporter* warned filmgoers that it was "overlong, inadequately organized and disjointed" and that much of the dialogue bordered on the "brink of absurdity."[26] *Variety* agreed that "beyond the sex attraction of Miss Russell's frankly displayed charms" the picture was horrible.[27] Quigley's *Motion Picture Herald* lambasted the film. Despite the fact that the it carried a PCA seal of approval, *Herald* critic William Weaver wrote that *The Outlaw* was made "in defiance of a number of principles and standards" established by the industry. The film "depicts . . . a hero without morals . . . and sends him out . . . at its close unpunished, unrepentant and triumphant over the minions and meanings of the law." Weaver noted the film featured "sex over six-shooters," and was outraged that it violated "with vigor the Hart–Mix–Jones–Autry tradition that sex has no place in a Western."[28]

When the ads and the reviews hit the papers, local Catholics peppered their parish priests with calls: Had the church cleared *The Outlaw?* What was the Legion rating? When it became apparent that the National Office of the Legion had not seen the movie and that Hughes had no intention of providing them with a print to preview, the local San Francisco branch of the Legion was given permission to classify the film. "If the objectionable parts were cut there would be nothing left," wrote one Legion reviewer. Another added: "Stupid, no changes could cure it."[29] A third objected to the way Russell was presented: "It makes woman a chattel equal to a horse." The San Francisco Legion condemned the film as immoral.

Despite critical disdain and the disapproval of the Catholic Legion – or perhaps because of it – there was a near-stampede at the box office when this modern cowboy saga opened at San Francisco's Geary Theater on February 5, 1943. Hughes brought a trainload of press representatives and Hollywood celebrities to San Francisco for the premiere, and the demand for tickets was so high that Hughes scheduled seats on a reserved-only basis at $2.50 apiece! The Geary was sold out, and *Variety* reported it did "a great $30,000" in business the first week and "a booming $25,000" the second.[30] After a two-week run the film moved to the Tivoli, where it ran for another month. *Variety* was amazed that after a six-week run *The Outlaw* was still "grossing $21,000, with waiting lines outside the theater."[31]

It was clear that Hughes and Birdwell had created a box-office sensation. After an incredibly successful run, Hughes, again inexplicably, withdrew the film from circulation for another three years.

At the end of the war in August 1945, Hollywood stood as the unchallenged leader in the production of mass entertainment for worldwide audiences. Awash in money, Hollywood could count on some ninety million customers consuming its product every week. With continental Europe in shambles, foreign competition was nil. Nevertheless, though few realized it at the time, the end of the war marked the end of the golden era for Hollywood. The industry's power and prestige would steadily erode over the next several decades. Perhaps symbolic of the end of the era was the resignation of "the Little General," the "Presbyterian pope," Will Hays, as movie czar.[32]

Hays had taken over a troubled industry in 1922 and for twenty-three years represented the interests of the industry; but the owners and producers had grown tired of Hays, who they felt was too ineffective to lead the industry in the postwar era. In March 1945 an ominous threat to the industry's economic security reappeared when the Department of Justice announced its intention to reinitiate antitrust action against the eight major studios. The industry executives, who believed Hays was no longer effective in Washington, gave him a golden parachute of half a million dollars. Hays gracefully retired to Indiana as a little-used consultant.

To replace him the moguls lured Eric Johnston, a solid Republican whose free-enterprise, anticommunist credentials were impeccable. A successful Seattle businessman, Johnston had been the president of the U.S. Chamber of Commerce during the war and had established important links between the business community and Washington. He was paid handsomely: $150,000 a year to promote the film industry and smooth over difficulties with censors and bureaucrats. Under Johnston the organization was renamed the Motion Picture Association of America (MPAA), but its goals remained the same.

Shortly after Johnston assumed power, Hughes decided to reissue *The Outlaw* through the distribution wing of United Artists.[33] With a limited number of prints available, Hughes contrived a road-show program with Russell making personal appearances to promote the horse drama. The original PCA seal, which had not been revoked, allowed access to industry theaters. Birdwell peppered the country with provocative ads again asking film fans if they would like "to tussle with Russell." Line drawings of Russell and Buetel clinching in a hay stack with CENSORED across their bodies announced the film's arrival in local cities.

Although the condemned rating from the Legion of Decency still stood, Hughes believed he could sell the film with or without Catholic approval.

The Legion rating simply played into his promotional campaign to sell the film as a property too hot for the censors. To prove the point, he opened the film in the second most powerful diocese in America: Chicago, long a hotbed of Legion support.

Hughes and Birdwell hit a last-minute snag when copies of Birdwell's ads, submitted to the MPAA's advertising code for approval, were "rejected in toto."[34] When Eric Johnston and the MPAA demanded that Hughes defend himself before an industry tribunal, Hughes resigned from the trade association in a huff and slapped a $5 million lawsuit on them (no idle threat from a man worth a reported $30 million). Hughes accused the MPAA of interfering with his ability to market his film, and his legal team quickly obtained an injunction that prohibited the MPAA from taking any action against the film until the dispute was resolved in court. It would take at least six months for the courts to rule, and Hughes used the time to exhibit the film.[35]

In March 1946 *The Outlaw* opened at the Oriental Theater in downtown Chicago. Aided by the personal appearance of Jane Russell, business was "colossal." *Variety* reported that a three-week run in Chicago generated almost $300,000 in box-office revenue despite Catholic protests and pickets.[36]

From Chicago the film moved to Los Angeles, where it opened at the four area Music Hall theaters. Newspaper ads told eager Angelenos that "The Music Halls get the big ones," and skywriters wrote *The Outlaw* in script followed by two huge circles with a large dot in each! Everyone got the message. The *Los Angeles Daily News* reported major "traffic jams" at all locations when the film opened.[37] At the Beverly Hills Music Hall all seats for a 10:00 A.M. showing were sold an hour before the theater opened. "Yells, whistles, screams and loud guffaws" greeted Russell's appearance onstage. The reviewer for the *Los Angeles Express* described the experience as more "appropriate to smoking room literature than a public theater."[38] The film broke all records at the Music Hall theaters during a two-week run.

In May *The Outlaw* moved to Father Daniel Lord's diocese, St. Louis. Picket lines greeted movie fans outside Loew's State in downtown St. Louis as children marched with banners urging "HELP US OUTLAW THE OUTLAW." Msgr. Alfred G. Thompson told the local press that "no decent person would go" to see the film; but once the St. Louis Police Department's Morality Squad viewed the film and found nothing objectionable in it, St. Louis cops chased away the Catholic kids manning the picket lines.[39] Even a weeklong rain could not keep people away from the theater. *Variety* reported that the "controversial flicker is the best coin getter" in the city. The film broke all local box-office records, generating more than $60,000 in a three-week run.[40]

Similar accounts drifted in from all over the country. In Louisville there were the "usual objections by religious groups," but Loew's State did a "mammoth $28,000" the first week. In Kansas City, Bible belters rushed the

Midland Theater for a glimpse of Russell. Indianapolis reported record business as well.

There were, of course, protests from Catholic groups nationwide over the next several years. In Harrisburg, Pennsylvania, Bishop George Leech called the film a "destructive and corrupting picture which glamorized crime and immorality." In Galveston, Texas, Bishop Christopher Byrne demanded a yearlong boycott of Loew's theaters in the Houston area for showing *The Outlaw,* which he judged was "indecent and immoral" and "basely offends in costume and action." The most effective protest came from Philadelphia, where Dennis Cardinal Dougherty threatened theater owner William Goldman that he would order a one-year boycott by Catholics of "any theaters that dare to exhibit this indecent film." Goldman appealed to Dougherty to no avail that the film had been approved by Pennsylvania censors. *Variety* reported that "roving bands of Catholics" threatened theater owners if they continued playing the film.[41] Under pressure Goldman withdrew the film.[42] In Memphis censor Lloyd Binford banned the film, stating it was, in his opinion, "a bad influence on the boys of today and I'm not going to let it show in Memphis."[43]

Critics savaged the film for other reasons. The *New York Times* called it "tedious," and judged Russell "hopelessly inept." The paper warned readers that the love scenes had been cut from the film.[44] Herb Sterne was merciless: "the film has an amateur air of a kind one might expect in a product confected by some grammar school cinema class."[45] Philip Hartung in the Catholic *Commonweal* dismissed it as a film that he found difficult to "take seriously." It was all "rather silly," he wrote.[46]

When *The Outlaw* finally reached San Francisco in late May for a return engagement, the police, aware of the national furor, seized the film as immoral. After it had been viewed by judge and jury, Judge Twain Michelson reprimanded the police for seizing a film that had already played in the city in 1943. He told the jury:

> I cannot bring myself to the legal conclusion that the picture . . . has left you . . . in a state of moral suspense, or of mental lewdness and licentiousness, bewitched and seduced.[47]

The judge even commented on one of the most controversial scenes in the movie. Censors were especially upset over the scene in which Rio climbs into bed with Billy to help break his fever. Judge Michelson was not convinced the scene was a corrupting influence, and told the women on the jury:

> I cannot bring myself to the legal conclusion . . . that you would at some opportune and clandestine moment abandon your hearths, your children and your husbands to lie in the bed of some invalided or dying man for one last moment of carnal or lustful experience.[48]

The good men and women of the jury agreed. The film opened to record crowds, raking in $158,000 in a seven-week run.

In early June the curious case of *The Outlaw* took another strange turn. The courts ruled that if Hughes wanted to keep the picture's code seal, he had to abide by the association rules. This ruling cleared the way for the PCA to withdraw its seal and prevent Hughes from showing the film in association theaters; but Hughes was free to continue to play the film at art houses and independent theaters – and he did just that.

Under normal conditions, inability to access industry screens meant death at the box office. The major studios still controlled all the first-run theaters in the major cities and, through their system of block booking and blind booking (requiring exhibitors to book films sight unseen), effectively tied up the national theater chains, which had agreed not to screen movies that bore no PCA seal.

Nevertheless, *The Outlaw,* to use theatrical parlance, had legs – strong legs, which continued to embarrass both the MPAA and the Legion. Prohibited from access to the first-run theaters in Dallas, Hughes opened his film simultaneously at twenty-one neighborhood theaters scattered throughout the Dallas area. Hughes's publicity agents hired helicopters with loudspeakers to drum up interest, startled Dallas pedestrians by projecting a trailer of the film across downtown streets, plastered local streetcars with posters of Russell, and used telemarketing teams to call local citizens. The results, *Variety* reported, were "nothing short of phenomenal": In a short three-day run more than 100,000 out of an estimated population of 375,000 paid to see *The Outlaw.* "Practically every one of the 21 houses had a queue standing in a misty drizzle . . . with traffic jams caused by motorists cruising from one theater to another hunting for the shortest line."[49] When the city commission in San Antonio banned the film, local entrepreneurs rented the Pan American Speedway, located a few hundred feet outside the city limits, and did a booming business with a makeshift drive-in in July 1947.

The Outlaw was an "industry phenomenon"; nothing, it seemed, could keep people away from this film. Secular and religious reviewers alike panned the movie without mercy, and to no avail. Trade magazines marveled that fans came despite bad weather, traffic jams, and second-rate theaters. The *Motion Picture Herald* admitted it was the "1946 wonder in the trade."[50] In rerelease in 1947, the film did even better business in the same cities it had played in 1946. Despite being limited to about two-thirds of the nation's theaters, the film grossed $3 million by mid-1947, and at the end of the decade was ranked eleventh-best box-office performer of the 1940s.

Record crowds followed the film to its European opening at the Pavilion in London. The critics again ridiculed *The Outlaw* as entertainment, but fans stormed the box office. The publicity campaign hit new highs when British press agent Suzanne Warner hired a psychologist to wire the Pavilion with a "psycho-galvanometer," a gadget used to measure audience emotional reactions during the film. Critic Walter Wilcox of the *Sunday Dispatch* panned the film, but registered a "warm 24 centimeters" when Russell appeared in the peasant blouse. A lady moviegoer who claimed indifference to screen sex hit a red-hot "29 centimeters" when Rio climbed into bed with Billy. Meanwhile, a soldier fresh from two years overseas duty blew the top off the "psycho-galvanometer" when Russell and Buetel tussled in the haystack![51]

It was very clear in 1947 that neither the lack of a Production Code seal nor condemnation by the Legion of Decency was any longer a portent of financial disaster. The message was pellucid to Bishop William A. Scully, who headed the Episcopal Committee on Motion Pictures in 1947. Scully wrote to his old friend Bishop John Cantwell that Legion efforts to stop *The Outlaw* had "been thwarted" by "the stubborn opposition" of Hughes, who simply refused to abide to Legion demands.[52] Hughes had successfully ignored not only the Legion but also Joe Breen. *The Outlaw* played throughout the country without a PCA seal until 1949, when additional cuts restored the MPAA's blessing.

The Outlaw demonstrated that there was a huge market for movies that stepped outside the restrictive codes that had determined movie content for close to two decades. Using a very aggressive (tasteless, many claimed) advertising campaign, Hughes made *The Outlaw* a box-office hit despite being frozen out of a third of the nation's movie theaters. The film grossed more than $5 million of box-office revenue, and Howard Hughes proved that the public would go to movies rejected by the PCA and the Legion.

It was a lesson that David O. Selznick, a Hollywood legend, would soon exploit and that, unfortunately, the rest of the industry would ignore. Selznick, like Hughes, was about to prove conclusively that censorship problems could not prevent a blockbuster film with a huge advertising budget from doing land-office business.

The Selznick family came from old Hollywood stock. Lewis J. Selznick, David's father, was an original Hollywood mogul. Born in Kiev, Russia, in 1870, he had immigrated to America at the turn of the century to escape dire poverty. Chasing the American dream, Lewis Selznick had quickly worked his way up from a lowly jeweler's apprentice to owner of a chain of very successful jewelry stores in Pittsburgh. In 1910 he had moved to New York and invested heavily in a new industry: the movies. After a short stint with Universal, Selznick had formed his own company and begun producing films. His sons, Myron (who became one of Hollywood's most famous talent agents) and David, worked for their father, learning every aspect of film production and distribution until he went bankrupt in 1923.

After several years of dabbling in other businesses, David moved to Hollywood in 1926 and was hired as an assistant story editor at MGM. One of the original "boy wonders" in Hollywood, Selznick quickly worked his way to the top of the industry. He left MGM in a huff in 1927 and by 1931 was vice-president in charge of production at RKO. He married Louis B. Mayer's daughter, Irene, in 1930 and returned to MGM in 1933 as vice-president and producer. After a highly successful run as a producer, he left MGM in 1936 and formed his own independent production company, Selznick International.

Selznick always viewed the producer, not the director, as the most important role in moviemaking. "The difference between myself and other producers is I am interested in the thousands and thousands of details that go into the making of a film. . . . The way I see it, my function is to be responsible for everything."[53] He put that attention to detail to work and reeled off a series of high-quality films: *The Garden of Allah* (1936) starring Marlene Dietrich, *A Star Is Born* (1937), and *The Adventures of Tom Sawyer* (1938).[54]

In 1939 his lavish production of Margaret Mitchell's *Gone with the Wind* solidified Selznick's reputation as one of the greatest filmmakers in Hollywood history. Selznick, one of the few producers who was willing to fight industry censorship, battled with Breen for months over whether or not Clark Gable could utter, "Frankly, my dear, I don't give a damn." Selznick won but he deeply resented Breen's interference. No one seemed too shocked by hearing "damn," and the film swept the Academy Awards, winning eight of its thirteen nominations, and brought in a staggering $77 million! (In 1939, when most ticket prices ranged from 15 cents to 50 cents, the second leading box-office hit, *The Wizard of Oz,* brought in less than $5 million; few films reached the million-dollar level.)

In 1940 the producer combined forces with Alfred Hitchcock to bring to the screen Daphne du Maurier's *Rebecca,* a haunting tale of infidelity and murder, laced with hints of abortion and lesbianism. Selznick, who prided himself on authentic adaptations of works of literary merit, fought both Hitchcock and Breen to maintain du Maurier's text. The novel centered around a wealthy widower on the rebound, Maxim de Winter, who marries a younger woman. It at first appears that de Winter's first wife, Rebecca, was beloved by everyone who knew her; but as the story unfolds quite another Rebecca emerges – a shrew, an adulterer whose viciousness drove her husband to murder.

Abortion and any hint of "sexual perversion" quickly disappeared; but a major problem remained because in the novel the husband is not punished for his crime. Breen balked when Selznick attempted to bring an unpunished murderer to the screen. Instead, he suggested the death be accidental, and Selznick was forced to make that concession to save the film. He complained to a friend: "Rebecca is the story of a man who has murdered his wife, and it now becomes the story of a man who buried a wife who was killed accidentally!" The code was, Selznick complained, "insane and inane."[55]

Despite the alternations, the film was a artistic and financial success. It won the Academy Award for Best Picture, giving Selznick a two-year sweep in that prestigious category. It garnered eight other nominations and came in a solid fourth in the all-important 1940 box-office sweepstakes.

Selznick, like the rest of Hollywood, was always looking for a hot property. In January 1944 Niven Busch published a novel, *Duel in the Sun,* which traced the history of a powerful Texas family, the McCanleses, in the 1880s. The patriarch of the family was Senator McCanles, who owned a million acres of Texas, ruled his empire with a iron fist, and was determined to prevent the railroad from coming through his land. He terrorized his wife, ignored his son Jessie, a lawyer who favored progress and the railroad, and doted on his no-good son Lewt. Busch's work differed from the typical western novel by focusing much of the action around the sexual exploits of Lewt and his torrid affair with Pearl Chavez, a half-breed Indian girl who lives on the McCanles ranch. The novel hit the best-seller lists almost immediately, and RKO bought the movie rights.

When RKO sent in a first script to the PCA offices, the reaction was rather predictable. Breen judged it unacceptable because it was littered with "illicit sex and murder for revenge, without the full compensating moral values required by the Code." The PCA also shuddered at the reaction religious organizations would have to the "Sin Killer," an uneducated, vulgar frontier religious figure who used unorthodox techniques to purge "sin" from sinners: The censors warned the studio to "make it quite clear that he is in no sense an ordained minister" and ensure that the character not be presented as "a travesty on religion." In addition, Breen worried about scenes implying that Lewt raped Pearl, or hinted that Pearl slept in the nude and went skinny-dipping with Lewt. As usual, Breen offered to work with the studio to make the property comply with the code.[56]

Selznick became involved when RKO asked him to loan out actress Jennifer Jones and director William Dieterle, both of whom were under personal contract to Selznick, for the film.[57] In 1943 Jones had won the Academy Award for Best Actress in her first starring role as a pious young peasant girl who has a vision of the Virgin Mary in *The Song of Bernadette.* In 1944 she had a major role in Selznick's popular war drama *Since You Went Away* and was considered strong box office in Hollywood. RKO wanted Jones to play opposite its cowboy hero John Wayne, whom the studio had scheduled to play Lewt. Selznick balked at pairing Jones and Wayne because he did not believe Wayne capable of playing a cowboy with an overly active libido and felt the pairing, not the role, would harm Jones's career. The negotiations quickly reached an impasse, but when Selznick offered to buy the screen rights from RKO in November 1944, they accepted.[58]

Duel in the Sun was an unusual choice for Selznick, who had a reputation for filming classic literature and was especially fond of Charles Dickens. Ben Hecht once told him: "The trouble with you, David, is that you did all your reading before you were twelve."[59] *Duel* was neither a classic novel nor one that would be read before the age of 12. It had been a popular best-seller but was not considered to be much more than good pulp fiction. Whether Selznick was drawn to the project because of the success of *The Outlaw* or because he saw it as a starring vehicle for Jones, with whom he was having an affair and would soon marry, is hard to tell. Whatever his reasons, Selznick was determined to turn this rather ordinary western novel into another *Gone with the Wind*. Writer Charles Brackett was closer to the truth, however, when he noted that *Duel* was "*The Outlaw* in bad taste."[60]

To replace the stodgy Wayne, Selznick settled on another Hollywood newcomer, Gregory Peck. Tall and lanky, Peck fit the cowboy image. Peck had came to Hollywood in 1943 and made an immediate impact as Father Francis Chisholm, a Catholic missionary in China, in *Keys of the Kingdom*. Selznick would soon turn Saint Bernadette and Father Chisholm into characters who lied, cheated, murdered, and died for lust.

Selznick moved quickly to bring the project to the screen. He began rewriting the script with screenwriter Oliver H. P. Garrett and recruited an all-star cast to work with Jones and Peck. To play the mean-spirited Senator McCanles he signed Lionel Barrymore, contrasting this old curmudgeon with Lillian Gish, who played Laura Belle, McCanles's saintly, frail wife. The charlatan minister, the Sin Killer, was played by character actor Walter Huston. Selznick paid Huston $40,000 for four days' work in a very minor role that would cause a major headache with both Catholics and Protestants. Joseph Cotton played Lewt's brother Jessie, a highly respected lawyer who loves Pearl and is shot by his jealous brother. Butterfly McQueen re-created her role from *Gone with the Wind* as the scatterbrained servant Vashti, and Hollywood regulars Harry Carey, Herbert Marshall, and Charles Bickford played supporting roles. Selznick lured Orson Welles to narrate and Dimitri Tiomkin to create a musical score, and filmed *Duel* in Technicolor.

After Dieterle refused the job, Selznick turned to King Vidor to direct. Vidor, a veteran of more than forty films including *The Big Parade, Our Daily Bread,* and *Northwest Passage,* battled Selznick for control; but it was clear from the beginning that Selznick, not Vidor, would dominate the set.

Selznick knew that he was going to have problems with the PCA over *Duel.* He desperately wanted to keep Lewt's seduction of Pearl and their fiery, violent, and passionate relationship; without it there was no movie. What he hoped to be able to do was to contrive enough "moral values" and severe punishment of the sinners into the script to satisfy censors and critics. The trick was how to illustrate this visually without offending the PCA and the Legion.

Selznick and Garrett began reconstructing *Duel* in early 1945. Pearl and Lewt were the keys to the new morality. Pearl tells everyone in the first third of the script that she wants to be a good girl. Her mother, a full-blooded Indian, had married a white man but was killed by him after he discovered her liaison with another man. Pearl has inherited her mother's blood and passion. Although she tries to be good, her fate is sealed after Lewt seduces her. Jessie then rejects her and she, despite her best intentions, is drawn to Lewt. She finally forces Lewt to propose marriage by refusing to see him otherwise. (To Selznick this established her good intentions.) The Senator, when he discovers that Lewt has proposed, is furious. Have your fun, boy, he tells Lewt, but no McCanles is going to marry a half-breed. Lewt assures his father that he has no intentions of marrying Pearl, he just wants to have a good time. The Senator is relieved that the "half-breed" will not marry into his family.

Lewt, however, had not been entirely truthful. He is obsessed with Pearl and extremely jealous of anyone else attempting to court her. When he learns that the foreman of the ranch, Sam Pierce (Charles Bickford), is sweet on her, he guns him down in a local bar. The sheriff immediately declares Lewt an outlaw and posts a reward for his capture. Lewt is now a fugitive from justice – an important point to the PCA, which always insisted that the justice system be shown as effective. When Jessie shows a renewed (nonsexual) interest in Pearl by bringing her to town so that she can get an education, Lewt risks capture, rides into town, and shoots his unarmed brother.

Pearl is finally outraged. She nurses Jessie back to health and, when a ranch hand tells her where Lewt is hiding, she rides off to kill him. When she arrives at his mountain hideout, they shoot each other. Then Pearl, bleeding from her wounds and overcome by grief, crawls to Lewt; they embrace, kiss, and die. Their duel in the sun has ended in tragedy.

Selznick felt this reworking established the moral base the PCA demanded in the script. Lewt was clearly depicted as evil: He destroyed Pearl, murdered, and was a fugitive from justice when he was killed. Pearl, having been drawn unwillingly into his web, suffered humiliation and death for her weakness. Selznick told his assistants to stress in all conferences with PCA representatives the point that "Lewt and Pearl are going to pay and pay the wages of sin." He believed that Breen and the PCA would be more receptive "toward the script . . . if they know that God punishes these two sinners." Lewt becomes a common outlaw, and he and Pearl die for their sinful relationship.[61]

Breen and the PCA were not totally convinced and worried about how these scenes would appear on the screen; but it was difficult for the censors to reject the script outright because Selznick kept rewriting it. In mid-March 1945 the PCA gave a tentative approval for the working script, and production began.

With approval from the PCA, Selznick packed up his cast and set off for the deserts of Arizona to film his western opus. He hired 6,500 extras to provide the massive look he wanted for the film. Vidor had little control over the interference of Selznick, who brought a host of directors to Arizona – William Cameron Menzies, Josef Von Sternberg, Sydney Franklin, and even William Dieterle – to help direct. Vidor was furious and walked off the set just before the last scenes were completed. According to Gregory Peck: "David was directing over his [Vidor's] shoulder and no real director will stand for that for very long. . . . King simply walked up to David and said, 'Take this picture and shove it.' He left and never came back. David finally said, 'Did I say something wrong?'"[62]

The filming took months, and costs soared above the $6 million mark, making *Duel* Hollywood's most expensive film to date. PCA representatives Geoffrey Shurlock and Al Lynch made periodic visits to the set to inspect costumes and to ensure that the seduction and swimming-hole scenes were not too explicit. Major cuts were made during production when the PCA objected to a dance Pearl performed at the swimming hole to lure Lewt into a marriage proposal. Lynch was shocked by this dance and told Breen that the "hip movements . . . might be interpreted as sex movements in connection with the tree in symbolism" – meaning Pearl made love to a tree to fire up old Lewt. Breen ordered Selznick to cut or trim the dance.[63] Selznick was furious. He told his assistant Dan O'Shea to tell Breen that redoing the scene would cost $25,000 and that it had been "photographed exactly as approved" by Lynch.[64] The PCA won out, however, and the scene was reshot. So was the first swimming-hole scene, which was shortened but did not remove the impression that Pearl was swimming nude – after all, she refuses to come out of the water until it is dark so that Lewt won't see her![65] Nonetheless, after much haggling over details, the PCA issued production seal number 11649 to Selznick in December 1946. Geoffrey Shurlock, who previewed the final print for the PCA, told Selznick he "was perfectly happy with the picture," which was "far superior" to anything he had seen in 1946.[66] Little did the producer realize his censorship problems were just beginning.

Selznick was eager to screen the film in December 1946 in order to qualify for the Academy Awards the following March. Unlike the major studios, Selznick did not have a string of first-run theaters on which he could depend to exhibit *Duel*. To distribute his film Selznick formed his own company, Selznick Releasing Organization (SRO), which he hoped could book enough first-run chain and studio theaters for *Duel* to make a profit. In desperation Selznick turned to his father-in-law, Louis B. Mayer, to book the Egyptian

Theater in Los Angeles for a two-week run opening on New Year's Eve 1946. Selznick booked one other theater in Los Angeles and qualified *Duel* for the 1946 Academy Awards.

Further complicating the distribution of *Duel in the Sun* was the lack of available prints. A strike at the Technicolor laboratory that December slowed production, and the company was able to deliver only four prints to Selznick less than two days before the scheduled premiere at the Egyptian.[67] Selznick shipped one print to New York for preview by the state censorship board, the National Board of Review, and the Legion; but in practical terms the result was that Selznick, like Hughes, opened a film on the West Coast without first submitting it to the National Legion of Decency in New York.

The press premiere at the Egyptian on December 30, 1946, went off without a hitch. The local Los Angeles papers, including the *Los Angeles Times,* were less than effusive but not hostile. *Variety* warned exhibitors that "rarely has a film made such frank use of lust" and still carried the PCA seal; however, the trade paper reminded theater owners that the "sex angle alone makes for boff b. o."[68]

Perhaps it did, but a bombshell hit Selznick when the January edition of the *Tidings,* the Catholic weekly of the Los Angeles Diocese, blasted the film as "plush pornography." Film critic William Mooring warned Catholic readers that *Duel* was much more dangerous "in a moral sense" than *The Outlaw* despite the fact that it carried the approval of the Production Code. In fact, PCA approval outraged Mooring, who believed the film violated the code by creating a mood of sympathy for sinners, detailing seduction, poking fun at religion, and generally violating provisions that a movie be made in good taste. Making a joke out of religion was especially galling to the Catholic critic. The Sin Killer's prayer for Pearl's soul – especially when he asked the Lord to give her the "strength not to go off in the tullies with worthless cowpokes" – brought, he wrote, "loud guffaws" from the audience. Even louder guffaws erupted when the Sin Killer prayed for Pearl's protection because of her tempting "female form."

This scene takes place late at night. Pearl is asleep in her room. Laura Belle, concerned that Lewt is leading Pearl astray, summons the Sin Killer to her home. After a short discussion, the Sin Killer asks Laura Belle to bring Pearl to him, and Vashti is dispatched to get her. As the servant enters the girl's room Pearl is sleeping face down, and the camera pans over her bare back. A semihysterical Vashti tells her that she must come immediately to Laura Belle's room. Pearl, not bothering to get dressed, simply wraps a short blanket from the bed around her. The implication was that she had been sleeping in the nude.

Pearl, surprised to find a man with Laura Belle, draws the blanket tighter around her, but there is plenty of bare flesh exposed: her legs and shoulders as the blanket sags here and there. The Sin Killer (Walter Huston, hamming up this scene for everything it is worth) turns Pearl around and around and carefully notes every curve of that tempting frame in front of him. As Pearl tries to keep herself covered with the blanket, the Sin Killer prays for her salvation. The scene enraged Mooring who believed it had "exposure far more objectionable than anything in the condemned *Outlaw*." He was incensed that Selznick had turned the "dignity and loveliness of . . . Saint Bernadette" into "a wholly immoral subject of the flesh."[69]

Within days Archbishop John Cantwell issued a stern warning to all Catholics in Los Angeles that "pending classification by the Legion of Decency they may not, with a free conscience, attend the motion picture *Duel in the Sun*." This motion picture, Cantwell warned, "appears to be morally offensive and spiritually depressing."[70] Another Catholic broadside hit Selznick when Martin Quigley, unofficial spokesperson for the Legion, told the producer that *Duel* "certainly would be placed in the 'Condemned' classification," and that in its present form would "create a wave of political censorship." Quigley warned Selznick that if he did not "materially alter" the film, the "outcome will be disastrous"; however, he offered a solution. Quigley believed that the original version of the film could be trimmed and reedited to satisfy Legion demands. He sent Selznick a list of thirty-two cuts that would take the sting out of *Duel*.[71]

Selznick was stunned. He did not believe the film was in any way immoral and viewed Quigley's cuts as harmful. He had cooperated with Breen, and in the prerelease previews in Southern California not a single person had indicated on preview cards that they had seen anything immoral in the film. The picture had been running in Los Angeles at four theaters and been doing excellent business. Selznick believed he had a hit movie and, based on an enthusiastic public reception in Los Angeles, booked seventy theaters in the Southern California Skouras movie chain. He planned a simultaneous opening in each in late February and was orchestrating a huge advertising campaign (having budgeted $2 million for promotion) to kick it off. Selznick hoped this would in turn create a national demand for *Duel*. However, by mid-January he still had only his original prints, and now the question was whether to print the PCA-approved version or to negotiate with the Legion through Quigley.

For a brief time Selznick contemplated ignoring the Legion, hopeful that the theater chains would honor their contracts. He commissioned the Gallup Poll to determine what impact a condemned rating by the Catholic Legion would have for the general public. He was delighted to learn that Gallup figures showed only 5 percent stated they would not go to a C-rated film. This loss would be more than offset, Gallup reported, by those who would be attracted to the film by the criticism and publicity generated.[72] Despite that good news, Selznick worried that a fight with the Legion would adversely damage his ability to produce and market other films. Before he took on the Legion Selznick wanted to know that he had the full support of both Eric Johnston and Joe Breen. The PCA had approved the film, and Selznick hoped that the industry and PCA officials would come to his defense.

At Selznick's request the MPAA conducted a quick survey of Hollywood studios: Were they prepared to help Selznick in a fight with the Catholic Legion of Decency? The opportunity seemed golden to challenge an organization that had been a thorn in their operations for over a decade. Every studio in Hollywood had at some point been forced by the Legion to remove material from one of its films; yet the producers were "completely, unalterably opposed" to meeting with Selznick or offering him any support. Leo Spitz, Universal's head of production, best summed up the industry point of view: He was, Spitz told the PCA, unwilling "to help Mr. Selznick pull his coals out of the fire."[73]

Spurned by his peers, Selznick realized that he was on his own in any dispute with the Legion. When he learned that many of the theater chains had a clause written into booking contracts that released them from their obligation to play a film if it carried a C rating, he decided to reedit his film along the lines suggested by Quigley.

The cuts were all relatively minor. Quigley suggested that Selnick trim the first swimming-hole scene to reduce the implication that Pearl was nude; cut some of the Sin Killer's speech, including one reference to him as "Padre"; trim the rape/seduction scene by shortening the struggle between Pearl and Lewt and the "passionate kiss" that followed the struggle; eliminate Pearl's seductive dance; and cut some dialogue between Lewt and Pearl discussing sex between horses, which he believed audiences would find offensive. Quigley was not offended by the ending of the film, however, which remained untouched. Although Selznick believed, as any producer would, that the cuts damaged the film's dramatic impact, they did not really change it. Both men hoped that trimming some of the more controversial scenes would allow the Legion to give it a B rating (i.e., some objectionable material), and that *Duel* could open to theaters nationwide without boycotts and pickets.[74]

"I have today completed some thirty-two cuts and trims . . . in *Duel in the Sun*, at the insistence of and in accordance with the suggestion of Mr. Martin Quigley," Selznick wrote Father Patrick Masterson of the Legion of Decency. In a long, detailed letter he told Masterson he had "personally made changes over and beyond what the Code authorities suggested" to ensure that the film had a proper moral tone. "I have acted in good faith," he concluded.[75]

From his Los Angeles office Quigley reinforced Selznick's plea. He told Masterson that the producer was hurt by the criticism that had come from

Catholic sources and that he had cooperated fully with both Breen and himself in editing the film. Quigley assured his friend at the Legion that some of the sordid characters "have been lightened," whole scenes "eliminated," and dialogue "dropped." From a moral perspective, Quigley stressed, the film had been "substantially changed."[76]

Duel was finally screened for the Legion in early February. Masterson was appalled. He fired off a letter to Breen informing him that "a serious mistake" had been made in issuing the film a seal. "The detail, the vividness emphasized by the color, the music and costuming, certainly leaves little to the imagination. Certainly such a presentation could not be called anything but explicit," he told Breen. It was the ending of the film, however, that upset both Masterson and the ladies of the IFCA who functioned as Legion reviewers. The two lovers, Masterson lectured Breen, "triumph." There is "not the slightest acknowledgment that what had gone on previously may have been wrong. There is no regret, no sorrow," just "one last lustful embrace."[77] Masterson demanded additional cuts, and Breen admitted that he had made a "serious error." He added, "I wish we might find some way to correct" it.[78]

It took another month of protracted negotiations among Selznick, Quigley, and the Legion to resolve their differences. Selznick trimmed additional footage from the swimming-hole scenes but refused to change the ending, which the Legion termed "immoral." Selznick scoffed at their interpretation and by April was fed up with the entire process. He told Neil Agnew, "my attitude is that [if] we are going to have a C [rating,] then let's have it and be done with it." He fired off letters to members of his organization complaining bitterly about the Legion. "We have suffered enough from the shenanigans of this organization."[79]

In frustration, he blasted Eric Johnston for his lack of support. He told Johnston that he believed it was "a rather shocking betrayal on the part of the industry that it sat silently by while attacks" were made on *Duel*. The industry, he wrote, was "completely yellow" in its refusal to back a picture "which has met with Code approval."[80] What good was a PCA seal, Selznick demanded, if every film had to be renegotiated with religious censors?

Johnston was quick to take offense. "I resent" your charge that the industry "has been yellow." "The records show," he told Selznick, "that we vigorously defend our Seal when challenged by censorship boards." Johnston then quoted various church groups that found *Duel* offensive. Johnston's letter, in fact, proved Selznick's point: The industry was not willing to take on religious organizations, especially if the offending film was made by an independent producer like Selznick or Hughes.[81]

Although the industry gave him no support, letters from moviegoers to Selznick ran three to one in favor of releasing *Duel* without the Legion cuts. Kathryn Allen from Manhattan Beach, California, told Selznick: "I hope you have the courage to stand by your great movie and display it without a single scene out." Mrs. Henry Murphy urged Selznick not to cut the film but "to put an age limit on it." Diane Hazel Sharp told Selznick that in deeply religious Salt Lake City *Duel* was extremely popular, and that the Sin Killer "found a place in the funny bone of Salt Lake."[82]

In the end, however, the Legion won. Selznick was able to keep his ending but had to agree to add a prologue and an epilogue to the film to satisfy Legion demands that all films make sin crystal clear. As audiences across America settled into their seats and began munching popcorn and sipping soft drinks, a warning about the passion they were about to see dramatized would scroll down the screen:

> *Duel in the Sun,* two years in the making, a saga of Texas in the 1880's, when primitive passions rode the raw frontier of an expanding nation. Here the forces of evil were in constant conflict with the deeper morality of the hearty pioneers. And here, as in the story we will tell, a grim fate lay waiting for the transgressor upon the laws of God and man.
>
> The characters in *Duel in the Sun* are built out of the legends of a colorful era, when a million acres were one man's estate, and another man's life was held as lightly as a woman's virtue.
>
> The character of the Sin Killer is based on those bogus unordained evangelists, who preyed upon the hungry need for spiritual guidance, and who were recognized as charlatans by the intelligent and God-fearing.

Those who remained in their seats after the movie to watch the credits would be informed by an epilogue, written by Msgr. John McClafferty of the Legion, that Pearl Chavez was "pursued . . . tortured by her own passion"; it was her "moral weakness" that led to "transgressions against the law of God." Lewt McCanles was "untamed . . . Godless"; a man whose "unbridled recklessness brings down upon him the frustration of his own hopes, and havoc and destruction upon others."[83] Having undergone forty-six cuts, *Duel* was given a B classification by the Legion.

Duel finally hit the theaters in May 1947. It was banned in Memphis and Bay City, Michigan, but had little problem with other censorship boards. The reviewers were less kind. *Time* told readers *Duel* was a "titillating blend of wild oats . . . in which virtue emerged triumphant, but low-bodiced vice seemed to have all the fun."[84] Jesse Zunser, film critic for *Cue*, dubbed *Duel* the "emptiest film since the Grand Canyon."[85] *Newsweek* renamed the film "Gone With the Sun" and warned readers it was a "grabbag of seduction, murder, hard riding, feuds and fisticuffs."[86] The *New Republic* panned *Duel* but admitted that "there are some hot scenes."[87] The *New York Times* found the film and "its juvenile slobbering over sex" boring. The review noted that although the Legion of Decency went to some lengths to make clear to audiences that the Sin Killer was not a real minister, "Huston's pungent thundering in this role is one of the bits of characterization which has real flavor and significance."[88] The Catholic publication *Commonweal* told readers that *Duel* had "little more to offer movie-goers than some hot love scenes."[89] Jesse Zunser was more on-target when he noted that "Its popeyed, hard-breathing innuendoes are aimed directly and without subterfuge at the peanut-munching, gum-chewing level of movie-goers – and will undoubtedly pay off heavily in proportion."[90]

Zunser was right: Peanut-munching fans flocked to theaters all over the country to watch *Duel*. Selznick saturated large urban areas, booking as many theaters for the film as he could. In Boston, despite "hostile reviews," *Variety* reported that *Duel* did "terrific" business at the Orpheum Theater because "the film is one of those things people figure they must see."[91] It did "near record" business at the State Theater in Providence, and in hostile Philadelphia the *Fox* reported that box office for *Duel* "looks like all-time record."[92] In Cleveland the Stillman Theater averaged four sellouts a day for the first week. In Kansas City, Pittsburgh, St. Louis, Denver, Detroit, and Cincinnati the film broke box-office records – and four of these cities were Legion strongholds. In Buffalo, another city with a large Catholic population, *Duel* was the only "bright spot" in an otherwise dismal summer box-office season.[93] The film generated more than $11 million in box-office revenue and by its final run stood second to *Best Years of Our Lives,* which had also been given a B by the Legion, for 1946 releases.[94]

In one of the more unusual ironies, and one that must have made Selznick chuckle with glee, *Duel in the Sun* was used as a highly successful fundraiser for the University of Santa Clara, a Catholic university in Santa Clara, California. In late April 1947 more than thirty-five hundred people crowded into an auditorium on the Santa Clara campus to watch *Duel*; another three hundred were turned away at the box office, and it took sixty off-duty policemen to control the crowd. Father Walter E. Schmidt, S.J., told Selznick officials he "was terribly grateful" that *Duel* helped raise $10,000 for underprivileged youth in the city. He told Selznick that he did not know anything about his battles with the Legion; all he knew was that the movie was rated B, which he viewed as acceptable, and that the audience seemed to enjoy themselves. Of course, Father Schmidt was wrong: The Legion's position was that a B movie contained material "unacceptable for all," and it discouraged Catholics from attending them. Schmidt, however, saw nothing immoral, and neither did his Catholic audience. It is also telling that a Catholic priest knew next to nothing about the Legion and did not bother to consult it before booking the film.[95]

Selznick later regretted that he had lacked "the guts and the courage and the intestinal fortitude" to challenge the Legion.[96] He was convinced that his caving in to the Legion had damaged the movie. The Legion cuts "completely destroyed the whole style and violence of the film," and what was left seemed "rather pointless." In the rape/seduction scene, Selznick argued forcefully that the passionate kiss that Pearl gives Lewt was absolutely necessary to show that Lewt did not rape her. Rape was never intended. According to Selznick: "Lewt is never punished for this rape; Jesse would become an utter imbecile and an extremely unattractive character, for he would be turning on the girl and destroying her entire life" if he turned away from her after she had been raped. Rather, Jesse turned away because he recognized that Pearl liked Lewt more than she liked him. The cuts made it extremely difficult for audiences to understand this key point of the film, and Selznick described this as "a substantial loss."[97]

He was also convinced that the protracted negotiations with the Legion had cost him millions of dollars in box-office revenue by forcing him to delay the release of the film after its original Los Angeles run. "Our best results were achieved in Los Angeles. . . . Even the reviews were splendid here, by comparison with what we got after we surrendered to the Legion's demands," he told his associate Neil Agnew. As he watched box-office returns roll in Selznick added, "It would also appear that the fears concerning bookings may have been completely unjustified."[98] "Reverend Masterson," Selznick fumed, "has not been designated by God as the final word in what is seriously offensive and we are damn sure that the non-Catholics of America, and a goodly percentage of Catholics as well, do not accept him."[99]

He was right, but it was too late. It is unfortunate that the industry did not have the collective will to stand up to the Legion. Selznick was not a rich industrialist who played with movies like Hughes; he was one of the most respected men in Hollywood and had a long record of producing quality films. Selznick operated within the system and had, despite some real misgivings, altered *Duel* to fit within the moral constraints demanded by Breen and the Production Code. The refusal of Breen, Johnston, and industry leaders to defend Selznick, and themselves, from Legion attacks simply encouraged the Legion to continue to demand that it be given the right of final approval of all films produced in Hollywood. It was a decision the industry would soon regret, and it would be another twenty years before the Legion stranglehold on Hollywood was broken. The industry had no one to blame but itself. The studios preferred allowing the Legion to dictate content in return for the stable market conferred by favorable classifications.

Darryl Zanuck, head of studio production at Twentieth Century–Fox, understood the role that censorship played in making movies. Before he started production on one of the most lavish productions in Hollywood history, one that would cost more than $6 million to produce, he told Joseph Breen: "In this particular case I set myself up as a censor."[100] What Zanuck wanted to censor was described by the highly respected *Saturday Review of Literature* as "the bawdiest novel . . . in years."[101] Kathleen Winsor's *Forever Amber,* a lusty tale of court life in Restoration England, traced the life of Amber St. Clare, a young Puritan maid, who rose from her humble rural home to become the mistress of King Charles II.

As the novel unfolds Amber has been pledged to marry a good Puritan pig farmer. She is appalled at the thought and when, by chance, she meets the dashing Lord Bruce Carlton, she begs him to take her to London. They have an affair and a child, but Carlton is unwilling to marry her. When the king sends Carlton away on a military mission, Amber decides to stay in London and sleep her way to success. She beds a long list of men in her determination to climb to the top of court life. Her ambition is finally rewarded when King Charles II takes her for his mistress; but through it all Amber still loves Carlton and constantly schemes to win back his love. Amber is crushed when Carlton marries and decides to move to the New World, taking their son with him. As the novel ends Amber has decided to go to the English colonies and win back both Carlton and her son. Most readers assumed she would succeed.

Despite a host of disparaging reviews from the literary community, the book soared to the top of the best-seller lists for 1944. It was banned in Boston until the Massachusetts Supreme Court ruled it was not a threat to public morals. Judge Frank Donahue told concerned citizens that *Forever Amber* was a "soporific rather than an aphrodisiac."[102] As screenwriter Philip Dunne remarked, it "appealed to the prurient in the great American reading public."[103]

It also struck a responsive note in Hollywood. Twentieth Century–Fox was interested in developing the novel into a film and, as was often the case in controversial material, the studio sent a brief synopsis of the nine-hundred-page tome to Breen for a predevelopment evaluation. Breen fired back that it was "utterly and completely unacceptable." The novel was, he wrote, little more than a "saga of illicit sex . . . bastardy, perversion, impotency, pregnancy, abortion, murder and marriage without even the slightest suggestion of compensating moral values."[104]

Breen worked behind the scenes to keep Amber St. Clare off the screen. While he admitted he had "no authority to forbid the studios" from attempting to develop a screenplay, both were worried about the adverse publicity a filmed version would cause. At a meeting of industry presidents the executives were warned of the damage a screen version of Amber's erotic exploits could have on the industry. The presidents agreed and expressed "overwhelming sentiment . . . that no company ought to attempt to develop a screenplay based on the novel."[105]

When word of this decision hit the trade press, author Kathleen Winsor classified the attitude of the industry as "absurd." "What a pity," she told reporters, "if all our historical annals were destroyed and our only remaining records were in Hollywood cans."[106] When *New York Times* reporter Frank Nugent later told her that the character of Lord Almsbury (Lord Carlton's best friend) "is to serve as the mouthpiece for the Purity Leaguers, bobbing up from time to time to shake his head over the immorality of the court," Winsor "winced."[107] She was mollified by the $200,000 for screen rights from Twentieth Century–Fox, who assured the MPAA they would develop an acceptable script.

That job was given to Darryl F. Zanuck, a short, cigar-chomping producer who was one of the old guard in Hollywood. He had come West from Wahoo, Nebraska, after World War I and hooked on at Warner Bros. as a writer for the Rin Tin Tin series. He soon graduated from canine capers and by 1930 had become head of production at the studio, but a fight over control forced him to leave Warner's. In 1933 he and Joseph Schenck formed Twentieth Century Productions, which merged with Fox Films in 1935 to become Twentieth Century–Fox. As head of production at the studio (and with Schenck, as chief executive of the corporation, based in New York), Zanuck produced such films as *Alexander's Ragtime Band* (1938), *Young Mr. Lincoln* (1939), *The Grapes of Wrath* (1940), *How Green Was My Valley* (1941), and *Wilson* (1944).

Like Selznick, Zanuck assembled production teams to oversee film production at the studio and reserved a central role for himself in each film. As an ex-writer he was convinced that the keys to good moviemaking were a good script and good tight editing. As he told one actor who wanted his part rewritten, "the treatment of the subject in script form should be left largely to the judgment and intelligence of our 'system.'"[108] The system that Zanuck used included constant story conferences, long meetings with writers, directors, and producers during which Zanuck talked through script problems and daily rewrites. His longtime associate Milton Sperling recalled that Zanuck would make the current writer or director sit in the middle of his office, in "the Hot Seat," around which everyone else formed a ring:

> Everyone else had to sit absolutely still and listen while Zanuck walked up and down the office, tearing ideas out of his head, suggesting scenes and special shots, and then swinging on the Hot Seat and rasping: "Whaddya think of that? Does it grab ya?"[109]

While he was not as likely as Selznick to interfere with the director during shooting, Zanuck "had absolutely no respect for directors until they got on the set" and insisted that the script he had approved be followed religiously. Zanuck, not the director, was responsible for the final editing.[110]

For *Amber* there were many story conferences. Jerry Cady, Philip Dunne, and Ring Lardner Jr. collaborated on the screenplay and shared the Hot Seat. Zanuck, unlike Selznick, felt no obligation to remain faithful to original material. He ranted during one conference: "It does not matter a tinker's damn whether or not you faithfully follow the continuity or structure of the book." In *The Grapes of Wrath* and *How Green Was My Valley,* he told his associates, "we violated the story line completely, yet we preserved the spirit, the theme, and the characters, and the results were successful." Zanuck believed that *Amber* would appeal to "a large bobby-sox audience who will come to see how Amber gets her man, and who will yawn right through" any attempt at historical background.[111] For Zanuck, the trick was to preserve the spirit of the novel, which was about a young unmarried woman who has no compunction about using sex for worldly gain, without invoking the wrath of Breen, the condemnation of the Catholic Legion, and additional cuts by state and municipal censors.

Zanuck knew that Breen, despite his initial reaction, would help him achieve his goal. As Dunne later recalled, Breen "warned us that . . . [they] would be keeping an eagle eye on us and that even the slightest transgression of the Code would bring lightning down on our heads." This self-imposed censorship system "was truly censorship, and in spades," wrote Dunne.[112] Zanuck understood Breen's power but also knew that with his support it would be possible to make *Amber*. A key element in eliminating costly post-production changes was to work closely with the censor during the story conference period. "I went to great lengths," he wrote, "to explain to Breen that this story is basically a tragedy. It is the story of a girl who tries to have a man who is above her. She repeatedly sins in order to get her man, and at the end she not only loses the man but she also loses her child who is the only link she has left with the man she loves."[113]

Zanuck's strategy worked: After reading an early script Breen told him he was "very pleased" with the way the overall moral tone of the film had improved but demanded that the producer strengthen the moral lessons of the film by having Lord Almsbury "become the voice of morality."[114] Zanuck readily agreed. As the script was revised over the summer of 1945, he told Philip Dunne to make certain that Almsbury continues "to warn Amber" that her behavior is wrong. He must be "the handwriting on the wall," "must try to show Amber . . . that she is going to end in eventual disaster if she" does not change her ways. An example of this voice of morality being inserted into the film is in a scene soon after Amber arrives in London. Almsbury, concerned for her future, urges her to leave the city before it corrupts her:

ALMSBURY: Amber I know London. Perhaps better than I should. Not only the city and the court, but the rest of it too – the slums and back alleys – the places no one mentions, except in whispers. We live in an evil age. Perhaps none in all past history has been so evil, no city reached the depths London has reached today. I'm partly responsible for your being here. I'll feel responsible for whatever becomes of you. It's a burden I don't want on my conscience. Go back. Please go back – while you have the chance.

AMBER: No my lord. I'll take my chances.

ALMSBURY: You're making a tragic mistake. [End of Scene]

To Breen, this brief scene made Amber's fall into sin acceptable under the code. A major character had offered her a choice, and she had rejected the moral road – life on the farm – and chosen instead the city and its corruption and sin. In Breen's mind, everyone in the audience would understand that Almsbury represented morality and proper behavior whereas Amber personified immorality. Moviegoers would also clearly recognize that Amber's gains were ill-gotten and that she would soon pay the price for her sins. It was also possible, of course, that the audience would read the opposite – that Amber had made the right decision in escaping life on the farm – but Breen did not care, believing most people would read the film as he did.

It is interesting to note that Breen was much more concerned that Amber pay a stiff price for her sins than he was in making sure that Lord Carlton was punished for his role in the illicit sexual liaison. Breen did ask Zanuck to insert some lines of dialogue for Carlton expressing his recognition that he and Amber had sinned, but Carlton suffered no loss of status.

After some additional minor changes, Breen gave basic script approval to Zanuck. There was concern in New York over this decision, but as Breen told the MPAA's Francis Harmon, "we have the competency to take out of novels like *Forever Amber* the good that is in them and to throw into discard that which is offensive and obscene." He admitted that the novel was one of "illicit sex," but the movie would have "sufficient compensating moral values to make it OK with the code." Audiences understood, Breen wrote, that over the years "the industry has . . . established the reputation for sponsoring only motion pictures that are reasonably acceptable to reasonable people."[115] *Variety* reported that the "expurgated screenplay . . . has made the original story hardly recognizable."[116]

With script approval in hand Zanuck rushed the project into production. He hired, then fired, John Stahl as director before settling on Otto Preminger. Preminger tried to beg off the project, telling Zanuck the book was "horrible," but the director was under contract, and Zanuck insisted.[117] Preminger wanted to replace Peggy Cummins, who had been signed to play Amber, with the more exotic Lana Turner; Zanuck insisted on Linda Darnell. Cornel Wilde played Lord Carlton, Richard Greene was Lord Almsbury, and George Sanders the debauched King Charles II. Breen had demanded, however, that almost all physical contact between Amber and her lovers be cut: With the exception of the odd kiss there was no hint of physical contact or any physical relationship between the characters. (James Agree told readers, "the famous hussy is never kissed hard enough to jar an eyelash loose.")[118] The baby that Amber and Carlton produce comes as a complete surprise because all Amber and Lord Carlton do in the film is stare at each other. The action was so wooden that one reviewer noted sarcastically, "Cornel Wilde . . . does his best to pass as flesh and blood, and George Sanders plays Charles II with an erotic lethargy that approaches coma."[119]

In fairness, though, there was little either Preminger or the actors could do with the material, which, according to Dunne, was "dreary" and "dutifully sanitized."[120] Zanuck had violated one of his basic concepts of good moviemaking by filming a bad script but compensated for the lack of substance with pure Hollywood glitz. He spent massive amounts of money on the film – $250,000 to recreate seventeenth-century London and thousands more to burn the set in a dramatic recreation of the Great Fire. The scene was so realistic that it panicked local residents, who called the fire department. To recreate the splendor of court life Zanuck spent $100,000 to build a set of Whitehall Palace, $90,000 for dresses for Linda Darnell (carefully designed to avoid plunging necklines), and $255,000 for other costumes. Filmed in glowing and expensive Technicolor, Zanuck expected his film to breeze through the final inspections from the Legion and the various state and municipal censorship boards. He scheduled his film for Legion preview ten days before its opening in New York in early October 1947.

At the National Legion office Father Patrick J. Masterson, the assistant executive secretary who was temporarily in charge of Legion operations, was suspicious "that an unsavory piece of celluloid was about to be foisted on an unsuspecting American public." It is unclear how the public was unsuspecting considering the fact that the novel had sold over three million copies and was read by millions more. That fact aside, *Amber* was scheduled to be previewed for the Legion on October 10, 1947, and, according to James Skinner, Masterson "was determined to impose his authority and kill what he considered must be a salacious picture" even before he and Legion reviewers screened it.[121]

Masterson was disappointed when Legion reviewers, comprising women from the IFCA and professional lay Catholics, were not offended by *Amber* and cast eight of nine ballots to classify the film as A2 (unobjectionable for adults) or B (objectionable in part for all); but he was determined to condemn the film. In a memo to New York's Francis Cardinal Spellman, Masterson argued that *Amber* was immoral, and that the movies in general were becoming increasingly daring and the PCA more and more lax in its enforcement of the code. In addition to *Amber* Masterson listed several films and projects then in production that he considered dangerous, including Zanuck's *Gentleman's Agreement* (because it presented divorce in a favorable light) and *The Snake Pit* (dangerous for its presentation of mental illness). Masterson told Spellman that Catholic opinion was "well-neigh unanimous that these [subjects] were grossly immoral."[122]

Whether Masterson was upset because the Legion had been unsuccessful in curtailing *The Outlaw,* which was currently playing throughout the country despite its C classification, or frustrated over the Legion's long battle with Selznick over *Duel,* or convinced that the industry was dominated by communists (the House Un-American Activities Committee hearings in Washington began the same day Masterson wrote his memo to Spellman), or determined to stop what he thought was a serious lessening of standards is unclear. It was most likely a combination of all those factors.

Cardinal Spellman readily accepted Masterson's assessment of the situation and immediately dispatched a letter to all priests in the archdiocese condemning the film as "a glorification of immorality and licentiousness" and warning Catholics that "they may not see *Forever Amber* with a safe conscience."[123] This lightning bolt sent shock waves through Hollywood. Once again a film that had been carefully and thoroughly cleansed by Breen had run into stiff Catholic opposition.

Then, for the first time since 1936, a major studio decided to challenge the Legion of Decency. Twentieth Century–Fox owned a chain of large first-run urban theaters and had a contractual arrangement to play *Amber* at many of the Paramount theaters. Thus, unlike Selznick, Twentieth Century–Fox had access to theaters, and the corporation decided to fight the Legion. The opening salvo came when company president Spyros Skouras bristled in a statement to the *New York Times* at the suggestion that the film was immoral. He called the Legion classification "unfair." *Amber* was "a sincere portrayal of the unattractive consequences of reckless personal conduct." As evidence that the film was not immoral, Skouras pointed to the PCA seal and the ease with which the film had been approved by state censorship boards in New York, Ohio, Virginia, Pennsylvania, Maryland, and Massachusetts and by municipal boards in Chicago and Milwaukee. The screen, Skouras said, must have "freedom within limits of decency."[124]

Most contemporary reviewers found the film lacking, but not because it was immoral. *Harrison's Reports,* which strongly favored the Legion of Decency and was quick to condemn movies it thought immoral, called *Amber* "great spectacle" that managed "to stay within the bounds of good taste."[125] *Time* chuckled that the film kept "sin carefully in its place – which is just about three feet offstage." They predicted, however, "it won't be enough to satisfy . . . the Legion of Decency."[126] Poor Amber, James Agree wrote, gets a crueler comeuppance in the movie than in the novel "without having much fun earning it."[127] The *New Republic* told readers, incorrectly it seems, that "the moral is bitter enough to satisfy the most vindictively upright."[128] Martin Quigley's *Motion Picture Herald* made no objection to the morality of the film and predicted it would "sell a torrent of tickets."[129] The Jesuit *America* called *Amber* "tawdry" but made no mention of the Legion's condemnation.[130] Father Daniel Lord's *Queen's Work* simply called *Amber* "dull and tiresome."[131] Philip Hartung, reviewer for the lay Catholic publication *Commonweal,* made no mention of the C classification by the Legion but instead complained that *Amber* "hardly comes to life"[132] – a less than honest evaluation because Hartung was a regular lay reviewer for the Legion and was well aware of the cleansing the movie had undergone.

While the reviewers were rather nonplussed by *Amber,* Catholic opposition picked up steam. In St. Louis Catholics were asked to abstain from attending the movie. Cardinal Dougherty went a step further in Philadelphia when he threatened, as he had with *The Outlaw,* that unless the local Fox theater withdrew the film in forty-eight hours, he would impose a yearlong boycott on all Fox theaters in the Archdiocese of Philadelphia. When Fox refused to cave in, Catholic War Veterans picketed Philadelphia theaters. Bishop James E. Kearney in Rochester, New York, repeated Dougherty's call for a boycott, as did the Catholic diocese in Buffalo. Chicago's Samuel Cardinal Strick did not call for a boycott but approved of the condemnation and urged Catholics to avoid the film.

The immediate reaction, however, was not what Legion supporters had in mind. "Oddly enough," *Variety* noted with some puzzlement, "in cities like Philadelphia, Boston and St. Louis where church influence is strongest, *Amber* is doing best."[133] In Rochester police admitted it was standing room only at the Paramount theater. *Variety* reported similar reactions throughout the country. *Amber* playing "big" in St. Louis "despite an upped scale, bad weather and a blast from the Archbishop." It was "gigantic" in Boston – so big that a local jewelry store located near the Paramount theater where *Amber* was playing sued for damages: Quadruple lines of eager fans waiting to see the film prevented customers from getting into the store.[134] In New York Cardinal Spellman's letter resulted in "an all-time record" at the Roxy of $180,000 for the first week. In Detroit the Fox did "smash" business at $50,000, with similar results pouring in from Cleveland, Chicago, Pittsburgh, Cincinnati, Louisville, Los Angeles, and San Francisco. In Buffalo the call for a boycott resulted in "block long queues." In nearby Geneva, New York Mayor Charles F. Neider campaigned for reelection on a pledge to ban *Forever Amber;* he was soundly trounced at the polls, and *Amber* played without controversy.[135]

In Los Angeles Breen watched the furor over *Amber* with some dismay. He told his boss Eric Johnston that his office had changed the novel to illustrate that "sin and crime are definitely and affirmatively shown to be wrong; they are not condoned, nor justified, nor made to appear right and acceptable."[136] When Abram F. Meyers, president of Allied States Exhibitors Association, complained that the PCA was loosening its standards and suggested that exhibitors try to cancel *Amber* contracts, Breen fired back that there was no loosening: *Amber* had been banned by the Legion, Breen asserted, "for religious reasons not moral."[137]

Despite an initial surge at the box office and some support from the MPAA, by late October Fox officials were becoming skittish. *Amber* continued to do well in large urban areas, but rural and independent exhibitors pressured the company to make peace with the Legion. As Zanuck later wrote: "The exhibitors wanted to support us . . . but when you gang up on a man and picket his lobby and threaten him with undermining the morals of youth, he finally gives in . . ."[138]

There was also pressure from another direction that influenced the decision to give in to the Legion. In Washington, the House Un-American Activities Committee (HUAC) hearings were in full swing and nerves were taut at the MPAA headquarters in New York. The hearings had started October 20, 1947, and a string of friendly witnesses accused a group of screenwriters, directors, and producers, soon to be called the Hollywood Ten, of planting communist propaganda in Hollywood films.

Eric Johnston was scheduled to testify on Monday, October 27, 1947. *Amber* had strong ties to the investigation and was certainly guilty by association. *Amber* screenwriter Ring Lardner Jr., who would soon become one of the Hollywood Ten, had been subpoenaed in September 1947 to appear before HUAC about his association with the Communist Party in America; he was scheduled to testify the week of October 27. His collaborator on *Amber,* Philip Dunne, was a founding member of the support group the Committee for the First Amendment. Both writers were in Washington preparing to fight HUAC when Twentieth Century–Fox officials decided to throw a white flag of surrender at the Legion.

On Saturday, October 25, Father Masterson and Martin Quigley representing the Legion and Spyros Skouras and Jason Joy representing Fox gathered at the Roxy Theater to implant a stronger moral lesson in Amber St. Clare. According to Otto Preminger, Skouras got on his knees and begged Masterson to help reedit the film;[139] this seems doubtful but illustrates that the industry had given up the fight. Masterson too was on thin ice: He could not or would not point to specific scenes that were offensive. Finally the four men agreed to limit changes to trimming a few lines of dialogue and inserting into all prints of *Amber* a prologue and epilogue that would, in Legion eyes, clarify the guilt of the sinners. The prologue, written by Masterson and Quigley, told the audience:

> This is the tragic story of Amber St. Clare . . . slave to ambition . . . stranger to virtue. . . fated to find the wealth and power she ruthlessly gained wither to ashes in the fires lit by passion and fed by defiance of the eternal command . . . the wages of sin is death.

For any who may have missed the point during the more than two hours it took to unravel *Amber,* a voice-over ended the film with a repeat of Lord Carlton's moral confession: "In heaven's name, Amber, haven't we caused enough unhappiness. May God have mercy on us both for our sins."[140]

The suggestion that sin, passion, and lust for wealth all result in unhappiness and death was Catholic to the core. For the Legion the point was to remind everyone in the audience that this sort of behavior would result in everlasting condemnation. Satisfied that audiences would draw the proper moral lesson from *Amber,* the Legion issued a B classification, and the film played without pickets and protests except in Philadelphia, where Cardinal Dougherty refused to lift his boycott.

Amber finished fifth on box-office lists for 1947, generating $5 million – significantly less than its reported $6 million-plus production costs. There is little doubt that the Legion controversy hurt the film at the box office, but more damaging was the original censorship enforced by Breen and the PCA. The novel *Forever Amber* was all about sex: about a beautiful young woman who uses sex to gain status and power. It was an old story and one that had been repeated countless times throughout history and would play again and again in modern life. The film, like *Duel in the Sun,* fared well on its original run, but in truth *Amber* was a dull film, and audiences stayed away because it was not good entertainment, not because they saw it as immoral. The Legion's willingness to reclassify the film with the addition of a brief moral lecture indicates how thin their position had been.

Moreover, there was little public support for the Legion beyond Catholic circles. *Amber* played to big crowds in urban areas, long considered Catholic strongholds; Fox worried more about small towns and rural areas, where exhibitors were far more susceptible to pressure from civic and religious groups than were those in the big cities. For example, in 1947, despite all the hoopla over *The Outlaw, Duel in the Sun,* and *Forever Amber, Woman's Home Companion* found that only 8 percent of its readers believed movies needed stricter controls. Few people stayed away when, for example, the Legion classified the smash hit of 1946, *The Best Years of Our Lives,* as B for containing a favorable view of divorce; nor were movie fans willing to avoid the 1947 winner of the Academy Award for Best Picture, *Miracle on 34th Street,* which the Legion also classified as "objectionable in part for all" because the female lead was divorced!

None of this is to suggest that the Catholic Legion was powerless; the organization was clearly very powerful and could, under certain circumstances, force Hollywood to bend to its version of moral behavior, as it did with *Duel in the Sun* and *Forever Amber*. Nonetheless, as the case histories in this chapter demonstrate, the Legion's power was often more illusory than real. Had the studios been determined to stand up to the Legion of Decency – to explain and fight for the PCA code – its hold on Hollywood might have been broken in the late 1940s.

The industry chose not to fight for a variety of reasons. One was that to reveal publicly the manner in which the PCA forced filmmakers to adhere to its moral code was to admit that filmmaking was a tightly controlled monopoly. Such an admission would add to the growing evidence the Justice Department was compiling in its long-running case against the industry as a restraint of trade.

There were, however, filmmakers who did not have to abide by a Production Code to make films. European directors, many of them Catholic, would challenge the very basis of censorship and marketing techniques that drove the studio system in America.

CHAPTER 3

A FOREIGN CHALLENGE

The influx of foreign motion pictures which is to be expected in this country will naturally serve as a challenge to Hollywood to meet this competition which it has not had since 1941. So as to keep our industry from descending to the moral levels of countries which have no Production Code, greater vigilance will have to be employed to preserve the objectives of the Legion of Decency, and to offset any departure from Christian ideals and ethics.
    – Father John Devlin to Msgr. John McClafferty, 1946

[W]e conclude that expression of motion pictures is included within the free speech and the free press guarantee of the First and Fourteenth Amendments.
    – Justice Tom Clark, U.S. Supreme Court, 1952

The major challenge to the cozy system of censorship maintained by the motion picture industry and the Catholic Legion of Decency since 1934 came neither from the Hollywood studios nor from independent producers like Howard Hughes or David O. Selznick. The Hollywood establishment had often threatened to challenge the legality of film censorship, but in reality it quietly complied with the demands of Breen and the Legion.

Ironically, the fight to end film censorship first centered around one man, Joseph Burstyn, who believed that film was an important means of communication and entertainment. Burstyn did not accept the view that films dealing in a direct and frank manner with such subjects as adultery, prostitution, drug addiction, or political corruption were automatically immoral. He loved movies – especially foreign films, in which he saw an honesty lacking in the slicker, more polished, and highly censored Hollywood product – and dedicated his life to bringing foreign films to American audiences. This eventually put him in the middle of a major legal battle: a challenge to the legality of state governments requiring that films and/or exhibitors be licensed.

Burstyn had immigrated to the United States from Poland in 1921 and worked in the family business as a jeweler in New York City, where he also developed a keen interest in literary expression. Following a stint as a stage manager for a Yiddish theater in New York, by 1936 he had formed a partnership with Arthur L. Mayer, a former publicity director for Paramount, to import foreign films. Mayer–Burstyn was the first distributorship to deal almost exclusively in foreign films. They concentrated most of their efforts in small art houses on the East Coast, especially in and around New York City.

In the immediate postwar era, they began to import a series of Italian films: *Open City, Paisan, The Bicycle Thief,* and finally Roberto Rossellini's *The Miracle,* which was condemned by the Catholic Legion as sacrilegious. When the New York State board of censorship denied a license to exhibit the film, Burstyn took the case to court and won a resounding victory for freedom of the screen.

From the end of the war in 1945 to the 1952 U.S. Supreme Court decision in *Burstyn v. Wilson* was one of the most tumultuous periods in the history of the Hollywood film industry. During these seven years the industry suffered tremendous economic loss, was branded as a hotbed of communism by the House Un-American Activities Committee, fired and blacklisted many of its most creative writers, directors, and actors, fought bitter and destructive labor battles between the unions and management, and had two of the major foundations of its economic success – control of theaters and control of film content – declared illegal by the U.S. Supreme Court. All of these issues became intertwined in the battle over the right to show foreign films in the United States.

The collapse of Hollywood in the decade following World War II has been thoroughly documented and chronicled in scores of books,[1] but the basic facts are so startling that they merit a brief summary. At the end of the war Hollywood was truly the entertainment capital of the world. In 1946 some ninety million fans jammed the nation's theaters every week, and the industry churned out 378 feature films to satisfy the seemingly insatiable demand of movie fans. Box-office revenues soared to a record $1.6 billion.

On the world stage Hollywood stood alone. The war had all but destroyed the vibrant prewar film industries in France, Italy, and Germany. In the immediate postwar period Hollywood flooded European screens with films produced during the war. To the casual observer everything pointed to Hollywood's continued worldwide domination of the industry.

Nevertheless, five years later the industry was drowning in a sea of red ink. By the mid-1960s the once powerful and glamorous studios were in disarray. Their fleets of huge, ornate picture palaces had been sold off by court order, their stables of stars were gone, the original industry moguls were retired, and the huge sound stages were reduced to producing TV sitcoms. MGM, Paramount, Twentieth Century–Fox, Warner Bros. – names that had evoked fascination, power, money, and glamour – were now mere cogs in international media conglomerates. The golden era of Hollywood was over.

This incredibly rapid demise of the industry, which began in 1947, is still shocking and hard to understand. For the next decade movie attendance declined steadily, with the industry losing almost half of its audience. Box-office receipts, which stood at $1.6 billion in 1946, had declined to $1.2 billion by 1956 despite a 40 percent rise in ticket prices. The ten leading production companies suffered a gross revenue loss of 26 percent, and profits collapsed from a high of $121 million in 1946 to a mere $32 million a decade later. Feature film production by 1956 had plummeted to 272 – one hundred fewer than a decade earlier.

Although television is most often cited as the main reason for the drastic declines in movie attendance, in 1950 there were only three million households with TV sets and fewer than a hundred commercial TV stations broadcasting. Nonetheless, by 1950 movie attendance had fallen from its 1946 peak of ninety million to sixty million weekly.

The reasons for the movies' lost popularity with American audiences and the collapse of Hollywood are in fact many, and most are beyond the focus of this book. One was the growth of the suburbs. Millions of Americans, using GI loans or savings from World War II jobs, were able to buy low-cost housing. In 1944 only 114,000 new houses were built in the United States, but 1.7 million were constructed in 1948! Millions more were built over the next several decades as the American exodus to the suburbs continued unabated. The GIs and workers who bought this low-cost housing also purchased cars, furniture, and carpeting and started the baby-boom generation.

Millions of GIs became the first in their families to go to college, taking advantage of the GI Bill created in 1944, which offered subsidies to finish high school, pay for advanced technical education, or go to college. These new students were older, often married, and had less time for leisure activities. It is not that they necessarily rejected Hollywood; they just could not afford to go as often as they had in the past. Monthly budgets were stretched to the limit as Americans used credit to consume goods at record levels.

Nor were movies the only leisure activity available: Life in the suburbs offered golf, tennis, Little League for the kids, and the all-American summer vacation, which consumed time and money. Although in 1946 movies took in 85 cents of every dollar spent on leisure activities, a decade later the figure had fallen to 74 cents, and by 1966 it was down to 50 cents. The American public by then simply had more options available.

This is not to say that television did not have a major impact on the movies; it did. By 1952, television sets had become a conspicuous fixture in half of American households. Relying on TV to bring them nightly entertainment, people no longer viewed a weekly trip to the movies as a necessity. Attendance slumped to under fifty million as the public went to see a blockbuster movie, ventured out for a 3-D film, occasionally piled the family in the car for a drive-in, or sought out their favorite stars. In other words, Americans came to attend movies *selectively*, largely ignoring the lower-budget, staple B features that the industry had once churned out by the thousands. Going to the movies became a treat, not a habit.

As if the loss in attendance was not enough, Hollywood suffered another and perhaps even more damaging economic blow in May 1948, when the U.S. Supreme Court declared the movie industry an illegal monopoly. Popularly known as the *Paramount* decision (334 U.S. 131), this case struck down the vertical integration of production, distribution, and exhibition that had been the economic foundation for the glitter and glamour of Hollywood.

Dominating the film industry were the five major corporations that owned their own fleets of theaters (Warner Bros., Paramount, Loew's Inc., Twentieth Century–Fox, and RKO) and the three minor studios that did not own theaters but cooperated with the majors (Columbia, Universal, and United Artists). These eight companies produced 70 percent of all feature films, were responsible for over 90 percent of the A (big-budget) features that played in the United States, and received 95 percent of all film rentals. In the area of exhibition they directly controlled about 2,800 theaters out of the roughly 17,000 in the United States, or about 16 percent. Although this would not on the surface appear to be a monopoly, the corporations restricted the first run of all of their A features to major theaters under their control. These theaters playing first-run features were responsible for the majority of film rentals.

The five majors divided up the country into "spheres of influence." Paramount controlled 50 percent of the theaters in the South, Twentieth Century–Fox had the Pacific Coast, Warner Bros. dominated the Middle Atlantic states, RKO controlled the states of New York and New Jersey, and Loew's reigned supreme in the most important market, New York City. Using traditional economic techniques, the majors fixed prices, pooled profits, set how long theaters could play a feature, agreed to exhibit one another's films, and forced independent theater owners to take all the films produced by a studio or take none (block booking).

Censorship was a major element of this monopoly. The majors had agreed they would neither produce, nor play in any theater under their control, a film that did not carry the industry PCA seal. Independents like Selznick who wanted, indeed needed, access to the first-run theaters either had to submit to the industry-code apparatus or book their films into second-class theaters. The whole economic structure of the industry was a textbook case of restraint of trade.

The original case, *United States* v. *Paramount Pictures,* had been filed by the Justice Department in July 1938. It charged the five majors with "combining and conspiring to restrain trade unreasonably and to monopolize the production, distribution and exhibition of motion pictures."[2] The three minors were charged with combining with the five majors. Specific allegations included price fixing, block and blind booking, excluding independent and foreign films from their theaters, and pooling profits.

A consent decree issued in November 1940 in federal court set up arbitration boards to try to work out the complaints of independent theater owners and increase competition. This decree limited block booking to five films, rather than the entire output of a studio, and forced the majors not to expand their ownership of theaters; but it did little to change the basic economic structure of the industry. In 1944, therefore, the Justice Department reactivated its suit and petitioned the District Court to implement a divorcement (i.e., separation) of exhibition from production in the movie industry. After a prolonged court battle, the Supreme Court ruled in 1948 in favor of the Justice Department, concluding:

> Divorcement is necessary to prevent the major defendants from being in a state of interdependence which too greatly restricts competition. Divorcement is a necessary remedy to introduce competition into defendants' system of fixed admission prices, clearances and runs, and to remove a major incentive to discriminatory trade practices.[3]

The Court ordered Paramount to divest itself of more than 700 theaters; Warner's had to sell 55 in major cities, Twentieth Century–Fox 100, and RKO more than 270; Loew's was forced to sell 24 of its holdings in New York City. The process was slow and it took almost a decade to complete; but the importance of the *Paramount* case for this study is that it broke the stranglehold of the eight largest studios on theaters in the United States. Theoretically at least, the divorcement decision meant that theater chains and independent owners could book any film they wished without fear of industry retaliation.

Divorcement also undermined the absolute power of the PCA, and would prove as important in the eventual elimination of film censorship as the Supreme Court cases of the 1950s that struck down the legal power of government to censor movies. The MPAA, through Breen and the PCA, had maintained absolute control of the product – movies – through its inspection process. The studios, by agreeing to submit their scripts and films for approval and not to exhibit, nor offer for exhibition, any film that failed inspection, had effectively excluded filmmakers from exhibiting films lacking a PCA seal. The key to this system was absolute control over theaters, which collected the revenue generated by the film. Once the theaters became independent of production, however, it was only a matter of time before the system of industry censorship collapsed. As film historian Tino Balio noted, the immediate impact of divorcement was that, "Without first-run theaters, the Big Five lost [their] power to enforce the strictures of the Production Code Administration."[4] Theater chains and owners were now free to choose whether or not to play films not bearing a seal, and to accept or reject a film condemned by the Legion of Decency. All this would take time to effect, but the path was clearly marked; the 1948 *Paramount* decision severely damaged the Legion and the PCA.

That the court recognized this was clearly signaled by Justice William O. Douglas, who added to his comments on divorcement that "we have no doubt that moving pictures, like newspapers and radio, are included in the press whose freedom is guaranteed by the First Amendment."[5] Justice Douglas was sending a clear signal that the industry system of self-regulation was as severe a restraint of trade as was industry ownership of theaters. Together they provided control of product and access to exhibition.

Separation from the theaters also meant that the studios did not have to produce as many films. Many of those made by the studios, especially the B features, had been produced to fill screen time at industry-owned theaters. Now that there was no longer a need for these films – and thus no need for a large and costly stable of actors and actresses, directors, and supporting staff – the studios dropped production of their B features and concentrated on large, expensive films. Total production of films declined almost as rapidly as attendance. In 1946 there were 378 features produced in the United States; a decade later there were only 272. The result was that divorcement opened theaters to competition from both domestic and foreign producers. As Garth Jowett noted in his study of American film, "movie theaters compensated [for the lack of domestic product] by filling their screen time with independent and foreign films."[6]

Foreign films, however, had never been very popular in the United States. They did find an audience during the silent era; but once sound (especially dialogue) was introduced, foreign-language films failed to attract an audience outside the large enclaves of ethnic populations found in a few American cities. From 1930 to the eve of the American entry into World War II, foreign films played with some regularity in around two hundred theaters in the United States – less than 1 percent of all American theaters. Most of these catered exclusively to ethnic audiences. In New York, for example, specialty theaters screened French, German, Italian, Russian, Greek, Hungarian, Chinese, and Yiddish films. Chicago, Philadelphia, Milwaukee, and San Francisco also had theaters that successfully marketed foreign films to specific ethnic audiences.[7] The limited market for foreign films – further restricted by the studios' tight control of access to theaters – meant that most were not submitted to the PCA.

An occasional foreign film might, however, break into wider release and enjoy some popularity. To get access to the best theaters, these foreign films had to be inspected by Breen's PCA and then pass the moral scrutiny of the Legion. Clearly, there was no opportunity to review scripts: The films had already been made without benefit of the tenets of the Production Code. A few were able to satisfy Breen, the Legion, and the American public – Jean Renoir's *Grand Illusion,* distributed by the major circuits in the late 1930s, being a rare example.

Hedy Lamarr was involved in a cause célèbre when she appeared nude in *Ecstasy (Extase)* in 1933 – a film banned as "obscene" in 1935 by Federal Judge John C. Knox not because of the nudity but because of the extended scenes of Lamarr's face as she experienced orgasm during intercourse with her lover. The original version of the film was burned by U.S. Custom's authorities. An edited version – no nudity, no orgasm, and recut to eliminate adultery – eventually played at some theaters but was denied a seal by the PCA and condemned by the Legion.

The experience of *Ecstasy* was not all that unusual. In 1936 the Legion condemned the highly acclaimed *Carnival in Flanders (La Kermesse hero-ïque),* which had passed the scrutiny of both PCA and New York censors, because of "subtle indecent dialogue and incidents."[8] In fact, three of the four films condemned by the Legion in that year were foreign.

In 1939 Martin Quigley reviewed thirty-eight French films for Breen. Appalled at their content – nudity, prostitution, suicide, vulgar comedy, free love, adultery, drugs, and murder were the dominant plot themes – he recommended that the PCA reject them all. *Le Messager* was "to be rejected by all means," Quigley wrote; it featured "divorce, adultery, nudes . . . cheap dancing . . . and suicide." Quigley warned Breen that *Coralie & Cie* was "highly perverse, glorifies adultery and free love, attacks marriage and favors divorce"; *Ménage Ultra Moderne,* in his view, was a "shameful" film "endorsing free love"; and *Mademoiselle Ma Mère* had to be rejected, he believed, because it made "religious marriage and fatherhood" a joke. In all, Quigley found nudity in fourteen of the films and adultery justified in eleven.[9] Needless to say, none of these films carried the imprimatur of either the PCA or the Legion.

Few foreign films were available during World War II, but by 1945 Quigley and Legion officials worried that a resurgent European film industry would ignore the code and, if allowed entry into the American market, could possibly undercut PCA and Legion authority. "I fear a rapid decline, especially in the European product," Quigley told Legion director Msgr. McClafferty in May 1945.[10] To counter the threat that he saw emerging from Europe, Quigley proposed worldwide adoption of the Production Code. As a first step his son, Martin Quigley Jr., had the code translated into Italian and pressed Vatican officials to push for its adoption for Italian films; but the proposal found few supporters outside the Vatican. The response of one foreign director to the code, with its clauses on crime, sex, profanity, vulgarity, nudity, and other taboos, was bemusement: "What a marvelous scenario!"[11]

The elder Quigley's fears were soon justified, however, when the film *Open City*, by unknown Italian director Roberto Rossellini, captured the imagination of film critics and a small but appreciative audience. Rossellini worked in the suburbs of Rome at Cinecittà, the largest film studio in Europe, during the Fascist regime. During the war years he made several documentaries and war propaganda films, but he maintained that he was neither a Fascist nor a supporter of the Mussolini government.[12]

Perhaps to prove that claim he began preparing *Open City*, about the liberation of Rome from Nazi occupation, while the Germans were still in Rome. The film was loosely based on the story of an Italian priest, Don Pietro Morosini, who was executed by the Germans for helping the partisan movement. The Allied invasion of Italy in 1943, the collapse of the Mussolini regime, and the Allied drive toward Rome prevented Rossellini from gaining access to Italian production facilities. He improvised by shooting scenes in the streets of Rome, used natural lighting, and saved money by using American GIs and, for the most part, nonprofessional Italians as actors. (Anna Magnani and Aldo Fabrizi were the only known professional actors.) He shot film without sound and dubbed dialogue and sound afterward, when studio facilities were available. As Rossellini later recalled, "there was only just enough [money] to pay for the raw film, and no hope of getting it developed since I didn't have enough to pay the laboratories. So there was no viewing of the rushes until shooting was completed. Some time later, having acquired a little money, I edited the film."[13] The result was a narrative structure that was difficult to follow at times and characters who drift in and out of the story. As Rossellini later recalled, his purpose was not to tell a story but to make "a film about fear, the fear felt by all of us but by me in particular. I too had to go into hiding, I too was on the run. I had friends who were captured and killed."[14] With a meager budget he managed to produce the entire film for $18,000.

Rossellini's concern (born of necessity) with constructing a cinema based on reality helped to create a style of filmmaking known as neorealism. Rossellini, Luchino Visconti, and Vittorio De Sica (director of *Shoeshine, Bicycle Thief,* and *Umberto D*) made earthy, often brutal, films about life in Italy during the period of liberation from fascism and the difficult and disappointing postwar era. They reflected life as it was: often unfair, painful, and at times morally ambiguous. It was not a cinema of mindless entertainment and studio formulas, nor one that could easily be fit into the absolute moral codes espoused by the Production Code and the Legion of Decency.

Open City attracted little attention when it opened in 1945 in Italy; in fact, it was booed by some Italian audiences because it reminded them of the terrible ordeal they had so recently suffered. However, when a print was brought to the United States in a duffel bag by an American GI, Rod Geiger, and picked up for release by U.S. foreign-film distributors Arthur L. Mayer and Joseph Burstyn, it created a sensation. *Open City* grossed some $3 million at the box office and was selected by the New York Film Critics as the Best Film of 1946. It was, said the *New Yorker,* simply "the best [film] that has ever come out of Italy."[15] It was also, however, a catalog of violations of the Production Code and of Legion of Decency standards, presenting rather matter-of-factly drug addiction, lesbianism, murder, a priest who helps leaders of the communist-led Italian underground, and the most graphic torture scenes ever projected on the American screen.

The film centers around a small group of people who are fighting alongside the Italian underground movement in the last days of the German occupation of Rome. Francesco (Francesco Grandjacquet), a printer of an underground newspaper, and Pina (Anna Magnani), an organizer, are dedicated anti-Fascists who are engaged. Pina has a young son by a previous marriage, Marcello; he too fights the Germans. The film opens on Francesco and Pina's wedding day. Pina is pregnant, but no one in the community, including the local priest, Don Pietro Pellegrini (Aldo Fabrizi), casts any moral aspersions on her; in fact, Don Pietro has happily agreed to marry them. The war, however, will prevent these lovers from living a normal life.[16]

The leader of the partisans is a communist, Manfredi (Marcello Pagliero, a journalist with no prior acting experience), who is on the run from the German Gestapo headed by Major Bergmann (Harry Feist, in real life a ballet dancer). Manfredi takes refuge in Francesco's apartment and recruits the priest, Don Pietro, to smuggle funds across German lines to the partisans. The Germans discover Manfredi's hiding place and raid the building, but he escapes; they arrest several men, including Francesco. When Pina sees her fiancé being loaded into the Gestapo truck she screams with terror. In uncontrollable rage she breaks away from her friends and runs frantically after the truck, hoping to free her lover. Although clearly no threat to the Germans, she is suddenly gunned down. Her young son witnesses her execution and is distraught, but no one else seems too surprised by the senseless killing.

The next scene makes Pina's death all the more meaningless. The partisans, led by Manfredi, attack the Germans and free Francesco. They both hide with Marina (Maria Michi), Manfredi's mistress. Marina, however, unlike Pina, is not a dedicated partisan: She is a drug addict and has been thoroughly corrupted by the war. As she tells one of her friends: "Of course I've had lovers. How else would I get this furniture. These clothes. My salary? It's just enough for cigarettes and stockings. I've known poverty and it frightens me." She asks her friend: "Should I have married that trolley conductor and had a brood of starving children?" Her answer was obvious: She wanted good times, and the Germans provided them. Her drugs were being supplied by Ingrid, a lesbian Gestapo agent who wants Marina as much as she wants information about the partisans. When Manfredi quarrels with Marina about her drug habit, she betrays him to Ingrid.

The Gestapo raid Marina's apartment and arrest Manfredi and Don Pietro. Determined to make Manfredi talk, they torture him in front of the priest. The Gestapo want to break Manfredi to get information on the partisans, but also to prove that they are the "Master Race." They believe that making him betray his friends will justify the war.

The scenes of Manfredi's torture are brutally graphic: The Germans use a blowtorch on him, then casually light their cigarettes with the same torch. They pull his fingernails out and they beat him senseless with whips.

Major Bergmann supervises the torture of Manfredi and interrogates Don Pietro in an adjoining room; he moves freely between one room and the other. Manfredi's screams often interrupt the interrogation, which terrifies Don Pietro but amuses the Germans. Bergmann taunts the priest: How could you – a man of God – help an atheist like Manfredi? The priest replies calmly: "I am a Catholic priest and I believe that a man who fights for justice and liberty walks in the pathways of the Lord – and the pathways of the Lord are infinite."

In a scene shockingly frank for American audiences, Marina and Ingrid are shown lounging on a couch drinking champagne in yet another room in Gestapo headquarters. Ingrid holds Marina in her arms. The lovers hear Manfredi's screams but are only mildly curious. Ingrid walks into the torture room to watch for a while before returning to Marina. The torture continues, and when Marina joins Ingrid in the torture room she faints when she realizes Manfredi has been killed. The Germans are furious because he did not break; they are not the master race.

The next morning a firing squad is assembled to execute Don Pietro. The children of his parish gather at a fence to watch in silence as their friend is killed. A momentary hope is given when the Italian firing squad purposely misses the priest. Don Pietro opens his eyes in disbelief but does not see the German who approaches him from behind and shoots him in the head. The children turn away slowly and trudge back home. The movie is over. Unlike in Hollywood, no last-minute heroics by partisan or Allied troops save Manfredi and Don Pietro. The Germans live, Marina survives, and the Italians who fought for freedom die.

The critics loved it. Ira Peck wrote in *PM* that what distinguished *Open City* was its utter honesty. "It leaves out none of the brutality, sordidness, and perversion that were the trademarks of the Nazis" and conveyed these "with a realism that Hollywood films have only been willing to suggest. One actually sees the Nazis performing the terrible physical tortures they inflicted on their victims."[17] *Cue* called it "memorable," made with the "utter honesty of the finest of the wartime newsreels."[18] Even the lay Catholic publication *Commonweal* was enthralled with *Open City:* Philip Hartung labeled it a "stirring film" in "a class by itself," but admitted "that it would never have been made" in Hollywood under the PCA. "The lesbian overtone, . . . the frankness in several of the discussions, the extreme brutality of the torture scenes, in fact the story's main theme" made it a film "for thinking people."[19]

Surprisingly, neither Hartung, who served as a consultant/reviewer for the Legion of Decency, nor the Legion was offended by the frankness of a movie that featured drugs, lesbianism, the church's official blessing of a marriage that ordinarily would not have been sanctified, and the open collaboration between a communist and a priest. Ordinarily, a film with any one of these themes would have automatically brought a stinging condemnation from the Legion and denouncement from pulpits all over America. *Open City* was certainly more frank than anything in *The Outlaw, Duel in the Sun,* or *Forever Amber;* yet the Legion hardly raised an eyebrow when it reviewed *Open City* and quietly issued a B rating, citing "deceit was sympathetically treated; excessive gruesomeness, suggestive costumes and implications; [and] use of narcotics."[20]

When *Open City* was submitted to the PCA there were few objections raised. Had it been reviewed in Los Angeles there might have been more; but because the film was not expected to play in many theaters outside of New York City, it was handled at the PCA's New York office by Arthur DeBra, who reported to Breen but had a certain amount of independence owing to the three thousand miles separating him from his boss. DeBra told importer Joseph Burstyn that the film was basically acceptable, but a shot of a young child sitting on a chamber pot should be cut and scenes that stressed Pina's pregnancy trimmed. Burstyn, however, refused to make any changes, and the film played in the New York area and a few other major cities for a year without a PCA seal. When Burstyn finally agreed to the cuts in July 1947, Breen issued the seal.[21]

It is very surprising that neither Breen nor DeBra insisted, as they did with so many movies, that some type of "voice for morality" be inserted into the film. Since the movie was already made it was not possible to have a character chastise Marina for her drug addiction or casual use of sex for profit, or have the priest mildly scold Pina for getting pregnant before marriage. Still, the PCA or the Legion could have insisted that some type of opening prologue be inserted to explain to audiences that Marina's actions were wrong and that the war did not justify Pina's indiscretion. Father Masterson had demanded a prologue for *Forever Amber,* and Marina's moral collapse is much more serious than Amber's.

Why, then, were the PCA and the Legion so lenient with *Open City?* There are several possible reasons, but perhaps most compelling is that the Vatican loved the film. *Open City* was approved by the Central Catholic Committee of the Vatican, and church officials were so enamored of the film that they requested a copy for the Vatican's film library. Despite the frankness of the sexuality in the film and its vivid brutality, *Open City* presents one of the most sympathetic portrayals of the Catholic church ever seen on screen. The typical Hollywood Catholic priest of the time, represented by character actors Barry Fitzgerald and Pat O'Brien, spun out pieties with moral absoluteness that allowed little thought for the other characters or audience members. In *Open City* the moral choices the partisans have to make are anything but clear-cut, and the church, represented by Don Pietro, is tolerant and understanding when war forces Francesco and Pina to violate normal conventions. Don Pietro is unalterably opposed to fascism and determined to fight for a better life for the people. In the film, the church has the total support of the people: Even the communists, who hate religion, turn to the church for help and support; what is more, the church is willing to help them because they are fighting fascism.

Open City presented a church that few in 1946 would recognize. The role of the Catholic church in Germany had been one of conciliation toward Hitler, with no bishop taking to his pulpit to denounce the campaign against the Jews. Moreover, Pope Pius XII had not spoken out against the Holocaust, and this silence on Nazi atrocities subjected him to severe criticism soon after the war. *Open City* offered a refreshing tonic for a church so stung.

American Catholics were not unaware of the controversy surrounding the pope. Given the position of the Vatican, it would have certainly been embarrassing for the American Catholic Legion of Decency to issue the film a condemned rating: The bishops would have been ridiculed in the American press and would not have relished explaining to Vatican officials why a film so favorable to Catholicism had been condemned in America.

Another reason for the lenient treatment of the film is that in the immediate postwar euphoria, it was very popular to make heroes of underground resistance movements. *Open City* presents an Italian people totally united in their opposition to the Germans and fascism. With the exception of Marina, all Italians are fighting the Germans. There is no reference in the film to the role played by the Italian armed forces in the Axis war machine, no hint of Italy's alliance with Hitler, no suggestion of the level of Italian collaboration with fascism, and no hint that Italian filmmakers willingly produced fascist propaganda films. Instead, the Italians, even Italian communists, emerge on the screen as heroic victims, not willing participants in the Nazi war effort. This theme of resistance to Nazi oppression was very popular in France, Italy, and even Germany in the period just after the war.

PCA officials may have believed this all to be true. In Los Angeles Breen, although concerned about the moral issues presented in *Open City,* did not challenge the decisions made by the New York office. He probably reasoned that Vatican approval and the limited number of theaters that would book the film made the decision more palatable; still, he remained on the alert.

Open City was the first in a trilogy of postwar films made by Rossellini. In 1946 he followed the success of *Open City* with *Paisan,* a tribute to the Allied liberation of Italy. Using the same techniques that marked *Open City* – nonprofessional actors, filming on location, and sound and dialogue added in the studio – the director captured the despair, the hopeless tragedy, as well as the humor and respect between the liberators and the liberated that marked the Allied drive to free Italy. Rossellini painted war as it was, often meaningless and brutal. Death is senseless: Heroes and the innocent die, the enemy often survives.

In this film, six separate and unrelated episodes chronicle the Allied march north from Sicily in 1943 to the Po Valley a year later. The opening sequence takes place in Sicily, where a small company of American soldiers is searching the coast for German snipers. A young Sicilian girl offers to help and takes the men to an area where she believes the Germans are hiding. The Americans are suspicious of her, and one soldier (Robert Van Loon) is left to guard her while the rest of the unit searches for the Germans. The two young people flirt, but neither can communicate with the other. They are careless, and both are killed by sniper fire.

The second segment is set in Naples. A young street kid (Alfonsino Pasca) steals the boots of a drunken American MP, played by African-American Dots M. Johnson. Once sober, the MP spots the child and forces him to take him to his home so he can recover the boots. The young boy, terrified of this huge foreigner, cooperates fully. When the MP sees the conditions under which this child is living, he suddenly understands why he steals. Nothing is said, but the message is clear. The MP just stares and then flees in horror.

The third episode was the most troubling to American censors. In Rome, a young prostitute, Francesca (Maria Michi), picks up Fred, just another drunken GI (Gar Moore). She takes him to a room, casually undresses, and gets into bed with him. Fred, however, is not really interested in having sex with her and complains, "You are all alike – all for sale, all cheap. What has happened to you? It was not like this when we arrived." He then tells a story in flashback of his first days in Rome, when he met a beautiful young girl. She was beautiful and pure, Fred said. They talked about their dreams and fell in love; but the war separated them. While the soldier is telling the story

Francesca realizes that she is that girl – a mere six months of war and poverty have forced her into prostitution. When Fred finally falls asleep she tiptoes out of the room, leaving him a note explaining who she is and asking that he meet her the next day so they can resume their love affair. She waits in vain: Fred, now sober, has forgotten her. The episode ends simply with Francesca standing on a street corner awaiting her lover. Reality will soon force her to turn another trick to survive.

The fourth section takes place in Florence, where a young American nurse (Harriet White) searches for her lover – a partisan leader. Her quest ends when she learns of his death. The fifth segment is set in a Franciscan monastery, where three Army chaplains are visiting. The monks (played by themselves), almost totally shut off from the world around them, are concerned when they discover that one of the chaplains is Protestant – and horrified to learn that the third is Jewish. They demand that the Catholic chaplain convert the two heathens to the one true faith. The priest gently refuses, and, in a touching scene at dinner, delivers a homily on religious toleration.

The final sequence takes place in the Po River Valley. OSS and British intelligence troops are parachuted into the marshlands in northern Italy to help partisans fight the Germans. It is hopeless: All are killed.

Variety called *Paisan* "a fine and moving human document" that must rank "near the great foreign pictures of all time."[22] *Time* judged the last segment "as fine a piece of war fiction as the movies have achieved."[23] "An unforgettably powerful film," said the British publication *Fortnight*.[24]

Although the critics again heaped praise on Rossellini, the film contained some very controversial material. The sequence set in Rome between Francesca and Fred, which *Variety* dubbed as the "best of the lot," was the most direct, frank, and perhaps honest treatment of prostitution and the effects of war seen on American screens since the early 1930s.[25] Had any Hollywood studio attempted a scene as candid as Rossellini's – a prostitute picking up a man, taking him to her room, casually undressing, and climbing into bed with him – Breen and the Legion would have raised a howl of protest; yet the film received a PCA seal of approval, and Catholic reviewers gave it a B, citing "suggestive sequences" and a tendency "to condone illicit killing."[26]

Why did the PCA approve this film when it had consistently demanded that all references to prostitutes and houses of prostitution be either struck from films or changed to imply that sex was never for sale? The explanation helps set the stage for Breen's later determination to bring foreign films under his control. His refusal in 1950 to issue a seal to the completely moral *Bicycle Thief,* as well as the uproar over Rossellini's *The Miracle* in 1951, must be viewed within the context of *Paisan*.

As in the case of *Open City, Paisan* was reviewed by Arthur DeBra of the PCA's New York office. There seemed no reason to bother Breen and his staff with a film that would have little play outside the East Coast art-house circuit. Although aware that the sequence between Francesca and Fred was "highly sexy," DeBra issued a PCA seal without demanding cuts.[27] In Hollywood, producers, directors, and writers quickly heard that these scenes had not been cut. Breen was seething; he fired off a letter to DeBra demanding an explanation.

DeBra was in a difficult position. He told Breen that when he had first seen the film he had insisted that Burstyn, who had attended the screening, cut the print "from the point when the girl and boy entered the bedroom and she started to remove her dress to the point where he begins to recite" his story. Viewing the film several days later, however, it now left the very clear impression that Francesca and Fred had had sex. "The inference," he wrote, "that an affair had taken place was unmistakable." DeBra had then spent several days studying the bedroom sequence but concluded it was next to impossible to cut it without "breaking into Fred's monologue and the subsequent dialogue, through which it becomes obvious that Francesca rues the fact that she did not remain the girl Fred returned to look for." To test his theory DeBra had two young, unmarried secretaries who worked for the MPAA view the film in its original form. Both agreed, DeBra told Breen, that "no one would consider her a prostitute and that the whole episode, as they saw it, was not only inoffensive but a tremendously moral lesson."[28]

"Sounds like an old wheeze to us," Breen fired back. He was furious with DeBra and the New York office. "I can tell you that we here, in this office, would, quite definitely, not have approved this picture if it were sent to us, because of its unacceptably offensive sex details." *Paisan* is "causing us no end of trouble," wrote Breen, adding for emphasis, "Your approval of this picture . . . is very much regretted."[29]

For Breen the final straw came when DeBra confided that he had talked censors in Boston and Pennsylvania into accepting the original version of the film. He proudly wrote his boss in Los Angeles that the Pennsylvania censor had told him that the film brought nothing but "praise in Philadelphia."[30] Breen was not pleased that a film he considered immoral was playing over his signature in his hometown.

In truth, the reading of the film by the young women in the MPAA office was far more sophisticated than Breen's. It is impossible to watch the episode and not feel that Francesca was forced into prostitution by the war. She did not have sex with Fred that evening, but she did survive by selling herself to soldiers. The scene certainly did not glorify prostitution and in no way would have led young girls into that profession.

Breen didn't care. It was his view that if the PCA began allowing this type of material in foreign films, the Hollywood studios would flood screens with similar depictions of down-on-their-luck girls who turn to prostitution. (This assumption was not necessarily valid: Breen could, and did, exert much more control over the studios than over foreign productions.) At any rate, he was determined to correct the mistake the New York office made; henceforth, foreign films would be sent to Los Angeles for screening and judgment.

Breen was ready when Rossellini and distributor Marcello Girosi, president of Superfilm, submitted the final film in the Italian director's trilogy of the moral decay in postwar Europe for PCA approval in 1949. Shot in Berlin in 1947, *Germany, Year Zero* tells the story of a young boy, educated under the Nazi regime, who murders his father because he is sick and can no longer provide for the family. Amid the ruins of Berlin Rossellini tried to convey the moral and spiritual decay that infected German society in the aftermath of total physical destruction. The film won the Grand Prize at the Locarno Film Festival in 1948 and opened in New York in the fall of 1949, after the dramatic Berlin airlift had saved that city from starvation.

Over the opening credits, journalist, and radio commentator Quentin Reynolds delivered a prologue:

> Berlin is a huge monument to death, not to the death of people who once lived and died here, but a monument to an evil dream of power that lies buried forever, the world hopes, under these ruins. . . . The defeated live in an almost lifeless country, victims of their own evil dream.

The film is centered around a 12-year-old boy, Edmund (Edmund Moeschke), who lives with his family in a small flat in Berlin. He and his family share the space with four other families. Their lack of privacy and their hopeless poverty cause the families to bicker constantly. For Edmund's family making enough money to feed themselves is a daily struggle. His father is sick and unable to work, his sister, Eva (Barbara Hintz) works as a hostess in a dance hall, and his brother, Karlheinz (Werner Pittschau) is a deserter from the German army, afraid to leave the house. Much of the responsibility for earning money falls on Edmund's shoulders.

As everyone struggles to survive, Edmund is left to wander the city. He sells goods on the black market and hooks up with a teenage street gang whose members survive by their own wits. He is befriended briefly by a young female prostitute his own age and spends a night with her. During his wandering he meets one of his old teachers, Herr Enning, an unreconstructed Nazi who has been fired from his job and now survives by providing young boys to an ex-Nazi General who lives with him.

Enning, who is clearly a pedophile, is delighted to see Edmund. He has the young boy sit on his lap and tell him about his current situation. While the boy is telling him about his family, the teacher cannot keep his hands off Edmund. He rubs his arms, his neck, hugs him – but Edmund is oblivious to it all. When Edmund complains about his sickly father, the teacher suddenly begins to spout Nazi doctrine about the strong surviving and the weak dying: "You're afraid Papa will die? Learn from Nature: the weak are always eliminated by the strong. . . . You must recognize your responsibilities."

Edmund takes this all too literally and returns home to poison his father. After his father's death, Edmund returns to his teacher's apartment and confesses to him. The horrified teacher screams, "You are a monster," but later tries to console Edmund, saying that he is just a young boy who misunderstood. Edmund stares at him for a few moments, then replies, "You should have told me that before."

Edmund again wanders the bombed-out city streets. He tries to regain his childhood by playing soccer with some kids, but it doesn't help. Instead of returning home he climbs to the top of an abandoned building across the street from his flat. From atop the building he watches his father's body being taken away. His sister frantically calls for him, but Edmund ignores her. When his family finally leaves for the funeral, he pauses for a moment, then leaps off the building to his death. The war and fascism have claimed another innocent victim.

The critics were split on the merits of the film. The *New Yorker* found, perhaps because the characters were German, "none of the warmth, humor, and understanding" that marked *Open City* and *Paisan*. The reviewer lamented that the film was "populated by characters for whom it is impossible to work up any sympathy."[31] Philip Hartung agreed: The film, he warned readers, while "interesting cinematically," ultimately "fails to stir our emotions."[32]

Others were more positive. One of the most conservative Protestant publications, the *Christian Century,* called the film "an unforgettable picture of corruption and despair suffered by victims of war." Readers were told that *Germany, Year Zero* "could hardly be improved upon."[33]

The censors were certain not only that could it be improved but that it was thoroughly immoral. Gordon White, director of the PCA code for advertising, told Breen that "no amount of argument that this is a pitiful portrayal of the physical and moral destitution that follows in the wake of war can gainsay the fact that the film is not fit for general family patronage."[34] PCA censor Jack Vizzard objected to Rossellini's lack of balance, telling Breen:

> No one would get the notion that possibly 20 percent of the people were damaged spiritually and morally, but that 70 percent or 80 percent of the people still retained some semblance of moral fiber. . . . I can hear him (the distributor) appealing that this is a great, artistic representation of the ravages of war, and an argument against war, since it shows the ravages of war upon the souls of people. All of which is a lot of high-flying sophistry.[35]

Breen agreed. He told distributor Marcello Girosi that *Germany, Year Zero* was "thoroughly and completely unacceptable" under the code. Breen was so outraged by the "unavoidable suggestion" that Edmund had sex with a 12-year-old prostitute who was generally available to "a whole gang of hoodlums" that he asked Girosi to withdraw his application for a PCA seal. No amount of trimming or cutting, Breen told Girosi, would make the film acceptable.[36]

In New York, the Legion of Decency condemned the film as "unfit for general movie audiences."[37] Negotiations opened quickly between the Legion and Girosi to make the necessary cuts to place the film in the B category. The Legion demanded that the scenes in which Edmund is fondled by his former teacher be eliminated and the scene in which the gang of boys offers Edmund the young girl also be cut. In addition, the Legion was deeply troubled by Edmund's suicide and wanted an epilogue added that would explain it to audiences. To avoid misunderstanding the Legion wrote the epilogue for the film:

> So ends the story of Edmund, who could not continue the arduous struggle for life in a land, from which had vanished all moral values, all religious principles. Too young for his burdens, nostalgic for childhood, Edmund tried to transcend the terrible pressures on a 12 year old of defeat and ruin. But, in a country which had rejected the lessons of the great teachers who brought mankind out of the darkness of barbarism into the light of Christian civilization, he could find no beacon of light, no out-stretched hand, no comforting word. Too young, too alone he could walk no further on so tortuous a path.

With the cuts and moral clarity added to the ending, the Legion raised *Germany, Year Zero* to a B rating; but Breen refused to budge, and his ban remained unchanged. It was becoming increasingly clear, however, that the PCA was out of touch. Breen must have felt betrayed when the Legion approved the film for adult audiences. Breen and the PCA took another body blow when the New York censorship board approved the film with *no* cuts. Ohio, Massachusetts, and Pennsylvania all gave their approval with minor cuts in the scenes with Edmund sitting on his ex-teacher's lap. Still, despite its slightly wider access to theaters, the film was a flop at the box office and quickly disappeared from view.

While Rossellini's *Germany, Year Zero* was playing to small audiences in a few urban theaters, another neorealistic Italian film was winning international acclaim. Vittorio De Sica's *The Bicycle Thief,* a poignant story of a poor man's struggle to escape poverty, won the Grand Prize at the Brussels Film Festival, was named Best Foreign Film by the New York Film Critics, and was given an Oscar by the Academy of Motion Picture Arts and Sciences as the best foreign-language film to play in the United States during 1949.[38]

Vittorio De Sica, like Roberto Rossellini, emerged as an important film director in the immediate aftermath of World War II. A popular heartthrob in Italian theater in the early 1930s, he began making movies in 1931. His directing debut was *Rose scarlatte (Twenty-Four Red Roses)*, a lighthearted romance-comedy that enjoyed some popularity in Italy. In 1943 he began his long collaboration with writer and director Cesare Zavattini.

De Sica and Zavattini gained worldwide attention with their 1946 *Shoeshine (Sciuscià)*, a powerful neorealist film that chronicled the tragic fate of two young Italian war orphans who attempt to carve out a living in the poverty and destitution of postwar Italy. The film was given a Special Academy Award in 1947.

The team followed their success a year later with *Ladri di biciclette (The Bicycle Thief)*. Set in contemporary Rome, where unemployment has forced millions of workers and their families into destitution, the film is centered on Antonio Ricci, played by Lamberto Maggiorani (a steelworker in real life). Antonio is one of the faceless army of unemployed; but inexplicably he is suddenly offered a job as a billposter, a position that promises to take his family out of poverty. There is one requirement for the job – he must have his own bicycle.

Antonio rushes home to tell his family the good news. His wife Maria, played by Lianella Carell (a journalist, not an actress), and his son Bruno, played by Enzo Staiola, are delighted. There is a problem, however. Antonio has had to pawn his bike to buy food for his family. Maria quickly decides to pawn the one remaining item from her dowry – the bed linens – to reclaim Antonio's bicycle. At the pawnshop they encounter long lines of people selling family heirlooms in order to survive; but for the Ricci family this humiliation is a necessary ordeal in order to regain their self-respect. With the money from the pawnshop Antonio reclaims his bicycle and his place as head of the family.

The next morning, Saturday, Antonio proudly goes to work. His son has polished the bicycle, and Maria has made her husband a fine lunch. Ironically, Antonio's first poster is a large, gaudy advertisement for a Rita Hayworth movie. As he struggles to paste it to a wall, a thief (Vittorio Antonucci, the only professional actor in the film) steals his bicycle. Antonio chases him, but the thief easily escapes into the back streets of Rome. When Antonio reports the incident to the police, they react with indifference, leaving him to return home dejected.

The next day, Sunday, Antonio and Bruno set off in a quest to find the thief. It is essential for their survival that they recover the bicycle. They enlist the help of friends, who take them to an open-air market where stolen bicycles are taken apart, refurbished, and reassembled for sale. There they search through bins of parts, but it is hopeless.

Their friends soon tire of the search and go home. As father and son take cover from a rain shower, Antonio sees the thief talking to an old man. When he runs after them, the thief escapes on the stolen bicycle. Bruno, who has followed his father faithfully, pauses by a wall and begins to fumble with his pants; he is going to urinate on the wall. When his father spots him, he yells, and poor little Bruno is so startled that he almost falls over. He runs to his father, and they follow the old man into a Catholic church that is offering a free shave and food to the downtrodden of Rome. Antonio badgers the old man during the church service and, when he is confronted for interrupting, the old man escapes in the confusion.

While it appears all hope is lost, Antonio again sees the thief, who this time ducks into a local bordello to hide. Antonio, who immediately recognizes the nature of the house, makes Bruno wait outside while he charges in after the thief. The madame is furious at his intrusion: Her house is closed, and all her ladies are in the dining room eating their breakfast. A comic scene follows in which everyone is yelling and gesturing wildly until finally both men are tossed out onto the street; but Antonio has his prey and is confident he will recover his bicycle at last.

It turns out, however, that the thief is a poor, destitute epileptic who is as desperate as Antonio. When Antonio begins to beat him to make him confess, neighbors rush to protect the thief. Antonio again turns to the police, who search the thief's apartment but find nothing.

In despair, Antonio and Bruno wander aimlessly through the streets, then stumble on a soccer stadium full of spectators and ringed with thousands of bicycles. Antonio, now convinced he will never recover his own bicycle, begins to contemplate stealing one. When the stadium empties, he grabs a bike and tries to blend in with the crowd; but the owner spots him, and Antonio is immediately caught by a mob of people. Bruno is mortified to discover his father has become a thief. When the owner of the bicycle sees the disappointment in Bruno's face, he orders the mob to release him. Bruno and Antonio walk away hand in hand. The film ends. There is no hope, no happy ending. A life of poverty and despair is their future.

Had Hollywood gotten its hands on the script, Antonio would likely have recovered his bicycle, and the last scene would have shown him riding off to work with his proud wife and son waving from the doorway. Breen would have insisted that the police be given a formal role in the recovery of the bicycle and the arrest of the thief. The critics, so used to classical studio formulas and PCA-enforced morality, were stunned by De Sica's refusal to end the film happily. His ability to illustrate visually both the desperation and dignity of Rome's unemployed overwhelmed audiences and critics. "None Better," the *New Yorker* headlined; it is "a masterpiece."[39] The *New Republic* told readers the film was "a work of art."[40] Bosley Crowther called it "a brilliant and devastating film" and predicted it would be an "absolute triumph."[41] Philip Hartung in *Commonweal* praised the film "as a realistic portrayal of emotions" full of "joyful sequences" that help the audience "bear the sorrowful ones"; it is "a gem."[42] To the *Christian Century* De Sica's film was a "sensitive study of a father–son relationship that becomes indirectly a plea for a chance at human dignity, [and] a condemnation of lack of concern for one's fellow men."[43]

The Bicycle Thief had been playing to large and enthusiastic crowds in New York City for over a month when film distributor Joseph Burstyn submitted the film to the PCA. As it had encountered no problems with municipal or state censorship boards, he was confident that it would win quick approval. The film had the Legion's blessing, and there was nothing remotely immoral in it. Burstyn hoped that with a PCA seal he could sell *The Bicycle Thief* to national theater chains and break out of the small but profitable art-house circuit to which he had thus far been limited.[44]

Even though *The Bicycle Thief* had won universal praise, however, Breen was deeply troubled by the film. He surprised almost everyone by declaring two scenes unacceptable: Bruno's failed attempt to urinate and Antonio's search for the thief in the bordello. If those scenes were eliminated from the film, Breen promised Burstyn he would issue a seal.[45]

The distributor was furious and told the censor that "under no conceivable stretch of the imagination can the scenes . . . be considered immoral." The film, he argued, had won international acclaim, and even the Catholic Legion of Decency had found nothing immoral in it.[46]

When Burstyn informed De Sica that in order to qualify for a PCA seal the two scenes would have to be cut, the director "was astounded." Unlike the Hollywood studios, De Sica refused to have his film changed. He told his American distributor that he would "prefer to protect [the] integrity of the picture" and hoped that an appeal would reverse Breen's ruling.[47]

To build public support, Burstyn took the controversy to the press. He charged Breen with using the Production Code to keep foreign films from competing with Hollywood by refusing seals under the pretext of morality. Elmer Rice, head of the ACLU's National Council on Freedom from Censorship and a Pulitzer Prize–winning playwright, agreed with Burstyn. He told Eric Johnston that Breen's refusal to issue a seal to *The Bicycle Thief* "deprives the American people of an opportunity to judge for themselves whether the film should be seen." It was, he wrote, a "shocking demonstration of censorship power and must be condemned as a violation of free thought and expression."[48] "Pure nonsense," countered Breen, who refused to reconsider; but Burstyn's instincts proved on target, and the press lampooned Breen, Johnston, and the MPAA for banning the film. *Life* told its readers that the only thing suggestive in the film was the poster of Rita Hayworth![49]

Martin Quigley came to Breen's defense, although less out of concern with the morality of the film than with the politics of the filmmakers. "*The Bicy-*

cle Thief," stated the *Motion Picture Herald,* "comes from that sector of Eurpean production which leans distinctly to the left." In a signed editorial Quigley charged that both De Sica and Roberto Rossellini were members of "the pro-Communist Italian Film Congress," which had "come out in strong support of Hollywood's Unfriendly Ten." When the National Board of Review announced it had selected *The Bicycle Thief* as Best Picture of 1949, Quigley was enraged. He blasted the decision as "alien and contradictory to the taste and judgment of overwhelming numbers of the theater-going public." Quigley's proof was the small box-office interest generated by the film. "The taste and judgment of the public will give preference not merely to a few but to several hundred pictures ahead of *The Bicycle Thief.*"[50]

Quigley, of course, was right in one sense: *The Bicycle Thief* would not have ended up a box-office champion of 1949 even if it had had a PCA seal. Despite the fact that the studios could no longer prevent theaters from booking the film, only a handful of exhibitors were prepared to open their theaters to controversial films. Quigley knew that as well as anyone, so his argument that box-office revenue was the only measure for quality was base hypocrisy.

In late March 1950 the MPAA Board of Directors gathered in New York to listen to the briefs presented by Joe Breen and Joseph Burstyn on *The Bicycle Thief.* The atmosphere was especially tense because the movie industry was once again under attack for promoting immorality. This time the cause was not another Hollywood scandal, but a torrid affair between an Italian director and a Swedish actress: Roberto Rossellini and actress Ingrid Bergman shocked American morality with a love affair that garnered international headlines and outraged condemnations from church groups, women's clubs, and politicians.

Bergman had come to Hollywood in 1939 under contract to David O. Selznick. Her screen image as a wholesome, almost saintly woman, was carefully crafted in such films as *Casablanca, For Whom the Bell Tolls, Gaslight, The Bells of St. Mary's,* and *Joan of Arc.* All this came crashing down when she deserted her husband, Dr. Petter Lindstrom, for Rossellini.

When Bergman joined Rossellini in Italy in 1949 they made *Stromboli,* a rather turgid film notorious only because of Rossellini and Bergman. Although both the PCA and the Legion passed the film, it was denounced in Congress and state legislatures, banned in Seattle, Memphis, and other cities, and flatly refused for booking by several of the large national theater circuits. When the lovers announced that Bergman was pregnant, shock turned to scorn.[51] All of this adverse publicity made the MPAA board nervous – so much so that they quickly cut Miss Bergman's death scene from *Joan of Arc* out of *History Brought to Life,* a publicity short that had been touring the country to demonstrate Hollywood's contribution to teaching history.

The board, well aware of the continuing, overall box-office decline, were certainly in no mood to be generous to an Italian director that March afternoon, despite *The Bicycle Thief*'s recent Academy Award. This was business, not art.

Breen went first. He admitted that the scene in *The Bicycle Thief* with Bruno attempting to urinate may "be humorous" or "cute" to sophisticated audiences. However, it was, in his judgment, in "bad taste per se" and likely to offend many viewers. He urged that it be removed from the film. The bordello scene had to be cut, he argued, "because such locales inescapably suggest commercialized vice and human depravity, and tend to arouse unwholesome interest and curiosity on the part of youth." It was, he concluded, "intrinsically offensive" to have any scene in any film set in a whorehouse.[52]

Burstyn was flabbergasted. No logical argument could be used to counter Breen's position. He simply recounted the awards the film had garnered and quoted from the glowing reviews, but to no avail: The board's decision was predetermined. The appeal was denied.

If the MPAA board believed upholding Breen's decision would bring the beleaguered industry some positive publicity, they miscalculated: The press had a field day. The *New Republic* told readers the decision on *The Bicycle Thief* "would be laughable if the MPAA were not as powerful as it is arbitrary."[53] *Life* said Breen's decision was "ridiculous" because it "effectively prevents all major U.S. movie houses from showing a film that has generally been acclaimed as one of the finest ever made."[54] Although technically this charge was untrue, in reality it was right on the mark.

Bosley Crowther, the movie critic for the *New York Times*, was indignant. He assured readers that "neither of the episodes which the Code Authority says must be cut are intrinsically indecent or offensive to morals and good taste."[55] Moreover, he pointed out that two Hollywood films with similar settings were then playing in New York: *Cheaper by the Dozen* had a toilet scene, and *Buccaneer's Girl* a bordello. Crowther, like Burstyn and Rice, wondered whether the code was being used to keep foreign films from national distribution.

The critics were right. While Breen maintained publicly that the code was not restrictive, privately he admitted that "under the operations of the Production Code a great amount of material has been kept from the screen"[56] – that, after all, was the point of his job. Breen bristled when individuals like writer-producer Mark Hellinger claimed: "Hollywood is gutless. You can't make an honest, forceful picture here." When asked why the Italians made such powerful films, Hellinger blamed censorship. "The code under which we now operate is highly restrictive. *Open City* . . . could never have been made here under any circumstances."[57]

Breen denied Hellinger's claim, but it is clear that the PCA and the Legion feared the ability of foreign films like *The Bicycle Thief* and *Paisan* to present themes like prostitution, drug addiction, lesbianism, and adultery in a manner that large numbers of people – the sophisticated audiences that Breen mentioned – found inoffensive.

Foreign directors and producers were able to do so because they were not forced to submit scripts to censors before they began filming. There were, of course, national censorship boards in all European countries, but these were often more understanding of human relationships and less likely to cripple severely their own products, which were competing for screen time with the constant flood of American movies. In the United States the audience for foreign films, although small in comparison to that for Hollywood features, nonetheless measured in the millions and was a significant source of income for foreign producers. The more foreign films played, the more Americans realized the extent of the system of censorship that kept Hollywood from the serious examination of serious topics.

Breen clearly recognized that if foreign films were allowed to present such themes, the entire rationale for the PCA and the Legion would be undercut. He was determined to prevent what he saw as a frontal challenge by foreign directors to his control of film content in America. It was a fight he was determined to carry forward but also one he was destined to lose.

This was made abundantly clear just a few months after the MPAA board meeting on *The Bicycle Thief.* As one Hollywood reporter noted: "[I]f a picture comes along which exhibs feel will be highly profitable and not cause them too much trouble, there will be more chance of selling it without a seal than there has been in the past."[58] De Sica's film fit the pattern perfectly. Three of the major national circuits, led by the decision of the powerful Skouras chain, flouted the MPAA and booked *The Bicycle Thief.* Their decision was a serious blow to Breen's authority and, as Leff and Simons have noted, broke the pledge that the major exhibitors had given not to book films that did not carry a PCA seal.[59] Exhibitors, increasingly desperate to bring people into their theaters, could no longer be counted on to reject automatically films that had incurred the wrath of the PCA and the Legion, especially for such minor infractions as those in *The Bicycle Thief.*

Another Italian film, one loaded with sexy women planting rice in the Po Valley and the hot-blooded men who worked with them, illustrated how much power Breen and the Legion had lost. When Breen and the PCA staff saw Italian bombshell Silvana Mangano planting rice in tight short-shorts and an even tighter and more revealing sweater, lounging about in revealing slips, enticing men with seductive dances, swimming in the nude, and expressing no moral qualms about hopping into bed with the man of her choice, Breen wired New York that they "were all speechless."[60]

The film, *Bitter Rice,* directed by Giuseppe De Santis, attempted to expose the horrible working conditions of women in the Italian rice fields, but it did so with a plot that included abortion, crime, illicit sex, a gruesome murder, suicide, nudity, and a realistic childbirth scene. As a statement on agricultural workers, *Bitter Rice* was no *Grapes of Wrath,* nor was it likely to be confused with the artistic achievement of *Open City, Paisan,* or *The Bicycle Thief;* but unlike those other Italian films, *Bitter Rice* clearly had the potential to pack theaters from New York to California. Mangano was far more sultry than Russell, and *Bitter Rice* was much more daring than *The Outlaw.*

In an interesting marketing strategy, the distributors, Lux Films, had not bothered to ask for a PCA seal. By the time Breen and his staff saw the film it was already playing to large audiences on both coasts.

Having received Breen's alert, Gordon White and Arthur DeBra of the New York office rushed to a local theater to see the film. White was shocked: He wired Breen that, in his opinion, *Bitter Rice* was the "most important problem we have to face in the near future."[61] He told Breen that the code was clearly violated because the "women rice pickers associate promiscuously with soldiers" and there was a great deal of "breast exposure." A chastened DeBra assured Breen that he recognized "every important tenet of the Code" broken in the film, which, he added, contained "flagrant and purposeful" exposure of thighs and breasts. Both, however, assured Breen that despite the generous amounts of flesh exposed, the film was "quite boring."[62]

Other forces of morality were quick to enter the fray. Martin Quigley dubbed the film one of "lust and unbridled violence" and "offensive to any reasonable moral and social standards." The Legion quickly gave it a condemned rating, citing its offensiveness to "Christian and traditional principles of morality."[63] William Mooring, the film critic for the Los Angeles Catholic newspaper *The Tidings,* charged that the film was "communist" inspired because of its "disregard of Christian morality."[64]

Secular critics were less offended. The *New Republic* predicted that "audiences whose innocence has been watched over by the American movie producers' code will be startled by some of the gamier passages in *Bitter Rice.*"[65] *Time* gave credit to De Santis for bringing a "sweaty authenticity" to the screen and for devoting "deserved footage to Silvana's Grecian profile and womanly body."[66] Despite the Legion's stinging condemnation, Philip Hartung, writing in *Commonweal,* did not warn Catholics of its immorality, but he admitted that De Santis "lets violence and sex run away with the story," which he believed prevented *Bitter Rice* from becoming "another interesting and honest Italian movie."[67]

Legion officials worried when reports began to drift into the national offices that *Bitter Rice* was attracting large crowds. Father Lawlar, a parish priest from Chicago, told Legion assistant director Msgr. Thomas Little that the film was having a "very successful" run in his diocese. It was playing, Lawlar told Little, in twenty-five local theaters, including several drive-ins.

Lawlar was furious with the Archdiocese of Chicago, which, he told Little, had done nothing to protest the film.[68] Little was powerless. The Legion had already condemned the film, and the PCA could not deny a seal because Lux Films had refused to ask for one. *Bitter Rice* was free to play theaters willing to book it – and many were.

Lux, however, eventually decided it would be more profitable to have the Legion lift the C rating. After months of protracted negotiations the distributor agreed to massive cuts and the film was reclassified by the Legion as B. Breen fumed over the Legion decision but could do nothing; and from the Legion's point-of-view, it had made the best of a bad situation.

All this was prelude to the main battle for control of the cinema. *Bitter Rice* played in theaters during the fall and early winter of 1950, but it would soon be upstaged by another Italian film: Roberto Rossellini's *The Miracle*, a forty-minute short that contained no nudity, crime, or tight-sweatered, buxom starlets. The film, a modern religious parable, outraged the Catholic church. The Legion quickly condemned it as sacrilegious and blasphemous. The New York State board of censorship, having originally passed the film, recanted and banned it from public exhibition.

Ordinarily, protracted negotiations would have begun among the producer, the distributor, and the censors to eliminate the offending material. The distributor, however, chose to challenge the legality of the state of New York to ban a film for religious reasons, and went to court to win the right to exhibition. The invitation to challenge the legality of government regulation of film – issued by Justice Douglas two years earlier in the *Paramount* case – was finally accepted. This legal battle over freedom of expression went all the way to the United States Supreme Court.

The Miracle was produced in Italy in 1947 and based on a story by Federico Fellini. Constructed in four short scenes, it starred Anna Magnani as Nanni, a poor, simpleminded goatherd who believes that a man she encounters on a mountain path is St. Joseph. When she first sees the man (played by Fellini) he is wearing a capelike coat and walks with the aid of a staff. She calls out to him, "St. Joseph. I knew you'd come. How beautiful you are." He looks quizzically at her for a moment, then turns and walks away. Nanni implores him to stay: "Give me your grace," she says. The man stares at her, unsure of what to do, then slowly returns and sits beside her. He says nothing, but offers Nanni some of his wine. She drinks and begins to babble on about saints, the people in her village, and the voices she hears in her head telling her, for example, to jump off the mountain. The man remains silent, and Nanni talks and drinks until she passes out. The scene fades to black.

Later Nanni is awakened by her goats. She looks around for the man, but he has disappeared. She slowly gathers her things and walks back to the village. She meets a monk near the church and asks him if the saints appear on earth. The monk assures her that they do, and that he sees the Madonna every day. Nanni is happy until another monk tells her that he has never seen a miracle in twenty years.

Several months pass. Nanni, while playing with a group of children in the courtyard of the village church, suddenly feels sick and passes out. A group of women help her to her feet and, when they touch her, discover that she is pregnant. Knowing that she is neither married nor mentally competent, the women begin to taunt her and laugh at her; but she dismisses them and announces, "It is the grace of God."

The news quickly spreads through the village that Nanni is pregnant and believes the father is St. Joseph. A nun, who is serving food to the poor, asks Nanni if she has gone to confession. "Of course, not," Nanni replies. The nun persists: "You must. You must be at peace with the Lord." Nanni is indignant. "I am at peace with the Lord. He loves me." "You have sinned," the nun says, and must go to the confessor for forgiveness. Nanni snaps back: "What does he know? I'm at peace with the Lord. He gave me HIS grace. My conscience is clear."

Some of the older women are understanding and try to help her. Most of the villagers, however, especially the younger ones, make fun of her: They fake a religious procession in her honor, sing hymns to "Mary," and crown her with a bucket. Nanni is humiliated and leaves the village to live in the mountains.

The last scene takes place as Nanni is about to give birth. When her time is near she starts to return to the village, but, seeing a group of villagers and recalling their taunts, she turns away. Nanni begins a long, painful climb up a narrow mountain path to another church. As she struggles up the mountain she cries out to God for help and protection. Her only friend, a goat, accompanies her. When she finally reaches the church she discovers it is deserted and locked. The goat gently guides her to a side door that is open. She enters the church and prepares for her delivery. The image dissolves. A baby cries. Nanni reaches out: "My son! My love! My flesh!"

Reception in Italy was mixed. The film was approved by the Italian censorship board for public exhibition, but the Catholic Cinematographic Center (CCC) – the Italian counterpart to the Legion – called *The Miracle* an "abominable profanation" and advised "everyone, nobody excepted, not to see the film."[69] The Vatican, however, made no attempt to suppress the picture. In *L'Osservatore Romano,* the semiofficial paper of the Vatican, film critic Piero Regnoli told readers that though "from a religious viewpoint" he had grave concerns about the film, "notwithstanding all this we still believe in Rossellini's art." *Il Populo,* the official paper of the ruling Catholic Christian Democratic Party, was effusive in its praise: *The Miracle,* the film critic wrote, was "a beautiful thing, humanly felt, alive, true and without religious profanation."[70]

Was *The Miracle* an open attack on the Christian belief of the Immaculate Conception and the Virgin Birth of Jesus? Or was it merely a stinging comment on intolerance in modern society? Did Rossellini mean that if the events in Bethlehem were repeated in modern Italy, Mary would be mocked and banished? Or was he saying that the institutional church was no longer capable of recognizing the basic fundamentals of Christianity: Love thy neighbor, care for the sick and the weak, be tolerant and understanding? Was it blasphemy, social commentary, or a parable? Whatever the interpretation, the film was a flop at the Italian box office, where it was completely ignored.[71] Only when it began playing in the United States did *The Miracle* become front-page news, and events soon made thoughtful analysis and discussion of the film's merits impossible.

The controversy over *The Miracle* began innocently enough. Booked by Joseph Burstyn into the Paris Theater on West 58th Street in New York City, the film had been cleared by U.S. Customs officials and approved for public exhibition on two different occasions by the New York State censorship board: The board, which was empowered to prohibit "sacrilegious" films, had passed *The Miracle* in March 1949 without English subtitles and then approved a second version with subtitles in November 1949. Burstyn did not seek PCA approval and did not need it for the art-house circuit to which the film would clearly be limited. In order to broaden the film's audience, *The Miracle* was combined with two older French short films – Jean Renoir's *A Day in the Country* (1936) and Marcel Pagnol's *Jofroi* (1934) – and released under the new title *The Ways of Love*.[72]

This trilogy of short foreign films opened at the Paris Theater on December 12, 1950, without much public attention. Critics were divided. Howard Barnes of the *New York Herald Tribune* advised readers "to skip it." Alton Cook of the *World Telegram and Sun* judged it "a very trying experience." Rose Pelswick in the *Journal–American* raved about Anna Magnani's performance but found the film "in questionable taste." Archer Winsten of the *New York Post,* in what proved to be a massive understatement, predicted that "the parallels with Christ's conception, birth in a manger . . . could well prove offensive to the religious. . . ."[73] The most influential reviewer in New York City, Bosley Crowther of the *New York Times,* brilliantly summarized the parameters of the ensuing debate. Crowther called *The Miracle* "overpowering and provocative" but warned readers that the character of Nanni could be interpreted as "a symbol of deep and simple faith, horribly abused and tormented by a cold and insensitive world; or she may be entirely regarded as an open mockery of faith and religious fervor. . . ." It depended, he wrote, on the viewer's perspective.[74]

Some eleven days after the film opened the Legion of Decency slapped a condemned rating on it and charged that *The Miracle* was "a sacrilegious and blasphemous mockery of Christian and religious truth." It was, Legion Executive Secretary Father Patrick J. Masterson told Cardinal Spellman, "a blasphemous mockery of the Virgin Birth," adding that, "In my opinion this is the most disgraceful thing I have ever seen on the screen." Masterson advised Spellman that "the usual means which the Legion uses to combat these films will not be effective": *The Miracle* was an independent foreign production that would play at only a handful of art houses in major urban areas and was therefore immune to boycott and protest. Masterson informed Spellman that he was going to "appeal to the civil authorities" and was attempting to contact New York City "[License] Commissioner [Edward] McCaffrey in the hope that he will see fit to take action."[75]

McCaffrey, a former State Commander of the Catholic War Veterans and an active lay Catholic, was eager to use his position to aid the church. On December 24, 1950, he leapt into action: McCaffrey informed the management of the Paris Theater that he found *The Miracle* "officially and personally blasphemous" and ordered it removed from the screen or else he would revoke the theater's license to exhibit films. In addition, he sent a letter to all New York City moviehouses threatening to withdraw their exhibition licenses if they dared to show *The Miracle*.

The threat was real, and Joseph Burstyn advised the management of the Paris Theater to pull the film, which it did. Burstyn, however, was determined to challenge McCaffrey's authority to ban a film that had been approved for public exhibition by the state censorship board. He went to court and in late December was granted a temporary injunction preventing McCaffrey from interfering with the exhibition of the film. The New York Supreme Court scheduled for early January 1951 a formal hearing on the legality of McCaffrey's ruling.

The Miracle was suddenly the hottest ticket in New York City. Newspapers chronicled the case on front pages. The New York Film Critics registered their displeasure with the attempt to censor the film by voting *The Miracle* Best Foreign Film of the year. The American Civil Liberties Union waded into the controversy by offering to defend any theater that showed the film. The publicity resulted in standing room only at the Paris Theater as curious movie fans braved miserable weather and Catholic pickets to see what all the fuss was about.

On January 5, 1951, the drama continued when the New York Supreme Court issued its ruling. The court held that McCaffrey had, in fact, overstepped his authority: "The right to determine whether a motion picture is indecent, immoral or sacrilegious is vested solely and exclusively in" the New York State censorship board. "It may not be amiss," the ruling continued, "to state that the Commissioner of Licenses is not the protector from affronts of a large portion of our citizens or even all of them."[76]

The ruling infuriated Cardinal Spellman, who issued a stinging rebuttal that was read at every Mass in the New York Archdiocese on January 7, 1951. The cardinal called on all American Catholics to boycott any theater that showed *The Miracle*. The film, he said, was "vile and harmful," and in licensing *The Miracle*, the state censorship board had "made a mistake." If the current law could not prevent such films from being exhibited, Spellman urged that federal and state statutes be strengthened.[77]

Why did Spellman consider *The Miracle* blasphemy? His rationale is curious: The film, he said, "is a despicable affront to every Christian. It is a mockery of our Faith. We believe in Miracles. This picture ridicules that belief." It also, Spellman believed, was a "vicious insult to Italian womanhood." "It presents," he claimed, "the Italian woman as moronic and neurotic and, in matters of religion, fanatical. Only a perverted mind could so represent so noble a race of women." In an undisguised swipe at the director and his affair with Ingrid Bergman, Spellman noted that the film "should very properly be entitled 'Woman Further Defamed' by Roberto Rossellini."

The Cardinal broadened his attack by placing the film in a political, not religious, context:

> The perpetrators of *The Miracle* unjustly cast their blasphemous darts of ridicule at Christian Faith and at Italian womanhood, thereby dividing Religion against Religion and race against race. . . . Divide and conquer is the technique of the greatest enemy of civilization, atheistic Communism. God forbid that these producers of racial and religious mockeries should divide and demoralize Americans so that the minions of Moscow might enslave this land of liberty.[78]

Spellman's message closed with a appeal "to all good Americans" to "unite with us in this battle for decency and Americanism." *The Miracle*, it seemed was blasphemy and must be banned from public exhibition, Spellman argued, because he believed it mocked a belief in miracles, insulted Italian women, and was communistic![79] One assumes Spellman saw no irony in his call for suppression of a film in his land of liberty.

Catholics rallied to Spellman's call to arms, and the situation quickly turned ugly. Catholic picket lines at the Paris Theater swelled to over a thousand men and women. It was, reported Bosley Crowther, "the most distasteful and disturbing" aspect of the case.[80] Picketers carried signs reading, "This Picture Is an Insult to Every Decent Woman and Her Mother," "Don't Be a Communist," and "Don't Enter that Cesspool." They also hurled insults and epithets at those who attempted to buy tickets – and buy tickets they did: Almost every performance in January was sold out. Even a series of bomb threats could not keep audiences away from the Paris Theater.

Emotions were ratcheted even tighter when Martin Quigley entered the controversy. In an editorial early in January Quigley labeled the film as communistic:

> With Americans dying daily in Korea, and the nation girding for total war if necessary to preserve our way of life, which is based on belief in God and the inalienable rights of man, it is intolerable that a film such as *The Miracle* should be shown in an American theater. Its logical birthplace in the modern world is the Soviet Union.[81]

Quigley may or may not have known that the Soviet Union rejected the film because it was, in their view, "pro-Catholic propaganda."

When Quigley discovered that the New York Film Critics were going to present their annual Best Foreign Film award to *The Miracle* at the Radio City Music Hall, he told the theater manager that the ceremony would be an insult to the Catholic church and might result in Catholic boycotts of all performances at that theater. This caused an uproar in New York City newspapers, with both sides hurling accusations and insults at each other. It quickly died when the film critics voluntarily moved their award dinner to another location.

By early 1951 it was very clear that the debate over *The Miracle* had moved far beyond anything that was on the screen: Perfectly intelligent people were arguing that, in order to protect democracy and the American way of life, the film had to be not just not censored but banned; Catholics from Cardinal Spellman on down freely tossed the charge of communism at all who favored showing the film; pickets lines and bomb threats were used in attempts to prevent audiences from seeing the film; those brave enough to run the gauntlet were accused of being communist or communist sympathizers; Protestant and Catholic representatives argued over what was and was not sacrilegious; and the professional film critics awarded *The Miracle,* at best a mildly curious picture, the Best Foreign Film of the year. No one, it seemed, could judge the film on its own merits – least of all, the New York State censorship board.

The board was now under tremendous political pressure to revoke the license it had originally granted to Burstyn. Its reviewers had originally missed the blasphemy, the insults to Italian womanhood, and the subtle communism that, Catholics believed, pervaded the film; now, not surprisingly, the board wanted to reconsider its approval. Burstyn submitted boxes of editorials, letters, petitions, and affidavits supporting *The Miracle.* He and his lawyers argued that the controversy over the film was Catholic, not Christian, offering as proof hundreds of letters of support from civic organizations, Protestant ministers, and spokespersons. The Reverend Karl Chworowsky of the Flatbush Unitarian Church in Brooklyn, for example, fought through picket lines and emerged from the film without the "slightest urge to think unkindly of Italian womanhood or of the Catholic religion."[82] He urged his congregation to see the film. Protestant Reverend W. J. Beeners of Princeton, New Jersey, told Burstyn that he had seen the film "and found no reason for the censorship being urged upon it."[83] Merrill E. Bush of the American Unitarian Association agreed, finding nothing in the film to be sacrilegious or "offensive on religious grounds."[84] Edward J. Smythe, editor of the *Protestant Statesman,* told the manager of the Paris Theater that the Catholic boycott was "dangerous and un-American."[85] The *Louisville Courier–Journal* sided with freedom of expression. "Nobody forces Catholics to see a picture of which they disapprove," the paper editorialized. "But there is no excuse for the theory that Catholic disapproval is the equivalent of moral outlawry."[86] The ACLU, Authors League of America, American Book Publishers Council, Society of Authors' Representatives, and Theater Library Association all gave their support to freedom of choice. The one organization with the most to gain – the MPAA – stood silently on the sidelines and watched Burstyn battle for freedom for the movies.

On February 15, 1951, *The Miracle* was screened for a ten-member committee of the New York State censorship board. After a brief deliberation the committee revoked the license on the grounds that New York law demanded that "men and women of all faiths respect the religious beliefs held by others." The film was sacrilegious, the committee held, because it associated the Protestant and Catholic versions of the Bible with "drunkenness, seduction and lewdness."[87]

Burstyn was not surprised by the ruling and immediately appealed the decision to the New York State Court of Appeals. He lost another battle when that court ruled on October 18, 1951, that the New York censorship board had been justified in its ruling. Determined to take the issue to the U.S. Supreme Court, Burstyn and his lawyer, Ephraim London, filed a petition with the Court on December 4, 1951; the Court agreed to hear *Burstyn* v. *Wilson,* and oral arguments were scheduled for April 24, 1952.

The legal precedent for government censorship of film rested with the U.S. Supreme Court decision of 1915 in *Mutual* v. *Ohio,* which had upheld the constitutionality of state censorship boards (see Chapter 1). Justice Joseph McKenna, who had written the opinion in that case, believed that movies had the power to communicate ideas that communities might not like, and that it was within the traditional powers of the state to grant or withhold "licenses for theatrical performances as a means of their regulation."[88] Burstyn was challenging this ruling.[89]

Representing Burstyn was Ephraim London. Counsel for the New York Board of Regents was Charles A. Brind Jr. The Court comprised Chief Justice Frederick Vinson and Associate Justices Hugo Black, Harold Burton,

Tom Clark, William O. Douglas, Felix Frankfurter, Robert Jackson, Sherman Minton, and Stanley Reed. Prior to hearing the oral arguments, the Court screened *The Miracle*. At issue were two basic points: the constitutionality of government licensing of films prior to their exhibition; and more specifically, the constitutionality of a New York statute that gave authority to ban films that were held to be "sacrilegious."

London began by summarizing the basic issues: Was the film censorship law of New York an unconstitutional abridgment of the right of free communication? Could a film be suppressed by a state because it was sacrilegious? London stressed in his arguments that film communicated ideas and was therefore entitled to the "privileges, immunities and freedom guaranteed the press by the Constitution." New York, which required a film to be licensed by the state before it could be exhibited, London argued, was violating the essence of the First Amendment, which was established to prevent government from prior restraint. When Justice Frankfurter asked if an exhibitor of obscene films could be prosecuted, London said he could under the provision of existing criminal law. What was unconstitutional, London stressed, was the requirement of prior licensing.

In clear reference to the *Mutual* v. *Ohio* decision London argued that film was more than just a business. It entertained to be sure, but it also communicated ideas. He cited contemporary filmed versions of George Bernard Shaw's *Caesar and Cleopatra,* Victor Hugo's *Les Miserables,* and T. S. Eliot's *Murder in the Cathedral* as examples of films that contained important ideas. "I do not think," he told the justices, "one can name a great novel, play or essay that does not both entertain and communicate ideas simultaneously."

The fact that millions of people went to the movies was hardly, he added, a constitutional argument for denying equal protection. Although close to sixty million people went to the movies each week, London pointed out that fifty-four million a week read newspapers. "The mere fact that a communication is effective does not mean it should be denied freedom guaranteed by the Constitution."[90]

London also attacked the perception that the film was sacrilegious. He cited hundreds of letters and petitions from Protestant theologians, ministers, and church members who found no offense in the movie. Could the state uphold the religious views of one group above all others, London asked? His position was that in doing so the New York exceeded the Constitution.

Charles Brind Jr. followed by arguing that the New York statute prohibited films that were "obscene, indecent, immoral, or sacrilegious," which meant that no film should be allowed to vilify the religious beliefs of any segment of the population. This did not, he argued, involve the religious beliefs of the censors: They prohibited any film that ridiculed or offended any religion. Frankfurter asked Brind, "How do you find out that it profanes a religious doctrine?" Brind responded by saying rather vaguely that the censors knew sacrilege when they saw it. Frankfurter pressed on, "I want to know what the sources are which lead them to say, 'Yes, this offends Jews, Catholics, . . . The criterion is in their minds. Is that it?" Brind replied meekly that it was.

Brind continued to try to explain how sacrilege was interpreted by New York censors. He told the justices that if, for example, a private foundation or church wanted to show *The Miracle* and did not charge a fee, the state would issue a license. Only when a film was exhibited publicly for profit did it have to be inspected for content. Justice Jackson was perplexed: "Suppose a church group that doesn't accept Divine Birth takes this particular film and says that we are going to show this film to show you that the doctrine is wrong. Could they show it?" Brind said they could. Jackson: "Then it comes down to this: That New York law prohibits sacrilegious for pay, but permits sacrilegious for its own sake." When laughter broke out in the Court, Jackson snapped at no one in particular, "Really, that isn't laughable."[91] It was not the best day Charles Brind had had as a lawyer.

A month after the oral arguments were presented, the U.S. Supreme Court handed down a reversal of the New York Court of Appeals decision. Justice Tom Clark wrote the unanimous decision for the Court.[92] After summarizing the events that led up to the case, Clark wrote that "the present case is the first to present squarely to us the question whether motion pictures are within the ambit of protection which the First Amendment, through the Fourteenth, secures to any form of 'speech' or 'the press.'"

Clark looked at each element of *Mutual* v. *Ohio*. "It cannot be doubted," he wrote, "that motion pictures are a significant medium for the communication of ideas." Their ability to communicate ideas "is not lessened by the fact that they are designed to entertain as well as to inform." Nor was it an important distinction in the Court's view that movies were a business conducted to make a profit. Books, magazines, and newspapers were all "published and sold for profit," and that fact did not "prevent them from being a form of expression whose liberty is safeguarded by the First Amendment."[93]

Clark then addressed the issue that movies had a greater capacity for evil than other means of communication. They could, he understood, communicate ideas to "the youth of a community" that other means of communication might not be able to do. In other words, most kids would eagerly go to movies but might be unwilling or unable to ferret out the same ideas from a novel, magazine article, or newspaper. This view that movies had a special capacity to captivate children was the essence of film censorship. Clark addressed that issue directly: "If there be capacity for evil it may be relevant in determining the permissible scope of community control, but it does not authorize unbridled censorship such as we have here."[94]

Clark then turned to the issue of sacrilege. The New York court had ruled that "no religion, as that word in understood by the ordinary, reasonable person, shall be treated with contempt, mockery, scorn and ridicule." This was not, Clark wrote, a narrow exception to freedom of expression. In attempting to apply a broad and inclusive definition of "sacrilegious" the New York statute had set the censor "adrift upon a boundless sea amid a myriad of conflicting currents of religious views, with no charts but those provided by the most vocal and powerful orthodoxies." The state has, he continued, "no legitimate interest in protecting any or all religions from views distasteful to them . . . ." Nor was it the business of government "to suppress real or imagined attacks upon a particular religious doctrine, whether they appear in publications, speeches, or motion pictures."[95]

The Court held that motion pictures were "included within the free speech and the free press guarantee of the First and Fourteenth Amendments," but in concluding added that the Court had not ruled "whether a state may censor motion pictures under a clearly drawn statute designed and applied to prevent the showing of obscene films. That is a very different question from the one now before us. We hold only that under the First and Fourteenth Amendments a state may not ban a film on the basis of a censor's conclusion that it is 'sacrilegious.'"[96]

Even with the added proviso that a censorship law carefully drawn to prevent obscene films might be legal, it was a stunning decision for freedom of the screen. In effect the Court ruled that the state censorship boards in New York, Ohio, Maryland, Pennsylvania, and Kansas, plus the two hundred or so municipal censorship boards (Memphis, Atlanta, Chicago) were unconstitutional because they all included some type of statement that prohibited films on sacrilegious grounds. One by one over the next decade these institutions of censorship would fall by the wayside.

While the Court made no statement about the self-regulation practiced by the motion picture industry, the ruling clearly undermined the power of Breen, the PCA, and the MPAA to demand that producers remove material that violated their code. Independent and foreign producers now had clear access to theaters and had firm legal ground for challenging adverse rulings by government (state and municipal) censors. Films like *The Miracle, The Bicycle Thief, Paisan,* and even *Bitter Rice* (which were by no stretch of the imagination obscene) could not be prevented from being publicly exhibited if a theater owner or theater chain decided it was in their best interests to do so. This does not mean that censorship disappeared with *The Miracle* decision; it just meant that the legal roadblocks were being taken down.

No organization suffered a greater loss of prestige over *The Miracle* than the Legion of Decency. From 1934 on the Legion had maintained that it did not censor movies but only rate them for Catholic audiences; but the Legion and the Catholic church had gone far beyond a mere classification of *The Miracle*, and had done so in a very public manner. The Legion had clearly tried to prevent all Americans, regardless of religious beliefs, from seeing the movie. In essence, the Catholic church through the Legion, had demanded that the state declare Catholic theology as offical dogma. Protestant organizations rightly opposed giving that kind of sanction to the Catholic church, as did the U.S. Supreme Court. The boundaries of separation between church and state remained firmly defined.

For well over a decade the Legion had carefully garnered a great deal of support from many religious organizations that may have resented Catholic influence, and even harbored anti-Catholic feelings, but silently approved of the Legion's efforts to prevent Hollywood from making movies on subjects that they did not want to see on the screen.[97] The Legion's position on *The Miracle* broke that uneasy relationship because many Protestants found nothing immoral or sacrilegious in that film. Protestant theology placed less reverence on the Virgin Mary than did the Catholic church; it was to be expected that Protestants would see *The Miracle* in a much different light than would Catholic theologians.

More important, the vicious nature of the Catholic action – the boycotts, the pickets, the accusation that anyone who saw the film was not only committing a sin but was also supporting communism – repelled many thoughtful Catholics as well as Protestants. William Clancy, a professor of English at Notre Dame University, for example, labeled the Church's position on *The Miracle* "a semi-ecclesiastical McCarthyism."[98] Frank Getlein, film critic for the *Catholic Messenger*, deplored the actions of Catholics and the Legion: "The worst point about this whole affair – the bitter personal attacks on Rossellini, the violence and threats of bombings . . . is that once again the Church has been viciously misrepresented . . . by the spokesmen of the Church themselves."[99] Otto Spaeth, director of the American Federation of the Arts and a very prominent lay Catholic, blasted the Legion in an editorial in the *Magazine of Art*. *Commonweal* reminded its readers that when "Catholics obey the voice of the Church, it is a free act; to pressure or force, even indirectly, others who do not believe, into the same kind of obedience is to ask for servility."[100] Even the very conservative *Indiana Catholic*, the newspaper for the Archdiocese of Indianapolis, told readers *The Miracle* was blasphemous but it was "hard to dispute" the Supreme Court's decision."[101]

Frank Getlein of the *Catholic Messenger* speculated that there was an even more basic reason for the Legion's attack on *The Miracle*: It was, he told his Iowa readers, pure revenge against a man who "had debauched a saint." Rossellini's unforgivable sin was that he had seduced Ingrid Bergman, whom American Catholics, Getlein said, "had just finished canonizing as a popular saint. She had played a nun a couple of times, and had played a saint. She had become, for the American Catholic fan, the symbol of feminine sincerity."[102]

This criticism, printed in respected Catholic and secular publications, severely damaged the Legion's reputation among its supporters. From this point on the Legion would increasingly be seen by a growing number of influential lay Catholics and leading Catholic clerics as an essentially negative force that had little moral authority to speak for all Catholics.

A final word about Joseph Burstyn before closing: Burstyn did not relish his role in fighting the Catholic church or in challenging the legality of film censorship in the United States. Bosley Crowther spoke of Burstyn's "grave anxieties and apprehensions" over challenging the laws of a country he loved. Although not a wealthy man, Burstyn spent over $60,000 of his own money because he believed the films he imported were important expressions of opinion and art. During his legal battles with the state of New York and before the U.S. Supreme Court, the MPAA offered him no support. Industry moguls, like David O. Selznick or Jack Warner, or the hundreds of others who had felt the wrath of the Legion and had grown wealthy from making and marketing movies, did nothing.

Ignored in his day and now largely forgotten,[103] Joseph Burstyn deserves recognition for helping to bring freedom of expression to an industry that had grown comfortable with its cozy relationship with censors and clerics.

CHAPTER 4

THE LEGION FIGHTS BACK

No one has the right to tell the American people what to see and
what not to see.

– Otto Preminger

Just one week after the Supreme Court delivered its decision on *The Miracle,*
the Court, in *Gelling* v. *Texas,* reaffirmed its conviction that movies communicated ideas and were therefore protected speech. This time the subject was
not religion but racism. The film was Darryl Zanuck's *Pinky,* a 1949 release
about a young, light-skinned, southern black woman who "passes" as white
when she goes north for an education. The woman, Pinky, played by Jeanne
Crain, becomes a nurse and falls in love with a white doctor. She is engaged
to be married but is suddenly called back home to help nurse an old family
friend – a white woman. In contrast to her professional career in the North
(and, by implication, an absence of racism), when she returns to the South
she encounters racism everywhere. Pinky is no longer a respected professional; she is a black woman. However, in the end Pinky decides not to marry into white society. Instead, she sends her lover away and stays in the South to
help fight for a better life.

The film, daring in its time, illustrated as few films had prior to 1949 the
nature of racism in American society. A plea for toleration and integration,
Pinky was based on Cid Ricketts Summer's novel *Quality* and adapted for
the screen by Dudley Nichols and Philip Dunne. In an effort to make the
film realistic, Zanuck consulted with Walter White of the NAACP and hired
White's daughter, Jane, to work on the screenplay. Zanuck constructed the
film to be pitched to white audiences because he wanted "the white majority of the United States [to] experience the humiliation and hurt and evil of
segregation and discrimination . . . [and] carry away a sense of shame [so]
. . . their feeling and thinking will be changed."[1]

He was certainly bucking tradition in Hollywood. From its inception, the
industry had reinforced the white American stereotype of black Americans as
lazy, stupid, and shiftless. D. W. Griffith's *The Birth of a Nation* established

a pattern that Hollywood followed faithfully until the late 1940s. Screenwriter Dalton Trumbo best summarized the industry's attitude toward blacks when he wrote that Hollywood made "tarts of the Negro's daughters, crap shooters of his sons, obsequious Uncle Toms of his fathers, superstitious and grotesque crones of his mothers, strutting peacocks of his successful men, psalm-singing mounteblanks of his priests, and Barnum and Bailey sideshows of his religion."[2] While Breen was highly protective of Catholicism and white Protestant ministers, Hollywood's view of black ministers brought no rebuke from the PCA or the priests of the Legion.

None of the censorship groups found Hollywood's traditional portrayal of black Americans offensive. In fact, they generally took the opposite position: Any film that suggested that black and white Americans shared a common heritage caused consternation at the PCA headquarters and was labeled "propaganda." Although the code presumably forbade racial discrimination in movies under the provision that no film could ridicule any nationality or religion, in practice stereotypical insults were ignored. The ultimate offense was a sexual union between a white and a black. In its final version, Father Lord's code stated quite explicitly that "miscegenation is forbidden."

One of the first scripts that Breen saw as head of the PCA in 1934 was that for *Imitation of Life,* and its theme of miscegenation caused him to fire off an angry letter of protest to Universal. The story, he wrote, "is founded upon the results of a sex association between the white and black race . . . which . . . will necessarily have to be rejected." Another PCA staffer contemptuously described the film as "an advertising campaign for Aunt Jemima Pancake Flour." Breen's views were shared by his superiors in New York, who told him, "it is our earnest hope that you will be able to persuade the company to abandon its plans for production."[3]

Hollywood usually pointed to the southern box office as an excuse for the racism that dominated its films. Industry spokesmen often claimed that any attempt to infuse racial tolerance into films would only result in the film being banned by southern censors. Breen made this very point on *Pinky,* warning Twentieth Century–Fox officials that there would be a southern backlash against the film.[4] There was, of course, some truth in that – southern censors such as Lloyd T. Binford of Memphis and Christine Smith of Atlanta routinely banned any film that did not pander to southern perceptions of blacks[5] – but Hollywood films perpetuated racism with insulting stereotypes of black Americans not out of fear of losing the southern box office, but because the filmmakers and the white audiences, in the North and South, held similar views. The censors made no objections because they too believed the stereotypes to be true.[6]

The PCA and the Legion certainly considered miscegenation immoral. When the script for *Pinky* hit the PCA desk, the censors warned Twentieth

Century–Fox to "avoid physical contact between Negroes and whites" and that the theme of the film might well cause "new political censor boards to be established."[7] However, 1949 was not 1934. World War II had exposed to many Americans the terrible consequences of racism. The Holocaust in Germany, the virulent hatred that many Americans felt for the Japanese, and of course the refusal to desegregate the armed forces revealed the contradictions between American rhetoric and reality.

Zanuck, fresh from his successful production of *Gentleman's Agreement*, which had confronted anti-Semitism in America, bristled at the less-than-subtle suggestions from the PCA and forged ahead with the project. Originally he hired John Ford to direct, but Ford clashed with black actress Ethel Waters and did not believe in the message Zanuck was promoting. Tension on the set forced Zanuck to fire Ford and bring in Elia Kazan to finish the project.

Despite Kazan's efforts, *Pinky* did not emerge as a great film, but it was a film brimming with ideas – controversial ideas. *Pinky* advocated education for blacks; showed that blacks and whites could fall in love; and suggested that, if allowed, blacks could play a meaningful role in American society. It stood with *Home of the Brave* (racism in the military), *Lost Boundaries* (miscegenation), and *Intruder in the Dust* (a black man accused of murder), three films playing in American theaters in 1949, as a plea for toleration and integration. Surprisingly, all four did good box office in the South, though they did incur pockets of resistance; for example, Atlanta and Memphis banned *Lost Boundaries* as "contrary to the public good."[8]

When *Pinky* hit the small Texas community of Marshall, a license to show the film was denied because it was judged "prejudicial to the best interests of the people."[9] The theater owner, W. L. Gelling, defied the city fathers and showed the film; he was arrested and convicted. When he appealed to the Texas Court of Appeals, the court upheld the original ruling. The case eventually went to the U.S. Supreme Court – and with the support of the MPAA. It would be almost three years before the Court would rule that censorship of controversial ideas was unconstitutional.

The drive to make films that communicated ideas was a growing force in Hollywood as the industry fought to keep its share of an ever-decreasing audience. Elia Kazan, for example, was not much interested in making lighthearted musicals or mindless westerns. Shortly before making *Pinky* he had begun a long collaboration with a southern-born playwright, Tennessee Williams, whose dark, perverse, violent, often depressing view of human relationships exploded on America's literary landscape.

Williams, widely recognized as one of America's most gifted writers and, in the 1950s, one of the most controversial, challenged censors, critics, and cinema enthusiasts alike on what was entertaining. His plays *The Glass Menagerie, A Streetcar Named Desire, The Rose Tattoo, Cat on a Hot Tin Roof,* and *Suddenly Last Summer* were all adapted to the screen and illustrated the deep divisions within the Production Code Administration, the Legion, and the Catholic community during the 1950s over what was acceptable entertainment for mature adults.

Born in Mississippi in 1911 to Cornelius Coffin and Edwina Dakin Williams, he had moved with his family to St. Louis in 1918. Williams suffered an unhappy childhood – his father was domineering, drank heavily, and fought with his strong-willed, Puritanical wife. Williams, like Tom in Robert Anderson's *Tea and Sympathy* (see Chapter 5), had preferred poetry and writing to football. His father, like Tom's, branded him a "sissy"; unlike Tom, however, Williams was in fact a homosexual, and he had turned to his mother for solace and love. He and his mother, like millions of other Americans, had often gone to the movies to escape their own reality. The movies held a special attraction for Williams: "When I was young I was obsessed with the screen. I went to the movies all the time. I used to want to climb into the movie screen all the time."[10]

In 1929 he had entered the University of Missouri, but a lack of money forced him to drop out of school. For several years he worked at a dreary job in a shoe factory; then, as the Depression tightened in 1934, he set out, like tens of thousands of others, for California.

This first trip to fantasyland brought no fairy-tale recognition from the dream factory. Williams lived in the shadows of the studios but was forced to work a series of odd jobs to pay his rent. He continued to write as much as he could, and his first recognition as a playwright came when he won first prize ($100) from a New York drama contest and was signed by literary agent Audrey Wood. Several years later, during World War II, Wood negotiated a contract as a studio hack for Williams at MGM. The salary of $250 a week seemed like millions to the young writer, but his work was unrewarding and unsuccessful. When the studio assigned him to write for child actress Margaret O'Brien, he rebelled. "Child stars make me vomit," he told his bosses. Both parties agreed to part company.[11]

At the time of his separation Williams had three months left on his contract with MGM, and he decided to stay in California and write a screenplay. What emerged was a synopsis he entitled *The Gentleman Caller* about an unhappy, young crippled woman whose domineering mother desperately tries to find a suitor for her. Williams pitched it to MGM, but the studio was not interested. He then expanded his idea into a play, which exploded on Broadway in 1945 as *The Glass Menagerie.*

The play ran for eighteen months, and Williams was awarded Best Playwright by the New York Drama Critics' Circle. In Hollywood, disgruntled

MGM executives lost the bidding war for this new talent to Warner Bros., which paid Williams $50,000 for the screen rights.

In retrospect, it is amazing that Hollywood would pay so dearly for a property from an unknown writer that had almost no action and very little prospect for visual appeal. The play opens with a narration by one of the central characters, Tom Wingfield. He tells the audience that they are about to see a memory play – a memory of his mother, Amanda, and his crippled sister, Laura. The setting is a shabby apartment building in St. Louis during the Depression.

Amanda is a strong-willed woman who lives mostly in the past. Her greatest fear is that her daughter – crippled at birth with one leg longer than the other and forced to wear a heavy brace – will not marry. The mother babbles about the long list of handsome suitors who had called on her and badgers her son Tom to help her find a mate for his sister.

Laura is unable to confront her mother and retreats into her own world. She has assembled a large collection of glass animals, which are scattered throughout the small, cramped apartment. In an effort to get Laura out into the world, Amanda has enrolled her in a local business college, which she hopes will produce a husband. Laura reluctantly starts the program but drops out after vomiting during her first speed-typing test. Unwilling, or unable, to tell her mother the truth, Laura leaves the apartment each day and wanders the streets of St. Louis in an attempt to make her mother believe she is still attending class.

Tom, who wants to be a poet, is also trapped in this small apartment with Amanda. Forced to work in a shoe factory, he longs to escape both job and mother. Unlike Laura, however, Tom can control his own destiny. He joins the Merchant Marine and will soon leave St. Louis; but that is in his future.

Amanda soon discovers Laura's ruse and is more determined than ever to marry off her daughter. She takes a job selling magazines to get some extra money, in order to entertain any potential suitors she might lure into her trap, and berates Tom until he finally agrees to bring someone home from the factory to meet his sister.

The evening the gentleman caller comes is full of excitement. When he appears, however, Laura is horrified: Her brother has unknowingly invited an old high school friend, Jim O'Connor. Laura had a crush on Jim in high school, but he was engaged to another girl, Emily. Naturally, Laura never told him about her feelings. After dinner Laura and Jim, left to themselves, fall into a relaxed conservation, despite their initial embarrassment. Jim tells Laura he is no longer engaged to Emily, and as music drifts into the apartment from a nearby nightclub, he convinces her to dance with him.

Laura has always been much too sensitive about her leg brace to dance with a man; but Jim is kind and gentle with her, and they dance happily about the small apartment. They accidentally bump into a table and knock off one of Laura's favorite glass figurines – a small unicorn – which breaks. Laura simply laughs and gives the broken figure to Jim, who is so taken with her inner beauty, her strength and personality, that he kisses her. She is overwhelmed, and Jim, who is a real gentleman, immediately recognizes that for her this moment is more than just a kiss: Laura is in love. Jim, deeply embarrassed by his impetuous action, confesses to Laura, and to Amanda who has just reentered the room, that he is engaged to another woman and is very much in love.

Jim quickly leaves the apartment, and Laura retreats back into her familiar world. The play ends, as it began, with Tom speaking to the audience from the fire escape. He has, he says, been haunted for years by the memory of his sister – her dignity, her beauty – and her tragic life. From his position above the stage Tom turns toward Laura and says: "Blow out your candles, Laura – and so good-bye." Laura, who is tidying up after Jim's hurried departure, leans over and blows out the candles. The curtain falls, and the audience knows that Laura will receive no more gentleman callers.

Warner Bros. brought the play to the screen almost fully intact. They cast Jane Wyman as Laura, Gertrude Lawrence as Amanda, Arthur Kennedy as Tom, and Kirk Douglas as Jim. Irving Rapper, whose reputation was established with the powerful *Now, Voyager* in 1942 and *The Corn Is Green* in 1945, directed. The only change was the ending – not because either the PCA or the Legion objected, but because Warner Bros. believed that an audience of bobby-soxers would not relate to Laura's impending spinsterhood. In the movie, Laura and Amanda are on the fire escape after Jim has left. Laura tells her mother, "I've had a lovely evening. I danced for the first time." As they enjoy the warm summer evening, a young man walks toward them. It is Richard, another male friend of Laura's. She introduces him to her mother as Tom's final narration tells the audience that "the long delayed but always expected something we lived for" has happened. Laura got her man, and millions of bobby-soxers sobbed with joy at yet another Hollywood "happy ending."

Tennessee Williams was enraged. "Imagine how I feel when someone mentions to me this most dishonest of all film adaptions of my work and says, 'Oh, it's so beautiful when that poor crippled girl has a new, promising beau at the end of the film.'"[12] Williams later noted that "[i]n *The Glass Menagerie* I said all the nice things I have to say about people."[13] For the remainder of the decade he filled his plays with dysfunctional southern families – characters who were obsessed with sex, who destroyed themselves and each other. His view of American families was considerably different from the myth of the happy, contented lives that dominated the American screen. In contrast Williams presented parents as ruthless tyrants and their children as psychological wrecks. The men were either brutes who beat and raped women or were impotent and tormented by their fear of their own homosexuality. His women were domineering, passionate, frustrated, and tortured creatures who sought physical love wherever they could find it. It would not be as easy for Hollywood to fasten a facile happiness on Blanche DuBois, the tragic heroine of *A Streetcar Named Desire,* as it had been to find a new beau for Laura.

In December 1947 Williams's *A Streetcar Named Desire* opened on Broadway. The play was directed by Elia Kazan and starred Jessica Tandy as Blanche DuBois, a faded southern magnolia who has come to New Orleans under rather mysterious circumstances to visit her sister Stella Kowalski (Kim Hunter) and her brutish husband, Stanley (Marlon Brando).

The plays opens as Blanche arrives in New Orleans. After traveling by train from Mississippi, she followed directions given by her sister and took a streetcar named Desire, transferred to another called Cemetery, and got off in the Elysian Fields district of New Orleans. She is shocked, however, to find herself in the squalor of the city's slums and her sister living in a cramped, shabby, two-room apartment with Stanley.

On the surface, Blanche seems to be a woman of some refinement: She is a teacher, has come with a trunkful of fine clothing, and until very recently has been living on the family estate, Belle Reve, in Laurel, Mississippi. She has all the affectations of a fine southern woman and immediately makes no secret of her disapproval of the brutish, hard-drinking, violent, crude "Polack," Stanley Kowalski. Blanche puts "on airs" in the Kowalski household and soon begins to urge her sister to leave Stanley: "He acts like an animal, has an animal's habits! Eats like one, moves like one, talks like one!"[14]

To Blanche's horror she discovers that her sister really loves Stanley. Stella is pregnant, and although they have a violent relationship, Stanley's power excites her sexually. One evening Stella and Blanche go out to dinner while Stanley and his cronies play cards. The men get drunk, and the card game is still going strong when the two women return. As they undress in the bedroom, Blanche turns on the radio. Stanley, furious that she would dare disturb his game, flies into a rage. He storms into the room, throws the radio out the window, and, when Stella screams at him, he punches her. Stella and Blanche take refuge in the apartment above. Stanley pleads for Stella to return, standing at the foot of the staircase and screaming: "Stell-lahhhh! . . . Stella! . . . STELL-LAHHHHH!" Hearing his cry she responds by walking slowly and sensuously down the staircase. Stanley buries his head in her stomach, pleading forgiveness. They kiss passionately, and Stanley carries Stella off to bed.

Blanche is dumbfounded. When she sees they are going into the bedroom she slinks outside the small apartment so she will not have to listen to them make love. The next day she scolds her sister for returning so quickly to this brute. Stella tells her simply, "there are things that happen between a man and a woman in the dark – that sort of makes everything else seem – unimportant."[15]

Stanley Kowalski may be crude and violent, but he is no fool. He suspects that Blanche has sold the family estate at a considerable profit and that he is entitled to a share of the money. Blanche tries to convince him that the family fortune was frittered away by her father and grandfather on "epic fornications," but Stanley remains suspicious and begins to ask questions about his sister-in-law. He discovers, to his delight, that this delicate southern flower is running away from her own sordid past.

Blanche, it seems, was married at a tender age to a young boy who wrote poetry and was extremely sensitive and tender. As she admits to Stanley's friend Mitch: "There was something different about the boy, a nervousness, a softness and tenderness which wasn't like a man's, although he wasn't the least bit effeminate looking – still – that thing was there." One evening she discovered just how different he was when she walked "into a room that I thought was empty – which wasn't empty, but had two people in it . . . the boy I had married and an older man who had been his friend for years." That evening her husband committed suicide.

This drove Blanche into her own world of debauchery. She took to the bottle and, as she tells Mitch – who had fallen in love with Blanche until finding out about her past – she had "many intimacies with strangers" and was run out of her teaching job in Laurel after the school authorities found out she was having an affair with a 17-year-old boy.

The audience discovers this was no passing fancy. Blanche, haunted by the memory of her dead husband, is still sexually attracted to youngsters. When a young man comes to collect for the newspaper, Blanche is overwhelmed by his beauty. She calls him over to her. "I want to kiss you, just once, softly and sweetly on your mouth." She kisses him, them says: "Now run along! It would be nice to keep you, but I've got to be good – and keep my hands off children."[16]

By fully exposing her past Stanley succeeds in destroying Blanche emotionally. Having driven away Mitch, her last hope for independence and respect, he then orders her out of the house. Blanche has nowhere to go. This hastens her descent into madness, and she begins to wander about the apartment fabricating a romantic story about an old suitor who has invited her on a cruise.

Stella suddenly goes into labor, and Stanley takes her to the hospital; but when the doctors tell him that she will not deliver until morning, he returns to the apartment. Blanche is concerned that the two of them are alone in the apartment, but Stanley is delighted at the prospect of being a father and suggests that they "bury the hatchet." However, when Blanche continues to babble about her rich suitor, Stanley is so enraged that he brutally rapes her.

The last scene of the play takes place several days later. Stella has returned from the hospital with her baby. It is clear that Blanche, who is packing for a trip, is emotionally disturbed. Stella whispers to her neighbor, "I couldn't believe her story and go on living with Stanley." Her neighbor agrees: "Don't ever believe it. Life has got to go on. No matter what happens, you've got to keep on going."[17] Blanche is still under the delusion that she is going on a cruise with a wealthy admirer; the truth is that she is being committed to a state hospital for the insane. As a kindly doctor leads her away, Stanley begins to console Stella. He holds her softly and in soothing tones whispers to her: "Now, love. Now, now, love. Now, now, love," and begins to unbutton her blouse.

The play stunned, shocked, infuriated, and fascinated audiences and critics alike. It was a smash hit on Broadway, winning not only the New York Drama Critics' Circle Award but also the 1947 Pulitzer Prize for drama. The theater critic for the *New York Post* called the play "feverish, squalid, tumultuous, painful, steadily arresting and oddly touching."[18] Harold Barnes of the *New York Herald Tribune* found it a play of "heroic dimensions."[19] *Streetcar* ran for two years on Broadway and, naturally, attracted attention from Hollywood.

Bringing this play to the screen would certainly challenge the creative talent of filmmakers. Williams managed to assault all the major provisions and assumptions of the Production Code: The play contained homosexuality, rape, and the pivotal female character, Blanche, was a lush and a borderline nymphomaniac with a particular attraction to underage boys. Stella – abused by her husband but so sexuality excited by his raw power that she continually returns to his bed no matter what he does – was hardly the vision of virtue that Hollywood and the Legion envisioned for America's mothers. In an era when "ladies" were supposed to be passive sexual partners, Stella was an eager participant. Moreover, the male "hero" in this slice-of-life drama was a sadistic brute who used his fists and sexual prowess to bend women to his will.

Almost two years after the opening on Broadway, Charles Feldman, agent and independent producer, announced that he had purchased the screen rights to *Streetcar* for $350,000. Feldman paid Williams a further $50,000 to help adapt the play to the screen, and stage director Elia Kazan signed on to direct for $175,000. Feldman cast aside Jessica Tandy, who had mesmerized New York audiences with her portrayal of Blanche Du Bois, in favor of screen star Vivien Leigh, who had captivated millions with her role as a tempestuous southern belle, Scarlet O'Hara, in *Gone with the Wind*. At the time Leigh was playing the role of Blanche in London, and Feldman brought the other players from the Broadway production to Hollywood – Brando, Kim Hunter, and Karl Malden – to re-create their roles.

When the script arrived in April 1950, Joseph Breen and his Production Code Administration were still a considerable force in Hollywood. Breen was deeply concerned with three main points in converting the play to the screen: homosexuality, nymphomania, and rape.[20] He told the producers to eliminate all three from the film. In various rewrites of the script, each of these potentially objectionable elements was softened but not totally eliminated. In the play, for example, when Blanche discovers that her husband is a homosexual she humiliates him: "I saw! I know! You disgust me!" This outburst drives him to suicide. In the film she still tells Mitch she caught him in bed with a man but says she confronted her husband with: "You're weak. I've lost respect for you. I can't pretend that I haven't."

Blanche's quest for sexual fulfillment is also toned down for the screen. She still admits that she has had many liaisons with strangers, is attracted to young men, and that drunken soldiers often came to her front lawn at Belle Reve and cried out for her. In the play, however, she discusses her sexual feelings quite openly with Stella – in fact, that is practically all the two women talk about onstage. For the film, most of that dialogue was either cut, shortened, or quickly glossed over so that Blanche does not appear to be as driven by sex as she was in the play. In the movie she does not discuss with Stella how much Mitch had pawed her, had lusted after her on their dates. In the play she tells her sister that she didn't mind all that much; rather, she was holding out on Mitch – not out of modesty – but cunningly planning just how much sex to give in order to lure him into marriage. Even though much of the overt frankness was cut, no intelligent adult could watch the movie and not realize that Blanche was a very experienced lady. However, the film was less direct than the play, and this took enough sting out for the PCA.

Altering the rape scene was more difficult. It was central to the entire play, but rape had been long banned as a subject by the PCA. Breen demanded that it be removed or, if it remained, be severely muted and Stanley be clearly punished. Kazan threatened to quit rather than eliminate the rape.[21] Williams pleaded that it was "a pivotal, integral truth in the play, without which the play loses its meaning, which is the ravishment of the tender, the sensitive, the delicate, by the savage and brutal forces of modern society."[22]

The compromise was an infusion of moral compensation in *Streetcar*: Stanley would lose Stella. Rather than refusing to believe that Stanley raped Blanche, and returning to him once again as the doctors take Blanche away, in the movie Stella reacts with rage when Stanley reaches to touch her, hissing, "Don't you ever touch me again!" She then picks up her baby and assures it (but, more important, the audience) that "I'm not going back in there again. Not this time, I'm never going back. Never." She slowly walks upstairs to her neighbor's apartment, and the film ends with Stanley screaming Stell-lahhhhh! Stell-lahhhhh! Stell-lahhhhh! – but she is never returning to Stanley's bed in this mass-entertainment version of *A Streetcar Named Desire*.

These changes, minor though they may seem, were enough to earn the film a PCA seal. The issue of homosexuality had been disguised. Most intelligent adults would certainly understand that when a male was referred to as "tender," "sensitive," and liking to read "poetry," this implied that he was homosexual; but the PCA was satisfied that Blanche did not *call* him a pervert or a homosexual. Blanche in the film seems more troubled emotionally than in the play, and less driven by raw sex. Finally, the character of Stanley was altered to make him appear like the animal that Blanche believes he is: sweaty, dirty, crude, and uncaring throughout the movie. Moreover, in the end, he pays dearly for his transgression by losing the one thing he really cares about: Stella.

Before the film was released to the general public the studios arranged "sneak previews" to try to measure audience reaction. *Streetcar* was shown to California audiences in Santa Barbara and Huntington Park and to audiences in New Jersey. The reaction was generally favorable: At Huntington Park preview cards ran "70 percent excellent, 30 percent fair to good with a few bad ones."[23] Many patrons thought the movie a bit long, so Kazan made several cuts in scenes to speed the action along. When the PCA seal was officially issued, he and Marlon Brando moved over to the Twentieth Century–Fox lot to begin work on *Viva Zapata!*

Kazan, however, did not anticipate that one additional preview group would play a major role in the finished look of *Streetcar*. When the Legion's Father Patrick J. Masterson, IFCA's Mary Looram, and Martin Quigley viewed the film they were shocked by its raw and lustful carnality. In another example of the very close working relationship between the PCA and the Legion, Jack Vizzard was in the screening room with Legion representatives when they viewed *Streetcar*. He later wrote: "When Martin Quigley walked out of the projection room in New York after viewing the picture, his face wore the ashen look of a man who had seen IT."[24] The Legion quickly sent word to Warner Bros. that they would condemn the film unless certain scenes were eliminated and others trimmed.

Warner Bros., terrified at the very thought of a Legion protest, never considered a challenge to Legion authority. Instead, fearful that Kazan and Williams might raise a fuss over religious censors tampering with their creation, the studio secretly hired Martin Quigley to reedit the picture, and dispatched David Weisbart, one of its best film cutters, to New York City to remove any scenes Quigley found objectionable.[25]

Quigley and the Legion objected to several scenes that they believed projected an atmosphere of lust and carnal desire. The most objectionable from their perspective was the scene in which Stella walks down the staircase and returns to Stanley after he has beaten her. Quigley, insisting that this was "too carnal," cut the close-ups of Stella as she walked seductively down to Stanley and eliminated Stanley carrying her off to the bedroom.[26]

Another scene disturbed Quigley, one implying that Stella loved making violent love to Stanley. The morning after the staircase scene, Blanche goes into Stella's bedroom. She is still in bed and is, by implication, nude (the audience sees her bare shoulder). The bed is a mess, and Stella is lounging, smoking a cigarette, legs spread apart and covered by a rumpled sheet. Blanche complains bitterly to her about Stanley's violent nature, but Stella is amused by her sister's reaction. Quigley demanded the following be cut:

> STELLA: Stanley's always smashed things. Why, on our wedding night as soon as we came in here, he snatched off one of my slippers and rushed about the place smashing the light-bulbs.
>
> BLANCHE: He did what?
>
> STELLA: He smashed all the light-bulbs with the heel of my slipper.
>
> BLANCHE: And you – you *let* him? Didn't *run*, didn't *scream*?
>
> STELLA: I was – sort of – thrilled by it.

The scene was indeed cut, as was Blanche's statement to the young newspaper boy: "It would be nice to keep you, but I've got to be good – and keep my hands off children." Blanche's admission that she had had "many meeting with strangers" and more than a few with drunken soldiers was also sent to the cutting-room floor by Quigley.[27]

When Kazan found out what was happening, he rushed to New York to try to prevent the Legion from destroying the film. It was September 1951, and in just four months the director would make his first appearance before the House Un-American Activities Committee. In his memoirs, published almost four decades later, Kazan wrote: "It was at this time that I became aware of the similarity of the Catholic Church to the Communist Party, particularly in the 'underground' nature of their operation."[28]

He discovered, much to his disgust, that the cuts had already been made in the film and there was nothing he could do about it. He sought an audience with Martin Quigley and Father Masterson to plead his case. The cuts, Kazan complained, changed the nature of the film. Masterson told Kazan that he was not a censor and that the Legion simply classified films; but Kazan noted, "He was damned patronizing."[29]

Quigley was more direct, but also treated Kazan with distain. The publisher told him that he had been hired by Warner Bros. and that Kazan was "really not in a position to ask anything of me." The cuts were made, Quigley asserted, to convert Stella into "a decent girl who is attracted to her husband the way any 'decent' girl might be."[30] The publisher repeatedly told Kazan that what was important was "the preeminence of the moral order over artistic considerations." When Kazan questioned the propriety of the Catholic church superimposing its set of moral values on all Americans, Quigley claimed a higher moral ground: The Legion censored according to the Ten Commandments, the director was told. The director was dismissed.[31]

Kazan complained bitterly to Jack Warner to no avail. "Warners," he later wrote, "just wanted a seal. They didn't give a damn about the beauty or artistic value of the picture. . . . They didn't want anything in the picture that might keep anyone away. At the same time they wanted it dirty enough to pull people in. The whole business was an outrage."[32]

When it was clear that the cuts would stand, Kazan wrote an article for the *New York Times* detailing the deletions forced on him by "a prominent Catholic layman." He concluded his article by stating: "My picture has been cut to fit the specifications of a code which is not my code, is not the recognized code of the picture industry, and is not the code of the great majority of the audience."[33] Kazan begged one last request: He asked the Legion to allow him to submit his version of *Streetcar* to the Venice Film Festival. The Legion refused. They warned the studio the film would be condemned if the original version was screened anywhere in the world. "I was the victim," he complained, "of a hostile conspiracy."[34]

Despite the cuts, "*Streetcar* made a bundle," according to Kazan.[35] It did well in the big cities. *Variety* reported that the film brought in over $100,000 in the first two weeks at the Warner Theater in New York City.[36] It did brisk box office in Washington, D.C., Chicago, Kansas City, Detroit, Denver, Cincinnati, and Toronto, and grossed $4.2 million by the end of its run a year later – not great, but respectable. More important, *Streetcar* was nominated for twelve Academy Awards and won four: Vivien Leigh for Best Actress, Karl Malden and Kim Hunter for their supporting roles, and Richard Day for Best Art Direction. Brando lost to Humphrey Bogart's touching portrayal of a gin-swilling riverboat trader in *The African Queen*, and Best Picture was given to more traditional Hollywood fare, *An American in Paris*.

Kazan and Williams lost their battle with the censors, but neither would forget the experience. Kazan was furious that "the gluttonous Pope of Fifth Avenue" (Cardinal Spellman) had "humiliated" him. He vowed, however, that the fight for freedom of the screen "wasn't over yet."[37]

He was certainly right on that score. Just a few months after the Academy of Motion Picture Arts and Sciences awarded four Oscars to *Streetcar,* the U.S. Supreme Court once again sent a message to clerics and censors that movies communicated ideas and were protected speech. On June 2, 1952, in a per curiam opinion, the Court cited the Burstyn decision in overturning the Texas conviction of W. L. Gelling for screening *Pinky* in Marshall, Texas. Justice Felix Frankfurter wrote that requiring a license to show a film "offends the Due Process Clause of the Fourteenth Amendment." Justice William O. Douglas concurred:

> The evil of prior restraint, condemned by *Near* v. *Minnesota*, 283 U.S. 697, in the case of newspapers and by *Burstyn* v. *Wilson,* 343 U.S. 495, in the case of motion pictures, is present here in flagrant form. If a board of censors can tell the American people what it is in their best interest to see or read or to hear then thought is regimented, authority substituted for liberty, and the great purpose of the First Amendment to keep uncontrolled the freedom of expression defeated.[38]

In one week in 1952 the U.S. Supreme Court had struck down as unconstitutional censorship either on religious grounds or of unpopular ideas, and had clearly given notice that states and municipalities that required exhibitors to obtain a license before exhibiting a film were in violation of the due-process clause of the Fourteenth Amendment and the prior-restraint concept of the First Amendment.

Despite the magnitude of the decisions rendered by the Court, however, the censors, the PCA, the state and municipal boards, and the Legion of Decency went about their jobs as if nothing had happened. The Legion was worried about the impact of the Court decisions but did not believe that it had to adjust its methods to fit within a broader definition of what was acceptable screen fare. From the Legion's point of view a film on divorce, for example, might be legal, but it would not be acceptable for a Catholic viewing audience. Had the Legion kept its criticism of films to a strictly Catholic viewpoint, it might have been able to function with much less controversy and with more support from the general population; but the organization would also have lost a great deal of its power. As we have seen, the Legion's goal was not simply to tell Catholic audiences what to see or not to see: The Legion insisted that its moral code was not Catholic but Christian, and attempted to prevent as many people as possible from seeing movies they adjudged immoral.

Although the censors and the Legion were still powerful, the Court decisions had weakened their authority and their ability to prevent films from being screened. Had Jack Warner possessed more fortitude, he would have backed Kazan. *Streetcar* would have still made money – not as much, perhaps, but enough theaters were willing to book films that had incurred the wrath of the censors to make films profitable. Their willingness in turn strengthened the determination of Hollywood filmmakers like Kazan to challenge both the PCA and the Legion.

One of these filmmakers was Cecil B. DeMille, who had fought censorship for years. DeMille specialized in gaudy biblical spectacles that often incurred the wrath of moral guardians. In 1932 his sexy, bloody Romans-versus-Christians epic, *Sign of the Cross,* had been at center of the censorship struggles that had resulted in the establishment of the Legion of Decency. De-Mille had sprinkled the film with naked slave girls and a requisite number of Roman debaucheries. Legionaries everywhere had picketed the film, and DeMille had been outraged at his critics.[39] Two decades later DeMille turned his cameras toward another spectacular setting: the circus.

In typical DeMille fashion *The Greatest Show on Earth* emphasized the spectacle of the circus. It featured beautiful women – Betty Hutton, Dorothy Lamour, and Gloria Grahame – dangling from a high-wire trapeze or performing dangerous feats with wild animals. Virile men were embodied by Charlton Heston, the boss of the circus, who loves Hutton and fights to keep his show on the road and to prevent Cornel Wilde, his handsome male aerialist, from seducing her. DeMille's big top also included a mysterious clown, played by Jimmy Stewart, who never took off his makeup. In one of the more bizarre plot twists, it turns out that Stewart is really a famous surgeon hiding from the law because he performed euthanasia on his dying wife. When Heston is trapped in the wreckage of a spectacular train wreck, Stewart saves his life with a emergency operation. The police, who have been following Stewart, now have proof that this clown is the famous doctor and quickly arrest him for murder. In true Hollywood fashion, the police triumph and the gigolo is jilted by Hutton, who returns to Heston's arms to live happily ever after.

When DeMille sent the script of his circus soap opera to the PCA, Breen made no objection other than to warn DeMille not to allow any excessive exposure of women's breasts in the film. A final review of the finished film brought no objection from the PCA or the state censors, but when the film went to New York for review by the Legion, it was given a B rating (objectionable in part for all). The Legion was disturbed by the costumes worn by the women and the "carnal, lustful characterization" of the character Sebastian, played by Cornel Wilde, who was, Legion reviewers (the ladies of the IFCA) believed, so "physically . . . irresistible" that the "virtue of the circus girls was in peril." The "mercy-killing" also "gravely concerned" the Legion. They feared that young people "might carry away a notion that this act . . . could not have been so bad or that nice clown would not have done it."[40] Privately, Legion assistant director Msgr. Thomas Little told DeMille that his organization did not "consider this particular type of entertainment fitting and proper for family consumption."[41]

Although ordinarily a B classification was not a problem with most filmmakers, who were delighted to have anything other than a C, a strict following of Legion guidelines maintained that *children* should not be allowed to attend a B film, and *The Greatest Show on Earth* was a wonderful circus show that kids loved. DeMille, who had experienced more than his share of censorship problems with his biblical films, was incensed. He publicly attacked the Legion's classification and refused to consider any changes in his film. In a very strongly worded letter to Little, DeMille took umbrage at the insinuation that his film was "capable of corrupting human souls." The character of Sebastian, DeMille told the priest, was a "flirtatious character, full of wit and fancy. I am sorry if you personally take offense" at the fact that there are men like him in the world.[42]

DeMille took special delight in informing Little that the costumes worn by the women in the movie "are the same costumes worn at every performance of Ringling Bros. and Barnum & Bailey" circus, which, he added, "is ritually blessed by a Catholic priest on its departure from Sarasota every year." It was possible, DeMille admitted, that "there are a few individuals so morbidly prurient that looking at someone dressed in a circus costume might constitute a moral danger for them." Still, DeMille deeply resented "your implied charge that I have been guilty of scandalous indecency in photographing costumes which happen to strike you as 'suggestive.'"[43]

Many Catholics agreed with DeMille. The editors of *Extension* were especially perplexed by the Legion reaction to the movie. Film critic William Mooring published a favorable review, and when the Legion flap with De-Mille became public some priests asked for a clarification: Could Catholic children see the film? The editors of *Extension* arranged a special screening with Paramount for four Catholic priests and the staff of *Extension* to examine the moral qualities of *The Greatest Show on Earth*. After the screening the managing editor, Rev. Msgr. J. B. Lux, D.D., was outraged – about the Legion's rating. This picture truly was, he believed, "The Greatest Show on Earth," and if Catholic children could not go to DeMille's film, he told the inquiring priests, then "no Catholic child could ever attend a circus – and that was ridiculous." Lux and his fellow staff members judged the costumes to be "ordinary circus" types, and they found "nothing suggestive in the dialogue." The charge that the film promoted mercy killing was "pure nonsense": The crime was "in no way condoned and DeMille could not have expressed disapproval of it more thoroughly unless he had actually put Stewart in the electric chair." The Legion's classification, Lux concluded, was wrong and would "undermine" Legion authority "in the minds of the people."[44]

In the final analysis, although the Legion did not condemn *The Greatest Show on Earth*, the B rating stuck. Perplexed priests who wrote to Legion headquarters for clarification on viewing by children were informed the Legion was "adamant" that DeMille's circus was objectionable.[45]

There is no indication that the rating hurt *The Greatest Show on Earth*; quite to the contrary, it was a box-office bonanza, topping the 1952 charts and bringing some $12 million into Paramount coffers. Moreover, there is no evidence that Catholic families stayed away because of the Legion: The film did especially well in the traditional Catholic urban areas of Buffalo, New York City, Chicago, Baltimore, and Pittsburgh.[46]

Perhaps more important to Hollywood, the film won Academy Awards for both Best Picture (beating *High Noon* for that honor) and Best Motion Picture Story. DeMille, nominated for the Best Director award, lost to John Ford for *The Quiet Man,* but was awarded the Irving Thalberg Memorial Award for his contribution to the industry. DeMille had proved that by 1952 it was possible to challenge Legion authority and still make money and garner accolades.

In New York, Otto Preminger, who was directing the stageplay *The Moon Is Blue,* was well aware of Kazan's losing battle with Legion censors and the flap over *The Greatest Show on Earth.* The very idea that the industry executives or a private religious organization could alter the artistic vision of a filmmaker was anathema to the director.

Born in Vienna, Austria, near the turn of the century, Preminger was the son of a very successful Jewish lawyer and government official. Despite having earned a law degree from the University of Vienna, his real love was theater. In Vienna he had studied with, worked for, and eventually replaced the legendary Max Reinhardt at the Josefstadt. In the early 1930s, he had been offered the directorship of the State Theater in Vienna, but declined because he would have had to convert to Catholicism. (For Preminger, it was a matter not of religion but of principle.) In 1936 Joseph M. Schenck offered him a directing contract with Twentieth Century–Fox, which Preminger eagerly accepted, fulfilling a lifelong dream of coming to America.

This young director, however, was as fascinated with the theatrical production in New York as he was by the glamour of the movies. With a temper that was mercurial, Preminger deeply resented any interference with his artistic vision. He wanted, and expected, complete artistic control over his projects and did not adjust well to the Hollywood system of collaborative production. Nor did this Viennese autocrat tolerate interference from prying censors: He described Hollywood's system of self-censorship as "absurd."[47] After directing two films for Zanuck, the two men happily parted company. Preminger went to New York and returned to directing theatrical productions on Broadway, where he had the control he demanded. Over the next several years Preminger established himself on the East Coast as an important and talented stage director.

He might have stayed on Broadway but for World War II. His autocratic personality, Viennese-German accent, cold scowl, shaven head, and strong physique made him a perfect German. Add a uniform and a monocle and, ironically, this Jewish Austrian was transformed into the perfect Nazi – a role he assumed with critical acclaim in Clare Boothe Luce's Broadway play, *Margin for Error,* which he also directed.

With Darryl Zanuck off at war, William Goetz was temporarily in charge of production at Twentieth Century–Fox. He lured Preminger back to Hollywood to play a Gestapo officer in *The Pied Piper,* a touching World War II drama about a group of schoolchildren who flee Nazi oppression with the officer's help. When Zanuck returned to the studio in 1944, he was shocked to find Preminger and vowed to get rid of the haughty Austrian once and for all. Preminger's first love, however, was not acting but directing, and he convinced Zanuck to give him one more opportunity, directing *Laura.* The producer's decision seemed brilliant when Preminger produced a haunting, gritty murder melodrama that captured the admiration of critics, fans, and even Zanuck himself.

Several years later, Zanuck turned to Preminger to rescue his overblown production of *Forever Amber.* Preminger, who described the book as "trite," agreed to complete the film; but when the Legion demanded a new ending, Preminger threatened to walk off the set rather than cave in to Legion demands (see Chapter 2). Zanuck, who was also furious over Legion interference, added a new voice-over written by the Legion and spared his director.

Over the next several years Preminger directed a number of respectable films but he was never totally comfortable in Hollywood. In 1951 he renegotiated his contract with Twentieth Century–Fox, accepting less pay for six months' freedom to pursue other projects.[48] "I demanded complete autonomy and the right to the final cut of the film," he wrote. "Nobody could overrule my decision. I had at last the freedom I had always wished for."[49] The first project that Preminger directed (and coproduced) under his new freedom was a Broadway play, F. Hugh Herbert's sex farce *The Moon Is Blue.*

The plot was rather simple: A handsome young New Yorker, Don Gresham, meets a cute young woman, Patty O'Neill, on the observation platform of the Empire State Building. He is a successful young architect, and she is a struggling actress. It is apparent from the beginning that they are attracted to one another. He invites her to dinner, and she accepts.

Using the pretext of a missing button on his suit, Don suggests that they stop at his apartment before going to dinner. This young woman, however, is neither shy nor demure but startlingly direct. Looking at him for a moment she asks, "Would you seduce me?" Don replies, "I don't know. Why?" Patty explains: "Why? A girl wants to know." Don is rather taken aback and, at the same time, amused by her directness. He pledges not to seduce her but admits he may try to kiss her. Patty is quite enthusiastic about that prospect: "Oh, that's all right. Kissing's fun. I've no objection to that." Gresham is now genuinely dumbfounded. He asks Patty if she is just teasing him or if she is serious. She is quite serious. If a girl goes to a man's apartment, she tells him,

it always ends one of two ways: "Either the girl's willing to lose her virtue –
or she fights for it. I don't want to lose mine – and I think it's vulgar to fight
for it. So I always put my cards on the table." When they arrive at Don's
apartment, Patty tells her date she is glad he doesn't mind. Mind what? he
asks. "Oh, men are usually so bored with virgins. I'm glad you're not."[50]

The rest of the play takes place in the apartment. Patty discovers that Don
broke up the previous evening with Cynthia, a strikingly beautiful woman.
"Was she your mistress?" she asks. Don is indignant. No, why are you so
preoccupied with sex? When Patty retorts that it is better for a girl to be preoccupied with sex than occupied, Don is speechless.

As this banter continues, Patty suddenly decides she would rather cook
than go out to dinner and sends Don to the store for steaks and staples. While
he is gone, Cynthia, who lives in the same building, comes to the apartment
determined to make up with Gresham. She is startled to find another woman there. Patty recognizes her from the pictures in the apartment and invites
her in; but Cynthia declines and goes home to plot against this interloper.

The sex farce continues when another neighbor, David, knocks on the
door. He is a wealthy, divorced, and slightly dissipated rake who specializes
in drinking and the seduction of young women. Unbeknownst to Patty, he is
Cynthia's father. David is immediately fascinated by Patty, who finds him innocently charming. She is not in the least bit bothered by any of his vices –
his drinking, the fact that he is divorced, nor his casual attitudes toward seduction; in fact she is rather amused. When, after several drinks, David suddenly asks Patty to marry him, she considers his offer for a moment but then
declines. (Later in the evening, the two have become good friends. Patty tells
David: "You're really horrible, and cynical and shallow and selfish and immoral and completely worthless – and I like you. I like you very much.")[51]

When Don returns he is furious to find David there, and even more upset
when Patty tells him she has invited him to stay for dinner. Three is a crowd,
to Don's way of thinking. While Patty is fixing dinner, David and Don talk
about Cynthia. The reason the two broke up is that Cynthia had wanted
Don to make love to her last night – was rather insistent about it – and Don,
uncomfortable with the passive role, had refused. A big fight had erupted,
and Cynthia had gone home in a huff. Now David is upset with Don for not
having made love to his daughter!

More sexual banter ensues. Cynthia lures Don out of the apartment and
sneeringly refers to Patty as a "professional virgin." Don is furious and returns home. There he discovers Patty's father, a tough old Irish cop, who
promptly busts him in the jaw and drags his errant daughter home.

The next day Don and Patty meet again on the observation platform at
the Empire State Building. Don proposes marriage; Patty accepts. The curtain falls, and everyone lives happily ever after.

Herbert and Preminger had a huge hit with the play. It was nothing very profound, but theater audiences loved its cleverness, wit, and fast-paced rhythm with a bit of slapstick tossed in for good measure. Sexual innuendo flew like machine-gun fire, but in the end virtue triumphed. The play ran for over three years on Broadway and toured more than thirty-five cities across the United States without "a peep from the censors, churchmen or public officials."[52] Even the Catholic church found some merit in the play: The Catholic Theater Conference Movement – the church's watchdog for theater – gave the play a B rating, objectionable in part.[53]

The play's popularity made it a natural for the movies. Preminger and Herbert formed an independent production company and struck a deal to release the film through United Artists, which agreed to distribute the film whether or not it had a PCA seal or received a condemned rating from the Legion. United Artists was not a member of the MPAA at that time and had little to lose by distributing a film without the industry seal. Preminger, who had struck up a friendship with William Holden while the two were filming *Stalag 17,* signed the Academy Award–winning actor to play Don. Holden, a sure box-office draw, was so intrigued by Preminger's plan to challenge Hollywood's censorship system that he agreed to play Don for a percentage of ticket sales. David Niven, who specialized in playing suave, debonair playboys, was perfect for David and leapt at the opportunity when Preminger offered him the role.[54] For the ingenue, Patty, Preminger gambled on a Hollywood unknown, Maggie McNamara.[55]

Breen and the PCA were prepared for someone to attempt to film *The Moon Is Blue.* When Paramount had asked for an opinion in June 1951, he had told them it was totally "unacceptable" because the entire play was centered around a light treatment of sex and seduction. The studio had dropped its plans because there seemed no way to remove the sexual innuendo from the zany stageplay.

Preminger and Herbert, on the other hand, had no intention of changing anything to suit the PCA. In late 1952 they submitted a script that was almost completely faithful to the play. Some scenes were rearranged, and they had struck a reference to marijuana, as well as several "damns" and "bastards," from the script. Otherwise, the plot and most of the dialogue were exactly the same.

When the script arrived at the PCA, Breen and his staff were concerned, but they had become accustomed to getting scripts that violated the code. The normal procedure was for a script to be assigned to one or more readers, who would report on the potential code violations at the morning "huddle," the daily PCA staff meeting. Once everyone was in agreement with the changes necessary to bring a script in compliance with the code, staff members would write, and Breen would sign, a letter to the studio head enumerating code problems. Those letters from Breen (some of which are detailed in preceding chapters) normally resulted in the script being rewritten and points of conflict being negotiated with the code office. The process might take a few days or several months, but normally the studios caved in to Breen's demands because they needed his seal for access to the vast majority of the nation's theaters.

The negotiations between the PCA and Preminger started quite normally with *The Moon Is Blue*. After reviewing the script, Geoffrey Shurlock and Jack Vizzard of the PCA met with Preminger and Herbert to discuss code problems. The code representatives expressed their objections based on the humor in the script concerning seduction, virginity, divorce, and sexual relations. They were not as concerned about the use of the word "virginity" as they were about the context in which it was used. The code stated that there were two types of love: pure and impure. The pure love of marriage was not based, the Catholic argument went, on sexual passion or attraction. Sex was a marital duty solely for the purpose of procreation. Impure love was lust. Sex, in the Catholic view, was sacred and serious and, as Father Lord wrote in the code, "must not be the subject of comedy or farce, or treated as material for laughter." Sex was not funny, nor was it to be fun in the movies.[56]

This attitude toward sexual relationship left little room for compromise. *The Moon Is Blue* made a comedy out of courtship and brought the issue of making love to the forefront. It verbalized thoughts and situations that almost everyone in the audience had had at some point in the process of dating. *The Moon Is Blue* struck a universal chord in men and women and made them laugh about role playing, flirtation, and seduction. It was the whole point of the play and the movie.

Preminger and Herbert listened politely to the censors' point of view. They offered a few minor concessions but basically informed the code administrators that they "intended to shoot the picture" more or less as it was written and could see "no reason to make any changes."[57] Moreover, they did not discuss scenes with the PCA during production. When the final, largely unaltered film was submitted to the PCA several months later, Breen accepted Preminger's challenge and rejected the film as "unacceptable because of the light attitude towards seduction, illicit sex, chastity and virginity."[58]

Preminger was irate, although his irritation seems more for the record than a genuine surprise. He told Breen the film contained "no scenes of passion" and no scenes of "crime or vice." It was, in Preminger's opinion, "a harmless story of a very virtuous girl . . . whose one aim in life is to get married and have children." As evidence of the broad appeal of the film, Preminger told Breen that no one protested the theme or the language at previews in the Los Angeles area; but, he added, several individuals wrote on preview cards that they hoped "the picture would not be ruined by censorship."[59]

Breen, who seemed sincere, replied that he was sorry that they simply could not agree. Since it was clear that neither side was willing to compromise, the only solution was to submit the film to the MPAA board of directors for a final ruling. Preminger complied and asked for a hearing. While the debates within the MPAA board meeting over *The Moon Is Blue* in mid-May 1953 were impassioned, the ruling was a foregone conclusion.

Breen went to New York, stopping only to brief MPAA officials before leaving for an extended European vacation. He turned his notes over to Gordon White, who argued the case before the board. White presented his argument against the film in personal terms: The film would be, he predicted, "highly offensive to many parents to whom the virginity of their daughters" is not a joke. Furthermore, it was not proper, he believed, for a movie to imply that it was acceptable behavior for an unmarried woman to visit the apartment of a man she had just met.[60]

Preminger and United Artists were represented by New York attorney and former New Dealer Samuel Rosenman. The lawyer was no stranger to MPAA hearings, having represented Eric Johnston against Howard Hughes over a PCA seal for *The Outlaw*. Now the tables were turned, and Rosenman argued for a seal for *The Moon Is Blue*. Rosenman followed the Preminger line: The theme of the film was moral; the young girl recognized the virtue of chastity. Although she was realistic enough to know that not all women valued virginity, she herself did. How, he asked, could a movie possibly have a better message?[61]

No matter how compelling the arguments presented, the MPAA board had no choice but to deny a seal to *The Moon Is Blue*. Preminger had openly bragged that he made the film exactly as he wanted to without making any concessions to the PCA. It was no secret within the Hollywood community that his contract with United Artists allowed him the freedom of producing a final product that did not carry the seal. UA was committed to distributing the film. If the MPAA ruling body were to give a PCA seal to Preminger, it would, in effect, have completely undercut what was left of Breen's authority to cajole filmmakers to abide by it. Not surprisingly, the MPAA ruled in Breen's favor.

Preminger, ever the showman, took his case to the public. He called the MPAA action "hypocritical" and threatened that if "the MPAA or any other group [the Legion] or individual should try to interfere" with the distribution of his film, he and UA would "take every possible step provided by law to protect ourselves." He further tweaked the MPAA by referring to Joseph Burstyn's victory over censorship: It was an individual, Preminger reminded reporters, who "after a long, costly struggle" had won a victory for freedom of the screen, not the MPAA.[62] It was clear that Preminger intended to follow in Burstyn's footsteps.

Everyone knew what was at stake. The MPAA action was, in 1953, no guarantee that the film would not be a box-office hit, but it was certainly going to make it more difficult to sell the film to distributors. Exhibitors had been reluctant to book films that did not carry the seal even after the 1948 *Paramount* decision. Darryl Zanuck warned Preminger, "Without the Seal there won't be five theaters in the United States that will show your film."[63] But even that vise grip of the MPAA was weakening. Exhibitors could not help but notice that the play had packed theaters on its national tour, and preview audiences loved the movie version.

The real question was what the Legion of Decency would do. Would it follow the rating of its sister organization for theatrical performances and rate *The Moon Is Blue* as objectionable in part, or would it condemn the movie as immoral? An even bigger question was how much weight a Legion condemnation would be given by distributors. Martin Quigley was sufficiently concerned about the movie that he appealed directly to UA headquarters during production for the distributors to edit out some of the scenes that he somehow believed advocated "free love." United Artists politely declined.[64]

At Legion headquarters in New York, Father Patrick J. Masterson and his assistant Msgr. Thomas F. Little prepared to classify *The Moon Is Blue*. Joining them in the reviewing room was Mary Looram and a committee of Legion reviewers from the IFCA. After the final credits had rolled, the two priests were shocked to discover that the IFCA representatives were *not* shocked; rather, Looram and her colleagues recommended a B classification for the film. In 1953 a B rating would have placed *Moon* in the same grouping as *Abbott and Costello Go to Mars; The Bad and the Beautiful; Come Back, Little Sheba; Singing in the Rain;* and *Snows of Kilimanjaro*. Almost ninety films were classified B in 1953, including *The Greatest Show on Earth,* and there was little if any stigma attached to this classification by most Catholics.

The priests outvoted the ladies of the ICFA and condemned *The Moon Is Blue* as immoral. On June 9, 1953, the Legion announced its decision. *Moon* was condemned because "the subject matter . . . in its substance and manner of presentation seriously offends and tends to deny or ignore Christian and traditional standards of morality and decency and dwells hardly without variation upon suggestiveness in situations and dialogue." That same day tragedy struck the Legion. Father Masterson, who had been executive secretary since 1948, died unexpectedly of a heart attack.[65] He was replaced by his longtime assistant Msgr. Little, who had joined the Legion staff in 1948. The two men had worked closely together for five years, and Little made a smooth transition to head of the organization.

Within days of Masterson's death Little penned a long memorandum to the local Legion directors advising them that *The Moon Is Blue,* while not "avowedly salacious," was "dangerous to the moral welfare" of movie audiences. Little asked local directors to be especially vigilant in directing Catholics to avoid this movie because "the strength of the Legion is going to be tested by the commercial success or non-success of this film."[66] It was, Little believed, necessary to remind all Catholics that when they took the Legion pledge they promised "to stay away altogether from places of amusement which show them as a matter of policy." In the past the Legion had invoked this part of the pledge only if a theater owner repeatedly exhibited C films, but the threat of *Moon* forced the Legion to up the ante: In Little's view, this clause now referred to any theater that played *The Moon Is Blue*. He asked local Legionaries to institute a "united protest" against the film that would include prohibiting Catholics from attending, in the future, any theater that dared to exhibit *Moon*. It was a gamble that could easily backfire if thousands of regular theaters booked the film.

Cardinal Spellman joined the attack when he declared *The Moon Is Blue* "an occasion of sin" and a violation of "standards of morality and decency" and repeated Little's contention that all Catholics must boycott any theater, in the present and in the future, that showed the movie. Spellman's message was repeated by his fellow bishops in Los Angeles and Philadelphia. (It is important to note, however, that most of the 103 bishops did not join Spellman's crusade.) This in turn prompted a reply from Elmer Rice, chairman of the National Council on Freedom from Censorship, who denounced Cardinal Spellman's appeal for a secondary boycott as "clearly contrary to the spirit of the First Amendment."[67]

Preminger joined the battle when he countered that Spellman's opinion was "of no concern" to him. "I like the picture as it is. I don't want to be a crusader," he told reporters; but, he added, "we are not going to change one line or one word." No one, he stressed, "has a right to tell the American people what to see and what not to see."[68]

While legions of Catholics worked to undercut *The Moon Is Blue*, the facade of Catholic solidarity was exposed when a Catholic publication unexpectedly endorsed the movie. Richard Hayes, film critic for *St. Joseph's Magazine*, billed as "America's Catholic Family Monthly," warned readers that some would find *Moon* "offensive or tasteless," but in his opinion the film was a "parable of the pure of heart" and "remarkably sane and wholesome." Hayes found the film "captivating,"an "irresistible entertainment piece," and predicted it would certainly be on every "moviegoers 'favorite' list as the brightest and most originally charming light comedy of the year."[69]

Hayes was wrong: It was not on the Legion of Decency's favorite list; in fact it topped their forbidden list for 1953. *Variety* lampooned the Legion with a headline that chuckled: "Moon Is Blue. Face Is Red."[70] Msgr. Little admitted the incident "was embarrassing."[71] Catholic publications were quick to denounce Hayes and echo the party line. In Los Angeles, William Mooring said *The Moon Is Blue* was dishonest because it "invites people to laugh at conventional views of chastity." Hayes, he wrote, did not fully appreciate its "dangerous inferences."[72] *Commonweal* dismissed *Moon* because "it added nothing to the art of the cinema," and predicted that the film would result in new local censorship boards.[73] Privately, Mooring told Little he was sure the film would be a "tremendous box-office success."[74]

Behind the scenes, the Legion worked furiously to make *Moon* a failure. Msgr. Little pressured distributors not to book the film into their theaters and implied that if they did, the Legion would call for Catholics to boycott them. He met with some success: On the West Coast, he told William Mooring, "the Skouras people have promised to cooperate." Each local Legion director was urged to call local theater owners to prevent *Moon* from penetrating his community. Msgr. Romeo Blanchette told Little he used phone calls and local high school students to pressure theaters in his community and was successful with all but one: the local drive-in, which combined *The Moon Is Blue* and Hedy Lamarr's *Ecstasy* on a successful double bill![75] The film was also pulled from exhibition in Putnam, Connecticut, after Catholic protest. Catholics were further encouraged when the film was banned in Maryland, seized as obscene in New Jersey, and limited to adults in Chicago.[76]

Despite these victories the Legion campaign against *Moon* fizzled badly. Little had to admit that the Legion of Decency was not successful in keeping the film out of theaters. Two of the nation's largest distributors, the Stanley Warner chain and United Paramount, refused to bend to Legion pressure and booked the film. In Florida, the Wometco chain turned down the Legion and brought the film to that conservative state. Legion efforts with state boards of censorship were mixed: Maryland, Ohio, and Kansas banned the film, but New York, Pennsylvania, Virginia, and Massachusetts approved it. In Kansas City, Missouri, Mrs. Lora Williams, head of the local censorship board, banned *Moon* as immoral but was panned for her actions by the *Kansas City Star,* which editorialized for an end to censorship.[77] In the end, the censors' victories were temporary. The courts eventually overturned as unconstitutional all the decisions to ban the film.

In many areas the publicity and censorship drove people away from their televisions into the theaters. *Variety* reported that in Omaha, where Archbishop Gerald T. Bergan denounced the film, *Moon* "drew long mobs nightly" after the denouncement.[78] Lloyd Binford, the 86-year-old censor in Memphis, created a similar reaction: He banned *Moon* from his city, but a theater a few miles south of Memphis, in his native Mississippi, "did SRO business" with *Moon.*[79]

Most reviewers failed to find anything offensive in the film. The *New York Times* called it "innocuous, even highschoolish."[80] Manny Farber of the

Nation assured readers that "everybody remains idyllically pure" despite some risqué dialogue.[81] *Time* said it was "scrupulously moral."[82] "Pure as Goldilocks," said the *Dallas Morning News*.[83] "What's blue is the censor's nose," wrote the *Chicago Daily News*.[84] William Wilkerson, a Catholic and editor of the *Hollywood Reporter,* agreed. He predicted that "there will be little objection on the part of adult audiences," and told readers, "It is a good picture."[85]

All the publicity translated into good box office. When *Moon* opened in Los Angeles at the Four Star Rialto theater, it was a "smash" doing $25,000 the first week; it continued to pack in customers throughout its run despite Cardinal James McIntyre's plea for Catholics to stay away. In Chicago, adults flocked to the Woods Theater, where *Moon* generated a "booming" $78,000 in the first two weeks and a month later was still "brisk" at $27,000.[86] Despite heavy Catholic pressure *Moon* was a "smash" in Buffalo and played to packed audiences in Boston, St. Louis, Denver, Portland, and Minneapolis.[87]

This is not to imply that the Legion campaign against *Moon* had no effect; it did, but not the effect the Legion anticipated. For example, *High Noon,* a tremendously popular horse opera, played in 19,000 theaters during 1952–3 and grossed $3.7 million at the box office. *The Moon Is Blue* was limited to a mere 4,200 theaters, and certainly the Legion's efforts helped keep it out of many others; but even with the limited number of play dates the film brought in $3.5 million to United Artists and ranked fifteenth at the box office in 1953. As *Business Week* noted: "With that kind of arithmetic, producers don't have to wonder which type of film the exhibitors will be bidding for."[88] To *Newsweek* the lesson was that "adult films . . . more or less on the sophisticated level" of *Moon* would capture a significant audience.[89]

Still, there was little doubt that *Moon* was controversial. Most adults thought it harmless, but many others found it offensive. The Legion's position was at least understandable within the context of the times: *Moon* was about sex, and the Legion believed it was harmful.

Few people outside of Catholic circles, however, could understand why the organization lashed out at a low-budget recreation of the life of Martin Luther that hit American theaters in 1953. There was nothing remotely sexual or immoral in the film. It contained no violence or anything else of a controversial nature that might cause it to be censored. Financed by six separate Lutheran organizations in the United States, the film was produced by Louis De Rochemont and shot on location in Germany.[90] Each of the six Lutheran sponsors had final script approval to ensure that the film was accurate.

The film is a rather straightforward accounting of Luther's life. After an unsuccessful attempt at studying law he enters the priesthood; but this young priest challenges his ecclesiastical superiors and is appalled by the Catholic practice, perfected by Pope Leo X, of selling indulgences. He is finally convinced that salvation comes through faith not the trappings of institutional religion. The most dramatic moments are the branding of Luther as a heretic and the re-creation of his famous trial at the Diet of Worms. The film concludes when Luther leaves the church in protest and marries a nun. The Reformation has begun.

   Martin Luther was, after all, a film, not a treatise on theology or history. Even secular critics noted that the film said little about the role of German nationalism in the rise of Lutheranism. There were points about which theologians might quibble – whether the selling of indulgences brought forgiveness (Catholic theologians argued it did not); the role of the Bible and individual interpretation of it; the level of corruption and superstition in the Catholic church in the early 1500s; and the personality and teaching of Luther – but when the film was submitted to the Catholic-dominated PCA, Joe Breen approved it without reservation, as did the various secular state and municipal censorship boards.

   To the complete surprise of filmmakers everywhere, this docudrama with little action, lengthy narration, and an almost gloomy reverence was a sensation at the box office. In a test run in the small town of Hickory, North Carolina (population 8,000), the film attracted more than 16,000 customers in an eight-day run. The manager of the Center Theater was so overwhelmed that he had to supply eager customers with popcorn from a rival theater! Urban audiences reacted with similar enthusiasm. In Minneapolis close to a hundred thousand fans packed the Lyceum Theater over a four-week period. *Martin Luther* outdrew every Hollywood film playing in the city. Houstonians, 22,000 in one week, flocked to the Kirby Theater to watch this tribute to a "monk who defied the Catholic church." Even in New York City, where it played at the Street Guild Theater, that cinema was the only one in town whose box office did not drop drastically when Twentieth Century–Fox opened its lavish Cinemascope spectacle *The Robe*.[91] By the end of its initial run, the film had accumulated more than eight thousand play dates and grossed more than $5 million on a total investment of less than $700,000.[92]

   Critics agreed with fans that *Martin Luther* was a good film. Manny Farber of the *Nation* called it "a nice, well-behaved little movie" that "makes its play more to the mind than to the eye."[93] Bosley Crowther judged it a "fully responsible job" and urged New Yorkers to see it.[94] The *New Yorker* noted that the film was "a box-office bonanza" as well as a "determined, reflective, persuasive and sanguine" portrait of Luther.[95] It was "distinguished fare for the serious movie-goer" to *Theater Arts*, and "Impressive" to the *Saturday Review*.[96]

   However, the Catholic church had not forgiven Martin Luther for his renunciation some four centuries earlier. The Legion, Catholic publications, and Catholic organizations all attacked the film as bad history, faulty theology, and potentially harmful viewing for Catholics. Although there was no sex or violence in *Martin Luther,* nothing that even remotely suggested impropriety or immorality, Church officials and the Legion attacked the movie with unrestrained vigor.

The Legion of Decency was faced with a potentially embarrassing situation: It would be extremely difficult to "condemn" *Martin Luther* and continue to argue that the only goal of the Legion was to purge immorality from entertainment films. The Legion had steadfastly maintained from its inception in 1934 that it represented Christian, not Catholic, opinion in classifying movies; but there was nothing to condemn in the film other than an unflattering view of the Catholic church in the 1500s. Nonetheless, many of the reviewers urged a condemned classification based on theology. As one Legion reviewer stressed to Msgr. Little, the film "not only teaches heresy but bears false witness against the Catholic Church's teaching."[97] Little realized, however, that a condemned rating would prohibit thousands of theaters from exhibiting the film and would bring a storm of Lutheran and Protestant protest against the Legion, open the organization to ridicule, and expose the strictly Catholic nature of Legion criticism of film.

Thus although Little believed the film could have a harmful influence on "weak Catholics" and that it was "heretical," he also recognized the potential harm a condemned classification could bring. Despite pressure to condemn *Martin Luther,* Little pushed for placing the film under the innocuous category of Separate Classification, which the Legion had previously used in 1938 when it disapproved of the politics of Walter Wanger's Spanish Civil War drama, *Blockade.*[98]

Little's position eventually won, and the Legion warned Catholics that *Martin Luther* "offers a sympathetic and approving representation of the life and times of Martin Luther, the 15th century figure of religious controversy. It contains theological and historical references and interpretations which are unacceptable to Roman Catholics."[99]

Once the Legion position was announced, Catholic publications were quick to do what the Legion itself could not: condemn the film. Readers of Catholic publications were warned to stay away from it. *Martin Luther* was so controversial in Catholic circles that Moira Walsh, the film reviewer for *America,* allowed James Brundage, a professor of Reformation History at Fordham University, to write a review. Brundage blasted *Martin Luther* as historically "inaccurate" and "misleading," which resulted, he claimed, in presenting an "essentially unfair" impression of the Catholic church.[100] Father James Gillis, C.S.P., editor of the *Catholic World,* charged that the film was "doctored."[101] In Buffalo, Father Nelson W. Logal asserted in a sermon at the American Legion Armistice Day–Gold Star Mothers Mass that the film was a false portrayal of Luther, who was "perhaps the most hysterically-voiced, vehement, immoderate and foul-mouthed preacher in history."[102] *Our Sunday Visitor,* the national Catholic newspaper, called the film "unhistorical, unbibical and unfair" and published a thirty-page pamphlet for Catholics explaining why the film was heresy.[103] Father Robert Walsh, writing in the *Catholic Messenger,* told Catholic readers the film makers "have deliberately twisted the truth."[104]

These attacks were mild compared to that of the *Wanderer,* a Catholic publication in Minnesota, which not only called the film dangerous but also described director Irving Pichel as "notorious for his multifarious connections with Communist-front organizations and activities."[105] The charge that *Martin Luther* was made by communists was leveled by several Catholic publications. Father Frederick J. Zwierlein, writing in the *Social Justice Review,* compared the film to the World War II production *Song of Russia,* which used "the best movie techniques to idealize Communist Russia"; *Martin Luther,* he told readers, "ignores historical research by depicting Luther as a champion of religious freedom" and, therefore, must "also be classed as lying propaganda."[106] In Los Angeles William Mooring raised a similar charge in *Tidings:* "If Martin Luther had been made by pro-Communists for the purpose of launching an attack upon the Catholic Church, it could not very well have been contrived with greater subtlety nor with more characteristic style."[107] When Allan E. Sloane, who wrote the screenplay, admitted before the House Un-American Activities Committee hearing in May 1954 that he had once been a member of the Communist Party, Catholic publications shrieked that the film was un-American.[108]

Lutherans had anticipated a Catholic attack on the film, although few could have predicted the vitriolic level of Catholic opposition. Dr. Paul Empie, Executive Director of the National Lutheran Council, warned members gathered at the annual meeting in February 1953 – months before *Martin Luther* opened – that the "film pulls no punches," and "its release will involve us in a certain amount of controversy, especially with members of the Roman Catholic Church."[109] Empie was right: Lutherans and Catholics traded gibes in the press throughout the run of the film.

None of this did the Catholic church or its Legion of Decency any good. At a time when the very concept of censorship was under attack, the Legion needed allies, not new enemies. Its position on *The Miracle* had cost it dearly among Protestants, who were potential supporters. Now the Legion, in essence, was calling Lutherans dupes of the commies and branding the Lutheran leadership as liars. It is hard to imagine an organization doing more to damage its appearance in the eyes of prospective allies than the Legion did regarding Protestant groups, who had generally supported the Catholic effort up to that time.

Perhaps even more harmful was the fact that the Legion's position and the ensuing strident Catholic attack destroyed the myth that the organization was concerned only with issues of morality in films. Attempting to connect *Martin Luther* with an international communist conspiracy exposed the Legion to ridicule – even during the anticommunist hysteria of the early 1950s.

By 1954 it was clear that the Legion's ability to rule Hollywood was coming to an end. Audiences were not shocked or scandalized by a film with a scene in a bordello, nor by the suggestion that ummarried people might have sex. *A Streetcar Named Desire* and *The Moon Is Blue* proved that there was a demand for adult entertainment. *Martin Luther* illustrated that non-Catholics paid scant attention to Legion opinions and that there was a market for films directed at specialized audiences.

A disappointed Martin Quigley told Cardinal Spellman that *The Moon Is Blue* "is attracting from large to very large audiences" in New England, New York, Texas, Chicago, and Denver. It was all very "disheartening" to Quigley, who had been instrumental in creating the Legion in 1934. Msgr. Little confirmed the bad news to Spellman.[110]

Even more disheartening to Quigley, Spellman, and the Legion was the action taken by the courts. Maryland's censor, Sydney R. Traub, had banned *Moon* because it was "immoral" and did not carry a PCA seal; but his decision was overturned by Judge Herman M. Moser, who held in December 1953 that *Moon* "is neither obscene, indecent, immoral, nor tending to corrupt morals." The judge also found the Production Code clause that stated seduction could never be subject for comedy "absurd if literally enforced and . . . fatally vague as a legal standard."[111]

The U.S. Supreme Court agreed with Moser. In 1953 and 1954 several cases involving banned films – *La Ronde,* a French import; *M,* a remake of the German classic; and *The Moon Is Blue* – percolated through the justice system. *La Ronde,* adapted from the play by Arthur Schnitzler and directed by the internationally acclaimed French director Max Ophuls, is set in Vienna in the early 1900s. The film portrays a series of casual love affairs all of which are interconnected – a prostitute and a soldier have an affair, but the soldier moves on to a housemaid, who in turn is having an affair with her employer, who is also having an affair with a married woman. (The playwright, also a medical man, intended his comedy to explain the spread of venereal disease.) It was all very "French" and was banned as "immoral" by the New York censorship board in 1951 and condemned by the Legion that same year. The distributor, Commercial Pictures Corporation, sued, and when the New York courts upheld the state board, Commercial pushed for review by the Supreme Court.

M had a similar history. The original version, made in Germany in 1931 and directed by Fritz Lang, was a chilling story of a child molester and psychopathic killer (Peter Lorre). The 1951 remake, directed by Joseph Losey, starred David Wayne as the killer and was set in modern Los Angeles. Despite very favorable reviews, the Ohio censorship board refused a license for the film on the grounds that it might have an unfavorable effect "on unstable persons of any age" and served "no valid educational purpose."[112] The distributor, Superior Films, sued, and the Ohio Supreme Court upheld the board's decision. That decision was then appealed to the U.S. Supreme Court.

In Kansas a similar process started when the state censorship board (Mrs. Frances Vaught, Mrs. J. R. Stowers, and Mrs. Bertha Hall) found that *The Moon Is Blue* was "obscene, indecent and immoral."[113] The board action was based on the Kansas statute empowering the censors to ban films that are "cruel, obscene, indecent or immoral, or such as tend to debase or corrupt morals." Holmby Productions and UA sued. The case went to the Kansas Supreme Court, which cited the U.S. Supreme Court decision in *Burstyn v. Wilson* in its decision – to uphold censorship! They ruled that the Kansas statute was neither a violation of the First and Fourteenth Amendments to the U.S. Constitution nor "so vague and indefinite as to offend due process." "We are of the opinion," the Kansas court wrote, that the words "obscene, indecent or immoral" have "an accepted, definite and clear meaning."[114] The court having ruled that the censorship board was acting within its power, the decision was appealed to the U.S. Supreme Court.

In each of the above cases, the Court issued a per curiam opinion with reference to *Burstyn v. Wilson* in reversing the state courts. The Court disagreed with Kansas that words like "immoral" and "indecent" had universally accepted meanings; rather, they were as vague and imprecise as the word "sacrilegious" and were not legal justification for banning a film.

Justice William O. Douglas, with concurrence from Justice Hugo Black, again spoke of the necessity for inclusion of film under the broad umbrella of protection offered for free speech by the First and Fourteenth Amendments. He disagreed with Ohio and New York that the states could censor movies: "I cannot accept that assumption," he wrote. Douglas reminded the states that in *Neer v. Minnesota* the Court had struck down a law aimed "at suppressing before publication" a malicious newspaper. The chief purpose of the constitutional guarantee of a free press, he wrote, was to "prevent previous restraints upon publication."[115]

Douglas understood the argument that movies were different from books, plays, and newspapers. "But the First Amendment," he wrote, "draws no distinction between the various methods of communicating ideas." He concluded: "In this Nation every writer, actor, or producer, no matter what medium of expression he may use, should be freed from the censor."[116]

The strength of that statement sent chills down the spines of censors and emboldened anticensorship advocates. The *Catholic World* called Douglas's conclusion that every writer, actor, or producer should be freed of the censor "the most disturbing" feature of the Supreme Court decision. If censors cannot reject films as immoral, "on what possible grounds can they reject them?" the magazine asked.[117]

The answer, which neither the Legion nor the censors liked, was on increasingly narrow legal grounds. The capricious denial by state or municipal censorship boards of the right to exhibit a film, refusing a license based on value-laden terms such as "sacrilegious," "indecent," or "immoral," was under attack. The U.S. Supreme Court was unmoved by arguments that portrayed film as a particularly seductive means of communication that needed special controls. The Court also found it difficult to determine whose moral standards were the benchmark. For example, there was clearly tremendous difference of opinion by thoughtful people of various political and religious backgrounds on the moral message of *The Moon Is Blue* or the sacrilege of *The Miracle*.

While it was clear that the U.S. Supreme Court was increasingly extending the net of protection of the First and Fourteenth Amendments to motion pictures, the Court did not take the next logical step and declare state and municipal censorship boards unconstitutional. Douglas and Black supported that extension, but the remaining justices were wary of totally removing local controls. The result was that, despite the Court's rulings, state and municipal boards continued to function in much the same way as they had over the previous several decades.

The Supreme Court decisions, the continuing decline at the box office, the silliness of the some of the censorship positions, and growing public support of a more adult cinema encouraged filmmakers, professional film critics, and anticensorship advocates to challenge the authority of the Production Code and the Legion of Decency. Samuel Goldwyn, one of the industry's founding moguls and one of its most respected voices, in late 1953 called for a revision of the Production Code. He warned that unless the code was brought "reasonably up to date," the tendency to ignore it altogether would increase.[118] Goldwyn, although clearly not advocating the code's elimination, believed that filmmakers had to be given more freedom of expression in making films for adults.

A *Variety* poll found that film exhibitors agreed with Goldwyn. Most were unwilling to pledge not to exhibit films that did not carry the PCA seal. Typical of exhibitors who wanted more freedom to book films was Richard Brandt of Trans-Lux, who said: "I don't think there should be a Code. I think motion pictures, like the press, should be free of censorship of any kind."[119]

Bennie Berger, a theater owner in Minneapolis, blasted the Production Code as "artificial." In his view "the public should be the only censor."[120]

Even some longtime supporters of the code and censorship agreed with Goldwyn. Philip Hartung, film critic for *Commonweal* and a consultant to the Legion of Decency, anticipated Goldwyn's alert by some six months: "Without doubt, the Production Code . . . has fenced in the movies . . . and . . . needs revision." The *Commonweal* promptly backed Goldwyn's appeal: "One simply can not," the editors wrote, "legislate a general code."[121]

The debate over the value of the Production Code reached a larger audience when historian Arthur Schlesinger Jr., writing in his weekly column "History of the Week" in the *New York Post*, asserted that many of the precepts of the code were "idiotic." An incredulous Schlesinger told readers the code simply had to be read to be believed. It would, he wrote, "have had the effect, if enforced through history, of aborting most of our great literary inheritance at the source, including probably the Bible itself." Although he did not believe that the current debate over the code would bring about its elimination, if Hollywood could "remove some of the more stupid and offensive prohibitions (miscegenation) it may increase the chances of maturity breaking into the film industry."[122]

Martin Quigley was furious with Goldwyn and Schlesinger, viewing any criticism of the code as a personal attack. He fired off a letter to the historian claiming the code was based on the Ten Commandments, not Catholic theology, and accusing him of creating a " shadow of bigotry" by inserting anti-Catholicism into his critique.[123] Quigley told MPAA President Eric Johnston that Schlesinger's article was "a particularly poisonous piece."[124]

Schlesinger, however, was not as easily bluffed as most of the moguls had been by Quigley's occasional tirades. He fired back at Quigley that the Ten Commandments were "statements of profound moral principles" and could not be compared to the "niggling detail" of the code. He defended the right of filmmakers to make films "like *La Ronde* or even *The Moon Is Blue.*"[125] "Do you seriously believe," Schlesinger asked Quigley, "that the literature and art of the world would have been improved if all writers and artists had been compelled throughout history to work under the principles of the Hollywood Production Code?"[126]

Radio programs and television shows suddenly featured debates over the need for a movie code. Newsman Charles Collingswood moderated a CBS-TV debate on January 23, 1954, which featured Otto Preminger and Otis L. Guernsey Jr., film and drama critic for the *New York Herald Tribune*, speaking against the code and MPAA representatives Manning Glagett and Philip O'Brien defending it. Preminger turned the tables and attacked the partnership between the Legion and the Code Administration. He could not understand, he told viewers, why the MPAA attacked political censorship boards yet worked closely with the Legion to prevent condemned movies from gaining access to theaters. The MPAA'ers stressed the fact that some eight thousand films had been made under the PCA, and counterattacked Preminger for cutting material from *The Moon Is Blue* for British censors that he had refused to cut for American exhibition. Neither side "won," but the debate was civil and intelligent and raised serious questions about the nature of the entertainment industry, censorship, and freedom of expression.[127]

The serious and thoughtful nature of the larger discussion over the merits of the Production Code died almost as quickly as it had begun. Neither Quigley nor Schlesinger, nor anyone else involved, convinced the opposition of his position, and events in Hollywood changed the debate from philosophical to emotional. Once again Catholic pickets hit the streets in front of theaters with placards pleading, "Help Save America from Moral Filth." Meanwhile, Howard Hughes, who had resumed leadership of the financially strapped RKO in February 1953, released a new film starring his favorite actress, Jane Russell. *The French Line* was a musical comedy filmed in Technicolor, with the added enticement of a 3-D format. The ads proclaimed, "Jane Russell in Three Dimension – and What Dimensions!" and "J. R. in 3-D. It'll knock both your eyes out."[128]

The French Line must rank as one of the worst movies ever made: As a musical comedy it was not in the least bit funny, and the musical numbers were embarrassingly wooden. The plot, such as it was, centered around a beautiful, extremely rich Texas oil woman (Mary Carson, played by Russell) who wanted nothing more than to be an all-American girl. She yearned for a husband and family and was more comfortable roping cows on her Texas ranch than she was wearing fancy dresses in high society. No normal man (or at least no real Texan) would marry her, however, because she was too rich: They all wanted to wear the pants in the family.

Early in the film, Mary's fiancé, Philip Barton (Craig Stevens), comes to the ranch to tell Mary he can't marry her because he has fallen in love with a normal woman – one who will allow him to be the boss. Mary is distraught and decides to travel to Paris to forget her troubles. She stops in New York to visit her old school chum Annie Farrell (Mary McCarty), who owns a super-chic fashion salon and has been invited to Paris to present her latest designs at an international fashion show.

They decide that Mary will accompany Annie as one of her models; perhaps in Paris she can meet a man who will love her and not fear her money. They set sail for France on the *Liberté* – symbolic, one presumes, for Mary's future liberation from being single (seen in the 1950s by Hollywood as representing failure for any woman). On the ship, of course, is the stereotypical French gigolo, Pierre Duquesne, played by Gilbert Roland, a Mexican actor who usually played Latin lovers. A series of supercilious subplots are inject-ed into the film that do nothing to enhance it. Suffice it to say that Pierre and Mary fall in love and that the film is moved along by several musical num-bers – the last of which caused an immense amount of trouble.

In the grand finale, Jane Russell sings and dances "Lookin' for Trouble" at the fashion show. Why she does this is not apparent, but one assumes the fashions were not good enough to keep the attention of the buyers. Russell struts out on the runway and shakes, quakes, bumps, and grinds while sing-ing that she is, in fact, lookin' for trouble. On this high point the film ends.

There was no real problem with the script or the content of the film. Breen passed it but he knew that the combination of Howard Hughes and Jane Russell was dangerous. Breen warned RKO to make sure the women in the film were appropriately covered.[129]

When Breen saw the finished film some nine months after reviewing the script, he was determined to fight Hughes. Russell wore several low-cut eve-ning gowns and a bathing suit, and most of the women in the cast appeared in dance numbers that featured low-cut outfits. (It must be noted at this point that the dresses worn by Russell and other cast members would not have raised much fuss in 1954 at any society ball in the United States; they were in fashion, much as the costumes in *The Greatest Show on Earth* had been typical of the circus.) The bathing suit was a typical one-piece suit. The re-newed battle between Hughes and Breen was as much about *The Outlaw* as it was about *The French Line*.

After reviewing the film the PCA staff concluded that *The French Line* did not conform to PCA standards because "it seemed quite apparent" that the costumes "were intentionally designed to give the bosom peep-show effect beyond even extreme décolletage and far beyond anything acceptable under the Production Code."[130] RKO's request for a code was denied.

Hughes's reaction was novel. The reclusive billionaire did not fight Breen, did not ask for a review by the MPAA Board of Directors, nor take his case to the press; instead he simply ignored Breen and the MPAA and scheduled the world premiere of *The French Line* at the palatial Fox Theater in St. Louis for December 29, 1953. The choice of St. Louis was no accident: It was the home of Father Daniel Lord, author of the Production Code, and had a Catholic population of almost half a million. As always Hughes flooded the city with radio, television, and newspaper ads, as well as billboards, includ-ing a two-story-high poster of Russell that adorned the Fox Theater and an-nounced the imminent arrival of her new picture, in magnificent Technicolor enhanced by 3-D. Russell did her part to generate publicity by telling the press that she agreed with the censors: Too much of her *was* exposed.[131]

Unlike United Artists, which was not an MPAA member when it released *The Moon Is Blue*, RKO was a member in good standing; thus Hughes's action amounted to open revolution. Eric Johnston and Joe Breen clearly understood the challenge to their authority. In another example of the close relationship between the PCA and the Legion, Breen dispatched PCA staff member Jack Vizzard to St. Louis to plot strategy with Archbishop Joseph E. Ritter. As Vizzard later wrote: "What was at stake was the survival of the whole system, and even the whole concept, of achieving decency in the movies. A successful breakthrough by Hughes, exploiting the bulge created by Preminger, would spell eventual doom for the entire experiment."[132]

A bit exaggerated, perhaps, but it was clear that the MPAA and the Legion were taking Hughes's challenge seriously. The Legion quickly issued a condemnation of the film due to "grossly obscene, suggestive and indecent action, costuming and dialogue." It further warned that *The French Line* "is gravely offensive to Christian and traditional standards of morality and decency and is capable of grave, evil influence upon those who patronize it, especially youth."[133]

Archbishop Ritter, Rev. John Cody, and Vizzard spent two days together plotting ways to prevent the film from luring in customers. After Protestant and Jewish groups politely turned down an invitation to join a common protest and the St. Louis Police Department refused to seize the film, the three men composed a letter that was sent to all priests in the St. Louis diocese. The letter warned that if *The French Line* was successful, it would do "irreparable damage" to the Legion of Decency and the Production Code Administration. Catholics must therefore make a "concerted effort on a nation-wide scale to ruin the box-office receipts of this picture," the recipients were informed.[134]

On New Year's Day 1954, Archbishop Ritter took a significant gamble. In a statement read at all masses in the diocese, Ritter told the laity that *The French Line* was a film that will "destroy our American sense of morality and degrades all womanhood." It was an irresponsible film, and "since no Catholic can with a clear conscience attend such an immoral movie, we feel it is our solemn duty to forbid our Catholic people under penalty of mortal sin to attend" it. Ritter further imposed a "grave obligation" on all St. Louis Catholics to boycott any theater, now and in the future, that showed the film.[135]

It was a gamble because by pronouncing attendance at *The French Line* a mortal sin – the most serious category of Catholic sins – it now entailed the same spiritual penalty as murder! A Catholic with a mortal sin on his or her soul, and who had not since gone to confession or received the last sacrament, would suffer eternal damnation. Thus if, for example, an extremely pious but curious Catholic went to the Fox Theater in early January 1954 to see what all the fuss was about and was killed in an automobile accident on the way home, that person would be damned for eternity. As Jack Vizzard, who had studied for the priesthood before becoming a censor, noted: "That the eternal fate of a human being should have to be connected to Jane Russell's mammaries, no matter how heroic, was a bit much."[136]

To the Catholic hierarchy and Legionaries, however, this was no joking matter. "French Line Turned into Crusade," *Variety* trumpeted,[137] and indeed it was; but the Catholic campaign against Hughes was quieter than prior protests. The Legion was by now well aware that noisy picketers generated good box office. The Legion told priests, "the more adverse publicity we give to an offensive picture, the more people throng to see it." Local priests were urged to call on theater managers and ask them "as graciously and as diplomatically" as possible not to book the film. If the film was shown, they were urged to make "a temperate but heartfelt appeal" from the pulpit for Catholics to boycott the film and the theater.[138]

Behind the scenes priests were asked to check on the religion of local theater owners. If they were Catholic, additional pressure could be applied, including refusal to administer the sacraments.[139] Cardinal Spellman, visiting in Los Angeles, huddled with MGM's Louis B. Mayer and Joe Breen to discuss methods of halting *The French Line.* The prelate was furious when Joe Breen told him that RKO President James Grainger was Catholic and that Grainger's son, Edmund, a graduate of Fordham University, had produced the film. Spellman vowed "to lambaste" the errant Catholics.[140]

Catholics were certainly not alone in their protest against the film. It was banned in Pennsylvania, Kansas, and New York State, as well as in numerous cities across the country. Major theater chains, such as United Paramount, Interstate, and Texas Consolidated – even RKO Theaters, no longer connected to the studio – refused to book the film.

Despite all this, Hughes refused to budge. The MPAA fined RKO $25,000, which Hughes ignored. He did, however, give in to some of the state censors' demands, thereby opening *The French Line* to the lucrative New York audience, which paid big dividends. In May 1954 the film opened in Buffalo, where Bishop Joseph Burke followed Archbishop Ritter's example and made attendance for Catholics a mortal sin; but business at the Basil Lafayette in Buffalo boomed. When the film moved into Cardinal Spellman's territory, the Criterion Theater in New York City did $73,000 in two weeks, which the theater reported was its "best business in months."[141]

In San Francisco *Variety* reported "French Smash $18,000 in Frisco." RKO found theaters in Dallas, Houston, and San Antonio willing to book Hughes's film, and it ran "without incident." In Charlotte, North Carolina, local Legion officials decided to picket *The French Line,* but this had "little effect on the size of the crowds." The film brought in $12,000 at the Trans-Lux theater in Washington, D.C.[142]

People flocked to see *The French Line* despite its universal panning by film critics. Bosley Crowther told his New York readers it was "a cheap, exhibitionistic thing."[143] *Newsweek* wrote it was "more to be pitied than censored."[144] To the *New Yorker* it was "trash."[145] *Time* warned that the film "was long on notoriety and short on entertainment."[146]

Variety, always able to cut to the chase, told exhibitors the film would appeal "mostly to distaffers"; but exhibitors who were willing to "join Howard Hughes in side-stepping the industry's code regulations would seem to be in line for a fancy b. o. buck – as long as the controversy continues to be fanned."[147]

In fact, enough exhibitors did join with Hughes to make the film a box-office success. A dejected Msgr. Little informed Bishop Scully in September 1954 that *The French Line* had managed to play in more than four thousand theaters in the United States and Canada and generate just over $2 million in its initial run. "Any film," the Legion director told the bishop, "which makes over two-million dollars is considered to have reached a good market." The projected profit for *The French Line* was in the $300,000–400,000 range.[148]

There is little doubt that Hughes and RKO would have made more money had they caved in to PCA and Legion demands. They might also have had wider booking had not Hughes been considered a pariah by the Hollywood community: Exhibitors who had been willing to challenge both the Legion and the PCA over films like *The Bicycle Thief, La Ronde,* or *The Moon Is Blue* were unwilling to cross the line for the Hughes–Russell film. At the same time, however, it was also readily apparent that the old order was on the decline. Neither the PCA nor the Catholic church could keep people away from films of which they disapproved. It is inconceivable that there were not large numbers of Catholics who helped fill theaters in New York City, Buffalo, San Francisco and other cities when *The French Line* came to town.

Joe Breen certainly recognized that fact. He had been at the helm of the Production Code Administration for almost two decades when he informed Eric Johnston in February 1954 that he intended to retire. Breen was in poor health and no longer had the strength to cope with the strenuous demands of the PCA. He also recognized that his view of American morals and movies was no longer widely accepted. The Supreme Court decisions had severely undermined the system of controls that Breen had helped construct. Films he had fought to keep from the screen, like *The Moon Is Blue* and *The French Line,* were now accepted as mainstream entertainment by millions of American moviegoers.

Just months before his decision to retire, Breen had fought hard to tone down the sexuality of the film *From Here to Eternity.* In March 1954, as the Hollywood censor settled into his seat at the annual Academy Award ceremony in Los Angeles, he heard Hollywood's elite nominate Maggie McNamara for Best Actress in *The Moon Is Blue;* she later lost to Audrey Hepburn for her performance in *Roman Holiday,* but the point was clear. It became even clearer as the evening progressed: *From Here to Eternity* swept the 1954 awards with eight Oscars including Best Picture. No one knows what went through the censor's mind when emcee Donald O'Connor announced the presentation of an honorary Academy Award to Breen for "his conscientious, open-minded and dignified management of the Motion Picture Production Code."[149]

It was a shallow tribute in the best Hollywood tradition: If one word captured the Breen years at the PCA, it was not "open-minded." The censor had viewed the code as a Bible to be literally enforced. His inability to be more flexible and to understand the changing nature of American society had led to his downfall. It was not that Hollywood needed to be more violent or more risqué; it was that the industry needed to be able to make films for adults as well as for children. Breen, Martin Quigley, Father Lord, the Legion, and the code all viewed movies soley through the eyes of children.

In the ensuing decade, between 1955 and 1965, the debate over films would center on the issue of what was acceptable screen fare for adults. Hollywood fought to liberalize the code and expand freedom of expression for the screen, yet stubbornly resisted all efforts to limit audience by age. It was, ironically, forces within the Catholic church that began to pressure the industry to restrict attendance by age in return for a more liberalized screen. This battle is played out in the remaining chapters of this book.

His Oscar in hand, Breen stayed on at the PCA for a few months until the controversy over *The French Line* died. He then left the industry quietly and remained – until the recent interest in film censorship – a forgotten man. For decades the Hollywood histories and documentaries that chronicled the industry failed for the most part to mention him, or did so only in passing; yet Joseph Breen had had more influence on the content and structure of films than any other single person in the long history of Hollywood. From 1934 to 1954, Hollywood's golden age of studio production, producers had submitted more than seven thousand scripts and films for his inspection. His word was law during this long reign as he forced producers to alter plots, directors to reshoot scenes, and writers to rewrite dialogue that changed hundreds of films in very significant ways. Without Breen and his view of the code, the films of this era would have had a much different look, structure, and feel.

With Breen retired, his longtime second in command, Geoffrey Shurlock, took the reins of a beleaguered censorship office. Shurlock, born in England, had begun his Hollywood career as a script reader for Paramount in 1926. After moving to the Code office in 1932 he had experienced many battles with producers over film content. Everyone in the industry wondered whether Shurlock would attempt to resist the changing times or adopt a more flexible attitude toward the code he now had to enforce.

In New York, Legion officials watched the passing of their ally with some trepidation. Although they had not always agreed with Breen, he had been a staunch Catholic and respected by the hierarchy. More often than not, the Legion and Breen's PCA had worked hand in hand to control the moguls. The Legion had counted on him to tip them off quietly about upcoming films to whose material the Legion might object, and to share scripts and confidential information about Hollywood producers, directors, moguls, and even MPAA activities. The files of the PCA are full of Legion correspondence, and vice versa. It had been a cozy, often volatile, relationship that endured for two decades. Now the Legionaries wondered what their relationship with Shurlock would be like.

Ironically, in March 1954 another titan of the old order died. Will Hays, the original czar of the movies, passed away in his hometown of Sullivan, Indiana; his death, far from the glitter of Hollywood, got little notice in a town devoted to the present. The following year, Father Daniel Lord – who had paid little attention to either the movies or the code since the beginnings of World War II – died in St. Louis, ravaged by cancer. Only Martin Quigley remained, and he was determined to continue to fight.

CHAPTER 5

DECLINING INFLUENCE

The Legion of Decency . . . is able no longer to exert its previous
practical influence.
    – Martin Quigley to Cardinal Spellman, July 1956

In many real ways, Martin Quigley was the driving force behind the Legion
of Decency. He had been instrumental in the crafting of the Production
Code in 1930 and four years later had helped create the Legion to ensure that
the moguls would not ignore his concept of movie morals. In fact, it is safe
to say there would have been no Legion had it not been for Quigley's efforts.

For the next two decades he carefully constructed his image in Hollywood
and New York as the power broker behind the Legion. Quigley was often
photographed in the company of priests, bishops, and cardinals and was
awarded the papal Medal of St. Gregory in 1950 for his role in the Legion.
Whenever Quigley went to Los Angeles, he was careful to consult with Archbishop John Cantwell as well with his successor, James Francis Cardinal Mc-
Intyre, on movie morality. He used the editorial page of his *Motion Picture
Herald* as a bully pulpit to blast films, producers, and studios that he believed
had violated his tenets of morality. The moguls quaked when Quigley fulmi-
nated. It was a heady brew and one that Quigley enjoyed to the fullest.

His efforts paid big dividends for the publisher. Over the years, he had
played a major role in securing a Legion blessing for a large number of important films including *The Merry Widow, The Garden of Allah, Anna Karenina, Two-Faced Woman,* and *Forever Amber.* In the production of a host
of other films, producers and clerics alike had turned to Quigley to help them
find a way to reconstruct a bit of dialogue, cut a scene, or write a prologue
that would bring an extra dash of "moral compensation" to films that had
offended the Legion.

Leff and Simmons, in their account of film censorship, *The Dame in the
Kimono,* state that Quigley used to parade through the Oak Room in New
York's Plaza Hotel, a favorite haunt of industry power brokers, "at one o'-
clock on weekdays, a Legion of Decency prelate on each arm."[1] This was

most likely an apocryphal story but an important illustration of Quigley's image in the industry. He may not have had a priest on his arm every day at lunchtime, but he did have the ear of Francis Cardinal Spellman, Joseph Breen, and the various Legion directors. He could also summon Eric Johnston and every important studio executive in New York to the phone.

As formidable as Quigley appeared, however, by the early 1950s his power base was eroding. The U.S. Supreme Court was moving steadily toward allowing filmmakers more freedom of expression. Distributors and exhibitors were certainly more willing to book controversial films, and it was increasingly evident that a large segment of the public was no longer troubled by a more realistic treatment of social issues on the screen. As we have already seen, the very necessity of a Production Code was under intense scrutiny by a wide variety of people.

As disquieting as these trends were to Quigley, he was even more concerned by the fact that large numbers of Catholics were no longer willing (if ever they had been) to follow Legion classifications blindly. *The Outlaw, Duel in the Sun, Forever Amber, The Bicycle Thief, The Greatest Show on Earth,* and *The Moon Is Blue* had not suffered at the box office in traditional Catholic areas despite Legion efforts to discourage attendance.

As if this were not enough, in the summer of 1956 a prominent Catholic theologian published an article on censorship that questioned whether Catholic adults had any obligation to follow restrictions imposed by the Catholic hierarchy on their consumption of mass media. John Courtney Murray, S.J., was a leading Jesuit intellectual and editor of the highly respected *Theological Studies.* His article, "Literature and Censorship," was originally delivered as a lecture to the Thomas More Association and appeared in print in the July 1956 issue of *Books on Trial,* a publication that reviewed contemporary literature from a Catholic perspective.

Murray aired an issue that had been raging within Catholic theological circles for several years: What was the ecclesiastical authority to prohibit Catholics from attending certain films? Was it a mortal sin, as some American bishops had maintained, to attend a condemned film? Could well-informed, intelligent Catholic adults make up their own minds on whether or not a particular film might lead them into "an occasion of sin?"

Murray argued that censorship in a democratic society was a dangerous infringement on freedom of expression and should be conducted only within a rigidly defined legal structure to prevent or restrict pornography. Those who do the censoring must be highly trained, intelligent professionals not amateurs, he wrote. No censor, he maintained, should ever be allowed to "display moral indignation," "fussiness," or use personal judgment in evaluating a creative work. There was simply no room, in his opinion, for the "personal, the arbitrary, the passionate" among censors. Rather, he argued, censorship decisions should be "calm and cool, objective and unemotional."[2]

Although Murray was primarily concerned with the censorship of books, he also addressed the problem of "voluntary agencies" that "exercise some measure of surveillance, judgment, and even control of various media of communication." He did not specifically cite the Legion of Decency, but there is little doubt that he had that organization in mind. Murray had no argument with the right of voluntary agencies to pressure the media, but he did fault their "methods."[3]

Murray wrote that there could not be even the "slightest quarrel" when these voluntary agencies appealed for "voluntary cooperation" from producers and theater owners. He was less comfortable with secondary boycotts against a merchant or theater owner, which he believed verged "upon the coercive" when used by "citizen-groups in the interests of morality in literature or on the screen." It might be legal to use coercion, but Murray argued that it made Catholics appear "ridiculous." Instead of carrying placards in front of movie theaters, Catholics, he believed, had "to stand before the world as men and women of faith, and . . . of reason too."[4]

Interestingly, Murray did not believe that intelligent men and women needed any help in determining what was obscene. They have, he wrote, "a fairly clear notion of what obscenity" is, and "can make, for themselves, a pretty good judgment on whether a particular work is obscene." According to Murray, "the Code of Canon Law [canon 1399 established eleven categories of books Catholics were forbidden to read] seems to suppose that the ordinary Catholic can make this concrete judgment for himself. I repeat, for himself."[5]

Murray's article, published "with ecclesiastical approval," signaled an internal shift developing within the Catholic church over the role of movies.[6] His thinly veiled references to "amateur" censors making "arbitrary" and "personal" decisions was a slap at the Legion. Central to the debate, which took place on an international scale, was the role and scope of the American Legion of Decency and the authority of the hierarchy to dictate what movies Catholics could see. On one side stood a number of intellectually progressive clergy including Murray; Father John G. Ford, S.J., Professor of Theology at Weston College, Massachusetts; Father Harold C. Gardiner, S.J., author of *The Catholic Viewpoint of Censorship;* Father Gerald Kelly, S.J., Professor of Theology at St. Mary's College in Atchison, Kansas; and Father Francis J. Connell, C.SS.R., Dean of the School of Sacred Theology at Catholic University, Washington, D.C.

These priests saw the Legion of Decency as an organization that badly needed reform. They were not necessarily opposed to censorship, but they believed it should be applied sparingly. They did not envision in 1956, nor would they have supported, the orgy of violence, full-frontal nudity, simulated sex, and the use of four-letter words as punctuation that have dominated filmmaking in recent years. They were saying, however, that in their view movies could deal in a more direct and honest fashion with subjects like drug addiction, adultery, corruption, prostitution, divorce, and crime without corrupting Catholics. It is doubtful that Murray and others like him would have worried much about *The Moon Is Blue*.

In their view, the Legion, by condemning films like *Moon*, promoted an old-fashioned and negative image of Catholicism as an anti-intellectual religion in which the hierarchy banned the members from seeing or reading anything not approved by the church. To condemn a film, to resort to pickets and boycotts because it might have one or two scenes, or even a general theme, of which the clergy did not approve, made the Catholic church appear, as Murray had written, "ridiculous."

This issue of whether or not Legion ratings were binding on all Catholics had been under discussion for some time. As early as 1946, Catholic University's Francis J. Connell had stated in an article in *Ecclesiastical Review* that there was "no strict obligation in obedience to follow the Legion's decisions."[7] He repeated that view in a private letter to Msgr. Little in 1954 in response to a letter sent by Msgr. J. B. Montini, Assistant Secretary of State at the Vatican, to the International Catholic Office of Film in Brussels and forwarded to all national offices. Montini asserted that all of the national offices created by the hierarchy in the various nations (and the Catholic church had agencies similar to the American Legion of Decency in many) had an explicit mandate to make judgments on the moral character of individual films. Therefore, he wrote, "The faithful . . . have a duty to learn what these judgments are and to make their conduct conform to them."[8]

Montini's letter was submitted to Father John C. Ford, S.J., a professor of moral theology at Weston College, to determine whether or not there was foundation within canon law for Montini's conclusion. Ford, in a private memo circulated among the Catholic hierarchy, asserted that there was no "ecclesiastical law which makes the classifications of the Legion binding on the consciences of all United States Catholics." There was, he informed his superiors, no general law in the "*Codex Juris Canonici*, or in *Vigilanti Cura*, or in any other Papal document" of which he was aware. Montini's views, he continued, deserve "our respect" but "they are not authoritative in the sense that they impose obligations on the conscience of the faithful."[9]

Ford expanded his argument by telling his readers that it was common knowledge that many Catholics "pay little attention to the classifications of the Legion." In his view, as a moral theologian, "more harm than good is frequently done by the imposition and multiplication of ecclesiastical obliga-

Figure 1 (right). Hollywood censor Joseph Breen. Courtesy the Museum of Modern Art.

Figure 2. Gregory Peck and Jennifer Jones in David O. Selznick's *Duel in the Sun*. Courtesy the Museum of Modern Art.

Figure 3. Silvana Mangano in *Bitter Rice.* Courtesy the Museum of Modern Art.

Figure 4. Silvana Mangano in *Bitter Rice.* Courtesy the Museum of Modern Art.

Figure 5. Anna Magnani in *The Miracle.* Courtesy the Museum of Modern Art.

Figure 6. Otto Preminger directs Frank Sinatra and Kim Novak in *The Man with the Golden Arm.* Courtesy the Museum of Modern Art.

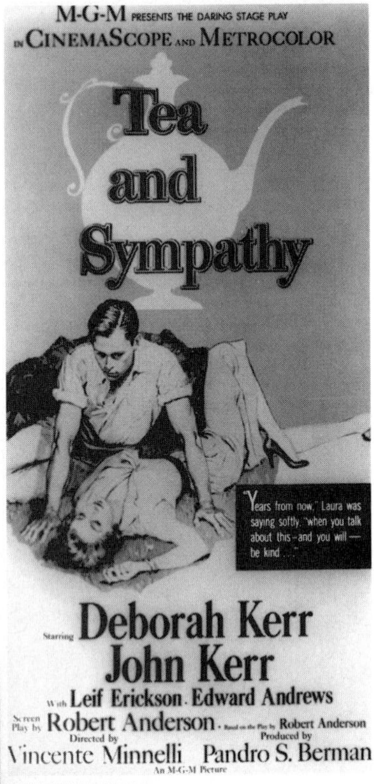

Figure 7 (right). Publicity poster for MGM's *Tea and Sympathy.* Courtesy the Museum of Modern Art.

Figure 8 (below). Deborah Kerr and John Kerr in *Tea and Sympathy.* Courtesy the Museum of Modern Art.

Figure 9. Carroll Baker in *Baby Doll.* Courtesy the Museum of Modern Art.

Figure 10. Eli Wallach and Carroll Baker in *Baby Doll.* Courtesy the Museum of Modern Art.

Figure 11. Paul Newman and Elizabeth Taylor in *Cat on a Hot Tin Roof.* Courtesy
the Museum of Modern Art.

Figure 12. Sue Lyon in *Lolita*. Courtesy the Museum of Modern Art.

Figure 13.
James Mason
and Sue Lyon in
Lolita. Courtesy
the Museum of
Modern Art.

Figure 14. Rod Steiger and Brock Peters in *The Pawnbroker.* Courtesy the Museum of Modern Art.

Figure 15. Richard Burton, Elizabeth Taylor, George Segal, and Sandy Dennis in *Who's Afraid of Virginia Woolf?* Courtesy the Museum of Modern Art.

tions binding under the pain of sin." Most Catholics did not understand – nor, as he told the hierarchy, did he himself understand – how "something is a mortal sin in one diocese or country and not in another." His conclusion was frank and direct: "There is no universal obligation binding Catholics in the United States under pain of sin to stay away from pictures classified as condemned by the Legion of Decency."[10]

Ford's memo was a bombshell at Legion headquarters in New York, and when Murray published a longer and more detailed version of his views (with coauthor Father Gerald Kelly, S.J.) in *Theological Studies* in 1957, it was clear to any interested Catholic that there was serious disagreement among clerics over the authority of the Legion.[11]

Not all Catholics agreed with Professors Murray, Connell, Ford, and Kelly, however. On the other side stood some of the most powerful members of the Catholic hierarchy, including Cardinal Spellman, Cardinal McIntyre of Los Angeles, Msgr. Little of the Legion and, of course, Martin Quigley, who was dismayed by the entire debate.

When Quigley saw Murray's article, he was outraged and fired off a letter to Bishop William A. Scully, Archbishop of Albany and Chairman of the Episcopal Committee for Motion Pictures. Quigley told Scully that Murray's position "reflects the whole chain of arguments we have been hearing from the Left" including, he added, "the Supreme Court." If Murray is correct in his assessment that individuals can make their own determination, Quigley concluded, then "all the agencies and all the persons who have been seeking to deal with the movie problem are in a straitjacket."[12] Scully was sympathetic. "The path is not easy for any of us," he told the publisher.[13]

As he often did, Quigley went around Scully and wrote directly to Cardinal Spellman. "Your Eminence, the situation is highly adverse," Quigley's letter began. "The prospect is that it will continue to worsen." Producers and directors "no longer abide by previous restraints," and the Legion "is able no longer to exert its previous practical influence," Quigley warned. "This seems mainly due to the failure of large numbers of the Catholic people to understand, accept or abide by the mandates of the Legion's classifications."[14]

In large measure, Quigley believed, Catholics ignored the Legion because of the "prevailing climate of thought relative to the individual's obligation under moral law." Quigley specifically cited Murray, and added that even in Spellman's archdiocese Catholics were being told that although the Legion's classifications are "a good sort of thing" they have no sanction of moral law. It seemed apparent, Quigley concluded, that "the moral line" for the movies can no longer be maintained.[15]

Spellman was upset by Quigley's letter, and especially distressed at the notion that parishioners in his diocese were being told that they did not have to follow Legion classifications. The Cardinal asked Quigley for specifics.[16]

Quigley was more than happy to oblige. In December, he told Spellman, he had gone to Mass at St. Augustine Church in Larchmont, New York, on the Sunday within the Octave of the Feast of the Immaculate Conception – traditionally the day on which the Legion pledge was administered. Father Joseph M. Moffitt, S.J., Assistant Dean at Georgetown, had given the sermon. The pledge, Moffitt had told the parishioners, was "a voluntary one" and did not bind them "under sin"; it "was not a sin to see a Condemned movie," he had stressed, and that anyone who did not wish to pledge should simply stand and remain silent.[17] One assumes that Quigley took the pledge, but he was not happy with Moffitt's assessment of the Legion.

It is not clear what happened to Father Moffitt, but it is doubtful that he was given clearance to appear in any official capacity by the Archdiocese of New York during the remainder of Spellman's tenure. What is certain is that by the late summer of 1956 there was strong disagreement within the Catholic church over the authority of the Legion to dictate to Catholics and that this debate had left academic halls and entered the churches. Catholics, in fact, may have been well ahead of the moral theologians. They were not especially shocked to learn they did not have to obey the Legion because there is little compelling evidence to suggest they had ever done so.[18]

Despite this lack of commitment on the part of millions of Catholics, Quigley, Spellman, Little, and Scully were determined to maintain as much Catholic control over the movies as they possibly could. Several films in the next few years would severely test their power as Hollywood experimented with themes that had not appeared onscreen in years.

In addition to all the problems faced by the Catholic hierarchy and the Legion, the Production Code Administration was undergoing its own internal debate over what was censurable. After Joseph Breen's resignation the directorship of the PCA had passed to his longtime assistant Geoffrey Shurlock. An Episcopalian and graduate of Dartmouth College, Shurlock had joined the staff of Hollywood censors in 1932, several years before Breen became director. He had served briefly as Acting Director during Breen's ill-fated attempt as an executive at RKO in 1940–1. When Breen returned to the PCA, Shurlock had faithfully returned to his role as second banana.

Shurlock, however, had not always agreed with his boss. For example, he had found the stage production of *The Moon Is Blue* to be "[a] lot of fun." The code provision stating that seduction could never be presented in a comedic manner was, in his view, "idiotic."[19] Jack Vizzard, who had worked with both Breen and Shurlock, wrote in his history of the PCA that Shurlock was much more willing than Breen to allow movies to portray sin. "If the Catholic Church," Shurlock told Vizzard, "is so weak that it cannot stand to see a little vice, then we cannot preserve it by hiding our heads in the sand."[20]

It was no industry secret that Martin Quigley and the Legion opposed Shurlock's appointment as director of the PCA; both were loath to see any non-Catholic assume a position of authority within the organization. Quigley lobbied hard for a candidate he and the Legion could influence, but Eric Johnston, well aware of Quigley's interference in PCA affairs, rewarded Shurlock for his long years of service with its directorship in 1954.

By the mid-1950s almost everyone except Quigley and the Legion agreed that some liberalization of the code was necessary. With little public fanfare, the PCA softened the old taboo on miscegenation, relaxed provisions on scenes with excessive drinking, and removed some of the "profane" words from the prohibited list; but the code, if taken literally, still prohibited any movie from dealing with narcotics, venereal disease, abortion, homosexuality, nudity, and crimes of revenge. It also prohibited filmmakers from making films that might feature a happy, fun-loving prostitute, or a hilarious bedroom farce, and discouraged films that featured divorce, organized crime, crimes of "apparent heroism," and corruption.

The question, however, was not what the code said, but how it would be interpreted in the atmosphere of the mid-1950s. State and municipal censorship boards were determined to continue as they had in the past, banning films they did not like. The Legion was determined to hold the line against films it considered immoral, but was sharply divided on where that line was. In contrast, the Supreme Court stood ready to overturn any censorship action that smacked of prior restraint.

In Hollywood, moreover, independent producers held the censors, the PCA, and the Legion in contempt. Even longtime supporters of the code within the traditional studios recognized that unless movies could deal with a much broader range of subjects fans would continue to sit at home in front of their televisions. Geoffrey Shurlock was under intense industry pressure to modernize the code yet maintain the PCA. Although he might be more liberal than Breen, he was still Hollywood's censor and had to enforce the code.

Over the next several years films with themes that had previously been banned from the screen – such as narcotic addiction in *The Man with the Golden Arm,* implied homosexuality in *Tea and Sympathy,* and unquenchable passion and lust in *Baby Doll* – would again test the limits of screen entertainment. Shurlock, the Legion, state and municipal censorship boards, the Supreme Court, and the American public would all attempt to define the limits of mass entertainment.

In 1949 a Chicago writer, Nelson Algren, published a "wonderfully poetic novel" about the pain and despair of drug addiction. Set in Chicago, it told the story of a young man, Frankie Machine, who fought and lost his battle to kick "the monkey off his back." He makes a living dealing cards but dreams of being a drummer in a band; yet escape from poverty and drugs is impossible for this dope addict.

His wife, who was crippled when Frankie smashed their car in a drunken stupor, nags him constantly about his weaknesses. She refuses to let him practice in their apartment and drives him into the arms of his beautiful neighbor, Molly, who lets Frankie practice in her apartment. Frankie, destined for self-destruction, rejects Molly's love and yields to the drugs he craves. He accidentally kills his pusher in a fight and, with the police about to arrest him, commits suicide. America's urban jungle has consumed another victim.

Algren, who lived in the slums of Chicago and hung out with drug peddlers and prostitutes, laced his book with colorful pushers, beautiful blondes, likable petty thieves, and an assortment of characters – some good, some evil – who inhabit America's urban underside. *The Man with the Golden Arm* was a best-seller and won the first National Book Award for fiction in 1950. *Time* found it "unbelievably sordid" but felt readers who stuck with the novel would emerge with some of Algren's "tender concern for his wretched, confused and hopelessly degenerate cast of characters."[21] Still, no matter how compelling was Algren's portrait of drug addicts, petty criminals, pimps, and prostitutes, the book was unfilmable under the Production Code: Any discussion of drugs, drug traffic, or addiction was banned by the code.

When first approached about adapting *The Man with the Golden Arm* in 1950, the PCA told independent producer Bob Roberts that the "basic story is unacceptable" and strongly suggested that he drop the project. When Roberts persisted, the PCA agreed to review his ideas but "gave him no encouragement and warned that he would encounter countless problems from the Legion of Decency, the Bureau of Narcotics, and state and municipal censorship boards if he attempted to film the novel."[22]

Roberts, however, was not easily discouraged. He bought the screen rights to the novel and signed the author to write the screenplay. Algren was not terribly excited about Hollywood or filmmaking and was never very comfortable in the glitter and glitz of Hollywood. He preferred the company of drug addicts, pushers, and prostitutes to Hollywood producers.

His politics were also all wrong for Hollywood circa 1950: He had openly supported the Hollywood Ten while living in Chicago, and in Los Angeles he made a point of hanging out with blacklisted screenwriters. Producer Bob Roberts tried to ignore Algren's politics, wining and dining him in the best Hollywood tradition. Algren saw through the sham and viewed Roberts "as a con man and a phony." He might have simply walked out of Hollywood except for the fact that Roberts had signed John Garfield to play the part of Frankie.[23] Algren and Garfield were soul mates and spent long hours together plotting Frankie Machine's screen image.

The early 1950s, however, were not the right time to do a film on dope addicts. FBI agents followed Algren around Hollywood, and Roberts had difficulty attracting financing and distributors to a project about dope written by a fellow traveler. When Garfield, harassed by the House of Un-American Activities Committee for his political views, died of a heart attack in 1952 there seemed little hope that *The Man with the Golden Arm* would ever appear on the screen.[24]

Just three years later conditions were vastly different. Otto Preminger did not care what the Production Code said about narcotics, was not frightened by the Legion or the Bureau of Narcotics, and was lucky that HUAC and McCarthy had by then been discredited. Preminger acquired the screen rights from Roberts, ignored Algren, and developed his own script, which he submitted to Geoffrey Shurlock in June 1955. Preminger told the censor that he believed "that this picture done with integrity can be a public service."[25]

Shurlock was not convinced; he flatly refused to consider Preminger's version. When a revised script was submitted three months later, Shurlock again rejected it and advised Preminger that in addition to drug problems the film had to avoid using suicide as a plot device, could not show women doing "bumps and grinds" in a strip bar, and had to tone down the general level of violence.[26] Preminger, as in the case of *The Moon Is Blue,* simply did not respond.

A rough cut of the film was completed in November 1955. It starred Frank Sinatra as Frankie Machine, a heroin addict; Eleanor Parker as his wife, Zosch; Kim Novak as Molly, Frankie's true love; Darren McGavin as Louie, Frankie's pusher; and Arnold Stang as Frankie's buddy, Sparrow, a street punk.

The film opens with Frankie returning to his old haunts in Chicago fresh from drug rehabilitation. He is determined to stay clean and refuses a standing offer to return to his old job as a dealer at an illegal poker game; but staying clean is never in the cards for Frankie. His wife, Zosch, is a bitter shrew who has been confined to a wheelchair after a drunken Frankie crashed their car. She constantly reminds him that her confinement is the result of his weakness.

Frankie dreams of escaping from his miserable life by becoming a drummer in a band. Zosch objects to his practicing in their apartment and urges him to return to his old job of dealing, which he does. His neighbor Molly, a B-girl in a low-life saloon in the movie, falls for Frankie and lets him practice in her apartment. The two misfits fall in love, but Frankie refuses to leave his wife because she is crippled. It appears, however, that he will finally break out of his vicious circle: He is invited to audition for a job with a band.

Fate, however, intervenes to prevent Frankie from grasping the American dream. His old boss begs him to deal one last game: a big-stakes ordeal that will last for days. Frankie agrees, and when he takes a fix to keep him going he quickly falls back into the horror of heroin. He is caught cheating at the big game, is beaten to a pulp, and then blows the audition when he tries to play in a drug-induced fog.

In the meantime, Frankie's pusher, Louie, discovers that Zosch is not crippled after all: She has been faking her injury to keep Frankie from leaving. When Louie threatens her with blackmail, she pushes him down a flight of stairs, and he is killed. The police, however, suspect Frankie is the killer. (In the book, recall, it was indeed Frankie who killed Louie.) Frankie knows he must face the police but also knows he can't do it high on drugs; so he stays in Molly's apartment to go through "cold turkey" withdrawal. For days Frankie goes through hell as his body demands a fix. The tormented junkie screams for drugs, but Molly refuses to let him shoot up. He emerges from his ordeal shaken but clean.

Free from drugs, Frankie summons up the courage to face the police and his wife. He goes to his apartment and confesses to Zosch that he and Molly are in love. Zosch is devastated and, as Frankie walks out the door, she leaps up from her wheelchair and runs into the hallway – where the police are waiting. When she sees the police Zosch knows immediately that they suspect her in Louie's death. In desperation she leaps out a window to her own death.

In the final scene Frankie looks at Zosch's body for a moment, and then he and Molly slowly walk away – not into the happy sunset of so many Hollywood fantasies, but into Chicago's urban maze of uncertainty. Whether they will move to the suburbs and live in middle-class respectability or fall further into drugs and despair is anyone's guess.

When Shurlock viewed the finished film he believed he had little choice but to reject it. Preminger had taken some of the sting out of the novel: Frankie is not a murderer and does not commit suicide; his wife kills the pusher and leaps to her death when she is about to be captured by the police; and Frankie and Molly, in the best Hollywood tradition, find true love. Nevertheless, Frankie is a junkie; no one could possibly miss that point. *The Man with the Golden Arm* not only dealt with drugs but did so in a very graphic manner. In one two-minute sequence, Frankie's pusher prepares his heroin in water, heats it in a spoon, and, just offscreen, injects Frankie with his fix. The America that Preminger painted in *The Man with the Golden Arm* was not the typical view of American life perpetrated by Hollywood; it was grimy and filled with a hopelessness that created little sympathy for the disreputable characters who fill the screen – and no one from the police, the church, or the state cared what happened to them.

When Preminger showed a rough cut of the film to United Artists President Arthur B. Krim, the executive declared: "We at U.A. are proud to be associated with a motion picture of this outstanding caliber. We are confident that the Motion Picture Association of America will recognize its immense potential for public service and grant the film a Production Code seal."[27]

The ball, as the saying goes, was clearly in the MPAA's court. The *New York Times* told readers that Shurlock had rejected the script and that it was "inconceivable that" he "could, of his own authority, do an about-face . . . and approve the picture." It would be, the paper reported, up to the MPAA board either to "suspend or alter the prohibitions" on drug addiction.[28] As the paper predicted, Shurlock denied a seal to UA, and the film went to New York for the judgment of the board.

The MPAA Board of Directors gathered in New York in early December to consider Preminger's *Man with the Golden Arm.* Even though MPAA President Eric Johnston told board members that in his view the taboo on films dealing with drugs needed to be revised, the board, still embarrassed by the flap over *The Moon Is Blue,* flatly refused to bend the rules for Otto Preminger.[29]

What was surprising was UA's reaction to the MPAA's refusal to grant a production seal. United Artists, which had rejoined the MPAA after the release of *The Moon Is Blue,* had issued a statement at that time qualifying the studio's commitment to the Production Code. "We have always made it clear that we were in favor of self-regulation to prevent obscenity from reaching the screen"; however, "[a]t the same time, we are interested in preserving the right of our independent producers to bring adult entertainment to the screen."[30] When the MPAA declared *The Man with the Golden Arm* unfit entertainment, UA withdrew once again from the organization and opened the film in New York after the state censorship board approved it.

"Why there should be any question about showing *The Man with the Golden Arm* . . . is a puzzlement," wrote *New York Times* film critic Bosley Crowther.[31] *Variety* told exhibitors it was "a gripping, fascinating film" that made a "powerful condemnation of the use of narcotics."[32] *Saturday Review* told its readers the film was worth "cheering about" and featured a "virtuoso performance" by Frank Sinatra.[33]

Those reviews greatly influenced the Legion of Decency, which was carefully monitoring public reaction to Preminger's latest challenge to the MPAA. A few days after the film opened in New York twenty-five Legion reviewers from the IFCA joined Msgr. Little and Mary Looram to watch Frankie Machine's battle with addiction. Some of the Legion evaluators voted for condemnation, but the majority favored a B rating. As Msgr. Little explained to Bishop Scully, *The Man with the Golden Arm* was no "lily," but Legion officials and reviewers did not believe a C rating would "be sustained by the public." Little noted that none of the reviewers in the secular press "raised the issue" of an immoral theme. He also told Bishop Scully it was clear that the code would eventually be amended to allow drug themes, and so it was pointless, he believed, to condemn the film.[34]

Little's assessment was right on target. Although some states demanded that the scene in which Frankie gets his fix from his pusher be cut or trimmed, the film encountered less opposition than was expected. The Legion's B allowed the theater circuits to book the film without fear of generating local protests. Loew's, for example, which had refused *The Moon Is Blue,* booked *The Man with the Golden Arm* into its circuit. *Variety* noted that *Man* was "giant" at the Victoria Theater in New York City in its opening week and was still doing a "smooth" $29,500 after a month at the theater.[35] It did excellent business as it traveled across the country. In Chicago, where Algren was well known, the film played to packed houses at the Woods Theater for over a month.[36] It did solid box office at the Fox Beverly in Los Angeles and broke records in Philadelphia at the Stanton Theater. *Variety* reported that it was "golden" at the Penn in Pittsburgh and, despite near-zero temperatures and a crippling snowstorm, it outgrossed all but two films playing in St. Louis.[37]

Although the PCA was determined to keep any discussion of drugs off the screen, it was obvious to most people that a film about drug addiction was not that shocking; in fact, stories about drugs were regularly beamed into American homes. Jack Webb, the producer and star of *Dragnet,* one of TV's most popular programs, told reporters in 1956 that thirteen of his segments had had a drug theme and "nobody got aroused over them." When he developed a feature-film script that contained a drug theme and was told by Shurlock that it could not be approved by the PCA, he was shocked. "They turned me down," Webb told *Variety.*[38]

Ironically, in many ways television had more freedom than the movies in the mid-1950s. Programs like *Playhouse 90, The Kraft Television Theater,* and *Studio One* often presented more realistic drama than was allowed on the screen. This fact was not lost on the industry, which had been steadily losing market share to its small-screen competitor for years. Within a few months after the release of *The Man with the Golden Arm* the MPAA began the process to amend the Production Code. In May 1956, a special ad-hoc committee of the MPAA began studying ways to modernize the code. The committee comprised Eric Johnston, Barney Balaban representing Paramount, Abe Schneider from Columbia, and RKO President Daniel O'Shea. O'Shea, a devoted Catholic, was a mole for the Legion of Decency, meeting regularly with Msgr. Little and Martin Quigley to report on committee activities.[39]

The ad-hoc committee deliberated code amendments for more than six months. Shurlock, summoned to New York to present his views, told the committee that in his opinion "almost anything can be treated as a story subject under the Code . . . provided it is done with taste." O'Shea immediately warned the Legion that Shurlock's views could "make for trouble" for the Legion.[40] His warning seemed accurate when Shurlock paid a courtesy call on Msgr. Little at Legion headquarters and told him that any subject could indeed be made into a movie if treated with "reasonably good taste."[41] Little was polite, but shuddered at what Hollywood might consider good taste.

In November, the committee recommended that the provisions in the code against any treatment of abortion, prostitution, narcotics, and miscegenation be lifted as long as the treatment was done in "good taste." Presumably, this would allow filmmakers and censors alike a bit more freedom and flexibility. While no other changes were recommended – nudity and sexual perversion were still banned – it was obvious that times were changing.

A film that alluded to homosexuality illustrated how far both Hollywood and the American public had come by 1956 – and, at the same time, how far there was yet to go for some of the realities of life to be approached on the screen.

In 1953 Robert Anderson's play *Tea and Sympathy* opened on Broadway. It was, along with *The Tea House of the August Moon* and *The Caine Mutiny Court-Martial,* a smash hit. The play, set at a private boarding school for boys, centered around a sensitive boy who is different from the others and is, in an atmosphere of conformity, falsely branded as homosexual. It was a daring theme in 1953, when Senator Joseph McCarthy was using investigations and innuendo to charge that liberals were either communists or communist sympathizers. McCarthy's assault on liberals created an atmosphere of fear in America that resulted in a national obsession for conformity. In the early 1950s people who were different – who dressed differently, who thought freely, and who did not run with the crowd – were often accused of subversion. *Tea and Sympathy* asked a very thoughtful question to a society beset by fear: What does it mean for an individual to be branded as different?

The play's central character, Tom Lee, is a young sensitive boy who hears the "beat of a different drummer."[42] Rather than the stereotypical rough-and-tumble teenager, he is solitary, pensive, and shy – an intellectual who enjoys reading and writing poetry more than playing the rugged team sports that all boys who want to become men play. At a school that worships manliness and rugged sports more than intelligence, Lee is a misfit. Even though he is an excellent tennis player, for example, his style is to hit lobs and drop shots. This infuriates his stronger opponents, who are humiliated to be defeated by such "girlish" methods.

As the play unfolds the audience learns that Tom's parents are divorced and that he has been shuffled off to one boarding school after another for most of his 18 years. His father is a boorish, dominating man who sired a son in a feeble attempt to save his marriage. When his marriage failed he gave little attention to Tom other than to develop a fetish that he would be a real man: wear his hair short, play football, and chase girls. Tom, much to his father's dismay, just doesn't fit this mold.

At school Tom is housed with housemaster Bill Reynolds and his vivacious young wife, Laura. Reynolds, a faculty member at the school, is obsessed with making men of the young boys in his charge. He takes them hiking, plays ball with them, and engages in rough-and-tumble games as if he were 16. It is quite clear in the play that Reynolds is resisting his own latent homosexuality by being overly aggressive in his manly role with the boys and inexplicably passive with his beautiful young wife. In the play it is clear that his marriage is unhappy and that his bluster is a cover for his own internal battles.

Laura's job as his wife is to mother the boys and give them "tea and sympathy" whenever they need it. She is frustrated in her marriage and furious at her husband and the other boys for the way they unmercifully razz Tom about his hair, his mannerisms, his love of poetry and books. Laura is really annoyed when she discovers that Tom has attempted to prove his manhood to them by arranging a "date" with the town whore, a waitress in a local dive. When Tom is unable to perform with this trollop, Laura alone realizes it is not his sexuality, but his personality. Tom must be in love in order to make love. At this point Laura realizes she must go beyond the traditional tea and sympathy.

After telling her husband she is leaving him, her final act of defiance is to help Tom prove he is a real man. Knowing that the boy has a crush on her, she enters his room and begins to unbutton her blouse. She walks across the room to Tom's bed, gently takes his hand, and, as the curtain begins to fall, says: "Years from now – when you talk about this – and you will! – be kind." When the lights came up, there was not a dry eye in the house.

The play, which starred Deborah Kerr as Laura, John Kerr (no relation) as Tom, and a hulking Leif Erickson as Bill, was a Broadway hit. Under the guiding hand of director Elia Kazan, it ran ninety-one weeks at the Ethel Barrymore Theatre on Broadway and immediately attracted the attention of many Hollywood studios and independent producers, even though its dual themes of homosexuality and adultery were sure to cause problems with the censors. *Variety* told readers that the play was "too strong a brew for the majors" and predicted that only an independent producer could bring it to the screen. The play would, *Variety* warned, "have to undergo drastic changes," no matter who produced it.[43]

It certainly worried the PCA that a studio might attempt to make a film from such a controversial property. The problem with a film version was twofold. First, in the play the theme of homosexuality was ever present. Although Tom was not gay, he was suspected of being gay and was the target of constant ridicule. When he was seen sunning and swimming in the nude with one of the teachers who was gay, the teacher was fired, and suspicions grew that Tom was also "funny." It was also strongly implied throughout the play that Bill Reynolds, Tom's housemaster, fought his own homosexual feelings and was so hard on Tom because he suspected him of being gay. Further, Reynolds was unable or unwilling to "love" Laura, who complained bitterly that his attempts at lovemaking were brutal. At one point in the play she reproaches her husband for his refusal to touch her.

On top of this basic theme of homosexuality was female sexuality. Laura is quite open in stating her needs. In the play one of the other faculty wives flaunts her sexuality at the boys for fun, purposely wearing low-cut dresses at the school dances and constantly flirting with the young men in her house. Laura, encouraged by her to do the same, refuses; however, she is clearly drawn to Tom and willingly commits adultery with him to prove to him that he is not "different."

From the PCA perspective it was seemingly a no-win situation: If Tom was gay, the film had to be banned; nor could it be implied that the faculty of a boarding school for boys was riddled with homosexuals and flirtatious faculty wives. If, however, Tom was not gay and made love with Laura, then the film justified not only adultery, but adultery between a schoolboy and a mature woman – the wife of a faculty member!

Despite the fact that Laura's husband was a brute, Tom's father a pompous fool, and the other boys at the school (with the exception of Tom's roommate) complete morons, the PCA was horrified that this type of situational ethics might be seen as acceptable by millions of young women. Moreover, the only characters in the play and movie who would generate any audience sympathy were Tom and Laura – and they, of course, were sinners. This challenged a fundamental precept of the code, that sin and sinners could never be presented in a sympathetic manner. The creative talents of Hollywood pondered this complex problem: If Tom was not homosexual, how does Laura convince him without having sex with him?

Martin Quigley was very worried. He admitted the play was "beautifully written, produced and performed," but was terrified that it might become a movie. He warned the Hollywood censors that the play was dangerous and was pleased when they assured him that the PCA would be "compelled" to reject it.[44]

Nonetheless, interest in *Tea and Sympathy* in Hollywood was very strong. Paramount, Columbia, MGM, and Twentieth Century–Fox, along with several prominent independent producers, including Samuel Goldwyn, sent queries to the PCA about the suitability of the play as screen entertainment. So many inquiries came flooding into the censorship office that a slightly harried

Shurlock admitted, "I rehearsed our Code reaction" in order to be sufficiently negative.[45] Those who inquired were told that "even inferences" of homosexuality would be unacceptable, and there could be no justification of adultery at the end of the story.[46] Columbia and the independents quickly bowed out of the running, but industry giants Paramount and MGM remained interested despite PCA objections. Both studios sent delegations of executives to the Ethel Barrymore Theatre in New York.

Paramount President Barney Balaban was "greatly interested" in the play. When the studio suggested that "moral compensation" could be satisfied by punishing both the boy and the wife who seduces him into manhood, the PCA stood firm: "If adultery achieves its purpose of awakening the young man's manhood, it is still justified" and thus unacceptable as screen fare.[47]

MGM executives also spent an evening on Broadway. After viewing the play, MGM President Nicholas Schenck told Shurlock that he "saw nothing objectionable" and committed the studio to the project.[48] The studio moved quickly, acquiring the screen rights for $200,000 and hiring Anderson to tone down his play for the movie version.

In order to help prepare an acceptable script, the studio asked the PCA for an unofficial evaluation of the Broadway production. Such a request was not unusual: The PCA often read novels and short stories in advance of script preparation, and the New York office often sent evaluations of plays to the PCA Hollywood office. It was unusual, however, for two members of the West Coast staff to travel to New York to do an on-site inspection. *Tea and Sympathy* was controversial enough for Geoffrey Shurlock and his assistant Jack Vizzard to take the long train ride from Los Angeles to New York to determine whether *Tea and Sympathy* could be granted a code seal.

After an evening on Broadway, the two censors met director Elia Kazan and author Robert Anderson. The meeting was friendly, but the PCA officials were discouraging, especially after Anderson insisted that in the movie Tom clearly be accused of being a homosexual, that he first attempt to prove his manhood with the local whore and, finally, that Laura seduce him.[49] Shurlock, not convinced that any of this was permissible, returned to Los Angeles without making any commitments.

After this initial meeting, it took almost two years for Anderson to develop a screenplay for *Tea and Sympathy*. He softened the homosexual theme for the movie by cutting the discussion of Tom sunbathing in the nude with a faculty member, and made it less clear that Bill Reynolds was fighting his own sexual identity. He completely cut the scenes of the other faculty wife telling Laura how much fun it was to show the young boys a little skin.

The script called for the film to open with Tom returning to the school for a ten-year reunion and quickly established that he was married, had children, and was a successful author. The audience thus immediately knew this man was not a homosexual, and soon learned he had written a successful novel based on his experiences at school. The book confronted his struggle with his own sexuality and, course, detailed his encounter with Laura.

As the film opens, Tom has returned to his school after a long absence for a class reunion. He drifts over to his old room, where he encounters an aging Bill Reynolds, who gives him a letter that Laura had written to Tom years ago. As a theatrical device the letter was intended as a confession of wrongdoing by Laura; in it she tells Tom (and the audience) that they were wrong to commit adultery and that it ruined her marriage.

From this beginning, the script flashes back in time as Tom relives his years at school. He is persecuted by the boys in the school because he walks in a funny manner, plays tennis strangely, puts up curtains in his room, and enjoys sewing. Shurlock, however, did not think the script went far enough, and told the studio that "no change can be made that will effectively meet Code requirements and still keep the story . . . as presented on the stage."[50] MGM was irate when it received a rejection from the censor. Instead of caving in, as the studios had for over two decades, they challenged the PCA verdict and demanded that Eric Johnston and the MPAA board of directors evaluate their script.

The topic for the MPAA board meeting on April 29, 1955, was the script for *Tea and Sympathy*. Dore Schary represented MGM; Shurlock presented the PCA's case. Schary emphasized the changes MGM had made and the broad popularity of the play. Few Americans, he stressed, were shocked by *Tea and Sympathy*. Shurlock countered that the basic theme of the play was banned by the Production Code and that the minor changes made by MGM had not altered that theme. After hearing both sides the board directed the two parties to negotiate a compromise that would allow MGM to make the film and the PCA to issue a seal. It took several months before Shurlock was satisfied that there was "no spot [in the script] where it could be inferred that anybody is afraid he [Tom] is a homosexual."[51] He told MGM that a seal was now possible.[52]

Although the PCA was now mollified, the Legion was horrified when a newspaper account of the compromise was published. Msgr. Little fired off a missive to Nicholas Schenck in New York warning him that the Legion viewed Anderson's play "to be gravely offensive."[53] The threat was clear: The Legion stood ready to condemn a filmed version of *Tea and Sympathy* no matter how sanitized it might be.

Legion threats no longer caused the studios to quake in fear. MGM went ahead with the project, confident that their version of life at an eastern boys' school would be a smash hit on the screen and would not in fact bring a Legion condemnation. Almost a year from the date of Little's warning to the studio, Legion reviewers Mary Looram and her IFCA colleagues, along with

Msgr. Little and his new assistant Father Paul Hayes, gathered to watch *Tea and Sympathy,* which had been granted PCA seal no. 18176 by Geoffrey Shurlock.

The women of the IFCA saw serious moral problems with *Tea and Sympathy.* They did not view Tom as a homosexual, and read Bill Reynolds as just another insensitive male. Shurlock and Anderson had succeeded, it appeared, in masking the theme of homosexuality. The women were instead concerned about Tom's evident virility! They saw a young man falsely accused who was secretly in love with a faculty wife and had allowed himself to be seduced by her. They were shocked that neither of the two sinners, Laura and Tom, appeared sufficiently remorseful about their act of adultery.

The negotiations with MGM were now in the hands of Msgr. Little, who was most concerned about the letter that Laura wrote to Tom. The purpose of the letter was to let audiences know that the act of kindness that Laura bestowed on Tom has ruined her life and her marriage. In the original letter, written by Anderson, Laura tells Tom she has just finished reading his novel. "It is a lovely book, tender and romantic and touching. And in it I come out rather like a saint. But, Tom, that isn't the whole picture, or even a true picture." She continues and tells Tom that their affair ruined Bill's life and that she sacrificed her marriage by making the easy decision. "The blame is all mine," she adds, because "you had no part in the decision I made." She concludes by reminding Tom that every decision is like a pebble dropped in the water because "there are ever-widening circles of ripples. There are always consequences."[54]

This confession of guilt, as strong as it seems, did not satisfy the Legion's demand for moral correctness. The religious censors demanded that some additional lines of dialogue (which could be incorporated into the Laura's letter to Tom) be inserted into the film that would "point up the immorality and the repercussions which came to the young man as result of Miss Kerr's so-called 'heroic act.'" The Legion wanted Tom punished for his participation in the sin.

To a point MGM was willing to appease the Legion because changing Laura's letter to Tom required only recording a new voice-over to the film. However, even this was complicated by the fact that Deborah Kerr was vacationing in England. Production chief Dore Schary approved a new letter drafted by Anderson in which Kerr told Tom he had "romanticized the wrong we did." Kerr cut her vacation short and dashed to a recording studio in London to read her new confession.

When Msgr. Little heard the new letter he was furious that the wording "had not been submitted to the Legion" before it was recorded, and again he threatened MGM with a condemnation. The priest told the studio that in his view Laura's admission that she had been "wrong" was "too elastic and needs replacement by something of a stronger nature to pinpoint the gravity of adultery."[55]

In an attempt to satisfy Little, Charlie Reagan, MGM vice-president, met with Martin Quigley, Looram, and Msgr. Little to try to compose a letter that would be both dramatically and morally correct. After several hours of work a new letter, written by Quigley, was approved by Msgr. Little. Quigley's letter, like Anderson's original, started with Laura telling Tom that she would probably not send him the letter, but then had several additions (shown here in italics): "Perhaps in the cold light of morning *it will be just another addition to my lengthening list of regrets.*" Instead of telling Tom that his book is "not the whole picture," Quigley's Laura states unequivocally that in the book "*I come out rather too well. You have romanticized the wrong we did, you have evaded the unpleasant reality.*" After admitting that their sexual encounter ruined her marriage, Laura now writes: "*In answering your cry I took the easier way, and unhappily the wrong way.*" Finally, Laura lectures Tom that "They say about dreadful experiences if they don't kill us, they make us strong *if we choose to learn their lessons. I now take much needed comfort in the thought that we both have chosen to learn.*"

With those added words of contrition Little believed audiences would clearly understand that Laura and Tom had sinned and suffered for their moment of weakness. He told Reagan that "this corrected version would raise the picture from C to B." It is clear that the real issue was power, not morality. The lines of voice-over Quigley wrote, and Little approved, did not substantially alter the moral message of *Tea and Sympathy;* they did, however, establish who was in control.[56]

Schary understood what the Legion was doing, and when he read what Reagan had approved he went ballistic. The studio had planned to open *Tea and Sympathy* at the Radio City Music Hall in New York City in late September. The production chief immediately called Russell Downing at the Music Hall to see if the theater had been pressured by the Legion to refuse the film if it was condemned. When Downing assured him that he had had no contact with the Legion, Schary sent word to Little that MGM was prepared to "release the picture as a Condemned product and reap the fruits of the added publicity." This decision, Schary told Little, had the full backing of the MGM–Loew's executives.[57]

Although Schary wanted to challenge the Legion, Reagan once again tried to reach a compromise among the warring parties. The MGM vice-president brought Robert Anderson, Martin Quigley, and Legion officials together for one last attempt to rewrite Laura's letter. Quigley did not help matters when he told Anderson that the film constituted "a serious moral danger." The playwright countered that the Production Code Administration "was perfectly satisfied" with the film and that he "had already gone too far as an artist" in changing his work. The whole point of his film, Anderson told Quigley and Little, was "to understand your fellow man and be tolerant towards him." It is not clear that they understood the point he was making. In frustration, Anderson stalked out of the meeting.[58] It seemed clear that a Legion condemnation was inevitable.

Three days later *Tea and Sympathy* was again screened by Legion officials. In addition to the IFCA staff reviewers, Little, in a highly unusual move, invited Bishop Scully and thirty-eight other prominent Catholics and clerics to judge the film. In this new group of movie critics were professors of moral theology from New York's Dunwoodie Seminary, a leading training ground for Catholic priests, and several influential priests from the Chancery Office of the Archdiocese of New York. Fifteen priests in total, including several critical of the Legion, were brought in to judge the morality of *Tea and Sympathy*. Added to this stellar panel of moralists were the leading lay Catholics in New York.

The version of the film that was screened for this august audience was exactly the same as the original version scheduled for condemnation by the Legion except for the revised letter (Anderson's version) read by Deborah Kerr. After the screening there was a very animated discussion. Martin Quigley was "vehemently opposed" to the film and argued that it must be condemned because Tom was a homosexual. Quigley was taken aback when many of the new consultants, including several priests, openly challenged his reading of the film. As Little later admitted, there was no consensus: Some judged the film offensive and agreed with Quigley that it deserved a C; others argued for a B or even for the recently adopted rating of A2 (unobjectionable for adults). Since no consensus was reached, each person was asked to submit a written evaluation of the film, to be considered in the Legion's final rating.

Two days after the screening Bishop Scully met with Martin Quigley and the Legion staff to classify *Tea*. Quigley continued to press for a condemnation. The clerics and Quigley poured over the advertising copy, the evaluations, the text of Laura's letter, and the Production Code. The position of the ad-hoc group of thirty-eight evaluators was interesting. Only four priests voted to condemn the film; eleven lay reviewers, however, thought it should be condemned. Eleven of the fifteen priests placed the film in either the B or the A2 category.[59] As one priest who recommended an A2 wrote, "we cannot deny the right to movies to present this subject matter [homosexuality and adultery]." A lay evaluator noted that in his view the film was "rather restrained": There was "no evil suggestiveness; no unhealthy arousal of morbid interest."[60]

John E. Fitzgerald, a respected film critic for *Our Sunday Visitor*, was not present for the meetings but had submitted his private assessment of the film to Little. In his view *Tea* was "a mature and moral film." He predicted that it would be a "box-office hit" and told the head of the Legion that he could not "find anything in *Tea and Sympathy* that would cause others to sin."[61]

Bishop Scully had the final word. He read all the written evaluations, considered Quigley's interpretation of the film as well as Fitzgerald's, and concluded that the issue of homosexuality had been sufficiently disguised and Laura's confession given enough "contrition and remorse" for the film to be granted a B classification.[62]

Scully's final ruling was based on several factors. First, he believed that the large group of Catholics called upon to judge the film accurately reflected the likely reception of the general public: Although the group was split, more individuals believed the film should not be condemned than believed it should be. It also is curious that the group included some highly visible critics of the Legion. Bishop Scully had had final approval of those invited, and that message was not lost on Msgr. Little. The bishop was also impressed by the effort MGM had made to satisfy Legion demands, despite its refusal to do absolutely everything Little and Quigley believed necessary. Although no direct evidence remains, it can be surmised that Scully did not agree with Little's insistence on another rewrite of Laura's letter to Tom. He judged Anderson's version satisfactory.

It was Bishop Scully who argued most strongly against condemnation, and the other clerics, Little included, followed his lead. Finally, like the clerical critics of the Legion, Scully feared that a condemnation of *Tea* would be a public relations error. After making his decision, Scully told Little to follow the "reaction of the public" closely.[63]

It did not take long to judge public reaction. *Tea and Sympathy* opened nationwide on September 28, 1956. As John Fitzgerald had predicted, it did a bonanza of business at the box office. The Radio City Music Hall took in $155,000 in the opening week, and MGM took in another $436,000 in the first week of national distribution. The film was not the box-office champion of 1956 – the Legion was pleased that Cecil B. DeMille's *The Ten Commandments* took that honor, generating more than $43 million – but *Tea* made a profit and, more important, drew hardly a peep of protest as it played throughout the country.

In New York, Martin Quigley was incensed that Bishop Scully had overruled him. For two decades Quigley's opinions on movies and morality had dominated the Legion. This was not the first time Quigley's views on a film were rejected, but it was the first time he had gone all out for a condemnation of a film and been overruled. The Catholic publisher was determined to fight to keep the Legion from becoming more liberal in its views of what was morally acceptable screen entertainment.

Quigley, however, seriously miscalculated his power base vis-à-vis Scully. The bishop was furious that Quigley had dared to tell him what was moral, and deeply resented his continuing efforts to control the Legion. Scully and Little had both heard the comments from Hollywood insiders that Quigley *was* the Legion. Shortly after the final confrontation between the bishop and and publisher over *Tea and Sympathy,* Scully ordered Msgr. Little "to break down the reputation" of Quigley "in the motion picture industry of being the 'Legion of Decency.'"[64] Bishop Scully wanted nothing more to do with Quigley, and instructed Little to do whatever he could to convince industry officials that Quigley did not speak for the organization.

The fight over *Tea and Sympathy* marked the beginning of a curious contest between the Catholic hierarchy and a Catholic layman over what subjects movies would be allowed to present. A significant issue in their growing disagreement over what was acceptable entertainment was which of the two men would control the Legion of Decency: the prelate or the publisher.

The war over who would control film content reached a fever pitch when a new Tennessee Williams–Elia Kazan film was released during the 1956 Christmas season. This one was centered on the marriage of a beautiful, voluptuous teenage girl to a sweaty, grimy, middle-aged man. Williams once again laced his story, set in rural Mississippi, with steamy sexuality. The twist this time was that the young girl, nicknamed Baby Doll, refused to consummate her marriage until she reached the age of 20. It was, said *Time,* "just possibly the dirtiest American-made motion picture that has ever been legally exhibited."[65]

Director Elia Kazan thought "*Baby Doll* was a lark from beginning to end"; it was, he said, "not to be taken seriously." Francis Cardinal Spellman did take it seriously, however, and condemned the film from his pulpit at St. Patrick's Cathedral in December 1956. As Kazan later admitted: "It took Cardinal Spellman to make it [*Baby Doll*] famous."[66]

The battle over *Baby Doll* was intense. Williams and Kazan had learned firsthand how powerless a writer and director were in the Hollywood system of production when the Catholic Legion had objected to *A Streetcar Named Desire.* Kazan was furious that Warner Bros. had been unwilling to fight the Legion, and by 1956 knew that if he wanted control over the content of a film, he had to produce it independently. With that goal in mind, he formed Newtown Productions and arranged financing and distribution through Warners; but it was to be Kazan's film, and it was he, and he alone, who would have final-cut authority.

Williams's screenplay was based on two of his one-act plays, *27 Wagons Full of Cotton* and *Unsatisfactory Supper,* written some years earlier. A black comedy set in the Mississippi delta, *27 Wagons* portrays Jake Meighan, owner of a run-down cotton gin, who is losing his business to a new gin owner named Silva Vicarro, a Sicilian immigrant who has recently moved to Mississippi. In a desperate attempt to regain his business, Meighan burns down Vicarro's gin.

Vicarro, an outsider, gets little support from the local police in tracking down the arsonist – he has ruined too many of the locals to get much sympathy or help; but he suspects that Meighan is guilty and takes twenty-seven wagon loads of cotton to his gin. While Meighan is busy ginning, Vicarro turns his attention to Meighan's voluptuous wife, Flora. After forcing Flora to admit that her husband was the arsonist, he brutally rapes her as revenge. When Jake finds out what happened, he agrees to let Flora "entertain" Vicarro whenever he brings cotton to be ginned.

The second one-act, *Unsatisfactory Supper,* was a short character sketch of an elderly spinster, Aunt Rose, who is dependent on the kindness of her relatives for room and board, cooking and cleaning in exchange for her keep. The vignette is set in rural Mississippi, where Aunt Rose is living with her niece, Baby Doll, and her husband, Archie Lee, in a rambling, dilapidated house. Archie Lee has no love and little patience for the doddering Aunt Rose, and when she serves a meal of greens that she forgot to cook, he orders her out of the house.[67]

Williams, after excessive prodding from Kazan, had brought the two stories together in a screenplay that he finally titled *Baby Doll*. Archie Lee (Karl Malden) and his young wife, Baby Doll (Carol Baker), became the central characters of the movie. Lee owns the run-down cotton gin and has lost his business to the new gin owner, now named Vacarro (Eli Wallach). Archie, a fading middle-aged man who has married a tender young girl of 18, has promised her father that he would not consummate their marriage until she reached the age of 20 – just a few days away when the movie opens.

Baby Doll, however, has imposed a condition before she will sleep with Archie: He must provide her with a suitable home. Unfortunately for Lee, and perhaps fortunately for Baby Doll, a local furniture company has chosen the day before Baby Doll's twentieth birthday to repossess all their furniture.

The poor man is desperate. He is driven to the point of complete distraction by sexual lust for his nubile young wife, who lounges about the house in her lingerie, provocatively sucks her thumb, and sleeps in a baby crib. Every time she takes a bath, Lee peeks at her through the keyhole in the bathroom door. When he is not drooling over his wife's body, he is trying to figure out how to make enough money to get his furniture back so he can finally take her to bed. In desperation, he sets fire to Vacarro's cotton gin.

As in the play, Vacarro gets little help from the police. Certain that Lee has destroyed his business, he drives out to Lee's place with several loads of cotton. While Archie is attending to business, Vacarro attends to Baby Doll.

Unlike in the play, Vacarro does not rape her, but he does awaken Baby Doll sexually. He pursues her with an intensity that reeks of sexuality. With

Archie Lee off on business, Vacarro spends the day alone with her. They sit in an abandoned car, where Vacarro alternates between an interrogation of Baby Doll and a seduction, questioning her as to Archie's whereabouts the night of the fire and wringing conflicting stories from this confused young woman.

Later, as the two of them sit in an old swing, Vacarro continues to press her about Archie while gently stroking her arm and face. Vacarro says, "every bit of you is delicate. Choice. Delectable, I might say. You're fine fibered. And smooth. And soft." Baby Doll squirms but smiles: "Our conversation is certainly taking a personal turn!" But she makes no real effort to escape and giggles when Vacarro tickles her. When he prods her with a whip that he carries, Baby Doll protests: "Mr. Vacarro, you're getting awfully familiar." But the protest is gentle. It is clear that she likes this attention and the compliments of this strange, powerful man. "You make me feel kind of hysterical, Mr. Vacarro," she says. He continues to stroke her arm, and Baby Doll tells him it makes her feel funny all up and down.

Later, that same day, Baby Doll is alone in the house making lemonade. It is extremely hot and she is dressed in a slip. (Williams's script described the scene: "Her slip hangs half off one great globular breast, gleaming with sweat.")[68] She carelessly cuts her finger slicing the lemons and runs upstairs to the bathroom for a bandage. She hears Vacarro enter the house, and they begin an adult game of hide-and-seek as he moves from one room to another. The game soon turns from fun to pursuit when Baby Doll attempts to take refuge in the attic. She crawls out onto weakening floorboards, which begin to creak under her weight. Vacarro refuses to leave until she signs a confession that Archie did indeed burn his gin.

By this time Vacarro is exhausted from his long night of fire fighting and his pursuit of Archie Lee and Baby Doll. He decides to take a nap, but the only bed in the house is Baby Doll's crib. He curls in it and begins to suck his thumb as Baby Doll snuggles up beside him on the floor. The scene fades out.

When Archie Lee finally comes home, he finds Vacarro in his house and his wife still dressed in her slip. Archie is suspicious, and Vacarro does little to ally his fears. When Archie steps out of the room, the two kiss. When Vacarro informs Archie that Baby Doll has confessed to his guilt in torching his business, and suggests that he and Baby Doll are more than just friends, Archie grabs his shotgun and chases Baby Doll and Vacarro out of the house. The police soon arrive, and Archie is taken off to jail. Vacarro leaves and Baby Doll is left alone wondering if either of these men will ever return. She turns to Aunt Rose and says: "We've got nothing to do but wait for tomorrow to see if we've been remembered or forgotten."

For two hours the screen pulsated with sexual tension. Archie Lee literally ached with desire for his wife. He did not love her, he wanted her. She claimed she "wasn't ready," but no one in the audience could believe for a minute that this healthy young woman, played so coyly by Carol Baker, was not ready – she just wasn't interested in getting into bed with her slimy, sweaty, panting, leering letch of a husband. She knew what he wanted and she was not about to give it to him if he could not at least provide her with decent furniture. She was interested in Vacarro and, while it was not directly evident that the two of them had had sex, it could be inferred that they had, or that they certainly wanted to.

This type of raw sexuality had been absent from the American screen since the creation of the Legion of Decency in 1933–4. When Kazan submitted the script to the PCA, they expressed concern about the "cold-bloodedness with which Vacarro" taunts Lee "with the fact that he is cuckolding him." The censors asked for the sexual tension to be lowered. Kazan assured them that "I . . . do not want there to have been a 'sex affair' between our two people." He told Shurlock that Vacarro's walking away from Baby Doll would "solve the adultery issue." He pledged to make the film "in good taste." "The boys [Shurlock and Vizzard] know," he told Jack Warner, "that when I say something, I make it good." Kazan also tried to brace up Jack Warner, who had caved in so quickly in 1951. He reminded Warner that "fewer and fewer people are leaving their TV sets," and filmmakers must provide "what they cannot and will never see on their TV screens."[69]

However, it really did not matter to Kazan what Warner, Shurlock, or Vizzard thought about the script. This time he had no intention of changing his film. Kazan and his production company set off for Benoit, Mississippi, in November 1955, where he stayed for some ten weeks capturing the feel of southern life. He completed the rest of the picture at the old Warner Bros. Vitagraph Studio in Flatbush, New York, and a rough cut was ready for PCA viewing in July 1956.[70]

Without any input from the censors, Williams and Kazan had known they had to tone down some of the more overtly sexual scenes of the short plays for screen treatment. Vacarro's character underwent the most obvious transformation. He, for example, does not rape Baby Doll for revenge: There is no rape, and his goal is to gather evidence that will stand up in a court of law because he knows that, as an outsider, the police will do nothing to help him. Archie, not Vacarro, is the heavy in the movie. He is dull, lazy, sweaty, mean-spirited, and destined for failure. He treats his wife like dirt and wonders why she does not respond to him. On the other hand, he does not, as does the husband in 27 Wagons Full of Cotton, offer her up as "entertainment" for future deliveries of cotton.

Geoffrey Shurlock was on vacation when the working print of Baby Doll reached PCA headquarters in Beverly Hills. The task of evaluating the movie fell to Assistant Director Jack Vizzard, who was aware of the history of the project. Vizzard was uncomfortable with several scenes. The general "sex frustration" of Archie and his peeking into the bathroom upset Vizzard, but not enough to withhold a seal. The scene in the swing, however, was another matter. Vizzard read the reactions of Baby Doll to Vacarro's stroking her arm and face as "reactions that were nothing if not orgasm."[71] If Baby Doll had an orgasm in that swing, it was the first seen in mainstream cinema since Hedy Lamarr's famous climactic scene in the 1932 Czechoslovakian film *Ecstasy* (which had been cut from prints that circulated in the United States).

Kazan argued passionately that Vizzard was reading too much into the scene. As Vizzard later recalled, "he sat down with us [other PCA reps] in the dark of the projection room and went over the footage frame by frame, showing why he could cut nothing and pleading the texture of the fabric would be damaged."[72] Vizzard did something Joe Breen never would have done: He gave in and issued *Baby Doll* a seal of approval.

Kazan got what he wanted: a PCA seal guaranteeing him and Warner Bros. that a large number of America's best theaters would play *Baby Doll*. It could not have been a surprise to them when the Catholic Legion issued a stinging condemnation of the film in late November 1956, just weeks before its scheduled release during the Christmas season.

Baby Doll, the Catholic censors wrote, was "morally repellent," with an "unmitigated emphasis on lust"; it was, in Legion opinion, "grievously offensive to Christian and traditional standards of morality and decency." The Legion quickly warned priests throughout America that *Baby Doll* was "replete with sordid details, Freudian symbolism and undertones of perversion." The sexuality was "so vividly presented . . . that neither deletions nor additions could salvage a basically bad theme." More important, the Legion added, Kazan had "made no attempt to contact the Legion for discussions." Msgr. Little called for local Legion directors to conduct a holy war against the film, which he hoped would "seriously affect the box office. . . ." The national Legion director warned: "Should this picture have commercial success it would strongly weaken the hands of the Legion in its negotiations [censoring] with the major producing companies of this country."[73]

Still, as Kazan noted, it took a cardinal to make *Baby Doll* a household name. On Sunday, December 16, 1956, Francis Cardinal Spellman, the "American Pope," slowly climbed to the pulpit of St. Patrick's Cathedral in New York City for the first time since February 1949, when he had denounced the jailing of Josef Cardinal Mindszenty. Spellman was a vocal cold warrior whose politics were firmly rooted on the right. He had made a point of riding in the ticker-tape parade with General Douglas MacArthur after the general was sacked by President Truman. He was an avid supporter of Senator Joseph McCarthy, long after McCarthy was discredited, and continued to sponsor a special "McCarthy Mass" at St. Patrick's on the anniversary of the senator's death. The cardinal led the Catholic crusade against communism and regularly denounced those he believed were communist supporters or fellow travelers.[74]

Given Spellman's politics and the brutal Soviet suppression of the Hungarian Revolt in early November 1956, many of the parishioners that Sunday in mid-December anticipated that some grave crisis in international affairs – perhaps a dramatic event involving Moscow, Washington, and the Vatican – had prompted the cardinal to address them. Moreover, as Spellman began to speak it did appear that international politics was his concern. After voicing dismay over the treatment of Catholics in Communist Hungary, Spellman intoned: "It is the moral and patriotic duty of every loyal citizen to defend America not only from dangers which threaten our beloved country from beyond our boundaries, but also the dangers which confront us at home."[75]

More than a few of the parishioners must have been bewildered when the cardinal informed them that the newest threat to American security was an American film: *Baby Doll!* It was, he said, "revolting . . . immoral and corrupting . . . evil in concept"; it "constitutes a definite corruptive moral influence." *Baby Doll*, Spellman charged, was unpatriotic – as much a threat to American security as international communism. "Such a subject," he told his captive audience, "constitutes an assault upon the honor, decency and moral fiber of a people which may be far more damaging than the external dangers" of communism. It was "astonishing and deplorable," Spellman continued, that the film carried a seal from "the so-called regulatory system of the Motion Picture Association of America," raising "a serious question as to whether this system has fallen into decay and collapse." He concluded with a solemn warning to New York Catholics: Those who went to see *Baby Doll* would do so "under pain of sin."[76]

When pressed by reporters for more information about why he believed the film was both immoral and unpatriotic, Spellman was forced to admit he had not bothered to see *Baby Doll.* "Must you have a disease to know what it is?" Spellman retorted.[77]

Spellman had read the statement; Martin Quigley was its author. The publisher certainly had lost no opportunity to brief Spellman on his problems with *Tea and Sympathy.* He told the cardinal that, in his view, it was no longer enough for the Legion simply to condemn a film: There was too much evidence that Catholics paid little, if any, attention, and too many priests telling Catholics that the Legion had no real authority. What was needed, Quigley believed, was a strong statement by an authority like Spellman to convince lay Catholics and his fellow bishops that movies were moral dangers. The Legion had agreed that *Baby Doll* was immoral, but Quigley wanted to send a pointed message to Bishop Scully, Msgr. Little, and those priests who were challenging Legion authority that he, through his protector Cardinal Spellman, was determined to resist a liberalization of Legion standards. Spellman was more then happy to oblige his old friend.[78]

Spellman's denunciation set off a firestorm of reaction. Tennessee Williams issued a statement from Key West: "I would like to say that as I wrote *Baby Doll* I was not conscious of writing anything that corresponded to the terms he has used against it. I don't think that it has any corrupting influence on audiences." Rather pointedly, the playwright added: "I cannot believe that an ancient and august branch of the Christian faith is not larger in heart and mind than those who set themselves up as censors of a medium of expression that reaches all sections of our country and extends over the world."[79]

More dramatically, but also to the point, Kazan stated he was "outraged by the charge that [*Baby Doll*] is unpatriotic. . . . In this country, judgments on matters of thought and taste are not handed down ironclad from an unchallengeable authority. People see for themselves and finally judge for themselves." Some years later Kazan was less charitable. Spellman was, he wrote in his memoirs, a "bag of sanctified wind."[80]

The *New York Post*, in an incredibly strong editorial, sided with Williams and Kazan. The paper granted Spellman's authority to speak for Catholics but noted that when he stated it was the patriotic duty of all Americans to refuse to see the film, "he trespasses beyond the bounds of democratic debate" and "confuses loyalty to country with fidelity to the moral decrees of a specific Church leader." The cardinal's attack, the *Post* noted, was somewhat ironic: The situation in Hungary, which the cardinal rightly noted was horrible, was "vaguely comparable" to "the terror to which the Legion of Decency has intermittently reduced Hollywood." All "cultural commissars," the paper warned, were dangerous, whether they be foreign or domestic. The issue at stake was broader than the mere freedom of moviemakers; it went, the *Post* believed, "to the very essence of the idea of cultural freedom."[81]

It did indeed; but it depended on where one stood. In the Bible Belt, the *Tulsa Tribune* blasted Catholic efforts to prevent everyone from seeing the film. "We are going to get into very deep water," the paper editorialized, "if religious pressure is brought to deny all people the right to see or read or hear what is otherwise lawful."[82] The Very Reverend Dr. James A. Pike, Dean of the Protestant Episcopal Cathedral of St. John the Divine in New York, agreed. He and his wife saw the film, and he told his congregation: "I don't think that I sinned in seeing it. Those who do not want the sexual aspect of life included in the portrayal of a real life situation had better burn their Bibles, as well as abstain from the movies."[83]

Most moviegoers seemed to agree. When *Life* interviewed people in the streets about *Baby Doll,* they found public opinion split. Frank Daley, an Irish-Catholic from Boston, judged it "immoral": "There is no doubt of that," he told the interviewer. Mrs. Maria Balestrieri, an Italian-American from Jersey City thought it was "very good." In her opinion it was not immoral, and she added: "I don't think the Cardinal fair to judge a film he has not seen. I'm a Catholic but I believe people must make up their own minds." Another Italian-Catholic, Mike Fezza from Brooklyn, was disappointed that "nothing happens." However, he thought "Carol Baker . . . pretty nice." Mrs. Ida Shindelman found it "trashy, but not immoral."[84] If this small sample was in any way indicative of Catholic opinion, Quigley was right: Lay Catholics made up their own minds about what films they saw.

The Legion, however, was determined to keep *Baby Doll* out of as many cinemas as possible. Aware that public protest drove curious fans to the theater, they had learned long ago that it was more effective to pressure distributors and theater owners. Joseph P. Kennedy, a friend of Cardinal Spellman and a father whose son would soon be president, readily agreed to ban the film from his theater chain. Kennedy told the press that *Baby Doll* "should be banned everywhere"[85] – and it was, in a few cities. Memphis and Atlanta prevented it from being screened, and several other bishops joined Spellman in declaring the film an occasion of sin: Scully in Albany, New York, Archbishop Francis F. Keough in Baltimore, Archbishop Joseph Francis Rummel in New Orleans, and Archbishop Dougherty in Philadelphia. The Knights of Columbus rolled out their picket signs in several communities, and the Catholic War Veterans vowed to do all in its power to see that *Baby Doll* would be a "financial fiasco for the company coffers and a grievous moral blow to Warners' reputation with the American public."[86]

Predictably, Catholic newspapers and magazines lambasted the film. The *Catholic World* called it a "masterpiece of decadence" that should have been rated "D" for "degenerate"; but several months after the release of the film the publication complained bitterly that "too many people have supported" it.[87] The *Commonweal* saw the film as an "unrelieved study of decay."[88] *America* told readers the industry had suffered a gross "dereliction of duty" in passing a film filled with "brutality, perversion [and] degeneracy."[89] To *Ave Maria*, *Baby Doll* was "repulsive."[90]

A slight break in Catholic unity erupted when Father J. A. V. Burke, S.J., director of the Catholic Film Institute, the British equivalent to the Legion, wrote that in his view *Baby Doll* could be seen at a "safe distance [by] adults . . . without contamination . . ."[91] Burke did not endorse the movie, which he described as "repellent," but he did believe that *Baby Doll* had "significant social background" for "thoughtful adults." So did the British rating system, which gave *Baby Doll* an X rating – adults only. From Burke's perspective, although children were prevented from attending the film in Britain, he saw no reason to protect adults from *Baby Doll*. Logical perhaps, but all hell broke loose when Burke's review was published in *America*. Burke wrote a long letter to Msgr. Little trying to explain his position, but, "the long arm of clerical vengeance . . . reached across the waters and touched him." Spellman had Burke terminated for, as Jack Vizzard recalled, "singing outside the chorus."[92]

Vizzard was personally stung by the vituperative nature of the Catholic attack on the PCA. In yet another example of the close working relationship between the PCA and the Legion, Vizzard called on Archbishop Timothy Manning in Los Angeles to try to explain why *Baby Doll* had received a seal of approval. Manning later wrote to Bishop Scully that even through Vizzard was an ex-Seminarian, "I could not compliment him for a good deal of his reasoning in view of his Catholic background."[93]

The Legion condemnation remained firmly in place and, in the final analysis, Catholic protest did hurt *Baby Doll* at the box office. Some four thousand theaters booked the film nationwide, far fewer than would have had it carried a B rating instead of the C. It eventually generated some $5 million in worldwide revenues, which was respectable but not great. Again, the film played to good audiences in urban centers. In Spellman's New York City the Victoria Theater took in over $100,000 in the first two weeks. The picture broke records at the Allen in Cleveland and packed in audiences in Detroit, Kansas City, Los Angeles, and Philadelphia. By the end of its initial run, *Baby Doll* had made $2.3 million in domestic revenues and stood a lowly thirty-eighth in the 1957 box-office chart.[94]

A disappointed Kazan admitted, "[T]he cardinal's attack hurt us. There'd be one good week, then a quick slide down. I never made a profit."[95] Hurt, but not crippled: Wherever it played, it did relatively well. The problem was insufficient play dates. Without a C rating the film could have expected some twenty thousand bookings. However, perhaps the fact that *Baby Doll* did not do all that well at the box office had more to do with the quality of the film than to the volume of Catholic protest. *Baby Doll* simply did not, in theatrical terms, have the legs to carry it beyond its initial run. The good week followed by a bad, to which Kazan referred, is more indicative of a mediocre film than of one hurt by a cardinal's fulminations.

Bad reviews in the secular press also hurt. Arthur Knight called it "one of the most unhealthy and amoral pictures ever made in this country" in his review in the *Saturday Review of Literature*.[96] *Newsweek* saw it as "a horrified visual report on a sordid environment full of appalling people."[97] Bosley Crowther, writing in the *New York Times*, found the characters "morons" without "character, content or consequence."[98] To the *New Republic*, *Baby Doll* was "The Crass Menagerie."[99]

Exhibitors in 1956 were more than eager to book a film that promised good box office, but they were leery of incurring Catholic protest over a film that did not promise to pack their theaters. Both Catholic and secular reviewers had trashed *Baby Doll,* albeit for different reasons. The marketplace, not the Legion, made *Baby Doll* a flop.

Despite some success in preventing *Baby Doll* from achieving star status at the box office, 1955–6 had not been good years for the Legion. Two of the most sensational images then on the American screen were James Dean as a teenage tough in *Rebel without a Cause* and a pouty, sex-kitten import, Brigitte Bardot. Dean's message of questioning authority appealed to teenagers, and Bardot portrayed a young woman whose sexuality was electric and natural in *And God Created Woman.* Audiences flocked to both films despite Legion objections.

The Legion made another dreadful mistake when once again it stepped outside its self-assigned role as moral guardian to attack a social-message picture. The film, about a small-town librarian accused of communist sympathies when she refuses to remove a controversial book from the library, contained no sex or violence; yet it was classified in the Separate Category by the Legion, which disapproved of its central idea: freedom of speech.

Storm Center was a collaborative effort of two longtime Hollywood figures: Julian Blaustein, who had joined Universal Studios as a story editor in 1935 and, by the early 1950s had worked his way to executive producer for Fox; and Daniel Taradash, a lawyer who became a successful screenwriter, winning a 1953 Academy Award for his adaptation of *From Here to Eternity.* The two men had been floating the script around Hollywood without success for several years. Not surprisingly, no one in Hollywood was eager to produce a film about a person falsely accused of being a communist sympathizer. [100]

Inexplicably, in 1956 Harry Cohn of Columbia gave the two men permission to produce the film, which the studio agreed to distribute. He hoped they could produce another *From Here to Eternity,* but instead Columbia got a film that the Legion would term "leftist propaganda."

The film starts off innocently enough: Alicia Hull, the widowed librarian (Bette Davis), is a respected member of the community. One book in her library, *The Communist Dream,* is controversial. She knows this and is very careful to warn anyone who checks out the book that its message may be dangerous. When the city council hears about the book, they order Hull to remove it. At first she is willing but upon further reflection she asks: "What would Thomas Jefferson say to a request like this?" She stands firm for the First Amendment and refuses to remove the book.

The council promptly fires her, and one of the council members, Paul Duncan (Brian Keith), vehemently denounces Hull as a communist. Duncan is a politically ambitious young man whose "voice, manner, and outlook seem unmistakably patterned after Senator Joe McCarthy."[101] His smear campaign quickly turns the community against Hull as a wave of fear sweeps the small town.

A young boy, who had worshiped Hull but who now has been consumed by the hysteria of the town adults, sets fire to the library. This act of violence suddenly brings the townspeople to their senses. They weep as they watch their beloved citadel of knowledge burn to the ground. After emotions cool, Duncan is exposed as a fraud, and Hull is invited back into the graces of the community.

The film was unquestionably preachy, and many of the reviewers judged it dull. Neither the script nor the film, however, encountered any problems with the PCA. In fact, the MPAA helped promote the film: Director of Community Relations Arthur DeBra wrote a promotional pamphlet that asked exhibitors to sponsor local discussions centered around the following questions: "Is the hysteria bred of prejudice and fear of Communism more dangerous than its political and economic theories?" "Can you intelligently and successfully defend Democracy without a knowledge of Communism?" "Should a book designed to deceive us about the true nature of Communism be labeled subversive?"[102]

This was a very strange set of questions for an industry that had enthusiastically cooperated in blacklisting suspected members of leftist organizations and had, for over two decades, purged films with controversial ideas. It is not clear if any cities actually held community discussion groups to deal with these thoughtful issues. One place that did not debate the difficult choices often faced in a democracy was Legion headquarters. The Legion branded the film as "highly propagandistic" and offering "a warped, over-simplified and strongly emotional solution to a complex problem of American life." Legion Assistant Director Father Paul Hayes attempted to clarify the unusual classification when he told reporters that "occasionally a movie comes along that's morally acceptable but harmful on philosophical or dogmatic grounds. *Storm Center* is one of these. The film confuses liberty with unrestricted freedom."[103]

The Legion's position that the film was heavy-handed propaganda was silly given the time period in which the movie was made. Just three years earlier Senator Joe McCarthy had launched his famous attacks on the Overseas Library Program, accusing the State Department of stocking the shelves of American libraries overseas with subversive books. In response, Secretary of State John Foster Dulles had ordered hundreds of books removed from the shelves. This action had infuriated President Dwight D. Eisenhower, who told the graduating class at Dartmouth College in June 1953: "Don't join the book burners. Don't be afraid to go in your library and read every book as long as that document does not offend your own ideas of decency. . . . How will we defeat communism unless we know what it is?"[104]

Interestingly, the Legion employed some of the same techniques that it held to be "propagandistic" in *Storm Center*. Msgr. Little was highly disturbed after previewing the film; perhaps he was upset by the obvious identification of Senator McCarthy with the heavy in the film. Whatever his reason, he launched an immediate investigation into the political backgrounds of both Blaustein and Taradash. When he discovered that Blaustein had been investigated for leftist connections by the California Senate Tenney Committee, Little immediately called Columbia Studios and, as he wrote, "reminded . . . Columbia [it] held itself vulnerable in view of the knowledge in the public domain that Julian Blaustein . . . had been cited by the Tenney Committee in California in 1948 of having association with various Leftist causes."[105]

This type of pressure would have caused heads to roll in 1953. In 1956, however, Columbia officials informed the Legion director that the film had the backing of Harry Cohn and there was nothing studio executives could, or would, do.[106]

The Catholic press launched a campaign of denunciation against the film. The *Sign* compared the film to propaganda movies produced in Soviet Russia and Nazi Germany – it was "pure hokum."[107] Patrick F. Scanlan, managing editor of the *Tablet*, found the film propaganda because elected officials were portrayed as "stupid and fanatical" while the librarian, "a champion of the Communist volume," was "depicted as intelligent and honorable."[108] Only *Commonweal* found the Legion action "regrettable."[109]

It was regrettable; it was also transparent. The Legion would have been on much more solid ground had it treated in the same manner all films that came out of Hollywood with a political message. However, the Legion had not, for example, given the same classification to such political-message films as *My Son John, Red Menace, I Married a Communist for the FBI*, or a host of other blatantly anticommunist films that had been produced by the studios as tokens of contrition to HUAC.

The Legion classification was condemned by industry officials, film critics, and anticensorship groups. The Motion Picture Industry Council called it an outright act of "censorship with the purpose of dictating and controlling the content of motion pictures."[110] Those Catholics who saw the Legion as a largely negative operation agreed; but few inside or outside the film industry or the Catholic church could have realized that because of decisions like the Separate Classification of *Storm Center* and the condemnation of frothy comedies like *The Moon Is Blue*, the Legion was about to undergo drastic changes in attitude, directed not from Legion headquarters at 435 Madison Avenue, but on orders from the Vatican.

CHAPTER 6

A NEW APPROACH

This Jesuit clique, which has dominated the conduct of the Legion office since 1957, is opposed to the condemnation of any motion picture – or any artifact by a Catholic agency – in this "pluralistic society."
            – Martin Quigley to Bishop McNulty

It is our opinion that the man [Quigley] suffers from megalomania.
            – Legion memo to Bishop McNulty

In January 1957 Catholic delegations from thirty-one European and American nations gathered in Havana, Cuba, to discuss the movies. They were welcomed by His Eminence the Cardinal Arteaga y Betancourt, Archbishop of Havana and Primate of Cuba, and Monsignor Andre M. Deskur, representative of Pope Pius XII; these were the official hosts for the Office Catholique International du Cinéma (OCIC), which sponsored the conference.

The OCIC, founded in 1928 at The Hague in Brussels, was an international Catholic organization dedicated to the study of cinema as an international form of communication. Although largely inactive from the mid-1930s to the end of World War II, it resumed activity in 1947. The OCIC sponsored a conference in Cologne, Germany, in 1954 to discuss "Moral Film Classification" and in Dublin, Ireland, in 1955 to study "Diffusion and Influence of Moral Film Classification."

In Havana the theme was "The Promotion of Good Films and Grouping of Cinematographic Culture." A papal message opening the conference praised the cinema "as a privileged instrument" given to man by God that, if used correctly, could "elevate" man. The pope urged the delegates to take steps to broaden film appreciation among Catholics through "real theoretical and practical instruction."

The delegates, leading clerics and prominent lay Catholics from Europe and the Americas, were cloistered far from the temptations of modern Havana in a beautiful New World setting: the Jesuit School of Belem (Bethlehem) in Havana. Huddled among the protective walls of Belem, their agenda was to construct a more positive Catholic approach to the movies. The OCIC wanted to encourage Catholics to study movies seriously, to have Catholic colleges, universities, and seminaries offer film-appreciation courses and sponsor film-study clubs, and actively to encourage Catholics to attend good movies.[1]

The American delegation included Msgr. Thomas Little and Mrs. Mary Looram from the Legion and, interestingly, Jack Vizzard of the Production Code Administration. Martin Quigley was conspicuously absent: He had been invited by Little but refused to attend, telling Little that in his view the record of the OCIC was "one of inept, unproductive dilettantism." Jack Vizzard later wrote that Quigley was convinced that the OCIC had been infiltrated by "left-wingers," who he suspected were going to subvert moral values.[2]

Quigley was infuriated, for example, when the OCIC awarded a Best Picture prize in 1956 at the Venice Film Festival to Luis García Berlanga's *Calabuch*. The film portrayed an American scientist who refused to allow his work to be used for military purposes. Quigley told Little that the OCIC had no business giving an award to a "film of trivial importance in the world market."[3] One suspects that Quigley was more upset at the message of the film than the fact that it would not make a killing at the box office.

Quigley was also upset that a 1954 film, Federico Fellini's *La Strada* – condemned by the Legion because of illicit sex – was praised by the OCIC. He told Msgr. Little that, in his view, the priests of the OCIC did not understand the "immediate moral and social problems of the cinema and how the Catholic influence might be brought to bear on a solution of these problems."[4] Quigley feared the Havana meeting would recommend an approach he had long opposed: praising good films (not criticizing bad ones) and taking a much more liberal view of films that presented adult themes seriously.[5]

The publisher's political antenna was right on the mark, as Msgr. Little would soon discover. The delegates to the OCIC, like many of the leading intellectuals within the Catholic church in the United States, believed the Legion of Decency was hopelessly out of step with the modern cinema. The first session of the conference proved the point.

Msgr. Little chaired one of the working subcommittees on film and morality. In his opening remarks he described with pride the working relationship between the PCA and the Legion and spent some time showing how the two combined to ensure that a "voice for morality" and "compensating moral values" were present in American films. He was, reported Jack Vizzard, "slightly triumphalistic" in his presentation.[6]

When Little finished his presentation, a "buzzing as from angry little swarms of bees" arose from the delegation. A Dominican priest from Belgium challenged Little's basic assumptions. "You think," he told the chief Legionnaire, that if "you can name a sin by this voice of morality of yours" or insert "compensating moral values" you "have punished sin" and "disposed of it." It was, the Belgian noted with heavy sarcasm, all "very American." Little tried to defend himself, but had, as Vizzard noted with some amusement, the "black-and-white Dominican up him, and down him, and around him, and in him, and out him like some frenzied Dalmatian."[7]

Mrs. Mary Looram, Chair of the Motion Picture Department of the IFCA since 1930, and in charge of the reviewing staff of the Legion since 1936, rose to defend the Legion and deflect criticism from a totally befuddled Msgr. Little. Looram selected a film condemned by the Legion to illustrate how the system worked; unfortunately, she picked the highly respected British picture *Black Narcissus* to illustrate her point. The film, which starred Jean Simmons as a Anglican nun who walks away from her religious order, had been condemned by the American Legion of Decency. Looram explained that one of the more troubling scenes in the film was one in which the young nun, who was supposed to be praying, was instead daydreaming of riding her horse through the woods. This, Looram announced, made religion appear unappealing and was one of the reasons the film was condemned for American audiences.

Jack Vizzard, who was in the audience, recorded that the delegates sat in stunned silence until a demure young woman from Latin America respectfully asked the older woman what type of daydream might have been acceptable to the Legion. Looram took the bait and charged ahead, confident that she was about to illustrate to the hostile audience how the Legion wanted films constructed. "Well," Vizzard quotes her as saying, "they could have shown her – if they had good will – in a nice kitchen with her mother . . . in a nice gingham apron . . . drying dishes . . . and smiling and talking to her. . . ." Before Looram could finish the audience erupted with a "scoff of derision."[8]

The following day Msgr. Little resigned as chair of the subcommittee. When the Legion representatives returned to New York, Looram tried to maintain a stiff upper lip when she told the *New York Times* that the delegates had agreed that Catholic policy toward the movies would be to "build up a good moving picture industry, not to tear down one."[9] Vizzard privately told Catholic authorities in Los Angeles that the Havana meeting concluded "the Legion of Decency was . . . too legalistic and negative."[10]

Ordinarily, one might simply dismiss the events in Havana as just another international conference, and in many respects it was. The American Legion was still under the direction and guidance of the American bishops, and there was no reason to suspect that the bishops wanted any radical change in the organization's operating procedures.

Nevertheless, the events in Havana were a clear signal to Catholic authorities that Pope Pius XII was calling for change. After all, the conference had been held under papal authority, and the opinions expressed represented thirty Catholic countries, all of which had groups similar to the American Legion. It is almost inconceivable that the open attacks on the American Legion would have been as forceful and direct had it not been understood that a broader, more liberal, more positive approach to film was in the air. There was, no doubt, personal jealousy operating within the conference – the American Legion, like Hollywood, dominated the Catholic approach to film – but Italian, French, and Spanish filmmakers, most of them Catholics, also deeply resented the American Legion's condemnation of their films, which they believed hurt their chances at obtaining access to the American market.[11]

That the papal signal was understood in America was apparent in March when Archbishop William A. Scully, chairman of the Episcopal Committee on Motion Pictures, published a call for the establishment of a more positive approach to the movies. Scully, calling on Catholics to continue to support the Legion, repeated the Catholic position that it was "not a 'censoring' body" but concerned only with "the moral appraisal of motion pictures." He strongly defended the right of the Legion to protest against films it believed immoral and called on Catholics to avoid all movies judged as objectionable in any part by Catholic authorities. The bishop admitted, however, that the public perception of the Legion was that it exercised a "merely negative" function. "It is luminously clear to me," Scully wrote, "that further affirmative work needs to be done." He praised the Havana Conference for suggesting that Catholics study movies and urged local priests and lay Catholics (there was no mention of a Legion role) to form study groups "dedicated to the analysis and criticism of motion pictures."[12] The movies were soon to become the cinema at Catholic schools and universities.

Scully's call for a Catholic program of cinematic literacy was a preface for a new papal encyclical, *Miranda Prorsus* (On Entertainment Media), issued in September 1957. Pope Pius XII told the faithful in his letter that the motion picture was one of the "most important discoveries of our times." The cinema, the pope stated, had the potential to be "a worthy instrument by which men can be guided toward salvation." It was, therefore, "essential that the minds and inclinations of the spectators be rightly trained and educated" to understand the art form used by filmmakers. The pope urged Catholics to "devote . . . deep and prolonged study" to the cinema in Catholic schools and universities.

By no means was the encyclical a rejection of the Legion of Decency: The pope urged that national offices continue to classify films using moral standards and that Catholics obey by not attending films judged to be immoral.

However, it was unmistakable that the tone of *Miranda Prorsus* differed radically from Pope Pius XI's 1936 encyclical *Vigilanti Cura* (Clean Movies), which called for a ban on improper movies. Strongly influenced by Martin Quigley, the 1936 papal statement had claimed that since the purpose of art was "to assist in the perfection of [the] moral personality of man," movies must above all be moral; but, the encyclical had warned, movies were far from moral because they seduced patrons in "a dark theater" by lowering the "mental, physical and often spiritual" faculties of the audience. In *Vigilanti Cura* the pope had labeled movies "a school of corruption" and praised the development of the American Legion of Decency for improving their moral message.[13]

Quigley, who had had no hand in drafting *Miranda Prorsus,* watched with some skepticism the developments toward a more positive and enlightened view of the role of movies. As we have already seen, he was horrified by the position taken by several leading Catholic intellectuals – Jesuits John Courtney Murray, Harold C. Gardiner, John C. Ford, and Gerald Kelly – that Legion classifications were only guidelines for Catholic adults. The Havana Conference, *Miranda Prorsus,* and Archbishop Scully's call for movie clubs confirmed his worst fears: He was in danger of losing his influence within the Legion. In a desperate move to maintain his position and prevent what he saw as a liberalization of the Legion, Quigley plotted to bring into the group a young Jesuit whom he could control. He believed – incorrectly, it turned out – that having a Jesuit in the organization would silence Jesuit criticism.[14]

Quigley picked Father Patrick J. Sullivan, S.J., to replace Assistant Director Paul J. Hayes. Sullivan was on the staff of Woodstock College, and Quigley was able to convince Cardinal Spellman, whose permission was necessary, that bringing the young Jesuit to the Legion would halt its liberalization.

This move, however, had little chance of success in the climate of change that was emanating from Rome and Catholic intellectuals. Within weeks it became apparent that the young priest was not going to be Quigley's puppet within the Legion. In November 1957 the Episcopal Committee on Motion Pictures met in Bishop Scully's suite at the Woodner Hotel in Washington, D.C. The meeting began at 6:30 in the evening with dinner and lasted until midnight. Joining the ECMP were Msgr. Little and Father Sullivan from the Legion. The main agenda for the meeting was the current classification system and *Miranda Prorsus.*

After dinner, Little took the floor and told the bishops that the Legion was being hindered by the current system of classification. A1 (morally unobjectionable for general audiences) and C (condemned) were working as intended; but the A2 and B classifications were not. The A2 category – morally unobjectionable for adults and adolescents – had become, Little said, increasingly restrictive over the years as Hollywood moved toward more adult themes. As Little explained, films that might be acceptable for a 30-year-old were not acceptable entertainment for a 15-year-old. At the same time a 17-year-old might view a film that was unacceptable for a 12-year-old. The result was that A2 had been redefined as "morally unobjectionable for adults." In fact, Catholic publications like *Catholic Preview of Entertainment,* the most comprehensive guide to the movies printed for Catholics, identified the A2 in that way.

This meant that in 1957 adolescents were prohibited from seeing filmed versions of literary classics like *The Hunchback of Notre Dame,* science fiction favorites such as *Lost Continent,* cowboy yarns such as *3:10 to Yuma,* and comedies like *My Man Godfrey* because Legion reviewers believed a scene or two therein might be inappropriate for young teenagers. By the same token adults were asked not to attend such B films as *Don't Go Near the Water, Gunfight at OK Corral, The Rainmaker,* and *Will Success Spoil Rock Hunter?* This type of classification damaged the Legion's credibility, Little advised, and everyone from the bishops to local priests admitted that the Legion could neither keep Catholics away from B-rated films, nor keep teenagers away from films like *Lost Continent.*

After several hours of debate, the Episcopal Committee accepted Little's recommendations to change the Legion's classifications:[15] A revised A2 category would classify films that were acceptable for both adults and adolescents; and a new A3 classification, "morally acceptable for adults," would list films that mature adults could attend. The bishops also empowered the Legion to recommend to Catholic patrons films it believed especially good. Thus for the first time in Legion history Catholics would be encouraged to attend films that it recommended, and adults and adolescents would be given much more latitude in choosing the movies they wanted to see.

In a letter sent to local priests to explain the new system, the Legion warned that the newly expanded A2 might include movies that had previously been given a B rating; the group believed that "excessive protection even for adolescents can prevent their normal maturation on the intellectual and emotional levels." The A2 category would be relaxed to "aid the adolescent," with the hope it would aid them in "growing up."[16] Local priests and lay leaders were charged with educating Catholic youth so that they could watch a more mature cinema.

The A3 classification, the Legion wrote, was "an attempt to provide for truly adult subject matter in entertainment pictures."[17] This, they hoped, would allow the Legion to avoid the embarrassment of having to place serious films with adult themes in the B category, which the Legion maintained were to be avoided by everyone. The new B would be restricted to those films that the Legion believed were truly "morally objectionable." The Legion never really addressed an obvious question: If B films were morally objectionable for all and no adult could go, how or why were they distinguished from the condemned films, which were also forbidden viewing? The distinction drawn – that the B film contained scenes or themes that were objectionable whereas the C film was totally objectionable – seems silly when the church maintained that no Catholic could see either one. The difference between the two classifications was very confusing: Some priests held that no adult could attend a B film; others told parishioners they were free to see any movie that was not condemned.

One other major change at Legion headquarters, which despite little public discussion had a major impact on Legion classifications, was the addition of a new group of reviewers. The women of the IFCA, under the direction of Mrs. Mary Looram, had been the Legion reviewing staff from the mid-1930s until the mid-1950s. They were, to put it mildly, conservative and often came under fire for their parochial interpretation of films. The *Motion Picture Exhibitor*, for example, labeled the IFCA as "a group of unskilled and untrained amateur 'Critics' who could not be relied upon to separate technical details from personal entertainment preferences."[18] Even Legion authorities questioned the competence of the IFCA. Bishop Scully, for example, told Jack Vizzard not to be too hard on Msgr. Little because he was surrounded by "old ladies, most of whom should be retired."[19]

The movement toward a more positive and enlightened Legion required new reviewers. The Legion did not fire the IFCA but weakened its voice by appointing a Board of Consultors comprising laymen and priests. This new board – teachers at Catholic schools and colleges, priests from the New York Archdiocese, Catholic film and theater critics, and Catholic lawyers, doctors, and professionals, often fifty or sixty in number and sometimes as many as a hundred – was much more sophisticated and worldly than the women of the IFCA and played a major role in the new Legion.

There were immediate, notable changes in Legion actions: By February 1958 teenagers could now view the cowboy thriller *3:10 to Yuma* and the classic story *The Hunchback of Notre Dame* without penalty of sin, and adults now were given the Legion's permission to see *Peyton Place*![20]

When the new classifications were announced and published, Martin Quigley could scarcely contain his rage. In an ill-advised tirade written to Archbishop Scully, he blasted Father Sullivan and the new Legion guidelines. Quigley told Scully that "my suggestion of last May [to replace Hayes with Sullivan] relative to a staff reorganization in the Legion . . . has grievously misfired." Father Sullivan, whom Quigley had hoped to control, was in fact out of control, he complained. The young priest, the publisher claimed, was "ladened with a mass of academic notions" garnered from his Jesuit colleagues and has "succeeded in imposing a new and different approach to . . . the Legion's function." Quigley told Scully that he viewed the revamped A2 classification as "an absurdity" and the A3 category as "a serious peril to the Legion's status and influence" within the industry. The Legion, Quigley warned, had embarked on "a course of disaster."[21]

The letter was ill-advised because, as Quigley clearly understood, Scully had approved all the changes in Legion classifications before they were made public. Although young Father Sullivan may have drafted the changes in the Legion classification system, and certainly had been influenced by those Jesuit intellectuals whom Quigley denigrated, nothing of import happened in the Legion without the approval of the chair of the ECMP (Scully) and the endorsement of the American bishops.

In fact, the bishops had approved the changes in classification at the November 1957 conclave in Washington, D.C., hoping they would "be helpful to our people by designating the B category as a serious menace to morals and by giving the mature adult mind an opportunity to witness pictures to be classified [A3] especially for them." In an unmistakable signal of their acceptance of a new, more positive Legion, the bishops had expressed their appreciation to "Fathers Ford, S.J., and Kelly, S.J., together with Father Francis Connell for their contribution towards a better understanding of the work of the Legion of Decency."[22]

For the first time since the late 1920s Martin Quigley found himself seriously at odds with the Catholic hierarchy regarding the movies. He was persona non grata at Legion headquarters and could no longer personally dictate Legion policy. Quigley did not take his fall from grace quietly: Over the next several years he would be engaged in a rather unfortunate and uncivil battle with the church hierarchy. It was a curious fight, with Quigley attempting to teach the bishops and priests what was and was not moral. Although this battle would rage over a large number of films in the late 1950s and early 1960s, three really illustrate the nature of the differences of opinion and the emotional level that both sides brought to the fight over morality and entertainment. These films clearly contained adult themes: Joseph Mankiewicz's *Suddenly Last Summer* (homosexuality), Federico Fellini's *La Dolce Vita* (modern life-styles), and Stanley Kubrick's *Lolita* (pedophilia).

Although he may have had no intention of doing so, it should be clear by now that Tennessee Williams played a major role in breaking down the barriers that moral guardians had so carefully erected around the movie industry. As we have already seen, filmed versions of *A Streetcar Named Desire* and *Baby Doll* caused censors and filmmakers to shroud Williams's overtly sexual characters in a camouflage of deception. Audience members who were familiar with his plays and short stories read through the attempts to conceal Williams's messages. Few adults, or even adolescents for that matter, could watch *Streetcar* and not know that Stella was sexually excited by Stanley's physical power; that Blanche was a very sexually active spinster schoolteacher whose first husband had been a homosexual; and that Stanley dominated women in life and in bed. In *Baby Doll* it was impossible not to understand that Archie Lee was being driven crazy because he could not make love to his wife – and Baby Doll herself understood it as well as anyone. While these sexual twists and turns were not, as we have seen, as apparent in the films as in the stage productions, they were there for all but the most naïve patrons.

By the late 1950s the necessity of disguising human sexual orientation and motivation in the movies had been significantly softened except in one very sensitive area: homosexuality. The Production Code still prohibited any presentation of "sex perversion," which specifically meant homosexuality but more broadly included any type of sexual behavior not normally associated with mom and pop in the missionary position once a year to produce another member of a growing, healthy, middle-class American family.

Tennessee Williams just did not write about this vision of sex and family. Williams's view of the American family was presented in his *Cat on a Hot Tin Roof*. The play opened on Broadway in March 1955 and was a smash hit. It won a second Pulitzer Prize for the playwright and strengthened his reputation as one of America's finest writers.

To use a 1990s term, Williams's archtypical family was dysfunctional. This was not the all-American family that had graced American screens for over two decades. The father, Big Daddy, was a mean, spiteful, tyrannical patriarch who bullies his family rather than loves them. His wife is terrified of him, as is almost everyone who comes in contact with him. Big Daddy is dying of cancer, but no one dares tell him the truth.

Big Daddy has two sons, Gooper and Brick. Gooper is married and has several children but has never won the respect of Big Daddy. Brick, on the other hand, is a former college football hero married to a beautiful, attractive woman, Maggie. Brick, Big Daddy's favorite son, on the surface has the perfect marriage; but underneath, sexual tension seethes. The audience soon learns that Brick cannot make love to his wife, and unless they produce an heir, Big Daddy will cut them out of his will.

Brick's problem seems inexplicable because his wife, Maggie (nicknamed the Cat) is sensual and sexual to her very core. She loves her husband and desperately wants to make love with him – not just to produce a child but for the pure enjoyment of it. Having resented Brick's relationship with an old football chum, Skipper – and suspecting that there was more to it than just football – Maggie had attempted to seduce Skipper. When Skipper could not perform with Maggie, he had phoned Brick to confess his true feelings toward him, but Brick had slammed the phone down in disgust. Humiliated, Skipper had turned alcoholic and committed suicide.

Brick, blaming himself and his wife for Skipper's death, has withdrawn into depression and alcoholism. Perhaps also worrying about his own sexual orientation, he is unable, or unwilling, to make love to his wife.

There was no pat happy ending in Williams's stageplay. Brick and Maggie do not hop into bed. Instead, Maggie tells the final lie when she proudly announces to Big Daddy that she is pregnant, and that she and Brick had reconciled. Everyone suspects it is not true, but no one challenges her. Big Daddy can now die happily.

Making a movie from *Cat on a Hot Tin Roof* was going to be a challenge to the creative talents of Hollywood. Although the central theme of the play revolves around the relationship between Brick and his father, the subplot of homosexuality caused problems for filmmakers. Brick never admitted to being a homosexual, but Skipper had, and Brick was consumed with guilt over his love for his friend. When one independent producer approached Geoffrey Shurlock in 1955 about making a movie of the play, the PCA director reminded him that the code still banned any discussion of homosexuality and made "it plain that it would be necessary to remove every inference . . . of sex perversion and to substitute some other problem for the young husband."[23]

The producer withdrew from the project, which was picked up by MGM later that year. After several failed scripts the studio hired writer-director Richard Brooks to adapt *Cat* to the screen. Brooks was an excellent choice. In 1945 he had published his first novel, *The Brick Foxhole,* which told the story of a group of bored soldiers who murder a homosexual. It was transferred to the screen by Edward Dmytryk as *Crossfire,* with anti-Semitism substituted for homophobia.

MGM wanted *Cat* to be big box office and was adamant, Brooks later stated, that the film earn the PCA seal and not be condemned by the Legion. Brooks was told "to find something to replace the unexpressed, latent homosexuality of Brick."[24] The solution was to blame Brick's inability to satisfy his wife on his refusal to grow up. It was his arrested development, his longing for the thrill of college football, the adoration of the crowd, not latent homosexuality, that caused him to reject his wife. In the movie Brick now thinks his wife successfully seduced his friend, which led Skipper to take his life. Skipper's homosexuality is purged from the film as is any concern Brick might have for his own sexual orientation.

When MGM submitted their revised version of *Cat* to Shurlock and Vizzard, the two censors were delighted that the studio had "corrected completely the problem of homosexuality that was in the play" and substituted more mainstream weaknesses of the flesh.[25] MGM got its seal, and under the Legion's newly revised classification system *Cat* was rated A3: morally acceptable for adults.

The film was a smash hit of the 1958 season. The box office was huge: *Cat* generated some $10 million in its domestic run and at least that much in the foreign market. Fans flocked to theaters to see Paul Newman slink away from a smoldering Elizabeth Taylor. Burl Ives was the very epitome of the public's image of a domineering southerner. Some critics panned the film – this *Cat* "is a formaldehyded tabby" chortled *Time,* and the *Nation* noted, "The taint of homosexuality has been wiped from this now-civilized tale"[26] – but most found it as hot as any film yet produced by a major Hollywood studio.

While *Cat* was playing to packed houses nationwide, another Tennessee Williams production opened in New York. In January 1958 the writer combined two one-act plays, *Something Unspoken* and his new *Suddenly Last Summer,* into an evening he titled *Garden District.* The second of these one-acts has been described as "a southern gothic horror tale" about homosexuality, Oedipal relationships, psychosurgery, and cannibalism.[27]

Suddenly Last Summer is set in the famous Garden District of New Orleans in the late 1930s. A wealthy matron, Violet Venable, has invited a brilliant young brain surgeon, Dr. Cukrowicz, from a public New Orleans mental hospital to her home to discuss funding work at the hospital. Venable knows the conditions at the hospital are primitive and that the staff is desperate to raise money to continue their work.

Cukrowicz is excited about the prospects of new funding for his work but quickly discovers that in order to get it he must perform a lobotomy on Venable's niece, Catharine Holly. Venable tells Cukrowicz a strange tale: It seems every year she and her son, Sebastian, a brilliant but unpublished poet, took a long vacation together, at the end of which, Sebastian wrote a single poem. Last summer, Venable says, she had a mild stroke and was unable to accompany her son, and he chose his cousin Catharine as a traveling companion; but tragedy struck when Sebastian died, suddenly, last summer, of a heart attack in the small Spanish town of Cabeza de Lobo. To complicate matters, Catharine returned in a state of mental distress, babbling obscene but mostly incoherent tales about Sebastian. No one is quite sure, Venable tells the doctor, what actually happened in Cabeza de Lobo because Catharine is hysterical and has been confined to a private sanitarium. Venable urges Cukrowicz to perform a lobotomy on her niece, whom she blames for Sebastian's death, to end her obscene babblings.

Cukrowicz suspects that Venable is not telling him the truth. As he interviews Catharine he begins to realize that she is not mad but highly disturbed by some terrible event in Cabeza de Lobo that she has blocked from her memory. Even if it means losing his funding from Venable, the doctor is determined to discover what really happened in Spain.

In a dramatic finale, Venable, Catharine, some family members, and Cukrowicz gather in a large garden in the Venable mansion. The doctor has given Catharine an injection of a "truth serum," and under his careful questioning the truth emerges. In Spain, she tells Curkowicz, he made her wear a scandalous white bathing suit that made her appear naked when she emerged from the water. Cukrowicz is confused. "Why did he do that?" he asks. Catharine screams: "I was PROCURING for him! She used to do it, too. . . . We both did the same thing for him, made contacts for him, but she did it in nice places and in decent ways and I had to do it the way that I just told you!"[28]

Catharine tells the doctor that as the summer progressed Sebastian no longer needed her help in seducing the young men of Cabeza de Lobo. Toward the end of their stay, however, something horrible happened. Catharine and Sebastian were having lunch at a cheap restaurant near the beach. Suddenly a mob of young boys playing an assortment of strange instruments descended upon them. The waiters tried to beat the band of urchins away, but they refused to leave. Then Sebastian made a fatal mistake: He panicked and raced out into the mob, running uphill into the village, from which there was no escape. The children quickly overtook him, and when Catharine found him he was dead, "lying naked as they had been naked . . . this you won't believe, nobody has believed it . . . They had devoured parts of him. Torn or cut parts of him away with their hands or knives or maybe those jagged tin cans they made music with, they had torn bits of him away and stuffed them into those gobbling fierce little empty mouths of theirs."[29]

Suddenly, just as Catharine finishes her story, Violet Venable leaps up and attacks Catharine, screaming at the doctor to cut this obscene story from her brain; but as the old woman is taken away everyone realizes the truth has finally emerged.

Although this distasteful subject matter would normally have given Hollywood pause, the recent success of movies like *A Streetcar Named Desire, Cat on a Hot Tin Roof, Tea and Sympathy,* and *The Moon Is Blue* convinced many producers that almost any topic could be screened.

Independent producer Sam Spiegel, like Otto Preminger, was not afraid to tackle controversial topics. Like Preminger he had been born in Austria and educated at the University of Vienna before coming to the United States. He had first entered the film business in 1927 and by the early 1930s was producing films in the United States and Europe under the pseudonym of S. P. Eagle. After the war he had produced Orson Welles's *The Stranger,* a haunting tale of a Nazi war criminal living in the United States; in the 1950s he had produced such popular hits as *The African Queen, On the Waterfront,* and *The Bridge on the River Kwai.* In 1959 Spiegel turned to the latest Tennessee Williams play, *Suddenly Last Summer,* which he hoped would be another box-office bonanza like *Cat*. So did Columbia Studios, which agreed to distribute.

Spiegel spared little expense in bringing the play to the screen. He inked Elizabeth Taylor, one of America's hottest and most expensive actresses, to play Catharine. British by birth, Taylor had evacuated to America during World War II and been quickly converted into the all-American teenager in such popular hits as *Lassie Come Home* and *National Velvet*. As an adult, Taylor had emerged as a sultry, aggressively frank, often neurotic, sex star in the 1950s. When her third husband, producer Mike Todd, was tragically killed in an airplane accident while she was filming *Cat*, she gave one of her greatest onscreen performances despite her mourning. She was nominated for, but did not win, an Academy Award for that performance and was a natural choice to play Catharine in *Suddenly Last Summer*.

Opposite Taylor, Spiegel cast the grand dame of the movies, Katharine Hepburn, to portray Sebastian's mother. Hepburn, who had captivated audiences with her portrayals of spinsters in *The African Queen, The Rainmaker,* and *Summertime*, was perfect as the devouring, domineering, protecting mother. Montgomery Clift, an icon of the 1950s, played Dr. Cukrowicz. Clift's powerful performances in *The Search, A Place in the Sun,* and *From Here to Eternity* had garnered the young actor three Academy Award nominations during the decade. He was solid box office. Gore Vidal adapted the screenplay, and Hollywood veteran screenwriter-producer-director Joseph L. Mankiewicz controlled the set.

Although he knew the subject matter was dangerous, Spiegel told the press he thought the film was about a mother "who is suddenly too old to procure boys for her son. Why, it's a theme the masses can identify with."[30] It was not clear what masses Spiegel had in mind. When PCA'ers Shurlock and Vizzard read Vidal's adaptation they objected to the fact that the leading character was identified as a homosexual, and threatened to withhold their seal. Sex perversion, they reminded Spiegel, was still taboo. He agreed to cut a reference to "procuring" but otherwise dismissed their objections as irrelevant and plunged ahead with the project. He told Shurlock that if the PCA denied a seal, he would appeal to the MPAA Board of Directors.[31]

When Shurlock and Vizzard viewed the completed film in October 1959 they kept their word and refused to grant a seal because, as they told Spiegel, "sex perversion or any inference of it is forbidden" by the code.[32] Spiegel, true to *his* word, appealed their decision to the MPAA and, surprisingly, was granted a certificate.[33]

The Legion of Decency was shocked. Msgr. Little protested to Shurlock that the film "violated the Code's provision of sex-perversion despite the changes that had been effected."[34] Little, however, was not entirely truthful with Shurlock: He implied that the Legion was going to condemn the film because of its presentation of homosexuality, and the old Legion certainly would have done so; but the new Board of Consultors was not so quick to condemn as the IFCA had been.

One consultor, a priest from Fordham University, told Little that *Suddenly Last Summer* was "the finest American movie" he had ever seen. Little must have shuddered when the priest added that, in his opinion, "no adult" would be harmed by the movie. Moreover, he did "not believe the Legion can condemn or put this movie in the B classification on any moral ground"; he recommended an A3 rating.[35] Another priest told Little that the "picture is a powerful one, and a very excellent attempt to show how evil corrupts completely those who are victimized by it." It was "magnificent entertainment," added another cleric, who also told the Legion director that *Suddenly* was "thoughtful . . . adult entertainment." Still another priest made no comment at all as to the homosexual theme; rather, he recommended a B classification "because of the undue exposure" of Catharine's white bathing suit! A lay consultor told Little it would be "a mistake to condemn a film of this stature."[36] *Our Sunday Visitor* film critic John Fitzgerald wrote to Little from his home in upstate New York that he did not view the film "as morally objectionable" and later published a positive review of it.[37]

There were others, of course, who believed the film should be condemned, but there was no consensus among those who viewed the film for the Legion. If the public at large was more willing to accept adult themes in its entertainment, so too were the new consultors of the Legion of Decency. In the end the Legion opted for a Separate Classification for *Suddenly*. The new Legion told Catholics that the film was "judged to be moral in its theme and treatment"; however, potential viewers were warned that because the subject matter "involves perversion" it was "intended only for a serious and mature audience."[38]

Catholic film reviews reflected the policy of the new Legion. The *Commonweal* told readers *Suddenly Last Summer* was "as chilling and decadent as anything ever told in the movies" but was also a "first-rate production" for "mature audiences who take their movies seriously."[39] Moira Walsh, writing in *America,* warned readers that the movie was controversial but added that "I belong to the school of thought that found much to admire both in the film's execution and in Williams' evident groping for the truths that give life its meaning."[40] The *Tablet* found the film "revolting" but "unlikely to do much harm."[41]

In an almost exact reverse of opinion, secular reviewers were harder on the film than were Catholics. *Time* dismissed it as "a psychiatric nursery drama."[42] The film was "a preposterous and monotonous potpourri of incest, homosexuality, psychiatry," according to John McCarten at the *New Yorker.*[43] "Tedious," wrote Bosley Crowther in the *New York Times.*[44]

Tennessee Williams agreed: He said the film "made me throw up."[45] The play was a personal statement by Williams. His sister, Rose, had been given a prefrontal lobotomy in the 1930s and was confined to a mental hospital the rest of her life. Williams suffered greatly for his sister, and the play helped him deal with this personal tragedy. Williams was also attempting to comment on the violence, prejudice, and greed that he saw in modern society, on the viciousness of man toward man. "Someone is always eating at someone else for position, gain, triumph, whatever," he said. He was distressed that Hollywood seemed to take such a literal view of cannibalism.[46]

The Legion classification and the supporting reception of the film in the Catholic press shocked many Catholics and industry insiders alike, who did not yet fully appreciate the internal changes that were taking hold of Legion operations and the Catholic attitude toward the movies. *Variety* reported, with some measure of disbelief, that a Legion spokesman told them *Suddenly* was about "a man who uses others and their love to his own ends and is finally devoured by the very corruption which he has sown." Tennessee Williams, the Legion spokesman said, perhaps "more than any other writer" in America, deals with the fundamental issues of man's relationship to God.[47]

Despite bad reviews in the lay press and the controversial subject matter, the public flocked to see *Suddenly Last Summer*. The film brought in some $6 million in domestic revenues to Columbia Studios – not quite the $8.7 million that *Cat* had generated in 1957, but still very respectable box office.

Martin Quigley watched the Catholic and public acceptance of *Suddenly Last Summer* with growing alarm. Being out of the loop at Legion headquarters he did not bother to protest to Msgr. Little; he went right to the top. In a long private conference with Cardinal Spellman, Quigley complained bitterly that the Legion was failing its charge of moral assessment of the movies.

Quigley's presentation convinced the cardinal to take action. Spellman asked his colleague, James McNulty, bishop of the Archdiocese of Paterson, New Jersey, to arrange a summit meeting between Scully and Quigley to thrash out their differences. The meeting took place at the Roosevelt Hotel in New York City in late July 1959. McNulty served as mediator. When Quigley arrived at the meeting he immediately protested that his benefactor, Cardinal Spellman, whom he expected to be present, was not. Nonetheless, McNulty reported, he "launched forth bravely on his present obsession" of the Jesuit conspiracy to control the Legion.[48]

When Bishop Scully sharply challenged Quigley to substantiate his allegation, the publisher could only repeat his charges that Father Sullivan was being controlled by Fathers Murray, Gardiner, and Ford. Under further interrogation, Quigley admitted his own role in placing Father Sullivan in the Legion. McNulty concluded in a report circulated among the bishops that Quigley's charges were groundless.

McNulty did much more, however. He added information to his report calculated to "undo Quigley's reputation." Quigley was upset, McNulty told his fellow bishops, because his "efforts to indoctrinate" Sullivan to his point of view had failed. Quigley had gone so far as to threaten Sullivan that "if he did not conform," he would be removed from the Legion. Quigley's reputation in the film industry, McNulty told the bishops, was that of "Mr. Fixit of the Legion." It was widely rumored, McNulty added, that Quigley billed each studio $5,000 "for services rendered" in solving Legion problems. Although McNulty admitted that Quigley denied the charge, he concluded that the publisher was "enhancing his trade position by his affiliation with the Legion." Quigley was, concluded McNulty, "continually a 'thorn in the side' of the executive personnel of the Legion Office."[49]

Quigley refused to retire gracefully from the Legion, and continued to appeal to Spellman. "Your Eminence," he wrote, the Legion classification of *Suddenly Last Summer* "represents a climactic demoralization in the work of the Legion." The Legion's position that the film was intended for mature audiences "displays a shocking ignorance of the motion picture business," he told Spellman. He reminded the cardinal that in previous conversations and correspondence he had predicted that "the uninformed and confused policies of 'liberalization'" in the Legion would produce this type of result. "I can now only say, in dismay, that the forecast has proved tragically true."[50] Spellman, who had read McNulty's report on Quigley, did not reply.

The furor over *Suddenly Last Summer* quickly faded. In 1961 the MPAA quietly changed the Production Code's position on homosexuality. By that time most Americans recognized that the ban was not only silly, but unconstitutional. That year the California Supreme Court ruled that Kenneth Anger's *Fireworks,* a film that dealt openly and directly with homosexuality, could not be banned in the state. The California justices noted that "homosexuality is older than Sodom and Gomorrah" and could certainly be the subject of drama and entertainment.[51] The MPAA recognized the inevitable in October 1961 when it announced that "[i]n keeping with the culture, the mores and the values of our time, homosexuality and other sexual aberrations may now be treated with care, discretion and restraint."[52] This was not terribly enlightened, but it was a far cry from Father Lord's total ban, which had been in effect for three decades.

None of this is to imply that the MPAA, Hollywood filmmakers, the Legion, or the American public was prepared to support films that featured homosexuals even in the negative terms of *Suddenly Last Summer.* It is hard to argue with Vito Russo, who noted that *Suddenly Last Summer* portrayed homosexuality "as the kind of psycho sexual freak show that the Fifties almost demanded."[53] This notion of homosexuals as freaks of nature was the way Hollywood chose to use its new freedom. Otto Preminger's *Advise and Con-*

sent featured a gay bar scene but presented homosexuality in highly negative terms. William Wyler's 1962 remake of Lillian Hellman's play *The Children's Hour* (which he had first filmed in 1936 as *These Three,* with the lesbianism removed) continued the freak theme of *Suddenly Last Summer:* Ad copy screamed, "Did Nature play an ugly trick and endow them with emotions contrary to those of normal young women?" But neither film was banned, and both received MPAA seals of approval. The Legion made no protest, giving the former a Special Classification and the latter an A3 rating.

When the delegates at the OCIC conference in Havana proposed that the Catholic church begin to treat the cinema as a serious artistic medium for international communication they may have had in mind a film like Federico Fellini's *La Dolce Vita.* It was a serious, thoughtful comment on modern life by a brilliant young director; but it was also controversial in its vivid display of sin and sinners.

Fellini had begun working in the Italian cinema in the early 1940s as a gag writer and in 1945 had collaborated with Roberto Rossellini in scripting *Open City* and *Paisan.* He had turned to directing in the early 1950s and gained worldwide acclaim with *La Strada* in 1954 (see Chapter 5). Although Fellini participated in the establishment of Italian neorealism, his films were more personal and spiritual. These aspects of Fellini's work burst onto the world film market in 1960 when he released his personal essay on the decadence and spiritual vacuum of modern society, *La Dolce Vita.*

Fellini's view of the sweet life was a bitter indictment of the aimless hedonism of the leisure class. The setting was modern Rome, but the intent was the modern world. The film opens with two helicopters racing across Rome: The first carries suspended a huge statue of Christ; the second, pursuing the first, contains Marcello (Marcello Mastroianni), a gossipmonger for a local scandal sheet, and several paparazzi, who are chasing after the story of the statue.

The film is constructed in a series of loosely connected episodes centered around Marcello, who longs to be a serious writer but has neither the talent nor the discipline to produce the book he wants to write. Instead, he fills his days and nights chasing scandal and women. In the first episode Marcello is picked up by a wealthy heiress, Maddalena (Anouk Aimée), who is bored by life. She takes Marcello to a prostitute's seedy apartment and makes love to him. When Marcello returns to his own apartment the next morning, he finds his mistress, who knows he is unfaithful, has attempted suicide.

Marcello rushes her to the hospital, but is soon called to the airport to cover the arrival of Sylvia (Anita Ekberg), a Hollywood starlet in Rome to star in some biblical potboiler. Marcello, who has forgotten about his mistress, is immediately infatuated with Sylvia and determined to add her to his long list of conquests.

That evening he attends a party in Sylvia's honor. She is ravishingly beautiful, dressed in a black evening gown with extreme décolletage. Sylvia has a fight with her drunken husband, Robert (Lex Barker, Ekberg's real-life husband) and runs away from the party. Marcello rescues her and takes her on an all-night tour of Rome's famous sites. His goal is to seduce her, but the sex star is not much interested in sex. Instead, she takes an erotic swim in the Trevi fountain. When she and Marcello return to her hotel at dawn, Robert beats both of them.

Marcello continues his aimless drift though life. He rushes to a small village where two children claim to have had a vision of the Madonna. The village turns into a circus, with reporters and hucksters clamoring everywhere. It is quickly established that the children and their parents have created a hoax. Nothing is what it seems to be in Marcello's life. He admires his friend Steiner (Alain Cuny), whose bohemian life-style Marcello envies. Steiner urges him to use his talents to write a book, but Marcello cannot escape the fast life. He is shocked and depressed when he learns that Steiner has murdered his two children and committed suicide. Nothing makes any sense to Marcello. He throws his mistress out and continues his downward fall.

The final episode takes place when Marcello's smart crowd breaks into the home of a friend for an orgy of drinking and partying to celebrate the annulment of the marriage of one of the women. To kick off the party she does a striptease; but even this fails to excite the lifeless thrill seekers, who are too jaded to participate in the orgy they thought they wanted. When the owner comes home, he kicks them out of the house.

The film ends as the disappointed revelers stumble out at dawn and walk to the beach. A transvestite, who was hired to entertain at the party, casually predicts to Marcello that soon everyone will be homosexual and the world will be in real trouble. Marcello pays no attention to him as he walks over to watch some local fishermen haul in a huge starfish they have caught. When he turns away he notices a young girl, whom he had met earlier in the film, waving at him from across a small inlet; but Marcello cannot hear her and turns and walks away. He has chosen to continue his hollow, meaningless life of debauchery.

Fellini's message was clear: The life-style of the rich and famous had no purpose. He illustrated sin and sex with graphic directness for 1960. Anita Ekberg spilled out of her evening gown in a way that Jane Russell never imagined. The fast crowd exchanged sex partners as they might exchange bridge partners. They knew nothing of life other than drinking themselves into oblivion and waking up in a new bed. That Fellini disapproved of this decadent life-style was only too clear to those who looked past the vivid bacchanal he put on the screen.

The Italians were outraged by Fellini's assessment of them. Despite the plea of the OCIC for greater freedom of expression for film, *La Dolce Vita* was condemned by the Catholic church in Italy for its casual depiction of sex and suicide. The Italian government followed suit when it banned the film for its scathing portrayal of modern Italy. Outside of Italy *La Dolce Vita* attracted a more tolerant reception. It was awarded the Grand Pix at Cannes, and the New York Film Critics judged it Best Film of 1961.

Could this film, which had been condemned in Italy by church and state because of its flagrant display of flesh and sex, win approval of the Production Code Administration and the new Legion of Decency? Would American audiences support such a picture?

La Dolce Vita was submitted to the PCA in 1961. There can be little doubt that Joe Breen would have been shocked by Fellini's film and would have denied it a seal of approval. Geoffrey Shurlock, however, was not the least bit offended by Fellini's vision of modern life-styles. The film hardly caused an eyebrow to be raised at the PCA offices. There were no requests to cut scenes, no comment about overexposure of actresses, and no discussion among the staff about the morality or immorality of *La Dolce Vita*. The PCA issued its seal of approval and congratulated the distributor, Astor Pictures, for "the dignified manner in which you are releasing this important, though controversial, picture."[54]

At Legion headquarters in New York City the film was much more troubling. Well aware that the Vatican strongly disapproved of the film and that conservative Catholics were unhappy with the Legion's growing liberalism, Msgr. Little and the Legion staff prepared to wade through the minefield that *La Dolce Vita* represented. Anything less than a condemned rating was sure to provoke rantings from Martin Quigley, who was certain to present his opinions directly to Cardinal Spellman.

Little, who was no novice to political infighting within the church, carefully planned the Legion's evaluation of *La Dolce Vita*. His first step was to write a report to his superiors sketching out what options were open to the Legion in 1961. Little stressed that unlike in the past, the Legion now had no power to keep *La Dolce Vita* out of theaters: It would be exhibited widely throughout the United States no matter what the Legion did and, he added for emphasis, "no industry or legal controls would be or could be applied" to it. The Legion "could effect some measure of control," Little wrote, either by pressuring the distributor to limit attendance or by invoking public pressure by condemnation. He added, however, that in recent years the evidence was overwhelming that a condemnation of the film "would not be supported by the public."[55]

Little also sketched out the Legion's available options to the 120 clerics and lay Catholics he brought in to evaluate Fellini's film. When he and Father Sullivan tabulated the reports from ninety-five of these consultors who submitted written evaluations, it was again clear that there was little consensus. Twenty-three, twelve of whom were priests, favored an A3 rating. One told Little that in his view the "theme of the movie is certainly a moral one"; there were shocking scenes in the film, he admitted, but they "were never exploited for sensual delight." A representative from the *Catholic World* pronounced it a "dull documentary on corruption" that would not harm "the average adult." Another priest judged it "a morality play" for adults.[56]

There was almost equal support for a condemnation: Twenty-two, including thirteen IFCA members, voted to condemn the film. One priest who voted for a Legion C was offended by the "suggestiveness" of *La Dolce Vita*. Another found its treatment of religion "scandalous" and "irreverent." One advocate of a C rating summed up the objections for his group: "The complete lack of all moral standards, the inclusion of male homosexuals and lesbians and transvestites together with all kinds of illicit intercourse and degeneracy can do no good whatever for the cause of decent entertainment." It was, he concluded, "first rate Communist propaganda."[57]

Twenty-two of the consultors, however, favored a B rating, and another twenty-eight thought the film deserved a Special Classification. All of the consultors who favored a B believed the overall theme of the film was "moral" but were squeamish about the flesh and sex in the movie. When Little and his staff read the various reports they were struck by the fact that so many of the consultors were convinced that Fellini was condemning the life-style he was illustrating. Everyone except those who recommended outright condemnation believed Fellini's overall theme was moral. "In a word," Little wrote in his report to Bishop McNulty, "the majority [76.8 percent] of our reviewers and consultors judged *La Dolce Vita* to be moral in theme and decent in treatment at least for mature audiences."[58]

Little worked behind the scenes to position Legion influence on the exhibition of the film. He did not want its distributor, Astor Pictures, to know the wide divergence of opinion within the Legion on *La Dolce Vita*. He knew he could no longer demand, as he once had, that scenes be cut or shortened, or that a prologue or epilogue be added to the film. The threat of condemnation would not work on an independent or foreign-produced film and, if democracy prevailed within the Legion, he did not have the votes. He also knew that large numbers of Catholics were going to see the film.

Little's goal, therefore, was to try to lessen the impact of *La Dolce Vita*. To achieve this goal he negotiated a threefold agreement with Astor Pictures that he hoped would limit attendance to mature adults. First, and most important to the Legion, Little asked that the film not be dubbed into English.

He was convinced that a subtitled version would restrict the appeal of the film to mature adults. The second condition Little requested was that Astor write into its contracts that theaters exhibiting the film limit attendance to those over age 18. The third condition was that advertising for the film not be exploitive. In exchange, Little agreed to issue a Separate Classification for *La Dolce Vita*.[59]

George F. Foley, president of Astor, readily agreed to the conditions. By doing so Astor avoided a public battle with the Legion and, in essence, won its blessing. With the agreement in hand, Little wrote to both Bishop McNulty and Cardinal Spellman for final approval. After summarizing the opinions of the Legion consultors, and stressing the overall moral theme of the film, he stated that in his view the three conditions imposed on its exhibition "will accomplish more for the common good than a condemnation." The subtitling, Little predicted, would severely limit its American exhibition. He admitted that the film had been condemned in Italy, but told his superiors that this had been for "political" not "moral" reasons.[60]

Both men supported Little, although it should be added that Spellman most likely did not agree with the decision but was unwilling to challenge it. When McNulty gave his approval, the Legion announced its Separate Classification several days later. In making the announcement the Legion informed Catholics that *La Dolce Vita* was "a bitter attack upon the debauchery and degradation of a hedonistic society of leisure and abundance." The Legion warned potential viewers that the film was at times coarse and exaggerated, but Catholics were assured that the overall "theme is animated throughout by a moral spirit."[61]

The decision of the Legion of Decency to approve *La Dolce Vita* brought a full declaration of war from the organization's creator, Martin Quigley. In a long missive addressed to Bishop McNulty and copied to Cardinals Spellman and McIntyre, friends in the Vatican, and conservative members of the Catholic press, Quigley let all his anger burst forth. He started his letter with the customary attack on the Jesuit clique that he believed responsible for approving Fellini's film. The Jesuits are, he claimed, "opposed to any condemnation of any motion picture . . . in this 'pluralistic society.'" They refused to recognize, Quigley fumed, that *La Dolce Vita* was "an obscene spectacle crowded with . . . immoral and sacrilegious representation – a burlesque on Fatima and Lourdes, sex perversion, strip-tease, prostitution, adultery, fornication and other . . . infectious violations of the moral law."[62]

Quigley accused the Legion of speaking "modernistic mumbo-jumbo" when it stated that the film was a bitter attack on debauchery and taught morality.[63] The publisher scoffed at the Legion contention that the film would appeal only to a "mature, adult, intellectually alert" audience fully capable of understanding its deeper meaning. The typical movie patron, Quigley told

McNulty, would see "no sardonic commentary" on modern society but rather only "vivid images of . . . adultery, fornication, prostitution" and striptease. Quigley held firm to his lifelong contention that the average moviegoer was not terribly bright and was openly susceptible to corruption by filmmakers.

La Dolce Vita was not a morality play for the masses, he argued; it was nothing more than a "vicious and degrading spectacle" that the Legion should condemn. Quigley was completely mystified that the Legion clerics failed to see the film as anticlerical.[64]

Ignoring the fact that the PCA had issued the film a seal, Quigley concluded his attack on the Legion by stating that its failure to condemn the film "has in effect administered a lethal blow to the Code which will result either in its being wiped out or its enforcement weakened to the point of literal ineffectiveness." To prevent this from happening, Quigley urged McNulty to take "remedial action" and condemn *La Dolce Vita*.[65]

"Mr. Quigley, this is unadulterated nonsense," countered Bishop McNulty. The claim that a Jesuit conspiracy was afoot within the Legion was completely "without foundation," McNulty told Quigley. "I find no happiness in writing a letter of this kind nor do I find happiness in your oft repeated, and, I think, unjustifiable attacks upon the National Legion of Decency."[66] Several days after McNulty scolded Quigley, Little told the bishop that in his opinion Quigley suffered from "a form of megalomania and unless he personally can make all the important decisions of this office he will remain unhappy until his dying day."[67]

The publisher did have his supporters, however. Archbishop Karl J. Alter of Cincinnati wrote Quigley of his support and to prove it condemned *La Dolce Vita* in his diocese. In Los Angeles Cardinal McIntyre supported Quigley's position but was unwilling to take any action that might embarrass the Legion publicly. William Mooring echoed McIntyre's line with a blistering attack on the film in *Tidings*.[68] In Albany, Bishop Scully, recently retired from his chairmanship of the Episcopal Committee, found himself agreeing with his old rival. Scully warned his flock to "pass this one up for the good of your soul." The prelate declared *La Dolce Vita* "out of bounds" in his diocese.[69]

For the most part, though, the Legion enjoyed the support of the Catholic press. *Ave Maria* editorialized that "the Legion should have our support for its adult response to a difficult task."[70] *Commonweal* congratulated the Legion for its "intelligent comment and evaluation."[71] The *Catholic Standard* told readers that the "Legion stuck its neck out . . . and undoubtedly gained stature in doing so."[72] The *Catholic Mind* called the Legion rating "correct and judicious."[73] Moira Walsh, writing in *America*, called Fellini's film a "salutary moral warning" and supported the Legion's decision.[74] Edward Fisher, reviewer for *Ave Maria*, after praising *La Dolce Vita*, reminded his readers of a basic fact about movies: "The only thing I can say definitely is that if anyone goes and finds this is too strong for him he can always get up and leave."[75]

Most moviegoers stayed glued to their seats. Quigley was right in predicting that the film would appeal to a much broader audience than the mature adults anticipated by the Legion. A New Orleans Catholic protested to Father Sullivan that when she saw *La Dolce Vita* the theater was full of adolescents under the legal age of 18 – something Quigley had also predicted – and she blamed it on the Legion. Father Sullivan firmly corrected her: The fault was not the Legion's or the theater owner's, Sullivan argued; it was the parents who were "guilty of delinquency in fulfillment of their parental responsibilities." The Legion, Sullivan wrote, gives guidance but "it doesn't exist to take over the role of parents in the home."[76]

According to Variety, *La Dolce Vita* brought in $6 million in rentals at the American box office. No doubt many who saw the film went for sexual titillation not moral instruction. There were no doubt many young teenagers who felt very grown up by posing as 18 year olds. Although the film was not a box-office champion in 1961, neither was it a dud. It ran for thirty-four consecutive weeks at the Henry Miller Theater in New York City and compared very favorably with the $6.3 million that *Suddenly Last Summer* generated. By the end of the year it ranked seventy-first on the *Variety* list of all-time box-office champions and proved that Americans would pay to see, and even read the subtitles of, foreign films.[77]

La Dolce Vita illustrated an important point in the history of the Legion and its attempt to control what the larger culture could see: Given a free choice, sincere, intelligent Catholics, clerical and lay, could no more agree on what was moral entertainment than could any other segment of the population. Martin Quigley believed to his core that his view of movie morality was correct. It is true he fought to maintain his influence in the Legion for personal reasons, but it is just as true that he was convinced his position was right. Where Quigley and his supporters saw only debauchery, however, many others saw moral lessons. Clerical professors of theology, whose entire lives were devoted to the study of ethical and moral dilemmas, were able to view Fellini's scenes of the false vision of the Madonna and nod knowingly – getting rich off religion had indeed become all too common a vocation. They saw the shallow life-styles of the rich and famous and recognized many around them; they saw moral comment where others saw only sin. Still, other clerics who watched the same movie – sincerely devoted men – saw the criticism of Western society as communist propaganda!

Even bishops could not agree on what was or was not a moral movie. Bishop Scully, for example, who had not been scandalized by *Suddenly Last Summer,* was shocked by *La Dolce Vita*. Archbishop Alter condemned it in Cincinnati, and it is clear that Cardinal McIntyre, and one assumes Cardinal

Spellman, did not approve of the film; yet Bishop McNulty was not shocked by it. Only one bishop of the more than a hundred in America took individual action against the movie.

If art is in the eye of the beholder, so too is the ability to pronounce a work of art, or a movie, moral or immoral. The diversity of opinion in the Legion on the morality of a particular movie was inevitable once a widely representative group of reviewers was allowed to voice opinions. The highly educated clerics and lay professionals rejected the narrow, negative, black-or-white view of movie morality that Quigley, the IFCA, and the leadership of the old Legion had carefully crafted and enforced for three decades.

It is very clear that the old Legion would have condemned *La Dolce Vita*. Of the twenty-one members of the IFCA who voted on the film, fifteen voted for a C or B classification. Quigley, who had always been invited to meetings on controversial films, would have won over to his position those IFCA reviewers who saw moral lessons in *La Dolce Vita*. The women of the IFCA were commonly pressured to toe the Legion line. As one recent study noted: "A reviewer who strayed from the Legion guidelines would receive a note in the next mail pointing out where she had gone wrong."[78] Expanding the pool of consultors had effectively limited the opinions of the IFCA and silenced Martin Quigley as the dominating voice in the Legion.

As a postscript to the story, in 1965 Edward Fisher, film critic for *Ave Maria,* was hired as a professor of Communication Studies at Notre Dame University. By the mid-1960s the Legion looked to Fisher, not William Mooring of *Tidings,* as its leading lay authority on the movies. Fisher's book, *The Screen Arts,* was recommended reading for Catholics, and he was the first movie critic for a Catholic publication to win the annual Critic's Award from the Hollywood Director's Guild for the quality of his reviews. In 1965 Fisher was teaching a course at Notre Dame, entitled "The Screen Arts," that featured *La Dolce Vita*. A nun attending the course described her viewing of the film as one "of the more powerful human, moral and religious experiences" she had ever had.[79]

In the 1950s Martin Quigley, in addition to having troubles with the Legion, faced financial difficulty in his publishing ventures. They had boomed during Hollywood's golden era, but now advertising revenue from the industry was declining. In middecade Quigley turned most of the day-to-day operations of his publishing business over to his son, Martin Quigley Jr., leaving the elder Quigley more time to dabble in Legion affairs and to capitalize on his reputation as "Mr. Fixit." He began with some regularity to sell his services as an expert on the PCA and Legion to producers. For a fee, Quigley offered to read scripts and help guide a project toward a favorable Legion rating.

Although it was clear to Legion officials that Quigley's role had waned, it was less apparent to producers and industry officials at the time. Publicly, he presented himself as an "unofficial Legion representative," and he was still in the good graces of two of the most powerful members of the Catholic hierarchy: Cardinal McIntyre in Los Angeles and Cardinal Spellman in New York. For $25,000 per film Quigley offered to guide producers toward favorable ratings by the Legion and a PCA seal.

From his New York City office Quigley must have seen the huge billboards overlooking the theater district in Times Square that featured a very young girl provocatively posed in a small bikini bathing suit and large sunglasses. The billboard asked New Yorkers: "How did they ever make a film of *Lolita*?" The implication was clear: Vladimir Nabokov's infamous novel about a middle-aged college professor's lust for a 12-year-old nymphet, Lolita, was too dirty for the movies. Those who bothered to read the staid *New York Times* saw movie critic Bosley Crowther's terse reply: "They didn't."[80]

They didn't because they couldn't. Nabokov's novel, first published in France in 1955, had been both praised as a literary masterpiece and denounced as pornographic trash. The book is narrated by Humbert Humbert, a middle-aged British widower who is a professor of French literature. The reader is informed that the author of the story, Humbert, has died of a heart attack in jail just before his trial is about to start. The reader knows Humbert has committed a crime but knows nothing else about the man. The novel unravels the mystery as Humbert tells his story in flashback narration.

Humbert has come to the United States to take a teaching position at a small midwestern college, but he decides to spend the summer before his teaching duties begin in New Hampshire. In the small town of Ramsdale he takes a room in the home of a local widow, Charlotte Haze. The widow Haze has designs on Humbert; but Humbert, a dedicated pedophile, has designs on Dolores Haze, nicknamed Lolita, Charlotte's 12-year-old daughter.

In order to remain as close as he can to Lolita, with whom he falls madly in love, Humbert turns down his teaching job and remains in Ramsdale. He marries Charlotte, though he despises her, in order to share a home with Lolita. He writes in his diary of his lust for the girl and his hatred for his wife. When Charlotte secretly reads his diary, she is horrified. She flees from the house and, in a freak accident, is killed by a passing car. Humbert is delighted by this unexpected good fortune because he is now the legal guardian of Lolita – and he intends to guard her very carefully.

After hastily making funeral arrangements, he rushes off to pick up Lolita at her summer camp, Camp Climax. Humbert makes up a story about Charlotte being very sick and in a hospital some distance from the camp. They will be forced, he tells Lolita, to spend a night in a hotel – a ruse on Humbert's part to get Lolita into bed. When they arrive at the hotel there is only one room available with one double bed. With great fanfare Humbert requests a cot for his daughter, but he has no intention of using it. When the two of them are alone, Lolita looks around the room and proclaims her suspicions. She tells Humbert her mother will kill her and divorce him if she finds out they slept in the same room. When he begins to stammer that her suggestions are out of line, she shouts back at him, "The word is incest."[81]

Humbert casually tells the reader he was not "unduly disturbed by her self-accusatory innuendoes." He had not, he assures his audience, intended to force himself on Lolita; instead, the professor had carefully planned to slip Lolita a strong dose of sleeping pills that would knock her out so he could then spend the night fondling her nude body. As he told the reader: "I was still firmly resolved to pursue my policy of sparing her purity by operating only in the stealth of night, only upon a completely anesthetized little nude." After all, Humbert reminds the reader, "Lolita was only twelve."[82]

After drugging her, Humbert goes down to the hotel bar to wile away some time while the pills take effect. When he returns to the room and climbs into bed with Lolita, she wakes up. The pills had not worked. Later he tries again: "After a long stirless vigil, my tentacles moved towards her again. . . . I managed to bring my ravenous bulk so close to her that I felt the aura of her bare shoulder like a warm breath upon my cheek."[83] And the girl re-awakens!

Poor Humbert spends a sleepless night so close to, yet so far from, his Lolita. He is afraid to touch her because he is convinced that she is a young, innocent virgin. A real surprise is in store for the old professor when Lolita wakes up and finds him beside her. Humbert, fearing reproach, pretends to be fast asleep, but he realizes that Lolita is looking at him. To his surprise and delight he discovers that "my Lolita was a sporting lass." They nuzzle and then kiss gently. Lolita excitedly asks Humbert if he had ever played the game she played with Charlie at Camp Climax. Humbert feigns ignorance. "You mean," she asks, "you never did it when you were a kid?" Never, Humbert replies. "Suffice it to say," Humbert continues, "that not a trace of modesty did I perceive in this beautiful hardly formed young girl whom modern co-education, juvenile mores, the camp-fire racket and so forth had utterly and hopelessly depraved." It was "she who seduced me," he joyfully confesses.[84]

Lolita, it seems, had spent much of her time at Camp Climax in the arms of Charlie Holmes, son of the camp owner, and Elizabeth Talbot, daughter of one of the most prominent families in Ramsdale. She was, by age 12, well instructed in the ways of love by both sexes.

The second volume of the novel continues as Humbert and Lolita spend a year traveling across the United States. Humbert is ecstatic: "For there is no other bliss on earth comparable to that of fondling a nymphet." Lolita is a willing if unenthusiastic sex partner for Humbert, who convinces her that if she tells anyone of the true relationship between them, he will be sent to jail and she to reform school. Each morning Humbert dutifully shuffles off to bring Lolita her morning coffee. "How sweet it was to bring that coffee to her, and then deny it until she had done her morning duty." "On especially tropical afternoons," Humbert tells the reader, "I liked the cool feel of arm-chair leather against my massive nakedness as I held her in my lap. There she would be, a typical kid picking her nose while engrossed in the lighter sections of a newspaper, as indifferent to my ecstasy as if it were something she had sat upon, a shoe, a doll, the handle of a tennis racket, and was too indolent to remove."[85] Lolita, however, soon tires of Humbert and his games.

When they finally settle down in Beardsley, where Humbert is take up his teaching duties, the pedophile professor's world begins to unravel. Humbert is insanely jealous and fears Lolita will tell someone about their relationship. He will not allow her to date boys or do the other things young girls normally do. He continually suspects that she has a young lover. Finally, in a desperate effort to keep her to himself, they depart on another cross-country trip; but this time Lolita is less willing to play Humbert's games, and he soon discovers they are being followed by a mysterious man.

Lolita, who had only agreed to go if she could set the itinerary, eventually ditches Humbert for this stranger, and the professor spends the next three years searching for her. When he finally finds her, she is married, broke, and pregnant. Humbert rushes to Lolita and attempts to lure her back into his arms. She is no longer a nymphet, but Humbert still loves her. She refuses. He does, however, force her to tell him who had stolen her away from him on their second trip. It was Clare Quilty, a famous writer who lived in Ramsdale. She matter-of-factly tells Humbert that Quilty later dumped her when she refused to make a pornographic movie he planned.

Humbert is crushed. He gives Lolita the money she needs and then murders Quilty, whom he blames for their separation. With Humbert in jail awaiting trial for murder the novel ends, but the reader knows he will soon have a fatal heart attack.

"There seems to be good indication that we are making excellent progress in our efforts to lift this notorious story out of the gutter," Quigley told a rather stunned Geoffrey Shurlock.[86] Quigley, the moralist, had been hired by director Stanley Kubrick and his partner James Harris to guide them through the labyrinth of codes and Catholics. Thus Quigley, during the same period when he was attacking the Legion over the classification of *La Dolce Vita*, was toiling as a paid consultant to secure approval for a film about a pedophile who drugs a 12-year-old child in order to have sex with her and then kidnaps her so he can continue to savor her sexual favors! Quigley's view of what was acceptable moral entertainment for the masses had undergone a radical – and remunerative – transformation.

At first glance it seems uncharacteristic that Kubrick, now recognized as a great auteur, would worry about whether or not the PCA or the Legion would approve of his film. He and Harris were independent producers and well aware of the recent success that independents had had in marketing films without a PCA seal or Legion approval. It is important to remember, however, that in 1960 Kubrick was a 30-year-old director with very little experience. He had directed a highly respected film about a mutiny in the French army in World War I, *The Paths of Glory,* and had one major Hollywood spectacular, *Spartacus,* to his credit. He would soon direct such important films as the black comedy *Dr. Strangelove, or How I Learned to Stop Worrying and Love the Bomb,* the science-fiction masterpiece *2001,* the deeply troubling *A Clockwork Orange,* and the horrifying thriller *The Shining;* but these films were in his future.

In 1958, when he and Harris had first pitched to the PCA a film based on *Lolita,* they were just another Hollywood production unit. Shurlock had been discouraging, telling them that a film featuring an "elderly man having an affair with a twelve-year old girl" was sex perversion and not acceptable under the code. The producers had assured Shurlock that their film would not be a story about perversion: They saw *Lolita* as a comedy that would illustrate the humor of a "mature man married to a gum-chewing teen-ager."[87]

Shurlock, however, was not convinced that *Lolita* was all that funny. When several studios approached him for an initial reaction to the project, he warned them that "a great deal of damage might be done to the industry" by a filmed version of the infamous novel.[88] When Kubrick and Harris inquired about funding and distribution at several studios, they encountered great reluctance. In fact, everyone turned had them down – unless, the studios added, the PCA and the Legion gave approval. It was one thing, the majors believed, to make or distribute a film that dealt frankly with adult sexuality; it was quite another thing to deal with pedophilia.

Kubrick and Harris persisted. Two years after they first approached Shurlock, they struck a deal with Seven Arts Productions, a Toronto corporation that produced television programs and occasional films, to finance *Lolita.* Seven Arts negotiated a distribution deal through MGM, which was willing to gamble on the project if Kubrick and Harris would make the film at its facilities in England: Trade agreements and British law had frozen some of its profits in England; the project was attractive to the studio if it could use those funds for production. Both MGM and Seven Arts insisted, however, that Kubrick and Harris receive PCA approval and a blessing from the Legion.

With financing and distribution assured, Kubrick and Harris bought the screen rights to the novel, hired Nabokov to craft a screenplay, and began working with Quigley.

Kubrick cast the film with some fanfare. Who would play Lolita was the question of the day in Hollywood. Tuesday Weld desperately wanted the part. "I don't have to play it," she said. "I was Lolita."[89] This may have been so, but the Hollywood veteran of such teen pics as *Sex Kittens Go to College* was, at the ripe old age of 17, long past her nymphet stage. Instead, Kubrick settled on an unknown actress from Davenport, Iowa: Sue Lyon. Born in July 1946, she was the perfect combination of fresh-scrubbed innocence and sophistication that Kubrick sought. She was 14 but looked much, much older. As her lover, Kubrick cast James Mason, a British actor who specialized in playing suave continentals. For Lolita's mother Kubrick cast blowsy character actress Shelley Winters, who gave an outstanding performance. The stranger who steals Lolita from Humbert, Clare Quilty, was played by Peter Sellers.

As Kubrick later admitted, "I wasn't able to give much weight at all to the erotic aspect of Humbert's relationship in the film."[90] Everyone agreed that much of the objection to the film would be eliminated if Lolita was older. A provocative teenager somewhere between 15 and 18 was easier to accept than a 12 year old. Even Shurlock bought into that concept when he told Quigley that the PCA might approve the story "provided the girl is at least fifteen."[91] Lyon was 14, but with a little makeup could certainly pass.

When Quigley read Nabokov's script he thought there was far too much erotic detail even for an older teenager. He carried on a long correspondence with James Harris and Seven Arts executive Eliot Hyman over script details. Quigley's greatest concern was the seduction scene between Lolita and Humbert. In the book they nuzzle and pet in bed, and then make love. Quigley wanted no such scene in the movie – and, in all fairness, neither did Kubrick or Harris. He was shocked, however, when he read how Lolita seduced Humbert in the proposed script: She awakens in the morning (undrugged) and finds Humbert sleeping, rather uncomfortably, on a hotel cot; she walks over to the cot and begins to tease Humbert; she bends over him, nuzzles his neck, then sticks her tongue in his ear.

Quigley must have had very sensitive ears. He informed Harris that this technique was a "notorious device for arousing sexual passion" and had been banned by the code out of fear that it would corrupt young people. "This technique," he continued, "cannot be used without arousing erotically the susceptible members of any audience, anywhere, any time." If this scene was in the film, Quigley predicted, it "would be enough to get a Legion of Decency condemnation" because it was "sharply in the direction of the pornographic." Let Lolita "tease, torment and bedevil Humbert," Quigley begged, but do not let her stick her tongue in his ear.[92]

He also suggested that the filmmakers include scenes of Humbert tucking Lolita in bed and giving her a "fatherly kiss on the forehead" to build audience sympathy for him and to make "more stark and dramatic Lolita's seduction." He urged them not to dress Lolita in a seductive Baby Doll outfit, and to delete as many of the double-entendre lines as possible to avoid offending moral guardians. He also expressed great concern over the scene in which Humbert is prone at Lolita's feet, carefully painting her toenails. The scene took place while Lolita was sunning herself, and Quigley suggested that she be completely covered "to make this toe-painting business without generating an odor of disgust."[93]

Although Quigley's opinions were valued, it was clear that he was viewed as a paid employee, not a censor or higher moral authority. Some of his suggestions were accepted, others dismissed. Harris assured Quigley that Lolita "could not be construed, in any way, as childlike." There were numerous scenes – a high school dance, her school chums – that would show audiences she was at least 15. Lolita would wear, he told Quigley, "a heavy flannel, long sleeved, high-necked, full-length nightgown." He assured Quigley that they would not have Lolita stick her tongue in Humbert's ear: The screenplay did call for it, but "what we will do is shoot 'clear daylight' between the two, and the audience will hear an inaudible whisper."[94]

Quigley was mollified and told Shurlock that he had successfully removed the most offending sections of the script. Shurlock was not so sure; he told Quigley that the "whispering in Humbert's ear will be interpreted as obscene" and would not be approved.[95] Quigley, disappointed, told Harris that the censor did not "seem disposed to extend himself in detailed and practicable helpfulness."[96] Shurlock was not disposed to help Quigley: According to Jack Vizzard, after one rather disagreeable phone conversation with Quigley on *Lolita*, Shurlock called him a "pious prick." *Lolita*, he told Vizzard, "better be clean, or I'm going to rub his nose it."[97]

He did so. In August 1961 a rough cut of the film was ready for PCA scrutiny. Kubrick opened the film with Humbert's murder of Clare Quilty, which not only eliminated the "mystery man" in the novel but also established that Lolita was an experienced young lady. The film was infused with a comedic flavor, and Humbert appears foolish, rather than evil, through much of the picture. He and Lolita exchange knowing glances, but not much more. The tension in the seduction scene is cut with a bit of slapstick humor when a bellboy shows up with a cot. The two of them fumble and bumble trying to get the cot set up. When Humbert finally gets in, it collapses, and he remains there the rest of the night.

Shurlock saw the film with Martin Quigley. Vizzard, who was also at the screening, later wrote that Shurlock taunted Quigley about several minor points in the film just to see him squirm. However, Shurlock turned serious during the seduction. Despite the slapstick nature of the cot business, Shurlock was worried about the following morning. In that scene, Lolita wakes up, goes over to Humbert, and asks him if he wants to play a game – a game she used to play in the woods at summer camp. Lolita, per the script instructions, applies "herself again to his tingling ear."[98] Lolita then asks: "Like me to show you?" Humbert twitches and replies: "If it's not too dangerous. If it's not too difficult. If it's not too – Ah, mon Dieu!" Lolita, the experienced seductress, soothes her trembling stepfather by wrapping her arms around his neck as the scene fades.

It was much too explicit for Shurlock. Despite vehement protests from Quigley, the Hollywood censor demanded the scene be edited. To rub a bit of salt into the consultant's wounds, Shurlock refused to discuss any further changes with him; instead, he called Harris and told him he wanted the seduction scene shortened and all the dialogue that implied playing games cut or so muted on the sound track that the audience could not hear it. When Harris agreed, Shurlock issued *Lolita* seal no. 2000. Quigley later cooed to Harris that it was "a good fat number," which, he hoped, would be "a good omen."[99]

Unfortunately for Quigley, it was not a good omen. The Legion of Decency was waiting for *Lolita* and Mr. Fixit. Writing to Msgr. Little as the Legion prepared to examine *Lolita*'s morals, Father Sullivan posed, and answered, several questions. Would the film harm adults? Sullivan was doubtful that it would. Could attendance be limited to 18 and older? Sullivan told Little that the producers were very agreeable to placing such a restriction on attendance and were also willing to write it into their contracts with exhibitors. Would a condemnation be effective? Sullivan was certain it would not be. The Legion had recently condemned *Never on Sunday*, which, Sullivan added grimly, was doing land-office business at the box office. He recommended that *Lolita* be given a Separate Classification. Would the film, because of the subject matter, open the door for further films on revolting themes? Perhaps. Finally, Sullivan asked Little to consider the "role of Martin Quigley in the making of this picture."[100]

Lolita was screened at least three different times and in two different versions for the Legion. The first screening took place in September 1961 and used the same version shown to Shurlock, including the longer, more detailed seduction scene to which the PCA director had objected. The fifty-two Legion consultants Little rounded up to judge the film were divided both on its merits and on the value of cutting the seduction scene. Nine, including four priests, saw *Lolita* as an A3 film that would do no harm to adults. A larger number, fourteen, including eight priests, were concerned enough to place the film in the B category. An even larger group, twenty-six, including eight priests, were shocked and voted for outright condemnation. A parish priest from Manhattan who favored a condemnation told Little the film had "no reason for existence." It was, he added, "stupid, dull and consistently boring." (He also voted to condemn *West Side Story*.) Another C vote came from a professor from the Fordham Law School, who called *Lolita* "a disgusting chronicle of perversion" that was "objectionable in its entirety." He did not believe Catholics would want to see either of the seduction sequences. Four voted to give *Lolita* a Separate Classification.[101]

The Legion staff, which voted separately, was also divided. Little was, "without qualification," in favor of condemnation, Sullivan held to his Separate Classification, and Mrs. Looram judged it a B. Again, little firm consensus existed: Twenty-seven total votes for a condemnation, twenty-six putting the film in some other classification. Little arranged a second screening, held on October 10, 1961, for the man who would cast the determining vote. Bishop McNulty, chair of the Episcopal Committee, would decide whether or not Martin Quigley had effectively purified the morals of the notorious young tart he had heard so much about. Just as Quigley was convinced that McNulty did not understand the moral dangers inherent in Fellini's work, McNulty was certain that *Lolita* was immoral. He dismissed the opinion of reviewers who saw morality in the film and ordered Little to condemn it out of hand.[102]

The film offers, the Legion told Seven Arts, "two and a half hours of exposure to an unrelieved . . . sexual depravity." It was "tasteless" and represented the "moral corruption" of the actress Miss Lyon, who had to be instructed in the ways of love in order to play the part. As for the comedic elements in the film, the Legion stated that "Quilty [Peter Sellers] as a psychotic clown does not add comic relief to the overall effect of the film but on the contrary serves to heighten the film's undercurrent of prurient morbidity."[103]

Kubrick and Harris, Seven Arts and MGM, and especially Martin Quigley were shocked by the Legion's actions. David Stillman, counsel for Seven Arts, wrote a letter of protest to McNulty. The corporation, Stillman wrote, was immediately withdrawing *Lolita* from public exhibition to protect its reputation. It is quite clear, Stillman said, that Legion action was "based on extraneous considerations" and not on the merits of the film. Stillman demanded to know why the producers were not given an opportunity to change the film to avoid condemnation. Was it, he asked, "to counter-balance the Legion's record of relatively favorable classification which has been given to many films which every informed person knows are far more condemnable on moral grounds. . . ?" In case the bishop found that reference too subtle, Stillman named *Suddenly Last Summer* and *La Dolce Vita* as movies that might more reasonably have been condemned. Stillman suggested that legal action might be taken if the Legion took the matter to the public press.[104]

"Although it would be difficult to prove in a court of law," Little told Cardinal Spellman, "Bishop McNulty, Father Sullivan and I . . . are convinced beyond doubt that Mr. Stillman composed his letter . . . with the advice and counsel of Mr. Quigley."[105] Little, aware that Quigley had appealed the Legion's decision to Cardinal Spellman, effectively countered his attempted intervention by citing the lengths to which Quigley was going in his attempt to control Legion classifications. The letter, Little pointed out, was deeply insulting to Bishop McNulty. Cardinal Spellman refused to enter the fray.

Lolita remained in purgatory for several months. A compromise agreement was finally negotiated in January 1962. The seduction scene was cut, even further than Shurlock had suggested, to a fadeout as Lolita bends over Humbert and begins to whisper in his ear. No details of the youthful seduction were left in the film. Attendance was limited to those 18 and older, and to ensure that exhibitors did not sensationalize *Lolita,* the studio gave the Legion final approval of the pressbook.[106]

Legion consultants were brought back for a third screening in January 1962 and asked to judge the effectiveness of the newest seduction scene. As a means of comparison they were also shown the previous version. A priest from St. Peter's College, who called the book "a great tour de force," argued that the longer, more detailed seduction sequence "was more convincing for the viewer who should know that Lolita's knowledge is not purely theoretical but experiential and authentic." He told Little that in his opinion "the picture is moral." Another priest from a local New York Catholic high school did not see that the "morality of the film is substantially affected" by the shorter seduction scene. He stated flatly there was nothing "in the film as a whole that would deserve condemnation." A local parish priest told Little that he saw no difference in the two versions of the seduction scene and "would not object to either one." Another priest wrote that the message he got from the film was that the relationship between Lolita and Humbert was "reprehensible, unnatural and altogether . . . unfavorable." He preferred the longer seduction scene because it clarified that Lolita was "a woman of experience." A professor of Communication Arts at Fordham thought the sensational aspects of the film were handled "in very good taste."[107]

Others continued to see the same problems with the film that they had seen at the first viewing. The overall numbers did not change substantially; but Sullivan argued, and Little finally agreed, that if the film was limited to adults it would not cause any harm. In April 1962 the Legion placed *Lolita* in the Separate Classification, noting that the film had been "sufficiently modified." It warned Catholics, however, that *Lolita* required "caution" and was "restricted to a mature audience."[108]

Father Sullivan went to considerable effort to explain the Legion's change of mind in an interview published throughout the country. Sullivan admitted that ten years earlier the Legion would have condemned the film; but in 1962, he added, audiences are more selective and more mature. Sullivan claimed that Americans no longer were passive receptors of media messages as they had been in the past: Modern audiences, he said, exercised "more judgment" and were "more selective" in the type of movies they chose to see. Nor was there, he stressed, any "widespread ground swell demand for control" of movie content. Adults did not want their movies censored. The Legion recognized this fact and was trying to create a system that would allow adults to see adult movies but would also prevent children from seeing films that were not appropriate for them. What the Catholic church wanted, Sullivan concluded, was "some type of voluntary classification by the industry and exhibitors" that would restrict attendance. In short, Sullivan was calling for the movie industry to initiate a rating system.[109]

The decision to place *Lolita* in a Separate Classification proved very controversial in Catholic circles. The *Sign* blasted it a "grotesquely unpleasant bit of erotica."[110] Philip Hartung told *Commonweal* readers that if they could forget the novel on which it was based, the film was "absorbing, well-acted with many sharp cinematic comments"; the editors, however, later countered that it "epitomized the vulgarity and tastelessness" of the novel.[111] To *Our Sunday Visitor,* however, it was "a kooky comedy done with skill and care" and "not a shocker."[112]

Secular reviews were equally divided. Stanley Kauffman dubbed his review "Humbug Humbug" and bemoaned the fact that Kubrick and Harris had solicited PCA and Legion approval, which had stripped the movie of its purpose. What is left, he wrote, was "a rather soggy odyssey of a rueful, obsessed mature man, a diluted *Blue Angel* with a teenage temptress instead of a tart."[113] *Variety* wrote that the "moralists can rest easy" because *Lolita* was like "a bee from which the stinger has been removed": It buzzed a lot but made "very little point as comedy or satire."[114] Not surprisingly, Quigley's *Motion Picture Herald* disagreed. It called *Lolita* "impressive" and predicted box-office appeal because the film combined "comedy and tragedy" so effectively.[115]

An audience survey conducted by the *New York Herald Tribune* confirmed that few were upset by the movie's morals. Women leaving the theater were asked what they thought of the film. Barbara Levine, 18, told reporters that she "liked the movie better than the book," but Lolita "should have been younger." Ellen Sherer, also 18, found "nothing in it to shock anybody." Barbara Puleo, 24, said she "felt very good about it. It happens to be true to life." Mrs. Alice Romanouski, a very mature 39 years old, said the film "was done with great finesse," and she would "recommend it for teenagers."[116]

As it worked its way across America's theaters there was little protest and much box-office appeal. *Lolita* ran for eleven weeks at Loew's State Theater in New York City, a month at Baltimore's Town Theater, seven weeks at the

Shady Oaks in St. Louis, and after nine weeks at the Loop Theater in downtown Chicago was still "sizzling" at $15,000 per week. By the end of 1962 *Lolita* stood at sixteenth in *Variety*'s annual box-office chart and had generated $4.5 million in rentals. It was not a smash hit, however: The box-office winner was *West Side Story*, which had raked in $11 million in cash.[117]

Priests and prelates, professors and lawyers, students and housewives, Catholic and secular reviewers who saw the same film came away with different perceptions. Some saw *Lolita* as harmless, with an overriding moral lesson; others saw perversion and degradation. Within the Legion there was no consensus over which seduction scene was better: Those who saw the film as moral favored the longer seduction sequence because it clearly established that Lolita was, as one member put it, "a woman of experience"; but others thought the longer sequence too detailed and preferred the shorter one, which they believed conveyed the same point.

By the early 1960s, it was becoming increasingly clear, even to the staff of the Legion of Decency, that personal opinion more than morality was the determining factor in whether or not individuals saw films like *La Dolce Vita, Lolita,* or *Suddenly Last Summer* as moral. The Catholic church and its Legion had made great strides in the five years following *Miranda Prorsus* in recognizing that adult themes in movies were not going to corrupt the morals of everyone who saw them. Father Sullivan led the movement toward a more tolerant view of movies for adults, but the Catholic bishops and the Legion remained adamant that these adult films not be shown to children. A key ingredient in classifying *La Dolce Vita* and *Lolita* was the willingness of the distributors and exhibitors to limit attendance to those over 18. Over the next several years the Catholic church and the Legion would continue to pressure the movie industry to adopt some type of ratings system that would restrict adult movies, as more than mindless entertainment for the masses, to adults.

The effort toward liberalization included not only expanded classifications and new consultors who brought a more tolerant view of what adults could handle, but also, in the mid-1960s, a replacement of the old Legion of Decency pledge with a new one written by Father Sullivan. The old pledge, written by Archbishop McNicholas, had called movies "a grave menace to youth, to home life, to country and religion" and had Catholics agree not to attend movies judged "vile and unwholesome."[118] The new pledge urged Catholics to promote good films and work against bad ones "in a responsible and civic-minded manner."[119] The influence of John Courtney Murray on Father Sullivan could not have been clearer. After Msgr. Little told the bishops that the old pledge "has become an object of criticism, dissatisfaction, indifference, and even hostility," they voted to adopt Sullivan's draft. It was mostly symbolic but an important symbol of change within the Catholic church.[120]

Martin Quigley fought this liberalization with all his might. He tried in 1961 to place the liberalization of the Legion on the agenda of the bishops' annual meeting in November. This time he appealed to Archbishop Alter in Cincinnati. Alter was sympathetic and wrote to Msgr. Paul Tanner of the National Catholic Welfare Conference in Washington asking for a debate on Legion policy. Quigley's request backfired, however, when Tanner asked Bishop McNulty for his views. McNulty recapped, in great detail, Quigley's recent history with the Legion staff, concluding that Quigley was a hypocrite who tried to use his Catholic connections "to derive more prestige, power and profit than he was entitled to."[121] Quigley was again rebuffed. It was clear that some bishops (Alter, Cardinals McIntyre and Spellman) might privately agree with Quigley, but they were not going to challenge a fellow bishop based on charges from a layman. Quigley never seemed to understand this fundamental point.

Occasionally, however, the Legion could still revert to its old self. Two films, *The Pawnbroker* and *Who's Afraid of Virginia Woolf?*, would propel the Legion and the movie industry further away from censorship and closer to a ratings system restricting film attendance by age groups. Ironically, this was a direction favored by the Catholic church and resisted by the movie industry.

CHAPTER 7

THE END OF THE LEGION

For two years the industry has not only refused to adopt [an age] classification but has unalterably opposed every effort at any form of film classification.
— Annual Report of the Legion, 1962

The 1960s were a turbulent decade of change in America. Although few people appreciated it at the time, the election of a young, handsome Roman Catholic, John F. Kennedy, marked the beginning of a new era. The safe, confident assumptions of the 1950s were challenged, assailed, and then junked by a new generation. Betty Friedan wrote in her ground-breaking study of feminism, *The Feminine Mystique,* that the American home, so celebrated in the 1950s, had become "a comfortable concentration camp" for women. Liberation from an oppressive society became the rallying cry for women, African Americans, Native Americans, and Hispanics.

The decade of the 1960s is synonymous with the civil rights movement. In 1960 four freshman students at North Carolina A&T College in Greensboro, North Carolina, sat down at the all-white lunch counter in a local diner and refused to leave. The movement exploded across America with dramatic, dynamic, and tragic results. In 1962 James Meredith entered a citadel of segregation, the University of Mississippi, and set off a firestorm of racial hatred. In 1963, the same year that saw Meredith graduate from Old Miss, hundreds of thousands marched on Washington for racial equality. Within the year assassins struck civil rights leader Medgar Evers and then shocked the world by killing President Kennedy.

Five years later the nightmare recurred: Martin Luther King Jr. was killed in Memphis, and then Robert Kennedy's bid for the Democratic nomination for the presidency was stopped with his assassination in Los Angeles. As tensions escalated, race riots erupted across the American landscape as millions battled for basic dignity and equal protection. A Gay Liberation movement was born when New York City police raided the Stonewall Inn in 1969. The clientele responded with anger and openly fought for a more tolerant society.

By middecade the United States had become involved in a war in Vietnam that would deeply affect the American psyche for the rest of the century. As troop buildups escalated into military stalemate, draft-age college students burned their draft cards and, in increasingly bloody riots on college campuses, fought the assumptions of cold-war architects President Lyndon Johnson and his Secretary of Defense, Robert S. McNamara. The war, still raging at the end of the decade, ended without honor in 1975.

Nowhere were the changes in American society more visible or apparent than in popular culture. In fashion, young women shocked their parents with miniskirts that topped the knee in 1965 and reached midthigh by 1969. Harvard psychologist Timothy Leary urged kids, to the utter horror of their parents and teachers, to "turn on, tune in, drop out." Millions did just that to the pulsating sounds of the Grateful Dead, Jimi Hendrix, and, of course, the Beatles. It was the dawning of the Age of Aquarius when more than four hundred thousand potheads, professors, hippies, and yippies flocked to Woodstock to celebrate a new age.

The movies flowed with the tides of change. The box-office champion of 1960 was the Walt Disney production *Swiss Family Robinson,* a film that fit more comfortably into the culture of the 1950s. More representative of the decade were films like *Psycho, Spartacus, Tom Jones, The Pawnbroker, Who's Afraid of Virginia Woolf?, The Graduate, Guess Who's Coming to Dinner?, Bonnie and Clyde, Easy Rider,* and *The Wild Bunch.* These films not only featured screen-splattering violence and casual nudity but also attacked, as other cultural icons had, the assumptions about love, sex, marriage, politics, and religion held so dearly by, as the new generation loved to say, the establishment.

The establishment was, in this case, the Production Code Administration and the Legion of Decency. As liberal as the Legion appeared to some Catholics like Martin Quigley, most Americans viewed it as an anachronism. By the mid-1960s, even the Legion conceded that few Catholics paid any heed to its judgments.

Suffering the same perception by the vast majority of the public was the PCA. No matter how enlightened Geoffrey Shurlock tried to be, any attempt to enforce Father Lord's 1930 code of ethics increasingly appeared hypocritical, if not ridiculous. The evidence was overwhelming that Americans did not want their films censored or self-regulated. They wanted films with adult themes and were not repelled by increasing violence and sexuality.

Even though the Legion recognized that its opinions were no longer followed – its 1960 annual report admitted there was "widespread apathy and indifference" among Catholics toward the classifications – it still fought fiercely to maintain some level of control over film content during its final decade. Despite a more positive approach to adult themes, the Legion often reverted to its more traditional role of censor as Hollywood films and foreign imports grew increasingly frank in their presentation of sexuality, violence, and important social issues.

The first five years of the 1960s were especially difficult for the Legion. It noted with dismay a "growing tendency" on the part of movies "to reject the traditional moral values in favor of the code of secular humanism or even nihilism whose basic premise is that the world is ridiculous and human existence meaningless."[1] The Legion bemoaned such films as *Splendor in the Grass,* which it believed told kids that "the denial of premarital relations may lead to serious mental problems." Based on a short story by William Inge, *Splendor in the Grass* is set in rural Kansas. The story revolves around a young high school couple, played by Natalie Wood and Warren Beatty, who fall in love but are not allowed to marry. The pressure to remain chaste or have sex with her true love causes the heroine to have a mental breakdown. The Legion objected to the "free love" theme and forced Warner Bros. to make several cuts in the film and limit attendance to a 16-or-over crowd in return for a B rating.[2] Director Elia Kazan was furious. He called the censorship "insulting to adults" but was powerless to prevent the changes.[3]

Billy Wilder's *The Apartment,* which starred Jack Lemmon as a rising insurance executive who loans out his apartment to his superiors for afternoon liaisons with their mistresses, was also troubling. It was rated A3. The Legion consultants were offended but believed, as one put it, that "middle-aged lechery is shown for the pathetic and grotesque thing it is."[4] On reflection, however, Little and Sullivan believed the rating was "a big mistake." They agreed with Hollis Alpert, who wrote in his review in *Saturday Review* that the real message of the film was that "every married executive has need for a hideaway, that a man who loans out his bed is likable . . . and the quickest way up the executive ladder is pimping."[5]

Stanley Kubrick's *Spartacus,* starring Kirk Douglas (who also produced the movie) as a slave turned freedom fighter, caused the new Legion concern on several levels. The historical Spartacus escaped from a Roman training school for gladiators in 73 B.C. He and a small band of followers soon freed thousands of slaves, and after two years of victories over Roman armies, Spartacus led an army of some ninety thousand soldier-slaves. His dreams of freedom were crushed when he led his troops into a pitched battle against the forces of Crassus. The slave army was smashed, Spartacus killed, and six thousand survivors crucified as a warning against further uprisings.

A film about Spartacus, in an age of increasing cinema realism, invited, as *Time* so aptly put it, "barrels of bright red, fresh-from-the-paint-can blood." With a budget of $12 million there was plenty of money for fake blood. The film flowed crimson for almost three hours: Necks were slit, arms and heads severed, bodies impaled – all filmed in Technicolor with Super Technirama-

70 and Panavision lenses. However brutal the film was, it paled by comparison with the actual cruelty and brutality of ancient Rome.

When the Legion saw *Spartacus*, it objected to the violence and to the sexuality that Kubrick brought to this tale of gladiators. Jean Simmons, who played Varinia, a slave girl who must relieve the sexual tensions of the gladiators, is nude in two scenes. When she is first thrust into Spartacus' cell, she calmly removes her dress. In another scene she bathes, as most people do, in the nude. The Legion objected, and both scenes were trimmed so that the camera focused on Spartacus looking at Varinia, not on her nudity.

The film also contained a scene between Crassus, played by Laurence Olivier, and his slave Antoninus, played by Tony Curtis. Antoninus is assisting his master in the bath. As Antoninus washes Crassus' back, the Roman speaks of his taste in food. He likes both snails and oysters, he tells his slave; it was all a matter of taste to like both and not just one to the exclusion of the other. Antoninus understood that Crassus was talking not about food but about his sexual tastes, and that as slave he was expected to do more than just wash his master's back. The poor Antoninus fled as quickly as he could to the noble Spartacus. This scene was eventually cut even though many of the consultants did not object: They felt that only adults would understand the subtext.[6]

The most violent scenes were shortened, trimmed, or cut. As one studio official admitted, "Realism has its place, but there may well be a limit to the shock audiences can be expected to take in Technicolor and on the magnified 70mm film." These scenes were trimmed as the Legion demanded because the production company believed it was urgent to make the film "as attractive and available to as wide an audience as possible."[7] With the offending scenes reconstructed, the Legion removed its original B and gave the censored version a more favorable A3 rating.[8] To the Legion this meant it was limited to adults, but one assumes that more than a few teens saw the film, which generated $13.5 million at the box office – a disappointing return on its huge budget, to be sure. However, *Spartacus* stood third in the 1960 box-office figures behind *Swiss Family Robinson* and *Psycho*, and by the end of 1962, with a strong showing in the foreign market, had made more than $18 million in total revenue.[9]

The studio gave into the Legion because Universal officials were convinced they needed as wide an audience as possible to make a profit on their $12 million investment; but they were wrong. There is no evidence that an A3 rating brought more people to the theaters than a B rating would have. Catholics made little or no distinction between these two, and non-Catholic audiences more than likely were totally unaware of any Legion rating other than a outright condemnation: Theater chains had no qualms about booking Legion B's.

Cleaning up bare breasts, blood, and bisexuals was easy because it was so obvious. Far more troubling to the Legion was the fact that the film was based on a novel by a writer who had been a member of the Communist Party – Howard Fast – and was adapted by one of the most famous of the Hollywood Ten, scriptwriter Dalton Trumbo.[10] Kirk Douglas openly challenged the Hollywood blacklist by buying screen rights from Fast and then hiring, and giving screen credit to, Trumbo.

A gifted writer, Trumbo had begun his Hollywood career in 1935 and had twenty screen credits, including such films as *A Bill of Divorcement, Kitty Foyle,* and *Thirty Seconds over Tokyo,* before being caught in the web of postwar anticommunism. Trumbo, an active member of the Communist Party in Hollywood, was jailed for his refusal to answer HUAC's litmus-test question: "Are you now, or have you ever been, a member of the Communist Party?"

Trumbo was too skilled a screenwriter to be banned by an industry desperate for good scripts. During 1947–56 he wrote eighteen screenplays under various pseudonyms for a fraction of his going price in 1946, which was $75,000 per script. A slightly embarrassed Academy of Motion Picture Arts and Sciences awarded best screenplay for 1956 to one Robert Rich (alias Dalton Trumbo) for *The Brave One.* In 1960 his name reappeared onscreen, first for Otto Preminger's *Exodus,* and then for *Spartacus.* Two legions, the American Legion and the Catholic Legion of Decency, were horrified.

At the headquarters for Decency, the priests worried that buried deep in this bloody tale of ancient Rome was a communist message. As one consultor noted, the politics of the film were clearly "subversive"; all the slaves being presented as "well-bred and utterly wonderful people [read communists] and all the Roman characters being ruthless, greedy, sick (etc.) [read capitalists] certainly follows the Lenin line."[11] Fathers Little and Sullivan, well aware of Trumbo's past, accused him of making *Spartacus* "anti-Christian" because he used such words as "reverence," "beatitude," "blessedness," and especially "your holiness," in reference to Roman leaders. The Legion demanded that a post-Christian lexicon be applied to a pre-Christian era because the writer was "subversive." What the Legion was really saying was that it was upset Universal had hired a blacklisted writer; but the studio cleverly took the Legion at its word, complying with demands for new words yet ignoring the larger point about Trumbo.[12]

When the film opened with Trumbo's name on the masthead, some Catholics protested to Legion headquarters. One, a lawyer from Kenosha, Wisconsin, found obvious communist propaganda in the mouth of a slave who uttered, "A man should be able to think as he wishes." This was, he informed the Legion, a clear attempt "to discredit agencies of our government that are concerned with our internal security." Father Sullivan replied by assuring the lawyer that "when we screen a film which has employed known Communists, we fine-comb it for subversive propaganda." Officially, Sullivan continued, the Legion is restricted to comments on the moral content of films; privately, he urged the lawyer "to register your criticism with the releasing company and with the Motion Picture Association of America."[13]

The American Legion posted pickets around theaters when *Spartacus* opened; perhaps the lawyer from Kenosha was among them. The Catholic Legion had long before given up picketing, having concluded that it helped promote a film. Despite the efforts by both Legions to brand *Spartacus* a communist tract, few outside the media paid any attention. Trumbo had two films playing at theaters nationwide during 1960; these generated almost $23 million in domestic revenue and ranked in the top five for that year.[14] The blacklist was not yet dead, but only because the industry allowed it to continue.

The Legion, too, was moribund. Studios, independent producers, and foreign filmmakers continued to submit their products for review despite growing evidence that Legion approval made little difference at the box office. They did so because they believed it would help attract more customers and because there was one remaining barrier in film exhibition: the continued reluctance of the major theater circuits to play films the Legion condemned. *The Moon Is Blue* and *Never on Sunday* had both sold over $4 million worth of tickets in the domestic box office but had been forced to play the so-called third circuit: small, independent theaters throughout the United States. The Loew's chain, for example, the most prestigious of the theater circuits, had never booked a film condemned by the Legion. That was about to change.

In 1962, producer Carlo Ponti brought three legends of Italian cinema, Federico Fellini, Luchino Visconti, and Vittorio De Sica, to direct separate, unrelated short films on the state of Italian mores – circa 1970. The films were very loosely based on the style of Giovanni Boccaccio's *Decameron,* a collection of ribald tales of twelfth-century Italy. *Boccaccio 70,* which premiered in Milan in February 1962, caused a mild storm of protest when shown at the Cannes Film Festival later that same year. It was brought to the United States by distributor Joseph E. Levine, whose Embassy Pictures made huge profits importing cheaply made but highly popular Japanese science-fiction films like *Godzilla* and Italian muscle features like *Hercules.*

When the print of *Boccaccio 70* reached New York, Levine did what most distributors who wanted to reach a large audience did: He sent it to the Legion. Levine told Father Sullivan he was very anxious "to avoid condemnation" and promised to cooperate fully with them.[15] Once Sullivan began to screen the film it was obvious why Levine was so eager to cooperate.

The first segment, "The Temptation of Dr. Antonio," was directed by Fellini and starred Anita Ekberg and Peppino De Filippo. It was, said Fellini, an ironic tale that pitted the power "of innocence and the strength of femininity against the imaginings of an over-zealous moralist."[16] More truthfully, the vignette (which ran for over an hour) was his response to a violent attack on his films by a Jesuit publication in Italy, which called for his arrest.[17] The moralist is Dr. Antonio Mazzuolo, an ardent crusader against all forms of vice. He is outraged when near his apartment a huge billboard is erected that urges the public to drink more milk. It is not the health message that has upset the moralist but the manner in which the milk ad is presented. The billboard includes a huge picture of a very voluptuous woman (Ekberg) who, while urging the public to consume milk, is spilling out of her dress!

Antonio is consumed by the billboard. He campaigns vigorously to have it removed, then slowly falls madly in love with the woman's picture. One evening he has a hallucination: The woman comes to life and tempts the moral crusader. Antonio imagines himself a knight in shining armor and slays the giant temptress – but it was all a dream, and in the morning Antonio wakes up to find himself clinging to the billboard. The police arrest him, and he is committed to an asylum.

The second story, "The Job," was directed by Luchino Visconti and starred Romy Schneider as Pupe, a wealthy, bored, and jilted wife of The Count, a typical playboy. Their marriage becomes front-page news when a scandal rag publishes the recent exploits of The Count in a $1,000-a-night Parisian brothel. Pupe vows to her wealthy father, who has been paying their bills, that she can support herself for a year. However, when she takes stock of her talents, she discovers she has none. She then strikes a deal with her husband: Whenever he is in the mood for a bit of dalliance, he must come to her, and she will entertain him. In return, he must pay her the going rate of $1,000 per session.

The third episode, "The Raffle," was directed by Vittorio De Sica and starred Sophia Loren as Zoe, the main attraction in a seedy traveling carnival. Zoe has no act; she is the prize in a weekly raffle that lures hordes of customers to the carnival. She, however, soon tires of her role when she falls in love. When a young, meek, church sexton wins her, she convinces him to take the raffle money in lieu of her charms. As part of the deal Zoe tells the villagers the young man ravished her. The sexton is hailed by the villagers, including his mother, as a hero.

There was lots of sex and plenty of flesh. Ekberg spilled out all over the screen as a fifty-foot-tall giant pursuing the moral reformer. Fellini was clearly poking fun at stern censors who attempt to protect the public's morals but who privately lust after what they ban. It was not a theme that Legion censors appreciated; nor did they care for Romy Schneider, who appeared nude in two scenes, nor for Loren, who sold raffle tickets by showing the leering, panting men what they would get if they won. All this was in yet another film made by Italian Catholics. Even a liberal Legion was disturbed by the loose morals of the Latins.

The film opened at art-house theaters in New York City, Los Angeles, Detroit, and Baltimore in July 1962 with neither a PCA seal nor a Legion classification. The film did excellent box office in those smaller venues, and Levine was eager to sell *Boccaccio 70* to major chains. To do so he felt he needed approval from both sets of censors. In this case the process was reversed: The Legion would see the film first and recommend cuts; then the film would be submitted to the PCA'ers for a seal. Sullivan told MPAA officials that he hoped this process "might set an important precedent for the future of foreign films in the American market."[18]

Msgr. Little was away from New York, so Father Sullivan negotiated for the Legion. His demands were consistent with past Legion policy. He wanted the distributor to cut Schneider's nudity, snip Ekberg rolling around on the ground, "which involves over-exposure of her breasts," and eliminate the scene of Antonio "pinching" Ekberg's breasts. The Legion also demanded "substantial trimming" of Loren's exposure and insisted that the film not be dubbed into English, on the assumption that fewer Americans would attend if forced to read subtitles. A final request, consistent with a major Legion objective, was that the film be restricted to "those over the age of 18." If those conditions were met, Sullivan was prepared to guarantee a B rating.[19]

The deal Sullivan thought he had negotiated suddenly collapsed, however, when Msgr. Little returned and saw the revised *Boccaccio 70*. Little told Levine that "he had decided to condemn the picture" and that "he was not interested" in any deals to which Sullivan had agreed.[20]

Rather than beg, as so many film executives had done in the past, Levine tried another approach. The timing was right, the information clear. *Boccaccio* was running "solid" after an eight-week run at the Fine Arts Theater in Los Angeles and was "lusty" after a similar run in Detroit.[21] It ran strong in Cleveland, where patrons had a choice of seeing two films condemned by the Legion: *Boccaccio* and Roger Vadim's *Les Liaisons dangereuses;* both were doing "pleasing" business at three different art houses in the city. New York and Baltimore reported similar results – the film did good business. So did another import condemned by the Legion: François Truffaut's *Jules et Jim,* a moving story of a woman (played by Jeanne Moreau) who is torn between two lovers, was condemned by the Legion as a film "alien to Christian and traditional natural morality." Cy Harver, president of Janus Films, which imported the film, responded by blasting the Legion as "a minority religious group" and used the text of the Legion condemnation in ads for the film. Predictably, fans rushed to see this French ménage à trois.[22]

It was certainly clear by September 1962 that low-budget films without a PCA seal and carrying a Legion condemnation could do excellent business at the box office, easily generating $2–4 million. Levine was able to convince the major circuits that playing *Boccaccio* would not harm them. In October 1962 he signed distribution deals with industry giants Loew's Theaters, National General, the Wometco Circuit, Chicago's Balaban and Katz, and others. The Legion countered with a press statement that labeled the film a "travesty upon marriage," and claimed it was "grossly suggestive."[23]

This action produced a totally unexpected result. Little and Sullivan were invited to a dinner conference to discuss the film. They must have expected what had usually happened in the past: They would be wined and dined and a compromise worked out that would satisfy the priests. They were flabbergasted when, during the three-hour dinner meeting with distribution officials, they were told that Loew's Theaters "is no longer interested in Code Seals for films which it books" and that "a Legion Condemned rating or no rating at all from the Legion means nothing."[24] The film had been booked into the nation's best theaters and, as Little later told reporters, "nothing could be done about it because the deal had been made."[25] *Variety* noted that if it could be shown that "large numbers of conventional circuits can play 'C' pic without ill economic effects, the Legion's influence on film content must inevitably diminish."[26]

That, of course, is precisely what happened over the next few years. A gigantic Anita Ekberg in a low-cut evening gown and chasing a do-gooder created a certain amount of curiosity at the box office. Sophia Loren was a major international star, and her fans went to the movie as did those aficionados of Fellini, De Sica, and Visconti. *Boccaccio 70* opened to a "torrid" $27,000 in its first week at the United Artists Theater in Chicago, a Catholic stronghold. In Washington, D.C., the film did a solid $70,000 in two weeks, and it opened strong in Minneapolis. There were a few cancellations here and there, but these were rare and usually caused by theater owners overreacting to a few angry phone calls or letters. *Boccaccio 70* was not a smash hit by Hollywood standards, but it did enough business to indicate clearly that most moviegoers by 1962–3 did not much care what the Legion or the PCA thought about a film. This had long been true, but finally it was clear even to those people who ran the movie business. For all intents and purposes the Legion was finished.

It was hard for the priests and bishops who had been so powerful in Hollywood to admit the game was over. To deal with adult films they added in 1962 the new classification A4, "morally acceptable for adults with reservations" to replace the controversial Separate Classification, and they lobbied the industry to adopt an age-based classification system, which the bishops believed would take them out of the censorship business. "For two years," stated the Legion's 1962 annual report to the bishops, "the industry has not only refused to adopt voluntary classification, but it has unalterably opposed every effort at film classification."[27] It was true; the industry did resist every attempt to impose age limitations on its product. Eric Johnston argued that the Hollywood self-regulation system was still effective, but critics pointed out that fewer and fewer films were submitted for evaluation. (By 1966, for example, only 59 percent of the films released in the United States would carry the emblem of the PCA.)[28] The Catholic church and the Legion remained insistent that age restrictions were the key to allowing adult themes in movies. The Legion had pointedly not condemned *La Dolce Vita,* for instance, when the distributor had agreed to limit attendance to those over 18.

The bishops were not foolish old men. By middecade they clearly recognized that the Legion had a negative image among Catholics and the moviegoing public. In an attempt to soften the concept of the organization as censors, they had created new categories of classification that allowed Catholics to see films that portrayed adultery in a nonjudgmental manner, or that discussed – however obliquely – homosexuality, drug addiction, impotence, divorce, and a multitude of other human activities that would have appalled Father Lord. In addition, the bishops approved a change of name: In November 1965 the Legion officially became the National Catholic Office for Motion Pictures (NCOMP). However, most people and even some Catholic publications still called it "the Legion," and its function was the same: to screen and attempt to alter the content of films of which it did not approve.

In 1965 the Legion had reviewed 269 films and forced producers to make changes in 32 in order to get a favorable rating. That same year the Legion had condemned fifteen films; twelve of these were foreign, and even the Legion admitted "most condemned films were of little importance." In its 1965 annual report to the bishops, the Legion admitted that 84.4 percent of the Hollywood films had been "found morally unobjectionable for some segment of the audience"; but with increasingly adult themes being inserted into movies – themes that incited even liberal Legionaries – the Legion accused Hollywood of playing a "dangerous game of moral brinkmanship."[29]

As more and more filmmakers broke the last taboo, nudity, the bishops and the Legion worried that if the Catholic church allowed them to do so without protest, nudity would become commonplace. In an attempt to keep nudity off the screen, the bishops instructed Msgr. Little and Father Sullivan to condemn all movies that contained it. In a press statement the bishops claimed that "nudity is not immoral and has long been recognized as a legitimate subject in painting and sculpture"; however, they maintained, the movies were a "very different medium," and screen nudity was "never an artistic necessity."[30]

The bishops' statement echoed the sentiments of Father Lord, who in 1930 had written that "the fact that the nude or semi-nude body may be beautiful does not make its use in . . . films moral. . . . Nudity can never be permitted *as being necessary for the plot.*" The code had argued that movies, because they appealed to a mass audience, did not have the same artistic freedom as other art forms. Thus the bishops were not announcing a new canon but simply reaffirming their commitment to one section of the old Production Code – the bulk of which they had long since abandoned.[31]

The Legion was right in claiming that nudity was being inserted into films with increasing regularity. It was commonplace in European features, and in 1964 fifteen American films that contained nudity had been submitted to the Legion. Msgr. Little and Father Sullivan had successfully removed the naked bodies from ten of these – Kim Novak in the remade *Of Human Bondage* and Carol Baker in *The Carpetbaggers* were two of the more famous – in return for favorable classifications. The five that had refused to delete nude scenes had not been produced by the major studios and did not play in major American theaters.

It was, however, only a matter of time before a serious American film would refuse to remove a nude scene. It happened in 1965. Sidney Lumet's *The Pawnbroker,* an independent American production, was an important and unusually strong film that made audiences think about the power of evil, man's inhumanity to man, and about group and individual responsibility. It was in every way a moral, even moralistic, film; nonetheless, it was condemned by the Legion for a few seconds of highly symbolic, nonerotic nudity. This was a desperate act by an organization trapped by its failure to see moral and ethical issues in all of their complexities. By condemning *The Pawnbroker,* the Legion handed another round of ammunition to its opposition. Even Catholics who had long been supportive of the Legion's overall goal were dismayed by the decision.

In 1961 Edward Lewis Wallant, a Jewish-American writer, published *The Pawnbroker,* a novel about a Jewish survivor of the Holocaust who is physically alive but emotionally dead – destroyed by the death of his wife and children in the concentration camps.[32] "Everything I loved was taken from me, and I didn't die," says Sol Nazerman. He is haunted by his dead loved ones and his inexplicable survival. He now lives, twenty-five years after the war, with relatives in a dreary suburban housing tract on Long Island. Every day Nazerman drags himself into Spanish Harlem, where he operates a pawnshop. An endless parade of the down-and-out of the ghetto plead for a few dollars from Nazerman for the worthless trinkets they hope to pawn. Nazerman barely looks at them because he considers them all to be scum; besides, the pawnshop is, in reality, a front for a local black racketeer, who uses it to launder the money from his whorehouses and drug trade.

As the book unfolds, the reader discovers that Nazerman's wife was forced to have sex with the Nazi officers before being tortured and killed by them. Adding to this tragedy was the fact that he was compelled by Nazi guards to watch his wife being used as a sexual toy. For twenty-five years he has attempted to suppress these images of his wife, but he is constantly reminded of the events in recurring nightmares. He confides in no one but his pain is evident; as one character in the book remarks when seeing Nazerman walk down a street, "that man suffers."

Eventually this man who has suffered so much is reawakened to the joys of life by his young Puerto Rican assistant, Jesus Ortiz. The young man is eager to learn the business, but Nazerman either ignores or insults him. Ortiz is so fed up with his treatment by the pawnbroker that he arranges with some local hoods to rob the shop. When the hoods enter the store and demand that Nazerman open the safe, he defies them and almost begs them to kill him. One of the hoods panics and shoots. Ortiz, who has had second thoughts about the robbery, tries to stop it, and when he steps in front of the pawnbroker, he is killed.

This suddenly jerks the pawnbroker back to reality. This death of a young man so full of life is so tragic that Nazerman is able to feel pain and grief. As the novel ends, Nazerman finally, after years of mourning, is able to say good-bye to his loved ones. "Rest in peace, Ortiz, Mendel, Rubin, Ruth, Naomi, David . . . rest in peace, he said, still crying a little, but mostly for himself."

Critics were divided about the merits of the book. Many felt it was forced and were unconvinced that the death of Ortiz would suddenly "cure" the pawnbroker.[33] Others were deeply touched by the novel's articulation of the continuing pain of this victim of hatred. Jewish reaction was critical of the negative image of the pawnbroker. In an America sharply divided along racial lines, in which people were still beaten and killed for drinking from the wrong water fountain, *The Pawnbroker* was seen by many as more than a historical novel about the Holocaust: It spoke about contemporary American race relations as well. It caught the immediate attention of Roger Lewis, a former executive at United Artists, who took an option on the novel and, after being rejected by every major studio, convinced independent producer-distributor Ely Landau to make the film.

Landau, who had begun in show business as a television director and producer, had entered the movie business in 1962 as executive producer of *Long Day's Journey into Night,* Eugene O'Neill's moving study of a doomed theatrical family. Landau negotiated a deal with Allied Artists, a member of the

MPAA, to distribute *The Pawnbroker,* which was produced by Lewis and Phillip Langner. The production company turned to Sidney Lumet to direct.

Lumet had grown up on the Lower East Side of New York. His parents had both been actors, and he was acting by the age of 5. He had debuted on Broadway in Sidney Kingsley's *Dead End* in 1935, and after military service in World War II had returned to New York, beginning his directing career on the television series *Mama.* For the next few years he had divided his time between the Broadway stage and television. His first feature film, *Twelve Angry Men,* had originated as a play written for and first presented on television; his filmed version looked much like a play, with most of the action confined to a single set – the jury room.

Lumet despised Hollywood, which he dismissed as a company town "not fit for human habitation." He worked mostly in New York, where he could direct for stage, screen, and TV. In 1962 Lumet directed Landau's production of *Long Day's Journey into Night;* the two men were reunited on the set of *The Pawnbroker.*[34]

They were fortunate to cast Rod Steiger as Sol Nazerman. Steiger, like Landau and Lumet, had been a seasoned television actor before being nominated for an Oscar for his supporting role in *On the Waterfront* in 1954. His career had taken off after that film, and he had played a series of character parts in such movies as *The Court Martial of Billy Mitchell, The Harder They Fall,* and *The Longest Day.* His performance as the tortured Jew in *The Pawnbroker* earned him an Oscar nomination for Best Actor. He lost, however, to Lee Marvin in *Cat Ballou.*

Lumet and screenwriters David Friedkin and Mortin Fine faced a crucial question in constructing a film from Wallant's novel: how to connect for the audience the horror of the pawnbroker's past to his present condition. They needed to illustrate what had turned this man into the uncaring, inhuman person he appeared to be. Immediately discarding the literary device of periodic nightmares that Wallant had used, they decided instead to use the more traditional Hollywood flashback, which would be triggered on the screen by everyday events in Nazerman's life. These flashbacks are, at first, extremely short – so short they are mere flashes of images to the audience. Gradually, as the movie progresses, they become longer and clearer. When the pawnbroker walks by a schoolyard fight, his mind flashes back to the camps. When he rides a crowded New York subway, he envisions his family's forced evacuation in packed railroad cars, which caused the death of his son. The screenplay was remarkably faithful to Wallant; but this device of visually illustrating the experiences the Jews faced in Nazi Germany would result in a condemnation from the Catholics and a refusal of endorsement from Shurlock and his PCA.

The problems centered around two scenes, both of which contained nudity. The first takes place in the pawnshop. Jesus Ortiz's girlfriend, played by Thelma Oliver, is a prostitute and deeply in love with Ortiz. When she finds out about his plans to rob the pawnbroker so he can set up his own business, she tries to prevent the robbery by raising the money herself. In a desperate attempt to protect her lover, she goes to Nazerman to pawn some jewelry and to sell herself to him. She tempts Nazerman by telling him how good she is, but when he does not respond to her, she goes a step further and removes her blouse. "Look, look," she says, "don't cost you nuthin' to look."

But Nazerman won't look. As the camera moves from the bare breasts of the prostitute, it captures the pain, shock, and horror of the pawnbroker, who is in another time and place. Rather than seeing the woman in front of him, he sees (and the audience sees) his wife, naked on a bed, a Nazi officer about to take her. Then he sees another woman being washed in preparation for her service to the Germans, and yet another stretched out, naked on a bed, waiting quietly for her degradation to begin. Slowly, Nazerman drifts back to reality and is so embarrassed by the nudity of the woman in front of him that he covers her with his raincoat and asks her to leave.

The nudity in these scenes was not fleeting, not presented in silhouette or hidden in any way. The camera focused directly on Thelma Oliver as she attempted to get Nazerman to look at her, and the shots of the pawnbroker's wife and the other women in the camp were also clear – they were nude; but there was no attempt on Lumet's part to make this nudity sexually stimulating. It was not erotic; it was tragic.

The film premiered at the Berlin Film Festival in June 1964, selected by the United States Information Agency and the Hollywood Guilds Committee of the motion picture industry as the official United States entry. It was the subject of extensive controversy. Critics hotly debated such diverse topics as: Who was responsible for the Holocaust? Was Lumet drawing a parallel between American racism and German anti-Semitism? Did this sort of brutality take place in the German camps? Yet as one participant at the festival noted, there "was no discussion whatsoever about the fact that the film contains a few scenes involving nudity."[35]

There was discussion of little else in the United States. *The Pawnbroker* was submitted to Shurlock and the PCA in January 1965. Shurlock denied it a seal because of the nude scenes but encouraged Landau to appeal to the MPAA board. The appeal was scheduled for March 23, 1965.

While awaiting the appeal, Landau scheduled the film to be screened for the Legion in early March. The consultants who saw it were once again divided on the matter of morality. One called the film a "tour-de-force" for Steiger but recommended a condemned rating because he believed the scenes of Ortiz and girlfriend in bed were "too graphic"; the nude scenes were not an issue for him. Another called the film "gripping" and recommended an A4 because of the nudity, which he found "poignant and jarring" with "no erotic atmosphere." Wrote a local parish priest who served as a consultor, "I am fully aware of the policy of the Legion in regard to nudity"; yet this film "is such a powerful – and artistic – presentation of a social issue" that he recommended an A4 rating. Still others, offended by the nudity, demanded a condemnation.[36]

Despite the divided opinion among the consultors, Msgr. Little informed Ely Landau that *The Pawnbroker* would be condemned "ipso facto" because it contained nudity.[37] It was, Little claimed, a "painful deliberation" but the Legion believed that only by condemning the film "could the flood of nudity be stopped." The decision taken "was in the common good" for "the greatest good for the greatest number."[38] He also told the producer that it was the opinion of the Catholic church that screen nudity "is never a necessary or indispensable means to achieve dramatic effect," and in this case the director could have achieved "his artistic objectives by the less literal and more demanding method of indirection."[39] There would be no public announcement of the classification, however, until after the MPAA appeal.

Privately, Little told Archbishop Krol that the film was "serious" and admitted that the nudity in question was "not necessarily salacious in its intent or execution." Little recommended, however, that the Legion stay the course because he feared an explosion of screen nudity. Krol agreed.[40] Little repeated the same points to reporters. He told Judy Stone of *Ramparts* that *The Pawnbroker* represented "a foot in the door"; if the Legion approved it, "nudity would become just as common as blowing your nose."[41] Father Sullivan was more pragmatic and perhaps more truthful. He told *Variety,* "we must maintain our position [no nudity] as a means of exerting influence."[42]

There was considerable tension in the air when the sixteen men who composed the MPAA appeal board screened the film. Some agreed with Shurlock and the Legion; others argued that the nudity was necessary, but there was too much of it. Stone wrote that the men watched carefully and saw the "pawnbroker tremble as the shock of her exposure broke through his painfully constructed protective wall to focus on the one image he had tried to forget: the sight of his wife, naked and ashamed before a Nazi officer." The board granted a PCA seal after lengthy deliberation, she wrote, which included "an unprecedented confrontation of hypocrisy."[43] The film was also approved by the New York state censors with the nudity intact.

The Pawnbroker opened in theaters soon after the MPAA ruling. "Don't miss this one," cooed *Cue;* it was "an unforgettable film that should take its place among the legendary ones." *Cue* warned its readers the film contained nudity and that the "guardians of the movie production Code" had "magnanimously bestowed dispensation." The magazine concluded, rather sarcastically, that no "discussion should have been required."[44] "Shockingly good," wrote *Life* critic Richard Oulahan.[45] It is a "brooding, disturbing drama that . . . commands attention and respect," wrote *Film Daily.*[46] Judith Crist told readers that it was "close to excellence" as a "harsh film and a compassionate one, achieving moments of unbearable cruelty and of total heartbreak."[47] Bosley Crowther in the *New York Times* called it "remarkable."[48]

Not all the critics agreed. Robert Hatch told readers of the *Nation* that "there doesn't seem to be a word of truth in it." He saw Nazerman as wallowing in "self-pity" and had little sympathy for his plight.[49] *Time* dismissed it as "seldom deeply moving."[50] Andrew Sarris blasted it as a "pretentious parable that manages to shrivel into drivel."[51]

Catholic critics were as divided as the secular ones. Moira Walsh, longtime film critic for *America,* opened her review by praising Landau for attempting to make serious, thoughtful films. It was unfortunate, she believed, that the Legion had over the years inhibited "the serious artist who might have raised the level of the screen" by its condemnation of important films containing scenes that its priests found inappropriate for Catholic audiences. *The Pawnbroker* was not perfect but it was thoughtful, and she assured her readers that the nude sequences were "not prurient" and had "some dramatic justification." Although she did not have the answer, Walsh wrote that somehow the bishops and the Legion had to find a way to "take a stand on principle without resorting to the misleading and damaging course of condemning a film like *The Pawnbroker.*"[52]

Philip Hartung, whose tenure as film critic at *Commonweal* paralleled Walsh's at *America,* told his Catholic readers that *The Pawnbroker* was "absorbing drama," and its "thoughtful themes" should make Americans think about "what's wrong today." He made no mention of nudity in his review.[53] *Sign* said the nudity "was unnecessary," but not shocking.[54] *Extension* found the film "inartistic" and noted the "static flashes of nudity" were vulgar; it was "not for the young, nor for perceptive and discriminating adults of refined tastes."[55] Neither *Sign* nor *Extension* made any reference to the Legion condemnation; but William Mooring, a longtime proponent of the Legion, certainly did. Mooring attacked the film from his base in Los Angeles, and his review was published in many Catholic publications. He dismissed *The Pawnbroker* as unimportant and was appalled at the "non-essential nude shots." The code, he told his readers, has been reduced to "a mere scrap of paper."[56]

There was further support for the *The Pawnbroker,* however, from some non-Catholic Christians. The Protestant *Christian Century* gave the movie a rave review: It was about "pain and sin," said film critic Malcolm Boyd, in whose opinion *The Pawnbroker* was "a unique expression of modern life." He mentioned the nudity only in passing.[57] James A. Pike, Episcopal Bishop of California, went even further, calling the movie "one of the truly significant religious films of our times." He wrote to Landau that he would not "hesitate to include the two brief scenes of relevant nudity in my recommendation."[58]

Although critics were divided on the merits of the film, most agreed that it was not immoral. Producer Joseph Mankiewicz, who participated in the MPAA appeal, wondered how an organization that condemned *The Pawnbroker* but approved of the trashy *The Carpetbaggers* could "expect its standards or reasons for its decisions to be taken seriously by adults."[59] (A nude scene had been cut from *The Carpetbaggers* in return for a better classification.) Judy Stone of *Ramparts* wondered the same thing. How, she wrote, could the Legion "expect its rating system to be taken seriously when it condemns one of the few significantly moral films made by Hollywood?" She pressed Msgr. Little: How could you condemn a film that argues that all men are responsible for each other when that same question was being hotly debated by Catholics and non-Catholics over Rolf Hochhuth's play *The Deputy* (which fell just short of accusing Pope Pius XII and the Catholic church of condoning the Holocaust)? Why, Stone insisted, did the Legion fail to see the moral question raised by *The Pawnbroker*? Msgr. Little refused to answer.[60]

Some Catholics raised similar questions. *Film Heritage*, a Catholic-edited film journal for teachers in Catholic schools and universities, condemned the Legion's condemnation of *The Pawnbroker*. "There is no place for the 'Legion' type of censorship"; Catholics need to understand, the editorial continued, that art "can be provoking" and even "dangerous." If Catholic culture was to achieve stature beyond that of narrow censors, then the Legion must, the editors stressed, "abolish the condemned rating" because it was a "brutalizing form of pressure."[61]

The condemnation of *The Pawnbroker* was a major miscalculation by the Legion and the Catholic church. It gave critics of the church's failure to speak out against the Holocaust additional evidence of Catholic insensitivity, if not overt anti-Semitism. It also reinforced the view of critics of film censorship who cast the organization as narrow-minded. As the editors of *Film Heritage* wrote: "If all he [a movie patron] can see is nudity in *The Pawnbroker* then all the censorship in the cosmos won't save him as a human being."[62] The Legion was being attacked from inside and outside the Catholic church. Few people saw any rationale for staying away from *The Pawnbroker*: If Catholics did not care what the Legion thought, who did?

Protected by a PCA seal, *The Pawnbroker* began a successful run in late April 1965. It did, reported *Variety*, a huge first week of $47,000 in three different theaters in New York City. After five weeks at the Beekman it was still doing a solid $5,000 at the box office. Following successful runs in Los Angeles, Boston, Baltimore, and Chicago, the film opened nationally in September 1965 in nine other cities. It played, despite the Legion condemnation, in Albany, Buffalo, Cleveland, Milwaukee, Philadelphia, Pittsburgh, and St. Louis – all cities with large Catholic populations. By the end of the year *The Pawnbroker* had generated more than $2 million at the box office.[63]

With the Legion – now newly rechristened NCOMP – tottering on the brink of elimination, Warner Bros. announced that they had paid half a million dollars for the screen rights to Edward Albee's critically acclaimed play *Who's Afraid of Virginia Woolf?* The play, a smash hit on Broadway during the 1962–3 season, contained no nudity but used language rarely heard in polite society – let alone on the stage or screen.

Set on the campus of a small liberal arts college in New England, the play dissects the lives of George, a mediocre, middle-aged professor of history, and his wife, Martha, the daughter of the university president. Martha is "a bitchy, aging man-eater with a father fixation and a casual lust for younger chaps."[64] The action starts late one evening after a faculty party. George and Martha have invited a new professor and his young wife to their home for a nightcap; the drink lasts all night. George and Martha's version of a parlor game is verbally to degrade and destroy everyone around them. They rip at each other as they get progressively drunker; then they turn their attention to the young couple in a "game" George calls "Get the Guests." Later, Martha beds the young professor, then pronounces him inadequate. The blood sport ends near morning when George destroys Martha's one remaining illusion: Throughout the evening both had made oblique references to their son; now George takes deadly aim when he announces that their son has been killed in an automobile accident. Ît slowly becomes clear that they in fact had no child: He was just another illusion they had created to help them survive.

The play contained a host of themes that would surely have been banned by the PCA of Joseph Breen and the Legion of his day. For one, the marriage of George and Martha was not the image of the idyllic, sanctified union demanded by Lord's code. However, strict adherence to that view of marriage had long since passed out of existence, and neither the PCA nor NCOMP would complain about the unholy alliance that George and Martha endured.

Neither group was much concerned about the drinking, the casual sex, or even the vicious nature of the relationship; but they *were* concerned about the language the characters use to describe their feelings. The play included, according to varying counts, over twenty "goddamns," five "sons-of-a-bitches," and seven "bastards"; colorful descriptions of body parts, such as "monkey nipples" and "melons bobbling"; and unusual parlor games like

"Hump the Hostess" or, more directly, "mount her like a goddamn dog." The language was delivered with such intensity and hatefulness that it left theater audiences drained. The play was quite daring for the mid-1960s, and such verbiage was clearly in violation of what was left of the MPAA's code.

Concern within the PCA and NCOMP ratcheted up another level when the studio announced it had signed Hollywood's most contentious couple, Richard Burton and Elizabeth Taylor, to play the parts of George and Martha. Warners chose Mike Nichols, a very successful Broadway actor-director with no film experience, to direct them. Cast as the foils for George and Martha were George Segal as the young biology professor and Sandy Dennis as his fragile wife. Ernest Lehman produced and adapted the play to the screen.

Shurlock, now 70 years old and nearing retirement, had been evaluating scripts in Hollywood since 1932; yet in more than three decades he had not read anything quite like *Who's Afraid of Virginia Woolf?* Rejecting the first script in October 1965, he told Jack Warner that "all the profanity and the very blunt sexual dialogue" must be removed if the film was to qualify for a PCA seal. Warner and Shurlock both knew that would eliminate most of the original play and would certainly sap it of much of its vigor.[65] Both were also aware of the long history of compromise that was part of Hollywood's adaptation process.

Nichols, a product of Broadway, was not used to Hollywood compromises. After an attempt to rewrite the dialogue, Lehman and Nichols restored Albee's barroom dialogue to the script and began shooting. The film was true to the stageplay, and when the studio submitted the finished product to the PCA in May 1966 Shurlock heard the same dialogue that had been heard by Broadway audiences. Feeling he had no choice but to reject the film, the censor urged Jack Warner to appeal his decision to the MPAA board. The studio did file for an appeal, which was scheduled for early June 1966.[66]

Warner Bros. wanted a PCA seal and Legion approval for its $7 million investment. The studio was cognizant of the box-office revenues generated by *The Moon Is Blue, Boccaccio 70,* and, most recently, *The Pawnbroker.* These had played nationally despite Legion condemnation and had taken in somewhere in the range of $2–4 million apiece – satisfactory revenue for a small-budget film but not enough to return profit on one costing $7 million. Warners took a calculated gamble by announcing that it would limit attendance at *Virginia Woolf* to "adults only" and by submitting the original version of the film to NCOMP in advance of the MPAA appeal.[67]

There is little doubt what the reaction of the old Legion would have been to *Virginia Woolf:* It would have been condemned in the strongest possible language; not as strong as Albee's, perhaps, but the moral indignation of the Catholic church would have been crystal clear. By 1966, however, moral issues were no longer as clear-cut as they had once seemed.

Father Sullivan screened the film for some ninety NCOMP consultors. All were aware of the nature of the play – many had seen it on Broadway – and they knew that this filmed version of *Virginia Woolf* had not been censored by the PCA.[68] The reaction of Legion–NCOMP reviewers was by 1966 predictable: There was no consensus on the morality or immorality of *Virginia Woolf.* Of the ninety consultors who were invited to see the film, fifty-three believed it fell into the A2–A4 range; forty-three of these voted for the newly created A4. Fourteen classified the film as a B, and eighteen felt it fully earned a traditional condemnation. In other words, sixty-seven out of ninety voted against condemnation.[69]

"Valid adult entertainment," wrote one consultor who recommended classifying the film as A4. "It's stark, loud, bitter, harsh, bleak," and "effective drama," wrote another consultor who had seen the play on Broadway and also favored an A4 rating. A New York parish priest found the strong language "uncomfortable" but recognized that "far too many people" were caught in similar situations. He too saw *Virginia Woolf* as acceptable adult entertainment because he perceived in it "a powerful sermonizing aspect." A cleric who taught at a boy's school told Father Sullivan the language of the film was "simply part of the ordinary speech pattern" of young people in college dorms. He recommended a B because of the language.[70]

Just as with *La Dolce Vita,* the consultors brought a much more tolerant view of what movies could do. The old IFCA reviewers of Mary Looram, on the other hand, voted overwhelmingly for condemnation: Eleven of the nineteen votes the women cast were for forbidding Catholics to see the film. However, wiser heads prevailed. As one seasoned veteran of these reviewing sessions predicted to Sullivan:

> [Y]ou can expect a storm of protest at the office from offended Catholics if this is rated A IV. Many will feel that this is giving some sort of approval to the use of such language. Or they will complain that they let their teenage children go to it since the film was given an A IV. But there is greater danger in classifying this as B or C. As I see it there is a major tendency among younger and well-educated Catholics to ignore the office's ratings. Giving this film a C or even a B would lead to an even further loss of the office's influence among these important groups.[71]

This argument carried the day at NCOMP. *Virginia Woolf* was awarded an A4 classification primarily because Warner Bros. pledged that it would write into all exhibition contracts a clause prohibiting anyone "under the age of eighteen unless accompanied by his parent" from buying a ticket.[72]

This decision put the MPAA in a very difficult position. As we have already seen, the film industry had fought every effort to impose age restrictions on film attendance at the same time that it insisted on bringing more adult themes and increasing violence and nudity into films. Will Hays and

Eric Johnston had steadfastly maintained that self-regulation was the key to effective control. Johnston had died in 1963 and been replaced, on an interim basis, by Ralph Hetzel, who continued to refute arguments for age classification; but it was an indefensible position.

When the MPAA board met in early June 1966 to rule on *Virginia Woolf* the industry had just elected a new president, Texan Jack Valenti. Like Hays, he had strong connections to the White House, having served as advisor to President Lyndon Johnson from 1963 until his appointment as the new movie czar. Valenti brought none of his predecessors' objections to age classification, and to the surprise of no one the MPAA granted a seal to *Virginia Woolf*. In so doing the industry ended over three decades of self-censorship.

It was the end of an era. It took another two years finally to develop a rating system, which the industry embraced in November 1968 with all the fanfare due a new Hollywood star. The creation of the Code and Rating Administration (CARA) brought the retirement of Geoffrey Shurlock, a veteran of four decades of censorship wars, who was replaced by another PCA vet, Eugene Dougherty. However, when Elizabeth Taylor and Richard Burton hit the screen screaming and tearing at each other with a hateful vengeance it was obvious that the movies had been changed forever. No longer were they going to be reigned in by codes.

Catholics knew it, but many did not like it. Letters of protest poured into NCOMP headquarters. More than a thousand concerned Catholics attacked the new tolerance endorsed by NCOMP. Father Sullivan patiently answered them all.

When a typical letter of protest came in to the Archdiocese of Wilmington, Delaware, Sullivan sent a long reply to the Reverend Michael Hyle explaining the decision. It was clear, Sullivan wrote, that many Catholics did not accept the right of the motion pictures to produce adult entertainment; nor did they understand Pope Pius's *Miranda Prorsus*, which called for a more tolerant view of movie entertainment. Catholics did not seem to understand, Sullivan continued, that NCOMP was "not urging" them to see *Virginia Woolf*. To those who complained that teenagers were seeing the film, Sullivan's response was pointed: "If any teenager sees this film and is 'corrupted' by it, it will be because his own parent has knowingly taken him into the theater." On the other hand, if adults wanted to see it, "we cannot intrude upon what is alone their right and obligation, namely, the exercise of individual responsibility in conscience." Adult Catholics, Sullivan argued, were perfectly capable of deciding whether or not they wanted to see this film. It was a matter of individual choice and conscience.[73]

Millions of Americans, including Catholics, did flock to see and hear *Virginia Woolf*. After viewing the film they themselves decided whether or not it was moral. Those who were into long-term relationships may have spent some time reviewing how they treated their loved ones. Albee's message certainly was not to uphold George and Martha as role models.

The film played at all the best theaters in America and generated more than $14 dollars at the box office. Their was no going back. The code was dead, censorship was dead, and the cultural war that had raged between the Catholic church and the movie industry was, at least temporarily, over.

CHAPTER 8

CONCLUSION

"Here we go again," wrote Moira Walsh in her review of *Darling,* a 1965 British film directed by John Schlesinger. The film starred Julie Christie as Diana Scott, a beautiful, amoral young woman who leaves her husband on a whim and consorts with a wide variety of gentlemen. Along the way she participates in an orgy, cavorts in a nude love scene, gets pregnant and induces an abortion, divorces her husband, and marries a man she does not love. Walsh realized that many Catholics were going to be "scandalized" by the film, but she admired it. "I question the premises of those who translate their personal distaste," she wrote, "into a general principle that finds the movie morally harmful for other people." This attitude, she observed, "embodies insufficient reflection and pious wishful thinking."[1]

NCOMP demanded that a few seconds of a naked Julie Christie be snipped from the prints to be shown in the United States, and then awarded *Darling* Best Picture of 1965 as "the film whose artistic vision and expression best embody authentic human values" for mature audiences.[2] One of those people that Walsh knew would be offended was Mrs. Van C. Newkirk, president and founder of Operation Moral Upgrade, who wrote Msgr. Little that the film made a heroine of "an amoral nymphomaniac" and was little more than an "exploitation of adultery, self-indulgence, homosexuality, sex-aberration, promiscuity, irresponsibility, illegal abortion, disbelief in marriage status, verbal profanity and obscenities."[3] She demanded to know how it could it be selected as Best Picture by a Catholic organization. Father Sullivan wrote back in much the same manner as he had to protests over *Virginia Woolf:* It was a movie for mature audiences, and individuals should decide whether or not to see the film.[4] Catholic publications backed NCOMP. *Darling* got from favorable to rave reviews in *Ave Maria, Extension, Catholic World, Commonweal,* and *Sign.*[5]

One by one the old forces of censorship departed. Joseph Breen, who had retired as PCA director in 1954, died in 1964. His mentor, Martin Quigley, died that same year. Msgr. Little, long since weary of his movie mission, retired with the quip that he wanted "to die in the Stations of the Cross, not looking at Gina Lollobrigida."[6] Several years later, however, he admitted that when he was younger moral issues had seemed "stark blacks and whites," whereas in the post–Vatican II revolution within the church those same "issues seemed less simple and more complex, and assumed various shades of gray."[7] Mary Looram remained at NCOMP until gracefully retiring in 1970.

Father Sullivan, a trooper to the end, stayed on at NCOMP for another decade. He worked with a small lay staff that continued to screen films, publish a newsletter for Catholic readers, and condemn those films that NCOMP found corruptive. The bishops made his job somewhat easier when they eliminated in 1969 the requirement that any film with nudity be condemned. It did not really matter, however: NCOMP condemnations no longer evoked the controversy that Legion condemnations had in earlier years. In 1971, for example, NCOMP condemned 76 of the 378 films it reviewed – some 20 percent of the total – but there was little controversy.

When in 1971 NCOMP condemned *The Last Picture Show,* Catholic film critic John E. Fitzgerald, whose column was printed widely in Catholic publications, made little note of it. Moreover, he listed Peter Bogdanovich's adaptation of Larry McMurtry's novel about coming of age in a small Texan town in his "Ten Best of 1971," which also included *Carnal Knowledge, A Clockwork Orange* (condemned by NCOMP), *The French Connection,* and *The Conformist.* He was not alone in praising *The Last Picture Show:* The *Catholic Free Press* headlined, "Despite 'C' Rating, Film Is Termed Masterful," with David Sebastian recommending the film "wholeheartedly" to his Catholic readers.[8] In Texas, Father Louis Reile, director of the Cinema-Arts seminar at St. Mary's University and film critic for the *Messenger,* told readers the film was "genuine Texas" and added offhandedly, it has been condemned by NCOMP.[9]

That same year, in protest over increasing sex and violence in films, NCOMP withdrew its support from the MPAA's rating system. The relationship between Jack Valenti and Father Sullivan had been strained from the beginning. Sullivan had expected CARA to continue to enforce a revised Production Code and then apply a ratings classification to the finished product. In his view, classification supplemented but did not replace self-regulation. In fact, however, the code was dead.

A series of meetings among Sullivan, the National Council of Churches (NCC), and Valenti failed to produce any changes. By 1970 both religious organizations were convinced that the industry was no longer responsive to their demands. They issued a joint report charging that theaters were not enforcing the age restrictions, that movies with increasing sex and violence were being placed in the G (all ages admitted) and GP (all ages admitted, parental guidance suggested) categories, and that trailers for X (only persons 18 and older admitted) and R (16 or with parents) movies were being shown with G and GP films.

When no action was taken by the MPAA, both NCOMP and the NCC withdrew their support in June 1971. This was not especially surprising. What was a surprise was the reaction of Jack Valenti: He blasted the joint NCOMP–NCC press release as "inaccurate and unfair." The rating system, Valenti claimed, has been "praised generally," and the "vast majority" of theaters are complying with the age restrictions. Valenti said his new system was a "bulwark for artistic freedom."[10]

NCOMP lasted another nine years. Increasingly the movies they reviewed were brutally frank portrayals of the human condition. Blood-spattering scenes became commonplace, nudity ubiquitous, and the language of the streets the lexicon of the new cinema. Hard-core pornography became chic.

Although many accused these new movies of corrupting American values, it is difficult to see Hollywood as the culprit. Americans eagerly read novels that would have been considered pornographic a decade earlier. Broadway plays exhibited the same type of frankness that dominated the screen, and when they toured Middle America attracted the same middle-class acceptance – with a few exceptions – that they did in New York. Moreover, the biggest cinema box-office sensation of 1973 was not a Hollywood product: The independently produced and distributed *Deep Throat* became the first hard-core film to attract serious attention from the critics and a cult following from respectable middle-class couples.

It was not very surprising that that same year a major star performed in the nude in what film critic Pauline Kael called "the most powerfully erotic movie ever made."[11] Her assessment of Bernardo Bertolucci's *Last Tango in Paris* echoed the views of many critics. Although Marlon Brando (Paul) keeps his pants on most of the time, in one scene he and Maria Schneider (Jeanne) make love in the nude. The film used sex to try to explain the mental breakdown of a middle-aged American expatriate living in Paris. Paul's wife has just committed suicide, and he is an emotional cripple. He meets Jeanne by chance when they both look at a vacant apartment littered with debris. In the squalor of this setting they begin a torrid, emotionless trip into degradation. Paul wants sex without emotion and refuses to allow either of them to use their real names or tell each other anything about their past.

He wants nothing from Jeanne but sex – and she is more than willing to do whatever he wants. After several traditional encounters, Paul demands that Jeanne bring him some butter. She does so dutifully. He rips down her pants, prepares her for anal intercourse and then, while brutalizing her, forces her to renounce family, church, and honor. It is a vicious scene, but Jeanne continues to return to the apartment of her own volition for more sex. Later, when Paul does open up a bit and tells Jeanne about his tortured youth, she wants to make love; but Paul refuses, and Jeanne is left to masturbate instead.

The movies ends with Paul regaining some semblance of his humanity. He tries desperately to win Jeanne to a more lasting relationship and declares his love for her; but she wants to marry her young lover who is making a film about her. When Paul forces his way into Jeanne's apartment (the same one they had been using earlier), she kills him.

It was, of course, tremendously controversial. Vincent Canby, writing in the *New York Times,* called it "the movie romance of the 1970s."[12] To others it was simply pornographic. Within Catholic circles both points of view emerged. Even NCOMP reviewers were split: One cleric asked, "What is all the hoopla about?" and recommended an A4 to warn those who might not like the language and the nudity. Another reviewer, who also recommended an A4, found the film a "stunning and overwhelming experience." Others denounced it as nothing more than a continuous series of "acts of sexual violence." One priest, with a clear sense of humor, called for a condemnation because the movie proved Brando could mumble "in French quite as well as in English."[13]

Catholic opinion in *Commonweal, America,* and the *Listener* reflected the radical change in America toward movies of this sort. There was no sense of moral outrage, no demand for a national boycott by Catholics. In reference to the anal intercourse scene, Gavin Millar in the *Listener* playfully chuckled that "Miss Schneider may have the most famous bottom in history."[14] *Commonweal* told readers that historically "sex has always been an invisible subject of movies." Just as a hero is about to "mount the heroine, Hitchcock cuts to the train entering a tunnel instead. In place of the ingenue's hymen, it is always a crystal goblet that is broken," he wrote. The review then discussed the anal sex, Brando making love "by sticking his penis out through his half-opened fly," and Schneider's fully exposed pubic area – all written as matter-of-factly as a plot summary of Disney's latest animated feature.[15]

Even more interesting was Moira Walsh's reading of the film in *America.* She found the current trend toward depiction of sex on the screen "a comparatively healthy development." This was not to say she necessarily approved of it, but because she believed that the underground pornographic industry "contributed to the continuing, unexamined degradation of, and acceptance of male myths about women. Ventilating the subject in public at least makes the dimensions of the problem visible." Bertolucci's film, she believed, was little more than a male fantasy: An aging man has a torrid affair with a beautiful young woman – "while he is fully clothed."[16]

Americans it seemed were not so upset by nudity as they were by the refusal of male stars to bare it all. Women wanted to see Brando's penis if Schneider's pubic hair was on full display. Stanley Kauffmann noted in his review in the *New Republic* that he had recently given a lecture on the film. When he told an audience that "Schneider frisks about in her pelt," but that "they wouldn't see Brando's organ," the women "groaned." *Newsweek* reported that audiences booed the film, hooting, "Take it off!" at Brando. Outside the theater in New York a reporter asked a middle-aged couple from Rhode Island what they expected from the film. The husband staunchly maintained no prurient interest in the film; his wife begged to differ. "Sure," she told the male reporter, "we're hoping it will be sexy." As her husband tried to meld into the crowd, she continued: "He likes to go to the porn films, but this will be my first one." It is unlikely it was her last one.[17]

This increasing acceptance of sex and violence in the movies and a willingness to discuss it in public illustrated how far the American public had come since the elimination of censorship. Martin Scorsese's *Taxi Driver,* released in 1976, underscored this point even more forcefully. The film presents a vision of America that had been banned from the screen during the PCA–Legion years. The hero of the film is an ex-marine, Travis Bickle (Robert De Niro), a New York City cabbie who is surrounded by pushers, pimps, and hookers. He lives in a seedy, filthy room and hangs out with fellow drivers in a greasy-spoon diner. He has little hope for escape from the sewer that New York represents to him.

The one counter to his life is a beautiful young woman (Cybill Shepherd) who works for a candidate running for the presidency, Charles Palantine (Leonard Harris). She accepts a date with Travis, but he is so unschooled in the rituals of dating that he takes her to a porno movie. She walks out in a huff, and Travis is both confused and hurt. He sinks further into depression and becomes obsessed with wiping away some of the sewage he is forced to confront every night in his cab. He first attempts to assassinate Palantine but is foiled by the presence of a very alert Secret Service.

He then turns his obsession to rescuing Iris (Jodie Foster), a young 12-year-old prostitute. When she rebuffs his efforts to have her leave New York with him, he decides to eliminate the pimps who have enslaved this young girl. In a dramatic gun battle, which features blood-spattering violence, he kills three lowlifes before the police arrive. Travis is wounded but recovers to find that, surprisingly, he is a hero for killing the pimps. This personal blood-letting has cured Travis of his depression, and the movie ends with Iris's parents thanking him for saving their daughter's life and Travis happily returning to his cab.

Although there was no nudity in the film, it was a litany of everything the old code and the Legion had feared in the movies. The dialogue was saturated with the language of the gutter, and the image of New York presented was of a grimy, seedy, flithy urban hell dominated by crime and corruption. Everywhere Travis looks he sees porno theaters and prostitutes. Moreover, the girls seem happy enough in their work. Iris tells him she rather likes her pimp and wants no part of returning home. She is quite eager to service Travis, and is genuinely confused by his refusal. Topping off this image of modern America is Travis's assassination of three people. Instead of the police arresting him and closing down the vice rings, they make him a hero!

In 1950, or even 1960, this film would have caused an outrage at the PCA and the Legion, but by 1976 the reviewers of NCOMP were rather unfazed. One local priest labeled the movie a "plumment into banality, ridiculousness, obscenity" with "too much violence and bloodshed," but recommended an A4 rating. Another noted that it was not a film "for the morally scrupulous" and agreed that it should be an A4. Others found it depressing, violent, and profane but did not consider condemning it. They all agreed it was not suitable for children, but if adults wanted to see it, they saw no harm in it.[18]

By 1980 even the Catholic bishops could see no point in supporting the continuation of NCOMP, which few Catholics supported. The conservatives within the church felt betrayed by its liberalism; the more liberal church members dismissed it as irrelevant. Father Sullivan informed his few remaining readers that NCOMP would no longer publish reviews after September 1980. What had started with such a fury in 1934 died in 1980 with hardly a whimper of protest.

What then to make of this long period of control by an American church of the movies? Were the movies better because of church interference? Was the Legion only a moral watchdog or was it a censor? What was the relationship between the Legion and the PCA? Did the Legion of Decency speak for the American public or for only a small minority of Americans? Did it speak for American Catholics? What ultimate responsibility does the movie industry have for its cooperation with the Legion? Finally, who killed the Legion?

It is clear that the movies were indeed different because of the existence of the Production Code Administration and its alter ego, the Catholic Legion of Decency. For more than three decades the industry's PCA and the Catholic church's Legion had demanded that the movies adhere to a moral code that had little to do with morality. The movies shunned presentation of important moral, political, and social issues of the day; on those rare occasions when they did present them onscreen they were forced to do so in a way that was fundamentally dishonest. This is not to suggest that Hollywood would have been a leader for a more realistic vision of the complexities of American life had neither the PCA nor the Legion existed. It would not have been – a point that cannot be stressed too strongly. The industry was not interested in presenting diverse opinions but in profits. Without censorship, novels, plays, and historical fact would still have emerged differently on the screen than in print or real life. Hollywood films were first and foremost entertainment, and because of the tremendous cost of making films the first priority was, and is, reeling in an audience large enough to make a profit.

There were filmmakers, however, such as Preminger, Selznick, Lumet, and Kazan, who did want to make films with ideas, and they were thwarted, both by their industry and by the Legion, from presenting films to the public that challenged the narrowly constructed vision of the PCA and the Legion. There were others who with a little encouragement would have been interested in making films that conveyed messages as well as entertainment. They did not want to corrupt American values or make obscene films; they simply wanted to make films that dealt more honestly with the human condition than the code or the Legion allowed. If you will, they wanted to present another point of view, one that may have been as fundamentally dishonest as the Hollywood product. They wanted to present their personal opinions on the issues of morality, politics, and social conditions; but they were simply not allowed to do so until this system of censorship passed. No other medium of communication in America accepted such restrictions on its ability to disseminate ideas to the public.

It should be clear that the Legion of Decency went far beyond its defined role as a moral watchdog. Had the Legion truly limited itself to rating films for Catholic audiences, it would have been much less controversial; but the organization refused to do so. Time after time, as this book has illustrated, filmmakers were forced to change dialogue, cut scenes, and add prologues and/or epilogues (which often changed the meaning of the film) in order to avoid Legion condemnation. Using the threat of condemnation, the Legion effectively censored films. It called for boycotts of any theater that dared exhibit a movie that failed to convey the morality espoused by the Legion. It demanded that its prescribed changes be incorporated into every print of the film screened for American audiences – and, in the case of American product, even foreign audiences. In return, the Legion gave films its blessing. Exhibitors, unwilling to challenge Legion authority, shunned condemned films like the plague. Filmmakers in turn bowed meekly to the Legion's demands.

The Legion of Decency's goal was that no one, Catholic or non-Catholic, see a condemned film. It was amazingly successful in achieving this goal: Only a handful of films produced by major Hollywood studios were condemned between 1934, the first year of the Legion, and 1953, the year *The Moon Is Blue* was released. Those few that were condemned were altered and released with a Legion blessing.

The premise of the entire history of the Legion was that if films on occasion showed sin not punished, crime profitable, corruption rampant, clergy hypocritical, or divorce possible that audiences would be corrupted. It is a premise that is highly questionable. Moria Walsh, in her review of *Darling,* struck at the very heart of the censorship issue when she noted that people translated their personal tastes into general principles. Msgr. Little came to much the same conclusion when he admitted that moral issues that had once seemed so clear were, in his later years, filled with shades of gray. Father Sullivan came to preach it: The decision to see any movie, he said, was an "exercise of individual responsibility in conscience."[19] The U.S. Supreme Court struck down a host of state and municipal censorship laws because, among other reasons, they were so vaguely worded that what was censorable was, in effect, what personally offended the censor.

The addition of some one hundred highly educated Catholics to the Legion's reviewing staff in the late 1950s further illustrated this point. The consultors came from many walks of life: teaching clerics from Catholic schools and universities, parish priests, and a wide variety of lay professionals. They were not intimidated by the fulminations of Martin Quigley, as the women of the IFCA had been; rather, they openly challenged his views of morality and refused to accept his contention that movies were only to entertain. They also argued among themselves and freely debated what was moral and what was not. In so doing they began a long process of opening Catholic minds to a wider view of the world. It is interesting to note that a review of a large number of Legion files indicates that the Catholic clerics, though more tolerant than the IFCA members, were also more willing to accept the presence of sin in drama than were the lay professionals brought into the Legion operation. The priests were, as a whole, much more tolerant of diverse views, as well as of sin and corruption, than their lay counterparts.

This same attitude was reflected in the position that theologians like Father John Courtney Murray took toward the Legion – and that the Legion finally came to accept. Murray viewed the Legion as only a guide for Catholics. It was not a sin to attend a condemned film; individuals, using their own consciences, had to decide what was acceptable entertainment. Catholics like Martin Quigley fought this concept of choice and individual responsibility. For him it was a matter of influence and power: He'd been the Legion for two decades, and he fought to maintain his level of power; but in the end he lost.

He lost because so many lay Catholics simply ignored the Legion. They stood in church each December and took the Legion pledge that was administered to everyone who went to Mass. However, taking the pledge in church was one thing; staying away from a movie was quite another. Millions of Catholics ignored the Legion ratings and flocked to see films that were condemned. It was evident even in 1934 that Catholics were not obeying the demands of the Legion, and it remained clear to Martin Quigley, Father Masterson, Msgr. Little, and the American bishops over the next three decades.

Time and time again Legion correspondence bemoans the fact that Catholics refused to support the organization's judgment. Catholics went to see *The Outlaw, Forever Amber, Duel in the Sun, The Moon Is Blue, The Man with the Golden Arm, Tea and Sympathy, Baby Doll, Suddenly Last Summer, Lolita, La Dolce Vita, The Miracle,* and a host of other films. While many perhaps were scandalized, many more wondered what all the fuss was about.

Martin Quigley charged that Father Sullivan "killed" the Legion. William Mooring claimed that the "ultra-sophisticated" Legion staff (meaning Sullivan and the consultors) had an "un-Catholic tolerance for immoral movies."[20] They were both wrong to their very core. The Legion was killed by Catholics, theologians, Legion officials, priests, bishops, and, most of all, lay Catholics exercising their rights of conscience.

The movie industry played almost no role in its demise; in fact, for decades Hollywood kept the Legion alive. The studios cooperated with Catholic censors because it was easier to remove material from films that offended Legion sensibilities than it was to defend the right for freedom of expression. It also protected them from increasing competition. This is said with no intention of defending Hollywood as an institution and in full recognition of what has happened to the industry in the past two decades. During the period covered by this book the position of the film industry was indefensible. The studios wanted to portray adult themes in movies without in any way conceding the right of all age groups to attend those movies. They fought restricting the audiences for such films to adults until they had no other choice.

Movies like *The Moon Is Blue, La Dolce Vita,* or *Baby Doll,* for example, were movies for adults. Few children under the age of 16 were likely to find much entertainment in any of them, and trying to retrofit them for children ruined them. The industry certainly could have stolen much of the thunder of Legion complaints had they done in 1934 (or 1947, 1953, or 1956) what they finally did in 1966 – that is, to identify certain films clearly as for adults only and to market them as such. "Adult" does not and did not mean pornographic; it simply meant adult. Hollywood, however, had refused.

Instead those in the industry had tolerated, cooperated, encouraged, and blessed the Legion by faithfully submitting every film they made for review by Catholic censors because it made good business sense to do so. As Otto Preminger noted: "The Legion of Decency has assumed an undue position of power because of the cowardice of some major motion picture companies. They're scared of the Legion; scared of losing money."[21] He was right on the mark. Any Legion classification other than a condemned opened up worldwide markets and allowed Hollywood to sell the product to everyone who had the price of admission. It also enabled the industry to exclude independent producers and foreign films from the American market. As long as the major studios submitted their films for purging, independent and foreign producers had either to do the same thing – thereby making their product indistinguishable from Hollywood's – or to play to a severely restricted market. Hollywood loved this system of protectionism and held on to it for as long as possible. It was easier to submit to religious censors than to compete freely in an uncontrolled market.

This comfortable system of cooperation between the industry and its critics was eventually challenged by the independent and foreign producers who were frozen out of the market. The industry was presented a golden opportunity to break the grip of the Legion in 1947 when David O. Selznick was set to release *Duel in the Sun* to the public. The maker of *Gone with the Wind* could hardly be branded as a pornographer or quick-buck artist; he was one of the most respected filmmakers in Hollywood. *Duel in the Sun* was not immoral, and Selznick's goal had not been to make an immoral film. The Gallup Poll he commissioned showed that only 5 percent of moviegoers were willing to stay away from a condemned film. Selznick believed that the publicity over a fight with the Legion would more than make up for that small loss, and he would have been right. Selznick wanted to challenge Legion authority, but the industry deserted him: The studios wanted to continue their domination of the market more than they wanted the freedom to make films that challenged the Legion's view of the world.

It was the independent producers and directors, men like Otto Preminger, James Harris, Stanley Kubrick, Elia Kazan, and Sidney Lumet, as well as the foreign-film distributors like Joseph Burstyn and Joseph Levine, who fought and broke this cozy system of self-mutilation. Bosley Crowther, who long opposed film censorship, recognized the pivotal role the independents played. *The Pawnbroker,* he wrote, "would not be here today if it had not been done by independents with imagination, integrity and zeal. And if it were not here, we would be missing a strong and disturbing film that has something to say – something trenchant – about an individual's responsibility in the modern world."[22] Directors who fought the system did so because it prevented them from making movies the way they wanted them made. It is no accident, it seems to me, that so many of them were trained for the legitimate stage and not weaned in Hollywood. They bristled at the charge that they were corrupters of American values, and they counterattacked – often in the courts. Eventually they won when the U.S. Supreme Court, from the early 1950s through the 1960s, consistently struck down attempts at prior censorship.

Many look back at this period and correctly point out that there were any number of films that seemed to "get away" with taboo topics, dealing with sex, sin, or politics in a more direct fashion than the PCA code allowed or the Legion tolerated. Clever directors, they note, managed to trick the dullwitted censors by inserting material that conveyed the intended message to audiences; and audiences, who were not as stupid as the censors, they conclude, did read the signals sent to them by filmmakers and understand the coded implications.

Although it is true that certain films do stand out in this manner, it seems to me that this argument not only totally misses the point but also misrepresents the history of filmmaking in Hollywood during the era of censorship. It is not a matter of how a few filmmakers got away with something, but that thousands upon thousands of films were refashioned to fit into the worldview of the censors. These censors were not dull-witted; they understood coded meanings as well as many in the audience did. What they did not want, and successfully squelched, was the overt visualization and discussion of controversial issues. Coded meaning was unimportant because, in their view, only a small minority of the vast audience would read a film for its deeper implications.

For more than three decades the Hollywood film industry allowed religious clerics to determine what was moral and immoral, what was socially acceptable political comment and what was not. They did so knowing full well that few Catholics and even fewer non-Catholics had much regard for the Legion of Decency. Hollywood allowed its films to be mutilated for profit. Those who challenged this system were consistently rebuked: There was no industry support for David O. Selznick in 1947, and even Selznick stood silent with the rest of the wealthy moguls while Joseph Burstyn spent the little money he had fighting for freedom of the screen. That was a freedom the industry executives were not interesting in having.

It is a sad commentary and a warning for those who would like to return to an era when the cinema seemed so innocent. There was no nudity, no on-screen intercourse, no spectacular orgasms, no spattered gore, no steady stream of four-letter words; but neither was there the freedom to explore important social, political, and economic problems without qualifying the solutions offered to make them palatable to the Production Code Administration and its alter ego, the Catholic Legion of Decency.

WORKING DRAFT OF THE LORD–QUIGLEY CODE PROPOSAL

Reasons Supporting a Code
TO GOVERN THE MAKING OF MOTION AND TALKING PICTURES
Formulated by
Association of Motion Picture Producers, Inc., and The Motion Picture
Producers and Distributors of America, Inc.

REASONS SUPPORTING PREAMBLE OF CODE

I.   Theatrical motion pictures, that is, pictures intended for the theatre as distinct from pictures intended for churches, schools, lecture halls, educational movements, social reform movements, etc., are primarily to be regarded as ENTERTAINMENT.

Mankind has always recognized the *importance* of entertainment and its value in rebuilding the bodies and souls of human beings.

But it has always recognized that entertainment can be of a character either HELPFUL or HARMFUL to the human race, and in consequence has clearly distinguished between:

a.   *Entertainment which tends to improve* the race, or at least to re-create and rebuild human beings exhausted with the realities of life; and

b.   *Entertainment which tends to degrade* human beings, or to lower their standards of life and living.

Hence the MORAL IMPORTANCE of entertainment is something which has been universally recognized. It enters intimately into the lives of men and women and affects them closely; it occupies their minds and affections during leisure hours, and ultimately touches the whole of their lives. A man may be judged by his standard of entertainment as easily as by the standard of his work.

So *correct entertainment* raises the whole standard of a nation.

Wrong entertainment lowers the whole living conditions and moral ideals of a race.

Note, for example, the healthy reactions to healthful, moral sports, like baseball, golf; the unhealthful reactions to sports like cockfighting, bullfighting, bear baiting, etc.

Note, too the effect on ancient nations of gladiatorial combats, the obscene plays of Roman times, etc.

II. Motion pictures are very important as ART.

Though a new art, possibly a combination art, it has the same object as the other arts, the presentation of human thought, emotion, and experience, in terms of an appeal to the soul through the senses.

Here, as in entertainment:

Art *enters intimately* into the lives of human beings.

Art can be *morally good,* lifting men to higher levels. This has been done through good music, great painting, authentic fiction, poetry, drama.

Art can be *morally evil* in its effects. This is the case clearly enough with unclean art, indecent books, suggestive drama. The effect on the lives of men and women is obvious.

Note: It has often been argued that art in itself is unmoral, neither good nor bad. This is perhaps true of the THING which is music, painting, poetry, etc. But the thing is the PRODUCT of some person's mind, and the intention of that mind was either good or bad morally when it produced the thing. Besides, the thing has its EFFECT upon those who come into contact with it. In both these ways, that is, as a product of a mind and as the cause of definite effects, it has a deep moral significance and an unmistakable moral quality.

Hence: The motion pictures, which are the most popular of modern arts for the masses, have their moral quality from the intention of the minds which produce them and from their effects on the moral lives and reactions of their audiences. This gives them a most important morality.

1. They *reproduce* the morality of the men who use the pictures as a medium for the expression of their ideas and ideals.
2. They *affect* the moral standards of those who through the screen take in these ideas and ideals.

In the case of the motion pictures, this effect may be particularly emphasized because no art has so quick and so widespread an appeal to the masses. It has become in an incredibly short period *the art of the multitudes.*

III. The motion picture, because of its importance as an entertainment and because of the trust placed in it by the peoples of the world, has special MORAL OBLIGATIONS:

A. Most arts appeal to the mature. This art appeals at once *to every class,* mature, immature, developed, undeveloped, law abiding, criminal. Music has its grades for different classes; so has literature and drama. This art of the motion picture, combining as it does the two fundamental appeals of *looking at a picture* and *listening to a story,* at once reaches every class of society.

B. By reason of the mobility of a film and the ease of picture distribution, and because of the possibility of duplicating positives in large quantities, this art *reaches places* unpenetrated by other forms of art.

C. Because of these two facts, it is difficult to produce films intended for only certain classes of people. The exhibitor's theatres are built for the masses, for the cultivated and the rude, the mature and the immature, the self-respecting and the criminal. Films, unlike books and music, can with difficulty be confined to certain selected groups.

D. The latitude given to film material cannot, in consequence, be as wide as the latitude given to *book material*. In addition:
   a. A book describes; a film vividly presents. One presents on a cold page; the other by apparently living people.
   b. A book reaches the mind through words merely; a film reaches the eyes and ears through the reproduction of actual events.
   c. The reaction of a reader to a book depends largely on the keenness of the reader's imagination; the reaction to a film depends on the vividness of presentation.

Hence many things which might be described or suggested in a book could not possibly be presented in a film.

E. This is also true when comparing the film with the newspaper.
   a. Newspapers present by description, films by actual presentation.
   b. Newspapers are after the fact and present things as having taken place; the film gives the events in the process of enactment and with the apparent reality of life.

F. Everything possible in a *play* is not possible in a film.
   a. Because of the *larger audience of the film,* and its consequential mixed character, psychologically, the larger the audience, the lower the moral mass resistance to suggestion.
   b. Because through light, enlargement of character, presentation, scenic emphasis, etc., the screen story is *brought closer* to the audience than the play.
   c. The enthusiasm for and interest in the film *actors* and *actresses,* developed beyond anything of the sort in history, makes the audience largely sympathetic toward the characters they portray and the stories in which they figure. Hence the audience is more ready to confuse actor and actress and the characters they portray, and it is most receptive of the emotions and ideals presented by their favorite stars.

G. *Small communities,* remote from sophistication and from the hardening process which often takes place in the ethical and moral standards of groups in larger cities, are easily and readily reached by any sort of film.

H. The grandeur of mass settings, large action, spectacular features, etc., affects and arouses more intensely the emotional side of the audience.

In general, the mobility, popularity, accessibility, emotional appeal, vividness, straightforward presentation of fact in the film makes for more intimate contact with a larger audience and for greater emotional appeal.

Hence the larger moral responsibilities of the motion pictures.

REASONS SUPPORTING THE GENERAL PRINCIPLES

I.   No picture shall be produced which will lower the moral standards of those who see it. Hence the sympathy of the audience should never be thrown to the side of crime, wrong-doing, evil or sin.
This is done:

1.   When *evil* is made to appear *attractive* or *alluring* and good is made to appear *unattractive.*

2.   When the *sympathy* of the audience is thrown on the side of crime, wrong-doing, evil, sin. The same thing is true of a film that would throw sympathy against goodness, honor, innocence, purity or honesty.

Note: Sympathy with a person who sins is not the same as sympathy with the sin or crime of which he is guilty. We may feel sorry for the plight of the murderer or even understand the circumstances which led him to his crime. We may not feel sympathy with the wrong which he has done. The presentation of evil is often essential for art or fiction or drama. This in itself is not wrong provided:

a.   That evil is *not presented alluringly.* Even if later in the film the evil is condemned or punished, it must not be allowed to appear so attractive that the audience's emotions are drawn to desire or approve as strongly that later the condemnation is forgotten and only the apparent joy of the sin remembered.

b.   That throughout, the audience feels sure that *evil is wrong* and *good is right.*

II.   Correct standards of life shall, as far as possible, be presented.

A *wide knowledge of life and of living* is made possible through the film. When right standards are consistently presented, the motion picture exercises the most powerful influence. It builds character, develops right ideals, inculcates correct principles, and all this in the attractive story form.

If motion pictures consistently *hold up for admiration high types of characters* and present stories that will affect lives for the better, they can become the most powerful natural force for the improvement of mankind.

III.   Law, natural or human, shall not be ridiculed, nor shall sympathy be created for its violation. By *natural law* is understood the law which is written in the hearts of all mankind, the great underlying principles of right and justice dictated by conscience.

By *human law* is understood the law written by civilized nations.

1.   The *presentation of crimes* against the law is *often necessary* for the carrying out of the plot. But the presentation must not throw sympathy with the crime as against the law nor with the criminal as against those who punish him.

2.   The *courts of the land* should not be presented as unjust. This does not mean that a single court may not be represented as unjust, much less that a single court official must not be presented this way. But the court system of the country must not suffer as a result of this presentation.

Reasons Underlying Particular Applications

Preliminary:

I. *Sin and evil* enter into the story of human beings and hence in themselves are *dramatic material.*

II. In the use of this material, it must be distinguished between sin which repels by its very nature, and *sins which often attract.*

    a. In the first class come murder, most theft, many legal crimes, lying, hypocrisy, cruelty, etc.

    b. In the second class come sex sins, sins and crimes of apparent heroism, such as banditry, daring thefts, leadership in evil, organized crime, revenge, etc.

The first class needs far less care in treatment, as sins and crimes of this class are naturally unattractive. The audience instinctively condemns and is repelled.

Hence the important objective must be to avoid the hardening of the audience, especially of those who are young and impressionable, to the thought and fact of crime. People can become accustomed even to murder, cruelty, brutality, and repellent crimes, if these are sufficiently repeated.

The second class needs real care in handling, as the response of human natures to their appeal is obvious. This is treated more fully below.

III. A careful distinction can be made between films intended for *general distribution,* and films intended for use in theatres restricted to a *limited audience.* Themes and plots quite appropriate for the latter would be altogether out of place and dangerous in the former.

Note: In general this practice of using a general theatre and limiting its patronage during the showing of a certain film to "Adults Only" is not completely satisfactory and is only partially effective.

However, maturer minds may easily understand and accept without harm subject matter in plots which do younger people positive harm.

Hence: If there should be created a special type of theatre, catering exclusively to an adult audience, for plays of this character (plays with problem themes, difficult discussions and maturer treatment) it would seem to afford an outlet, which does not now exist, for pictures unsuitable for general distribution but permissible for exhibition to a restricted audience.

I. Crimes Against the Law

The *treatment of crimes* against the law must not:

1. *Teach methods* of crime.

2. *Inspire potential criminals* with a desire for imitation.

3. *Make criminals seem heroic* and justified.

Revenge in modern times shall not be justified. In lands and ages of less developed civilization and moral principles, revenge may sometimes be presented. This would be the case especially in places where no law exists to cover the crime because of which revenge is committed.

Because of its evil consequences, the *drug traffic* should not be presented in any form. The existence of the trade should not be brought to the attention of audiences.

The use of liquor should never be excessively presented even in picturing countries where its use is illegal. In scenes from American life, the necessities of plot and proper characterization alone justify its use. And in this case, it should be shown with moderation.

II. SEX

Out of regard for the sanctity of marriage and the home, the triangle, that is, love of a third party by one already married, needs careful handling. The treatment should not throw sympathy against marriage as an institution.

Scenes of passion must be treated with an honest acknowledgment of human nature and its normal reactions. Many scenes cannot be presented without arousing dangerous emotions on the part of the immature, the young, the criminal classes.

Even within the limits of *pure love,* certain facts have been universally regarded by lawmakers as outside the limits of safe presentation.

In the case of *impure love,* the love which society has always regarded as wrong and which has been banned by divine law, the following are important:

1. Impure love must *not* be presented as *attractive and beautiful.*
2. It must *not* be the subject of *comedy or farce,* or treated as material for laughter.
3. It must not be presented in such a way as to *arouse passion* or morbid curiosity on the part of the audience.
4. It must not be made to seem *right and permissible.*
5. In general, it must *not* be *detailed* in methods and manner.

III. VULGARITY; IV. OBSCENITY; V. PROFANITY; hardly need further explanation than is contained in the Code.

VI. COSTUME

General Principles:

1. The effect of nudity or semi-nudity upon the normal man or woman and much more upon the young and immature person, has been honestly recognized by all lawmakers and moralists.
2. Hence the fact that the nude or semi-nude body may be beautiful does not make its use in the films moral. For, in addition to its beauty, the effect of the nude or semi-nude body on the normal individual must be taken into consideration.
3. Nudity or semi-nudity used simply to put a 'punch' into a picture comes under the head of immoral actions. It is immoral in its effect on the average audience.

4. Nudity can never be permitted as being *necessary for the plot*. Semi-nudity must not result in undue or indecent exposures.

5. Transparent or translucent materials and silhouette are frequently more suggestive than actual exposure.

VII. DANCES

Dancing in general is recognized as an *Art* and as a *beautiful* form of expressing human emotions.

But dances which suggest or represent sexual actions, whether performed solo or with two or more, dances intended to excite the emotional reaction of an audience, dances with movement of the breasts, excessive body movements while the feet are stationary, violate decency and are wrong.

VIII. RELIGION

The reason why ministers of religion may not be comic characters or villains is simply because the attitude taken toward them may easily become the attitude taken toward religion in general. Religion is lowered in the minds of the audience because of the lowering of the audience's respect for a minister.

IX. LOCATIONS

Certain places are so closely and thoroughly associated with sexual life or with sexual sin that their use must be carefully limited.

X. NATIONAL FEELINGS

The just rights, history, and feelings of any nation are entitled to consideration and respectful treatment.

XI. TITLES

As the title of a picture is the brand on that particular type of goods, it must conform to the ethical practices of all such titling.

XII. REPELLENT SUBJECTS

Such subjects are occasionally necessary for the plot. Their treatment must never offend good taste nor injure the sensibilities of an audience.

NOTES

Introduction

1 *Ave Maria* 70 (Oct. 15, 1949), 483.
2 Russell Whelan, "The Legion of Decency," *American Mercury* 60 (June 1945), 655–63, at p. 655.

1. A Catholic Coup against Hollywood

1 *New York Times,* Apr. 7, 1996, E, p. 1.
2 Kevin Brownlow, *Behind the Mask of Innocence,* p. xv.
3 Kay Sloan, *Loud Silents,* p. 3.
4 Janet Staiger, *Bad Women,* pp. 29–52.
5 Jane Addams, *Spirit of Youth and the City Streets,* pp. 78–80.
6 It was renamed in 1915 to remove the stigma of censorship.
7 Gregory D. Black, "Hollywood Censored: The PCA," p. 169.
8 "Censorship of Motion Pictures," *Yale Law Journal* 49 (Nov. 1939), 88. See also "Film Censorship: An Administrative Analysis," *Columbia Law Review* 39 (1939), 1383–1405; Douglas Ayer, Roy E. Bater, and Peter J. Herman, "Self-Censorship in the Movie Industry: An Historical Perspective on Law and Social Change," *Wisconsin Law Review* (1970), 791–838; Felix Bilgrey and Ira Levenson, "Censorship of Motion Pictures – Recent Judicial Decisions and Legislative Action," *New York Law Review* 1 (1955), 347–59.
9 Garth Jowett, "A Capacity for Evil: The 1915 Supreme Court Mutual Decision," *Historical Journal of Film, Radio and Television* 9 (1989), 59–78, at p. 66.
10 *Mutual Film Corporation* v. *Ohio Industrial Commission,* 236 U.S. 230, U.S. Supreme Court (1915), p. 238.
11 Ibid., pp. 242, 230.
12 Ian Jarvie, "Dollars and Ideology: Will Hays' Economic Foreign Policy, 1922–1945," *Film and History* 2 (1988), 207–21, at p. 210; Alva Johnston, "Profiles: Czar and Elder," *New Yorker* 9 (June 10, 1933), 18–21; Albert Shaw, "Will Hays: A Ten-Year Record," *Review of Reviews* 85 (Mar. 1932), 30–1.
13 Garth Jowett, *Film: The Democratic Art,* p. 475.
14 Raymond Moley, *Hays Office,* pp. 59–63; Will Hays, *Memoirs of Will H. Hays,* p. 431.
15 Moley, *Hays Office,* pp. 59–63; Daniel Lord, *Played By Ear,* p. 296.
16 Joseph Breen to Father Wilfrid Parsons, box C-8, Wilfrid Parsons Papers, Georgetown University [hereafter as PP].

17 Lord, *Played By Ear,* p. 289.

18 In *Queen's Work*, for example, he continually wrote serial novels with strong moral lessons. See his *Clouds Over the Campus* or *Murder in the Sacristy,* both from 1940.

19 Lord, *Played By Ear,* p. 289.

20 Daniel E. Doran, "Mr. Breen Confronts the Dragons," *Sign* 21 (Jan. 1942), 327–30; Walter Davenport, "Pure as the Driven Snow," *Collier's* 94 (Nov. 24, 1934), 10–11, 34–7; J. P. McEvoy, "The Back of Me Hand to You," *Saturday Evening Post* 211 (Dec. 24, 1938), 8–9; Timothy Higgins, "No-Man in Yes-Land," *Catholic Digest* 4 (May 1940), 92–6.

21 Breen to Father Wilfrid Parsons, Sept. 9, 1929, and Jan. 14, 1930, PP.

22 Breen to Father Corrigan, Oct. 17, 1930, box 42, Will Hays Papers, Indiana State Historical Society, Indianapolis, Indiana [hereafter as HP].

23 McEvoy, "Back of Me Hand to You," 8–9; Elizabeth Yeaman, "The Catholic Movie Censorship," *New Republic* 96 (Oct. 5, 1938), 233–5, at p. 235.

24 The details of the controversy regarding the code's authorship are beyond the scope of this chapter. Quigley campaigned for twenty years to have the credit for the code bestowed on him. At one point he softened his feud with Breen and asked for a formal letter from the PCA director crediting him with authorship (see Breen to Quigley, June 19, 1937, box C-81, PP). The debate really heated up when Lord's autobiography was published shortly after his death in 1955. The debate simply represents the deep levels of disagreement over the direction of the entire movement. In 1929, when relations were friendly, and perhaps more accurate, Quigley wrote to Lord: "I have received this morning your final draft of our code." Only a few minor changes were made in the document approved by the industry. There is little doubt that Quigley contributed many ideas that were incorporated into the code, but Lord wrote it. See Quigley to Lord, Nov. 26, 1929, Daniel Lord Papers, Jesuit Missouri Province Archives, St. Louis, Mo. [hereafter as LP].

25 Several drafts of the code are in Lord's papers. The code has been printed in a variety of film books. For an excellent discussion see Jowett, *Film: The Democratic Art*, pp. 240–3, 468–72; and Gregory D. Black, *Hollywood Censored,* pp. 21–49.

26 "Suggested Code to Govern the Production of Motion Pictures," n.d., LP.

27 Stephen Vaughn, "Morality and Entertainment," pp. 39–65. Vaughn's article is by far the most complete analysis of the adoption of the code by the industry.

28 Hays, *Memoirs,* p. 439.

29 Ibid., p. 440.

30 William Halsey, *Survival of American Innocence,* pp. 107–11.

31 "General Principles to Govern the Preparation of a Revised Code of Ethics for Talking Pictures," n.d., LP. The copy of the document in Lord's papers has "Irving Thalberg" written on it. Whether this means that Thalberg wrote the document or merely presented it to the meeting is unclear. There are no known records of the meeting; but it is clear that the producers had a radically different view of the movies and their role in society than did Lord.

32 Ibid.

33 For accounts of the various meetings see: Quigley to Lord, Jan. 3 and 10, Feb. 17, 24, and 28, and Mar. 1, 1930, LP; Lord to Mundelein, Feb. 14, 1930, LP. Lord, *Played By Ear,* pp. 298–304; Hays, *Memoirs,* pp. 439–43.

34 *Variety*, Nov. 5, 1930, p. 30.

35 John Baxter, *The Gangster Film* (New York: A. S. Barnes, 1970), pp. 119–60.

36 For a summary of newspaper editorials against gangster films see "Protests against Gangster Films, 1931," box 42, HP; see Gerald Peary, ed., *Little Caesar*, pp. 21–8, for the controversy over that film; Joy to McKenzie, Jan. 30, 1931, and Joy to Wingate, Feb. 5, 1931, *Little Caesar*, PCA.

37 Joy to Hays, Dec. 15, 1931, *Possessed*, PCA.

38 Wingate to Hays, Feb. 13, 1933, and Wingate to Hurley, Jan. 11, 1933, *She Done Him Wrong*; Wingate to Botsford, Sept. 18, 1933, *I'm No Angel*, PCA.

39 Stark Young, "Angels and Ministers of Grace," *New Republic* 76 (Nov. 29, 1933), 73–6; *New Orleans Tribune*, Jan. 4, 1934. For an excellent account of West see Ramona Curry, *Too Much of a Good Thing*.

40 For a more detailed discussion of the period 1930–3 see Black, *Hollywood Censored*, pp. 21–148.

41 Daniel Lord, "The Code – One Year Later," Apr. 23, 1931, box 42, HP.

42 Raphael M. Huber, *Our Bishops Speak* (Milwaukee: Bruce, 1952), p. 199.

43 *New York Times*, Nov. 20, 1932, p. 30.

44 Francis X. Talbot, "Smut," *America* 48 (Feb. 11, 1933), 460–1, and "More on Smut," ibid. (Feb. 25, 1933), 500–1. See also *New York Times*, Feb. 23, 1933, p. 15.

45 Fred Herron to H. A. Banday, Sept. 2, 1930, *A Farewell to Arms*, PCA.

46 For a more complete account of the censorship involved see Black, *Hollywood Censored*, pp. 87–91.

47 *New York Times*, Mar. 7, 1933, p. 18.

48 Breen to Wingate, May 5, 1933, *Ann Vickers*, PCA.

49 Cooper to Wingate, May 11, 1933, *Ann Vickers*, PCA.

50 Wingate to Hays. Aug. 26, 1933, *Ann Vickers*, PCA.

51 Hays to Kahane, July 31, 1933, LP. The letter was sent to all studio heads; a copy of the letter was sent to Daniel Lord.

52 Breen to Parsons, Oct. 10, 1932, box C-9, PP.

53 Ibid. Breen's rabid anti-Semitism is present in a large number of letters he sent to Lord, Parsons, Dinneen, and Quigley. It is unclear whether or not they shared his beliefs: In return correspondence they make no mention of his anti-Semitic views – neither agreeing with him nor taking him to task for his obvious racism. Lord, who published *Dare We Hate the Jews* in 1939, would seem an unlikely anti-Semitic; but anti-Semitism was an issue in the campaign against the movies, and Jewish domination of the movie industry was often given as a reason for "indecent films."

54 Quigley to Parsons, Aug. 27, 1934, box C-76, PP.

55 Henry James Forman, *Our Movie Made Children*, pp. 1–100.

56 Quigley to McNicholas, Oct. 4, 1933, U.S. [National] Catholic Conference [of Bishops] Archives, Episcopal Committee on Motion Pictures, Catholic University, Washington, D.C. [hereafter as NCCB–ECMP], 1933–44.

57 Cantwell summarized an article that would be published under his name in the February issue of *Ecclesiastical Review*, a publication read by Catholic priests. The article was ghosted by Breen and also contains much of Daniel Lord. See John Cantwell, D.D., "Priests and the Motion Picture Industry," *Ecclesiastical Review* 90 (Feb. 1934), 136–46. See also "Minutes of the Annual Meetings of the Bishops of the United States, *1919–1935,*" NCCB–ECMP. These minutes were printed but not published.

58   "Minutes of the American Hierarchy," Nov. 15, 1933, NCCB–ECMP. Cantwell did not want to be chair because he believed he would be subjected to too much pressure from the Hollywood community. McNicholas was a perfect choice – far away from both coasts.

59   Paul W. Facey, S.J., *Legion of Decency*, p. 45.

60   Gerard B. Donnelly, S.J., "The Bishops Rise against Hollywood," *America* 51 (May 26, 1934), 152.

61   "Compensating Moral Values," June 13, 1934, box 47, HP.

62   *Nation* 141 (Oct. 2, 1935), 391.

63   Breen to Hays, Aug. 31, 1935, *Barbary Coast*, PCA. See also Black, *Hollywood Censored*, pp. 218–20, for more details on the censoring of this film.

64   "Minutes of the Annual Meetings of the Bishops of the United States, 1919–1935," Nov. 13, 1935, pp. 9–14, NCCB–ECMP.

65   Ibid.

66   Mary Harden Looram, "National Recognition for Our Motion Picture Bureau," *Quarterly Bulletin of the International Federation of Catholic Alumnae* 5 (Mar. 1936), 15. See also McNicholas to Cardinal Hayes, Jan. 1, 1936, and McNicholas to Cicognani, Jan. 11, 1936, NCCB–ECMP, for details.

67   Edward Moore to McNicholas, Jan. 18, 1936, NCCB–ECMP.

68   Ibid. By 1937–8 the B rating was read as "objectionable in part for all."

69   Donnelly, "Bishops Rise against Hollywood," p. 152. See also Black, *Hollywood Censored*, pp. 167–8.

70   "National Legion of Decency," Feb. 1936, NCCB–ECMP.

71   Black, *Hollywood Censored*, p. 229.

72   Frank Walsh, *Sin and Censorship*, p. 144.

2. Cowboys and Courtesans Challenge Censors

1   For the latest biography of Hughes see Peter Harry Brown and Pat H. Broeske, *Howard Hughes: The Untold Story* (New York: Dutton, 1996).

2   Tony Thomas, *Howard Hughes in Hollywood*, pp. 22–33.

3   For a more complete account of the production of *Scarface* see Gregory D. Black, *Hollywood Censored*, pp. 124–32; Thomas, *Hughes in Hollywood*, pp. 71–6; Jay R. Nash and Stanley R. Ross, *The Motion Picture Guide*, pp. 2759–63; and Gerald Mast, *Howard Hawks, Storyteller* (New York: Oxford University Press, 1982), p. 74.

4   Thomas, *Hughes in Hollywood*, p. 75.

5   Ibid., p. 131. For criticism of Hughes see Martin Quigley, "Hughes and Censorship," *Motion Picture Herald*, May 28, 1932, p. 17.

6   Joseph Breen to Will Hays, May 1, 1935, *Cock of the Air*, PCA.

7   "Memo to Files," Apr. 19, 1940, *The Outlaw*, PCA. To read some of the PCA letters to Hughes see Gerald Gardner, *Censorship Papers*, pp. 26–31.

8   Breen to Hughes, Dec. 27, 1940, *The Outlaw*, PCA.

9   Nash and Ross, *Motion Picture Guide*, p. 2305.

10   Breen to Hughes, Mar. 28, 1941, *The Outlaw*, PCA.

11   Breen to Hays, Mar. 29, 1941, *The Outlaw*, PCA.

12   *Newsweek* 17 (Apr. 21, 1941), 52.

13   Carl Milliken to Hughes, May 16, 1941, *The Outlaw*, PCA.

14   Ibid.

15 Breen to Lord, Mar. 1, 1941, LP.

16 *Newsweek* 17 (May 12, 1941), 61.

17 It is hard to know whether RKO hired Breen just to get him out of the PCA or if the studio sincerely believed he could be a successful studio executive. One major criticism of Breen that was well known in Hollywood circles was that he was a poor administrator. The PCA, with a small staff and budget, was a one-man operation, and Breen often bragged, "I am the Code." Internal Legion documents show that Breen was in trouble within a few months of his RKO tenure. The fact that the studios insisted on Breen's return to the PCA illustrates how fully the self-regulation system had been integrated into the Hollywood production system.

18 The Catholic church received assurances from Hays that a Catholic would be named. See Archbishop John Cantwell to Archbishop John McNicholas, Sept. 22, 1941, NCCB–ECMP.

19 Memo for the Archbishop, Feb. 2, 1942, NCCB–ECMP.

20 Quigley was furious but powerless to prevent the reappointment. See McClafferty to McNicholas Apr. 1, 1942, NCCB–ECMP. McClafferty also told McNicholas that Breen originally turned down the offer to return as censor in early Mar.; but when it became clear he was not going to survive at RKO, Breen accepted his old position. See McClafferty to McNicholas, Mar. 6, 1942, NCCB–ECMP.

21 For a complete analysis of the role of OWI and Hollywood see Clayton R. Koppes and Gregory D. Black, *Hollywood Goes to War: How Politics, Profits, and Propaganda Shaped World War II Movies* (New York: Free Press, 1987).

22 Ibid., pp. 67–71.

23 Ibid., p. 206.

24 Leonard J. Leff and Jerold L. Simmons, *Dame in the Kimono*, p. 123.

25 For an interesting account see Jane Russell, *An Autobiography: My Path & My Detours* (New York: Franklin Watts, 1985), pp. 69–71.

26 *Hollywood Reporter*, Feb. 8, 1943, p. 8.

27 *Variety*, Feb. 10, 1943, p. 8.

28 *Motion Picture Herald*, Feb. 13, 1943, p. 1157.

29 For Legion reviews see Carl Milliken to Francis Harmon, Apr. 4, 1943, *The Outlaw*, PCA.

30 *Variety*, Feb. 10, 1943, p. 10. Normally ticket prices ran from 25 cents at local neighborhood theaters to $1.00–$1.50 at first-run theaters.

31 Ibid., Feb. 17, 1943, p. 10.

32 The term "Presbyterian pope" was coined by Kenneth Macgowan. See John Alan Sargent, "Self-Regulation," Ph.D. diss., p. 116.

33 His original contract with RKO had expired.

34 *Variety*, Jan. 23, 1946, p. 8.

35 *Business Week*, May 4, 1946, p. 20.

36 *Variety*, Mar. 20, 1946, p. 20.

37 *Los Angeles Daily News*, Apr. 4, 1946, in clipping file, *The Outlaw*, PCA.

38 *Los Angeles Express*, Apr. 4, 1946, in clipping file, *The Outlaw*, PCA.

39 *Variety*, May 15, 1946, p. 6.

40 Ibid., p. 12, and *Variety*, May 22, 1946, p. 22.

41 *Variety*, Jan. 12, 1947, p. 4.

42   Dennis Cardinal Dougherty to William Goldman, Nov. 3, 1947, box 2, Dougherty Papers, Archives of the Archdiocese of Philadelphia, Overbrook, Pa.

43   *Variety*, Feb. 20, 1946, p. 3.

44   *New York Times,* Sept. 12, 1947, p. 18.

45   *Rob Wagner's Script Review* 32 (Apr. 27, 1946), 14.

46   *Commonweal* 44 (July 26, 1946), 360.

47   *Variety*, May 22, 1946, p. 6.

48   Ibid.

49   *Variety,* Jan. 15, 1946, p. 21.

50   *Motion Picture Herald*, Apr. 17, 1946, p. 6.

51   *Time* 49 (Feb. 17, 1949), 102.

52   Bishop Scully to Archbishop John Cantwell, Apr. 5, 1947, box 58, Archdiocese Archives of Los Angeles, Mission Hills, Calif. [hereafter as AALA].

53   Rudy Behlmer, ed., *Memo from David O. Selznick* (New York: Avon Books, 1973), p. xiii. This wonderful collection of Selznick correspondence documents vividly his obsession with the detail of filmmaking.

54   For more on Selznick see Schatz, *Genius of the System*, pp. 48–57.

55   For an excellent discussion of *Rebecca* see Leonard J. Leff, *Hitchcock and Selznick: The Rich and Strange Collaboration of Alfred Hitchcock and David O. Selznick in Hollywood* (New York: Weidenfeld & Nicolson, 1987), pp. 36–84; see also Frank Walsh, *Sin and Censorship*, pp. 165–6.

56   Breen to William Gordon, Aug. 2, 1944, and Breen to Margaret McDonell, Jan. 24, 1945, *Duel in the Sun*, PCA.

57   Selznick maintained a small stable of stars and directors whom he often loaned out to other studios. For example, Selznick made a profit of over $450,000 in one year for "loaning" Joan Fontaine and Ingrid Bergman. Fontaine and Bergman each earned less than $90,000 that same year.

58   James Skinner states in his study of the Legion that Breen had bought the screen rights for *Duel in the Sun* when he was at RKO but had refused to go beyond script stage. Selznick, during his battles with the censor, told the press that Breen had first brought the project to RKO. However, Breen does not appear ever to have been involved with *Duel* in his brief stay at RKO. See Skinner, *Cross and the Cinema*, p. 87, and Breen to Paul MacNamara, July 7, 1947, box 3368, SP.

59   Quoted in Ethan Mordden, *The Hollywood Studios: House Style in the Golden Age of the Movies* (New York: Knopf, 1988), p. 205.

60   Quoted in Otto Friedrich, *City of Nets: A Portrait of Hollywood in the 1940s* (New York: Harper & Row, 1986), p. 228.

61   Stephen C. Lee, "Pending Catholicization: The Legion of Decency, *Duel in the Sun* and the Threat of Censorship," M.A. thesis, Radio, Television and Film, University of Texas–Austin, 1985, p. 16.

62   Vidor was given directorial credit for the film but records in the Selznick collection show that he directed only about half of the total footage. Out of the 14,310 feet of film in the final cut Vidor was credited with some 6,800 feet, Dieterle with 3,275, and Von Sternberg with 457. Second-unit directors Otto Brower and B. Reeves Eason did much of the rest of the film. Dieterle was furious when he discovered that Vidor had demanded that his credit on the title be "King Vidor's *Duel in the Sun*." Dieterle protested to the Screen Directors' Guild, demanding codirectorial credit for *Duel*. He lost, but the title belonged to Selznick, with Vidor listed as director and credits to both Brower and Eason.

See Dieterle to Screen Director's Guild, Apr. 5, 1946, box 3369, David O. Selznick Papers, University of Texas–Austin, Austin, Texas [hereafter as SP]. For Peck quote see Doug McClelland, *Forties Film Talk: Oral Histories of Hollywood* (Jefferson, N.C.: McFarland & Co., 1992), p. 423.

63 Breen to Selznick, July 13, 1945, *Duel in the Sun,* PCA.
64 Selznick to Glett and O'Shea, Oct. 23, 1945, SP.
65 Jones was not nude. She wore a bathing suit during the scene, but the implication was that she was nude.
66 Jim Steward to Selznick, Sept. 9, 1946, box 3368, SP.
67 Lee, "Pending Catholicization," pp. 34–7.
68 *Variety*, Jan. 1. 1947, p. 14.
69 William Mooring, "Hog-Wash Served in Golden Canteen," *Tidings,* Jan. 3, 1947, p. 15, and "Selznick's Film Makes Sham of Movie Code," *Tidings,* Jan. 17, 1947, p. 1.
70 Father John Devlin to Rev. Patrick J. Masterson, Oct. 4, 1947, box 57, AALA.
71 Martin Quigley to Selznick, Jan. 10, 1947, box 3368, SP.
72 Selznick to Scanlon and O'Shea, Feb. 8, 1947, box 596, SP.
73 Lee, "Pending Catholicization," pp. 70–1.
74 "Duel in the Sun – Legion Cuts," n.d., box 3368, SP.
75 Selznick to Rev. Patrick Masterson, Feb. 3, 1947, box 3368, SP.
76 Quigley to Masterson, Feb. 3, 1947, box 3368, SP.
77 Masterson to Breen, Feb. 18, 1947, *Duel in the Sun,* PCA.
78 Breen to Masterson, Feb. 21. 1947, *Duel in the Sun,* PCA.
79 Selznick to MacNamara, Aug. 11, 1947, box 3368, SP.
80 Selznick to Eric Johnston, Feb. 18, 1947, box 3368, SP.
81 Johnston to Selznick, Mar. 17, 1947 (and see Selznick's reply Mar. 24, 1947), box 3368, SP.
82 Kathryn Allen to Selznick, Jan. 27, 1947; Mrs. Henry Murphy to Selznick, Jan. 23, 1947; Diane Hazel Sharp to Selznick, July 29, 1947, all box 3368, SP. Selznick kept hundreds of letters on *Duel* (see box 3368, SP) and claimed that writers favored challenging the Legion by a 3:1 margin.
83 Selznick to Quigley, Apr. 10, 1947, box 3368, SP.
84 *Time* 49 (Jan. 27, 1947), 86–7.
85 *Cue* (May 10, 1947), p. 11, in clipping file, *Duel in the Sun,* National Legion of Decency Papers, Catholic Archdiocese of New York, New York, N.Y. [hereafter as NLOD].
86 *Newsweek* 29 (Mar. 3, 1947), 81–2.
87 *New Republic* 116 (May 19, 1947), 34.
88 *New York Times,* May 17, 1947, p. 30.
89 *Commonweal* 46 (May 23, 1947), 142.
90 *Cue* (May 10, 1947), p. 11, in clipping file, *Duel in the Sun,* NLOD.
91 *Variety*, May 14, 1947, p. 13.
92 Ibid., June 4, 1947, p. 15.
93 Ibid., June 25, 1947, p. 13.
94 Other films that got a B from the Legion included *All My Sons, Anna Karenina, Forever Amber, Paleface, Red River,* and *Yellow Sky.*
95 Walter E. Schmidt, S.J., to Selznick, May 23, 1947, and Willson to Selznick, Apr. 28, 1947, box 3368, SP.
96 Selznick to MacNamara, Aug. 11, 1947, box 3368, SP.
97 Ibid. See also Skinner, *Cross and the Cinema,* p. 90.

98 Selznick to Agnew, Oct. 29, 1947, box 596, SP.
99 Walsh, *Sin and Censorship,* p. 209.
100 Darryl Zanuck to Breen, Oct. 9, 1945, *Forever Amber,* PCA.
101 *Saturday Review of Literature* 27 (Oct. 14, 1944), 44.
102 *Variety,* Oct. 29, 1947, p. 18.
103 Philip Dunne, *Take Two: A Life in the Movies and Politics* (New York: McGraw–Hill, 1980), pp. 183.
104 Breen to Jason Joy, Oct. 4, 1944, *Forever Amber,* PCA.
105 Memo to Files, Nov. 2, 1944, *Forever Amber,* PCA.
106 *New York Herald,* Oct. 11, 1944, p.31.
107 Frank Nugent, "Forever Amber or 'Crime Doesn't Pay,'" *New York Times,* Oct 23, 1947, p. 31.
108 Schatz, *Genius of the System,* p. 138.
109 Leonard Mosley, *Zanuck: The Rise and Fall of Hollywood's Last Tycoon* (New York: McGraw–Hill, 1985), p. 175. The story conferences were transcribed and often circulated in the studio. The transcripts have survived and are in the 20th Century–Fox collection at the Doheny Library on the campus of the University of Southern California–Los Angeles [hereafter as TCF–USC]. They offer a unique insight into moviemaking during the studio era.
110 Ibid., p. 176.
111 Zanuck to William Perlberg and Jerome Cady, May 1, 1945, *Forever Amber,* TCF–USC. This memo is reprinted in Behlmer, *Memo from Darryl F. Zanuck,* p. 91.
112 Dunne, *Take Two,* p. 183.
113 Zanuck to Perberg and Philip Dunne, Oct. 16, 1945, TCF–USC.
114 Ibid.
115 Breen to Francis Harmon, Dec. 13, 1945, *Forever Amber,* PCA.
116 *Variety,* Jan. 1, 1946, p. 3.
117 Otto Preminger, *Preminger: An Autobiography,* p. 104.
118 *Time* 50 (Nov. 3, 1947), 99.
119 *New Republic* 117 (Oct. 27, 1947), 36.
120 Dunne, *Take Two,* p. 184.
121 Ibid.
122 Skinner, *Cross and the Cinema,* p. 84.
123 *New York Times,* Oct. 23, 1947, p. 36.
124 Ibid., Oct. 25, 1947, p. 12.
125 *Harrison's Reports,* Oct. 18, 1947, p. 166.
126 *Time* 50 (Nov. 3, 1947), 87.
127 Ibid., p. 99.
128 *New Republic* 117 (Oct. 27, 1947), 36.
129 *Motion Picture Herald,* Oct. 18, 1947, p. 3885.
130 *America* 78 (Nov. 8, 1947), 166.
131 *Queen's Work* 40 (May 8, 1948), 20.
132 *Commonweal* 47 (Oct. 31, 1947), 71.
133 *Variety,* Nov. 12, 1947, p. 4.
134 Ibid., Nov. 5, 1947, p. 24.
135 To follow box-office returns see *Variety,* Oct. 29, Nov. 5, 12, 19, 1947.
136 Breen to Johnston, Oct. 23, 1947, *Forever Amber,* PCA.
137 *Variety,* Dec. 19, 1947, p. 63.
138 Behlmer, *Memo from Darryl E. Zanuck,* p. 203.

139   Preminger, *Preminger: An Autobiography*, p. 106.
140   Stephen Jackson to Johnston, Nov. 26.

3. A Foreign Challenge

1   The ensuing discussion draws on Garth Jowett, *Film: The Democratic Art,* pp. 347–60, especially for the various statistics; Douglas Gomery, *Shared Pleasures: A History of Movie Presentation in the United States* (Madison: University of Wisconsin Press, 1992), pp. 230–46; and John Izod, *Hollywood and the Box Office, 1895–1986* (New York: Columbia University Press, 1988), pp. 134–50.

2   Michael Conant, *Antitrust in the Motion Picture Industry* (Los Angeles: University of California Press, 1960), p. 94.

3   Ibid., p. 103.

4   Tino Balio, *The American Film Industry* (Madison: University of Wisconsin Press, 1976), p. 405.

5   Conant, *Antitrust,* pp. 94–105.

6   Ibid. See also Jowett, *Film: The Democratic Art,* p. 346.

7   Gomery, *Shared Pleasures,* p. 177.

8   Reported in *Box Office,* quoted in Quigley to McNicholas, Oct. 30, 1936, NCCB.

9   "French Films," n.d. (production dates ranging from 1932 to 1936), box 2, MQ.

10   Quigley to McClafferty, May 26, 1945, box 1, MQ.

11   Martin Quigley Jr. to author, Jan. 28, 1997. The quotation is from Ezra Goodman, *The Fifty Year Decline and Fall of Hollywood* (New York: Simon & Schuster, 1961), p. 421.

12   For an excellent portrait of Rossellini see that by Patrizio Rossi in John Wakeman, ed., *World Film Directors, I, 1890–1945,* pp. 959–70.

13   Pierre Leprohon, *The Italian Cinema,* trans. Roger Greaves and Oliver Stallybrass (New York: Praeger Publishers, 1972), p. 92.

14   Rossi in Wakeman, *World Film Directors, I,* p. 961.

15   *New Yorker* 22 (Mar. 2, 1946), 81.

16   For an excellent analysis of *Open City* see Marcus, *Italian Film in the Light of Neorealism,* pp. 33–53.

17   *PM* (Feb. 10, 1946), p. 10.

18   *Cue* (Mar. 2, 1946), p. 14.

19   *Commonweal* 43 (Mar. 22, 1946), 574.

20   Richard Corliss, "Legion of Decency," p. 31.

21   Arthur DeBra to Burstyn, May 6, 1946; Gordon White to Files, July 17, 1946; and DeBra to Burstyn, July 30, 1947, *Open City,* PCA.

22   *Variety,* Feb. 11, 1948, p. 14.

23   *Time* 51 (Apr. 19, 1948, 96.

24   *Fortnight* 6 (Mar. 4, 1949), 30.

25   *Variety,* Feb. 11, 1948, p. 14.

26   Corliss, "Legion of Decency," p. 31. The Legion file for *Paisan* is missing from the NLOD. Mr. Henry Herx, Director, Department of Communications, Office of Film and Television, U.S. Catholic Conference, New York, N.Y., told me that Legion offices moved several times during the 1960s and 1970s, and that some of the records were lost. Herx was aware of the historical importance of the records and has maintained them in spite of a lack of storage space. Although

a few files from before 1967 have been lost, most of the controversial files remain under Herx's control. He has generously made them available to scholars interested in the history of the Legion.

27 Jack Vizzard to Files, Mar. 14, 1949, *Paisan,* PCA.

28 DeBra to Breen, Mar. 24, 1949, *Paisan,* PCA. It is not clear why the Legion of Decency was so lenient toward *Paisan*; its file is missing from Legion archives.

29 Breen to DeBra, Mar. 28, 1949, *Paisan,* PCA.

30 DeBra to Breen, Mar. 24, 1949, *Paisan,* PCA.

31 *New Yorker* 25 (Sept. 24, 1949), 54.

32 *Commonweal* 50 (Oct. 7, 1949), 632.

33 *Christian Century* 67 (Jan. 25, 1950), 127.

34 Gordon S. White to Breen, Nov. 15, 1949, *Germany, Year Zero,* PCA.

35 Vizzard to Breen, Jan. 25, 1950, *Germany, Year Zero,* PCA.

36 Breen to Fred Levenstein, Oct. 12, 1949, and Breen to Marcello Girosi, Oct. 21, 1949, *Germany, Year Zero,* PCA.

37 *Tidings,* Nov. 18, 1949, clipping in *Germany, Year Zero,* NLOD.

38 David A. Cook, *A History of Narrative Film,* 2d ed. (New York: W. W. Norton, 1990), pp. 430–1.

39 *New Yorker* 25 (Dec. 10, 1949), 140

40 *New Republic* 118 (Dec. 19, 1949), 23.

41 *New York Times,* Dec. 13, 1949, p. 44.

42 *Commonweal* 51 (Dec. 23, 1949), 319.

43 *Christian Century* 67 (Mar. 15, 1950), 351.

44 Pennsylvania, Maryland, and Kansas passed the film without comment. Massachusetts snipped a bit of the scene in the bordello but left untouched the one of Bruno attempting to urinate. New York, with a huge Italian population, cut a few lines of dialogue from the film but otherwise approved it without change. See *Bicycle Thief,* PCA.

45 Breen to Arthur Mayer and Joseph Burstyn, Jan. 31, 1950, *Bicycle Thief,* PCA.

46 Breen related the conservation to Francis Harmon. See Breen to Harmon, Feb. 6, 1950, *Bicycle Thief,* PCA.

47 Vittorio De Sica to Burystyn, n.d., *Bicycle Thief,* PCA.

48 Elmer Rice to Johnston, Mar. 3, 1950, *Bicycle Thief,* PCA.

49 *Life,* 13 (Mar. 1950), 40.

50 *Motion Picture Herald,* Feb. 18, 1950, p. 20.

51 For a good summary see Leonard J. Leff and Jerold L. Simmons, *Dame in the Kimono,* pp. 155–60.

52 Breen to Board of Directors, Mar. 21, 1950, *Bicycle Thief,* PCA. Breen offered no evidence for either claim.

53 *New Republic* 122 (Mar. 13, 1950), 9.

54 *Life* 13 (Mar. 1950), 40.

55 *New York Times,* Apr. 2, 1950.

56 Breen to Quigley, n.d., box 1, MQ. The letter was attached to Breen to Eric Johnston, Mar. 10, 1949, ibid. Both were written during the *Bicycle Thief* controversy.

57 Goodman, *Decline and Fall of Hollywood,* p. 421.

58 Leff and Simmons, *Dame in the Kimono,* pp. 155–6.

59 Ibid., p. 161.

60 Breen to White, Oct. 9, 1950, *Bitter Rice,* PCA.

61 Gordon White to Breen, Oct. 4, 1950, and see also White to Steve Schreiber, Mar. 15, 1951, *Bitter Rice*, PCA.

62 Gordon White to Files, Oct. 9, 1950, and Arthur DeBra to Files, Oct. 9, 1950, *Bitter Rice*, PCA.

63 Quigley to E. R. Zorgniotti, Lux Films, July 31, 1951, and Masterson to Rev. John Mets, Mar. 1, 1951, *Bitter Rice*, NLOD.

64 *Tidings*, Mar. 16, 1951, clipping in *Bitter Rice*, NLOD.

65 *New Republic* 123 (Oct. 9, 1950), 30.

66 *Time*, 56 (Nov. 6, 1950), 104.

67 *Commonweal* 52 (Oct. 6, 1950), 632.

68 Little to Files, June 25, 1951, *Bitter Rice*, NLOD.

69 *The Miracle* was passed by the Italian censorship board on Aug. 30, 1948, and issued certificate no. 4472, which was never withdrawn. See Joseph Burstyn Papers, box H-208, Museum of Modern Art, New York, N.Y. [hereafter as JB].

70 All the Italian papers cited here are quoted in Allan F. Westin, *The Miracle Case: The Supreme Court and the Movies*, p. 10. See also Little, "Memo to the Files," Nov. 23, 1951, NLOD.

71 The film only grossed $30,000 in Italy.

72 Bosley Crowther, "The Strange Case of 'The Miracle,'" p. 36. For a detailed analysis of the legal battles see Westin, *Miracle Case*. For an excellent account of the press coverage of the film see Jay Turner, "Public Reaction to the Legion of Decency in the Public Press, 1934–1952," M.A. thesis, Mass Communications, University of Texas–Austin, 1984, pp. 109–34. For a summary of the legal history of film censorship see Douglas Ayer, Roy E. Bater, and Peter J. Herman, "Self-Censorship in the Movie Industry: An Historical Perspective on Law and Social Change," *Wisconsin Law Review* (1970), 791–838. See also Richard S. Randall, *Censorship of the Movies* (Madison: University of Wisconsin Press, 1968), pp. 20–32.

73 All quoted in Westin, *Miracle Case*, p. 4.

74 *New York Times*, Dec. 13, 1950, p. 50.

75 Patrick Masterson to Francis Cardinal Spellman, Dec. 20, 1950, *The Miracle*, NLOD.

76 *New York Times*, Jan. 6, 1951, p. 1.

77 Ibid., Jan. 8, 1951, p. 1.

78 Ibid.

79 Ironically, the film was rejected for exhibition in the Soviet Union on the grounds that it was pro-Catholic propaganda.

80 Crowther, "Strange Case of 'The Miracle,'" p. 37.

81 *Motion Picture Herald*, Jan. 2, 1951, p. 2.

82 Turner, "Public Reaction to the Legion of Decency," p. 119.

83 Rev. W. J. Beeners to Burstyn, Jan. 26, 1951, box H-211, JB.

84 Merrill E. Bush to Ephraim S. London, Jan. 26, 1951, box H-211, JB.

85 Edward J. Smythe to Manager, Jan. 8, 1951, box H-211, JB.

86 *Louisville Courier–Journal*, Jan. 23, 1951, clipping in box H-211, JB.

87 Westin, *Miracle Case*, p. 15.

88 *Mutual Film Corporation v. Ohio Industrial Commission*, 236 U.S. 230, U.S. Supreme Court (1915), p. 242. See also Gregory D. Black, *Hollywood Censored*, pp. 15–18. For an excellent discussion of the case see Garth Jowett, "A Capacity for Evil: The 1915 Supreme Court Mutual Decision," *Historical Journal of Film, Radio and Television* 9 (1989), 59–78.

89 Many Catholics were confident the Court would uphold *Mutual.* See Harry Feldman, "'The Miracle' and the Constitution," *Sign* 30 (May 1951), 13–14.

90 *Burstyn v. Wilson,* 343 U.S. 495 (1952), pp. 17–18.

91 Ibid., p. 19.

92 The decision is reprinted in Kenneth S. Devol, ed., *Mass Media and the Supreme Court,* 3d ed. (Mamaroneck, N.Y.: Hastings, 1982), pp. 274–7.

93 Ibid., p. 275.

94 Ibid.

95 Ibid., pp. 276–7.

96 Ibid., p. 277.

97 For a history of the early years of the Legion see Black, *Hollywood Censored.*

98 William P. Clancy, "The Catholic as Philistine," p. 567.

99 Quoted in *Magazine of Art* 44 (May 1951), 194.

100 *Commonweal* 53 (Mar. 2, 1951), 507.

101 Quoted in Turner, "Public Reaction to the Legion of Decency," p. 131.

102 Quoted in *Variety,* Mar. 28, 1951, p. 13.

103 Burstyn is strangely missing from most film reference books.

4. The Legion Fights Back

1 Zanuck to Francis Harmon, Mar. 30, 1949, *Pinky,* PCA.

2 Clayton R. Koppes and Gregory D. Black, "Blacks, Loyalty, and Motion Picture Propaganda in World War II," *Journal of American History,* 73 (1986), 383–406.

3 Breen to Harry Zehner, Mar. 3, 1934; Maurice McKinzie to Breen, Apr. 3, 1934, *Imitation of Life,* PCA.

4 Breen to Joy, Feb. 28, 1949, *Pinky,* ibid.

5 Thomas Cripps, *Making Movies Black: The Hollywood Message Movie from World War II to the Civil Rights Era* (New York: Oxford University Press, 1993), p. 8.

6 For an excellent discussion of how the PCA dealt with racial issues see Thomas Cripps, *Slow Fade to Black: The Negro in American Film, 1900–1942* (New York: Oxford University Press, 1977), and his *Making Movies Black.*

7 Breen to Jason Joy, Feb. 28, 1949, and Joy to Breen, Mar. 2, 1949, *Pinky,* PCA.

8 *Newsweek* 34 (Oct. 10, 1949), 89–90; see also Ira H. Carmen, *Movies, Censorship and the Law* (Ann Arbor: University of Michigan Press, 1966), p. 55.

9 *Gelling v. Texas,* 343 U.S. 960 (1952).

10 Gene D. Phillips, *The Films of Tennessee Williams* (Philadelphia: Art Alliance Press, 1980), pp. 39–43.

11 Ibid.

12 Ibid., p. 61.

13 Ibid., p. 65.

14 Tennessee Williams, *A Streetcar Named Desire* (New York: Dramatists Play Service, 1947), p. 50.

15 Ibid., p. 49.

16 Ibid., p. 60.

17 Ibid., p. 98.

18 Richard Watts Jr., "*Streetcar Named Desire* Is Striking Drama," Dec. 4, 1947, reprinted in Jordan Y. Miller, ed., *Twentieth Century Interpretations of 'A Streetcar Named Desire'* (Englewood Cliffs, N.J.: Prentice–Hall, 1971), p. 30.

19 *New York Herald Tribune*, Dec. 14, 1947, reprinted in ibid., p. 35.

20 Breen to Jack Warner, Apr. 28, 1950, *A Streetcar Named Desire*, PCA. This memo is also reprinted in Gerald Gardner, *The Censorship Papers: Movie Censorship Letters from the Hays Office, 1934–1968* (New York: Dodd, Mead & Co., 1987), pp. 202–3. For a detailed analysis of the changes from the play to the screen see Ellen Dowling, "The Derailment of 'A Streetcar Named Desire,'" *Literature/Film Quarterly* 9 (1981), 233–40.

21 Kazan to Jack Warner, Oct. 19, 1950, quoted in Rudy Behlmer, *Behind the Scenes* (New York: Samuel French, 1990), p. 222.

22 Quoted in ibid., p. 221.

23 Ibid., p. 230.

24 Jack Vizzard, *See No Evil: Life Inside a Hollywood Censor* (New York: Simon & Schuster, 1970), p. 177.

25 Mort Blumenstock (WB) to Patrick Masterson, Aug. 7, 1951, *A Streetcar Named Desire*, NLOD. The letter details the cuts made by Warner Bros. after meeting with the Legion.

26 Ibid.

27 Ibid.

28 Elia Kazan, *A Life* (New York: Alfred A. Knopf, 1988), p. 432.

29 Quoted in Richard S. Randall, *Censorship of the Movies* (Madison: University of Wisconsin Press, 1968), p. 195.

30 Kazan, *A Life*, p. 435.

31 Ibid., pp. 434–5.

32 Ibid.

33 Elia Kazan, "Pressure Problem," *New York Times*, Oct. 21, 1951, p. 34.

34 Kazan, *A Life*, p. 436.

35 Ibid., p. 437.

36 *Variety*, Oct. 10, 1951, p. 8.

37 Kazan, *A Life*, p. 438. Kazan wrote in his memoirs that his article in the *Times* was too temperate, reasonable, and balanced, and that his real feelings were just the opposite. He was irate and determined to challenge again.

38 *Gelling v. Texas,* 343 U.S. 960 (1952), p. 960.

39 Gregory D. Black, *Hollywood Censored*, pp. 65–70.

40 Little to Rev. Michael O. Driscoll, July 28, 1953, box 1, MQ.

41 Little to DeMille, Dec. 11, 1951, box 651, Cecil B. DeMille Archives, Harold B. Lee Library, Brigham Young University, Provo, Utah [hereafter as CBDA]. I am thankful to James V. D'Arc, Curator of the DeMille Archives, for sending me the correspondence between DeMille and Little.

42 DeMille to Little, Dec. 26, 1951, box 651, CBDA.

43 Ibid.

44 Rev. Msgr. J. B. Lux to Rev. John McGrath, Apr. 7, 1952, box 651, CBDA.

45 Little to Driscoll, July 28, 1953, box 1, MQ.

46 See *Variety* "Box-Office Survey," Feb. 27–May 28, 1952, for figures from each city.

47 Otto Preminger, *Preminger: An Autobiography*, p. 110.

48 Leonard J. Leff and Jerold L. Simmons, *Dame in the Kimono*, p. 189.

49 Preminger, *Preminger: An Autobiography*, p. 108.

50 F. Hugh Herbert, "The Moon Is Blue," reprinted in *Theater Arts* 36 (Jan. 1952), 51–74, at p. 52.

51 Ibid., p. 65.

52   "Hullabaloo Over 'Moon Is Blue,'" *Life* 35 (July 13, 1953), 71.

53   Richard Hayes to Mrs. Looram, n.d., Legion of Decency, box 56, AALA.

54   Leff and Simmons, *Dame in the Kimono*, p. 191.

55   McNamara, who had played Patty in Chicago, would appear in three other films: *Three Coins in the Fountain, Prince of Players*, and finally in Preminger's *The Cardinal*. She committed suicide in 1978.

56   This comedy aspect of the code and sex was the downfall of Mae West. Her films made sex and sexual banter harmless fun. It was the way adults entertained each other, and was seen by the censors as subversive.

57   Shurlock to Files, Jan. 6, 1953, *The Moon Is Blue*, PCA.

58   Breen to Preminger, Apr. 10, 1953, ibid.

59   Preminger to Breen, Apr. 13, 1953, ibid.

60   Quoted in Leff and Simmons, *Dame in the Kimono*, p. 196.

61   Ibid.

62   *Variety*, June 10, 1953, p. 3.

63   Preminger, *Preminger: An Autobiography*, p. 108.

64   Skinner, *Cross and the Cinema*, p. 113.

65   Ibid.

66   Little to Diocesan Directors, June 11, 1953, *The Moon Is Blue*, NLOD.

67   *New York Times,* June 26, 1953, p. 16.

68   *Newsweek* 41 (June 29, 1953), 88.

69   *St. Joseph's Magazine* 54 (July 1953), 18. Hayes wrote his review before the Legion's position was known. The editor of *St. Joseph's Magazine*, Father Albert Bauman, found out just before the July 1953 issue went to press. In an act of journalistic bravery he allowed the review to run but editorialized that the review did not mean endorsement by the magazine.

70   *Variety*, Jun. 3, 1953, p. 6.

71   Little to Mooring, July 23, 1953, *The Moon Is Blue*, NLOD.

72   "Free Screen Without Honor?" *Tidings,* Aug. 7, 1953, clipping in Legion of Decency, box 56, AALA.

73   *Commonweal* 58 (July 17, 1953), p. 369.

74   Mooring to Little, June 26, 1953, *The Moon Is Blue*, NLOD.

75   Msgr. Blanchette to Little, Sept. 20, 1954, *The Moon Is Blue*, NLOD.

76   *New York Times,* June 23, 1953, p. 26, and Oct. 15, 1953, p. 53.

77   *Variety*, Aug. 12, 1953, p. 3.

78   Ibid., Aug. 5, 1953, p. 3.

79   Ibid., Sept. 9, 1953, p. 5.

80   *New York Times,* June 3, 1953, p. 6.

81   *Nation* 177 (July 4, 1953), 18.

82   *Time* 62 (July 6, 1953), 84.

83   Quoted in Milton Lehman, "Who Censors our Movies," *Look* 18 (Apr. 6, 1954), 86.

84   Ibid.

85   Quoted in *Newsweek* 41 (June 29, 1953), 88.

86   *Variety*, July 22, 1953, p. 11.

87   Ibid.

88   *Business Week* (Jan. 9, 1954), p. 33.

89   *Newsweek* 41 (June 29, 1953), 88.

90   The six organizations were the National Lutheran Council, the United Lutheran Church in America, The Lutheran Church–Missouri Synod, the American

Lutheran Church, the Evangelical Lutheran Church, and the Augustana Lutheran Church. Together they formed Lutheran Church Productions and raised $500,000 for production costs.

91   Alfred P. Klauser, "Martin Luther – The Story of a Film," *Christian Century* 70 (Oct. 21, 1953), 1195–7.

92   The film continued to circulate for showings in church basements for years. When WGN-TV tried to air the film in 1957 Chicago-area Catholics raised such a fuss that the station pulled the film. See "The 'Martin Luther' Controversy," *Commonweal* 65 (Mar. 15, 1957), 615–19.

93   *Nation* 177 (Sept. 26, 1953), 258.

94   *New York Times,* Sept. 10, 1953, p. 22.

95   *New Yorker* 29 (Sept. 19, 1953), 108.

96   *Theater Arts* 37 (May 1953), 83; *Saturday Review* 36 (June 13, 1953), 30.

97   Skinner, *Cross and the Cinema,* p. 63.

98   For a discussion of the Catholic reaction to *Blockade* see Clayton R. Koppes and Gregory D. Black, *Hollywood Goes to War: How Politics, Profits, and Propaganda Shaped World War II Movies* (New York: Free Press, 1987), pp. 24–6. *Blockade* had also been panned by the trade union IATSE, which told projectionists not to run it; Leff and Simmons, *Dame in the Kimono,* p. 108.

99   Memorandum on "Martin Luther," Dec. 9, 1953, National Catholic Welfare Conference Papers, Media/Motion Pictures, box 30, Catholic University, Washington, D.C. [hereafter as NCWC].

100   *America* 90 (Oct. 10, 1953), 53.

101   *Wanderer* 23 (Oct. 22, 1953), p. 4.

102   NCWC News Release, Nov. 16, 1953, box 30, NCWC.

103   Quoted in NCWC News Release, Nov. 30, 1953, box 30, NCWC.

104   Quoted in NCWC News Release, Nov. 9, 1953, box 30, NCWC.

105   *Wanderer* 23 (Oct. 22, 1953), p. 4.

106   For clipping see NCWC News Release, Nov. 30, 1953, box 30, NCWC.

107   Quoted in Skinner, *Cross and the Cinema,* p. 64.

108   See Martin Work, Executive Director of the National Council of Catholic Men, to Msgr. Paul Tanner, May 11, 1954, NCWC.

109   *New York Times,* Feb. 5, 1953, p. 26.

110   Quigley to Spellman, July 27, 1953, and Little to Spellman, July 18, 1953, *The Moon Is Blue,* NLOD.

111   See *The Moon Is Blue,* PCA. *United Artists and Holmby Productions* v. *Sydney R. Traub et al.,* Baltimore Docket 295, Folio 16, Dec. 7, 1953.

112   Edward deGrazia and Roger Newman, *Banned Films: Movies, Censors and the First Amendment* (New York: R. R. Bowker, 1982), p. 236.

113   *Holmby Productions and United Artists* v. *Vaughn,* no. 39699, 177 Kan. 728, 282 P.2d 412, p. 1227. See also L. S. Colby to Breen, Apr. 9, 1953, *The Moon Is Blue,* PCA.

114   *Holmby and UA* v. *Vaughn,* p. 1227.

115   *Superior Films* v. *Department of Education of State of Ohio,* 346 U.S. 587 (1954), p. 286.

116   Ibid.

117   *Catholic World* 78 (Mar. 1954), 403.

118   *New York Times,* Dec. 29, 1953, p. 19. For a general discussion of code revision see "Revising the Code," *Commonweal* 59 (Jan. 22, 1954), 392.

119 *Variety*, Dec. 30, 1954, p. 11.
120 Ibid., Jan. 20, 1954, p. 5.
121 *Commonweal* 58 (July 17, 1953), 369, and "Revising the Code," p. 392.
122 *New York Post*, Jan. 10, 1954, clipping in box 1, MQ.
123 Quigley to Schlesinger, Jan. 12, 1954, box 1, MQ.
124 Quigley to Johnston, Jan. 12, 1954, box 1, MQ.
125 Schlesinger to Quigley, Jan. 21, 1954, box 1, MQ.
126 Schlesinger to Quigley, Feb. 10, 1954, box 1, MQ.
127 For a detailed account of the program see *Variety*, Jan. 13, 1954, p. 20.
128 Skinner, *Cross and the Cinema*, p. 117.
129 Breen to William Feeder, Mar. 25, 1953, *The French Line*, PCA. Although Jack Vizzard states in his *See No Evil* (p. 174) that Breen sent a "long and bristling" letter citing code violations, Breen's letter to Feeder gives little indication of such violations other than the warning about the costumes.
130 "Memo to the Files," Jan. 13, 1954, *The French Line*, PCA.
131 *Business Week* (Jan. 9, 1954), p. 33.
132 Vizzard, *See No Evil*, pp. 173–4.
133 Little, "Memo to the Files," Jan. 8, 1954, *The French Line*, NLOD.
134 Rev. John Cody to Little, Jan. 4, 1954, *The French Line*, NLOD.
135 *Boston Pilot*, Jan. 9, 1954, and *St. Louis Register*, Jan. 8, 1954, clippings in *The French Line*, NLOD.
136 Vizzard, *See No Evil*, p. 207.
137 *Variety*, May 12, 1954, p. 7.
138 Rev. Michael Owen Driscoll to Dear Rev. Father, Feb. 15, 1954, *The French Line*, NLOD.
139 Rev. Paul Lackner to Little, May 18, 1954, *The French Line*, NLOD.
140 Little to Bishop Scully, Jan. 14, 1954, *The French Line*, NLOD.
141 *Variety*, May 5, 1954, p. 9, and May 19, 1954, p. 11.
142 Ibid., May 5, 1954, p. 8; Mar. 31, 1954, p. 12; Mar. 10, 1954, p. 7; and May 26, 1954, p. 8.
143 *New York Times*, May 15, 1954, p. 13.
144 *Newsweek* 43 (May 31, 1954), 85.
145 *New Yorker* 30 (May 22, 1954), 112.
146 *Time* 63 (May 31, 1954), 72.
147 *Variety*, Jan. 6, 1954, p. 52.
148 Little to Scully, Sept. 23, 1954, *The French Line*, NLOD.
149 *Variety*, Mar. 31, 1954, p. 13.

5. Declining Influence

1 Leonard J. Leff and Jerold L. Simmons, *Dame in the Kimono*, p. 228.
2 John Courtney Murray, S.J., "Literature and Censorship," *Books on Trial* 14 (July 1956), 393–5, 444–6, at p. 445. The article was reprinted in several Catholic publications including *Catholic Mind* 54 (Dec. 1956), 665–77.
3 Ibid., p. 445. Murray must also have had in mind the Catholic National Office of Decent Literature, which pressured publishers and book and magazine sellers to remove publications of which it did not approve. The NODL was especially effective in pressuring corporations not to advertise in publications on its condemned list.

4 Ibid.

5 Ibid., p. 446.

6 Quote from ibid.

7 Francis J. Connell, "How Should Priests Direct People Regarding Movies?" *American Ecclesiastical Review* 114 (Apr. 1946), 241–53, at p. 245. See also Connell to Little, Apr. 19, 1954, box 1, MQ.

8 John C. Ford, S.J., "Moral Evaluations of Films by Legion of Decency," n.d., box 56, AALA.

9 Ibid.

10 Ibid.

11 Gerald Kelly, S.J., and John C. Ford, S.J., "The Legion of Decency," *Theological Studies* 18 (Sept. 1957), 387–433. The U.S. Catholic Conference sent a letter of appreciation to Kelly and Ford stating that the article represented the views of its bishops. See "Bishop's Minutes," Nov. 12, 1957, NCCB–ECMP.

12 Quigley to Scully, June 25, 1956, box 1, MQ.

13 Scully to Quigley, July 3, 1956, box 1, MQ.

14 Quigley to Spellman, July 30, 1956, box 1, MQ.

15 Ibid.

16 Spellman to Quigley, box 1, July 30, 1956, box 1, MQ.

17 Quigley to Spellman, Legion of Decency Files, Archives of the Pastoral Center, Catholic Diocese of Albany, Albany, N.Y. [hereafter as AANY].

18 For more detail on lay Catholics ignoring Legion classifications see Gregory D. Black, *Hollywood Censored,* pp. 187–92.

19 Leff and Simmons, *Dame in the Kimono,* p. 192.

20 Jack Vizzard, *See No Evil,* p. 178.

21 *Time* 54 (Sept. 12, 1949), 104.

22 Breen to R. B. Roberts, Mar. 7, 1950, *Man with the Golden Arm,* PCA.

23 Bettina Drew, *Nelson Algren: A Life on the Wild Side,* p. 213.

24 Breen to R. B. Roberts, Mar. 7, 1950; E. Dougherty to Files, Mar. 25, 1950; and Breen to Roberts, June 21, 1950, *Man with the Golden Arm,* PCA. Sal Mineo recalled that during the filming of *The Gene Krupa Story,* released in 1958, federal narcotics agents descended on the set and insisted on monitoring and measuring the amount of marijuana that Mineo ingested during the "smoking scenes." According to Mineo he was limited to "three takes" to keep him from going "one toke over the line." See the radio series, *That Other Generation: 1950s* (written and produced by Joan and Robert Franklin, Cinema Sound Ltd., New York, 1978).

25 Preminger to Shurlock, June 27, 1955, *Man with the Golden Arm,* PCA.

26 Shurlock to Preminger, Sept. 16, 1955, *Man with the Golden Arm,* PCA.

27 *New York Times,* Nov. 13, 1955, p. 31. See also ibid., Oct. 25, 1955, p. 38.

28 *New York Times,* Nov. 13, 1955, p. 31.

29 *Motion Picture Daily,* Dec. 8, 1955, p. 1.

30 Ibid., p. 6.

31 *New York Times,* Dec. 16, 1955, p. 38.

32 *Variety,* Dec. 14, 1955, p. 6.

33 *Saturday Review of Literature* 38 (Dec. 17, 1955), 26.

34 Little to Scully, Dec. 21, 1955, *Man with the Golden Arm,* NLOD.

35 *Variety,* Dec. 28, 1955, p. 15, and Jan. 11, 1956, p. 11.

36 Ibid., Jan. 18, 1956, p. 9.
37 Ibid., Jan. 25, 1956, p. 7, and Feb. 1, 1956, p. 9.
38 Ibid., Jan. 18, 1956, p. 17.
39 O'Shea to Bishop Scully, Dec. 17, 1956, Legion of Decency Files, AANY.
40 Ibid.
41 Father Paul Hayes, Assistant Director LOD, to Scully, May 16, 1956, AANY.
42 Thomas Adler, *Robert Anderson* (Boston: Twayne Publishers, 1978), p. 72.
43 *Variety*, Dec. 14, 1953, p. 3.
44 Quigley to Breen, Oct. 13, 1953, and Breen to Quigley, Oct. 15, 1953, *Tea and Sympathy*, PCA.
45 Shurlock to Files, Nov. 9, 1953, *Tea and Sympathy*, PCA.
46 Breen to Harry Cohn, Oct. 20, 1953, *Tea and Sympathy*, PCA.
47 Shurlock to Files, Oct. 10, 1953, *Tea and Sympathy*, PCA.
48 Shurlock to Files, Nov. 6, 1953, *Tea and Sympathy*, PCA.
49 Memo to Files, Oct. 29, 1953, *Tea and Sympathy*, PCA.
50 Memo to Files, Mar. 25, 1955, *Tea and Sympathy*, PCA.
51 Memo to Files, Aug. 26, 1955, *Tea and Sympathy*, PCA.
52 Shurlock to Schary, Sept. 1, 1955, *Tea and Sympathy*, PCA.
53 Little to Schenck, Sept. 27, 1955, *Tea and Sympathy*, NLOD.
54 Haven Falconer [MGM] to Little, Aug. 9, 1956, *Tea and Sympathy*, NLOD.
55 Little to Files, Aug. 14, 1956, and Aug. 23, 1956, *Tea and Sympathy*, NLOD.
56 Little to Files, Aug. 29, 1956, *Tea and Sympathy*, NLOD. The Legion files contain various versions of the letter written by Quigley and Anderson.
57 Little to Files, Aug. 30, 1956, *Tea and Sympathy*, NLOD.
58 Hayes to Files, Sept. 7, 1956, *Tea and Sympathy*, NLOD.
59 Ibid.
60 Ibid. All the written comments by the various evaluators are in the file. Henry Herx has asked that individual evaluators not be identified.
61 John Fitzgerald to Little, Sept. 6, 1956, *Tea and Sympathy*, NLOD.
62 Little to Files, Sept. 14, 1956, *Tea and Sympathy*, NLOD.
63 Ibid.
64 See "A Short Biobraphy of Martin Quigley, Sr.," in Little to McNulty, May 24, 1961, *Tea and Sympathy*, NLOD.
65 *Time* 68 (Dec. 24, 1956), 61.
66 Elia Kazan, *A Life* (New York: Alfred A. Knopf, 1988), pp. 561–3.
67 Gene D. Phillips, *The Films of Tennessee Williams*, pp. 88–9.
68 Tennessee Williams, *Baby Doll*, p. 96.
69 Kazan to Warner, Nov. 15, 1955, *Baby Doll*, PCA.
70 Phillips, *Films of Tennessee Williams*, p. 94.
71 Vizzard, *See No Evil*, p. 207; idem, "Memo to the Files," July 25, 1956, *Baby Doll*, PCA.
72 Vizzard, *See No Evil*, p. 207.
73 Little, "Memorandum to Diocesan Directors," Nov. 27, 1956, *Baby Doll*, NLOD.
74 John Cooney, *The American Pope*, pp. 202–3.
75 *New York Post*, Dec. 18, 1956, clipping in *Baby Doll*, NLOD.
76 Ibid.
77 Quoted in Kazan, *A Life*, p. 564.
78 Quigley to Spellman, Dec. 14, 1956, box 1, MQ.
79 Phillips, *Films of Tennessee Williams*, p. 99.

80 Kazan, *A Life*, p. 564.
81 *New York Post*, Dec. 18, 1956, clipping in *Baby Doll*, NLOD.
82 *Boxoffice*, Jan. 26, 1957, ibid.
83 *Los Angeles Times*, Dec. 24, 1956, clipping in *Baby Doll*, PCA.
84 *Life* 42 (Jan. 7, 1956), 60–5.
85 *New York Times*, Dec. 27, 1956, p. 21. See also ibid., Dec. 17, p. 28, and Dec. 24, 1956, p. 24, for various opinions on the movie.
86 *Variety*, Dec. 19, 1956, p. 10.
87 *Catholic World* 184 (Jan. 1957), 245, 302; ibid., 185 (Apr. 1957), 62.
88 *Commonweal* 65 (Dec. 28, 1956), 335.
89 *America* 96 (Jan. 5, 1957), 386.
90 *Ave Maria* 85 (Jan. 12, 1957), 5.
91 *Tablet* 209 (Jan. 5, 1957), 8.
92 Vizzard, *See No Evil*, p. 210.
93 Archbishop Timothy Manning to Scully, Dec. 26, 1956, box 56, AALA.
94 *Variety*, Jan. 2, 1957, p. 9, Jan. 16, 1957, p. 9, and Jan. 8, 1958, p. 30.
95 Kazan, *A Life*, p. 564.
96 *Saturday Review of Literature* 39 (Dec. 29, 1956), 22.
97 *Newsweek* 48 (Dec. 17, 1956), 106.
98 *New York Times*, Dec. 19, 1956, p. 40.
99 *New Republic* 136 (Jan. 21, 1957), 21.
100 See *New York Times*, Oct. 14, 1956, III, p. 5, on problems in getting the film produced.
101 Arthur Knight, "The Lady's Not for Banning," *Saturday Review of Literature* 39 (June 16, 1956), 16.
102 Arthur DeBra to Dear Friend, July 1956, *Storm Center*, PCA.
103 *New York Times*, Oct. 22, 1956, p.25. The Separate Classification had been used for only three entertainment films in Legion history: *Blockade*, *Martin Luther*, and *Storm Center*.
104 Chester J. Pach Jr. and Elmo Richardson, *The Presidency of Dwight D. Eisenhower*, rev. ed. (Lawrence: University Press of Kansas, 1991), p. 66.
105 Little to Files, June 1, 1956, *Storm Center*, NLOD.
106 Ibid. The Motion Picture Industry Council called the Legion position a form of censorship. See *New York Times*, July 23, 1956, p. 16.
107 *Sign* 35 (August 1956), 31.
108 Scanlan to Little, n.d., *Storm Center*, NLOD.
109 *Commonweal* 64 (Aug. 3, 1956), 431.
110 *Variety*, July 25, 1956, p. 7.

6. A New Approach

1 For a summary of the meeting see "International Study Days," Jan. 4–7, 1957, box 1, MQ.
2 Jack Vizzard, *See No Evil*, p. 250.
3 Quigley to Little, Sept. 10, 1956, box 1, MQ.
4 Ibid.
5 Quigley had long been opposed to any attempt by the Legion to praise good films. When Father Joseph Daly proposed awarding a monthly Gold Medal Award to the film that most closely conformed to Legion standards, Quigley told Archbishop McNicholas that Daly was "an unfortunate choice" as Legion

director. McNicholas replaced Daly with Father John J. McClafferty, and the Legion never again attempted to recognize films in a positive manner. See Quigley to McNicholas, Mar. 7, 19, and 24, 1936, NCCB–ECMP.

6   Vizzard, *See No Evil,* p. 252.
7   Ibid., pp. 252, 254.
8   Ibid., p. 256.
9   *New York Times,* Jan. 13, 1957, p. 31.
10 Archbishop McIntyre to Files, Feb. 14, 1957, box 56, AALA.
11 In 1957 the Legion had seventy-eight films on its condemned list, of which forty-eight (61 percent) were foreign. Only two films on the condemned list – *The Moon Is Blue* and *Baby Doll* – could be considered major Hollywood productions. The remainder were "exploitation" productions such as *Mom and Dad* and *Garden of Eden.*
12 William A. Scully, "The Movies: A Positive Plan," *America* 96 (Mar. 30, 1957), 726–7.
13 *"Vigilanti Cura,"* *Catholic Mind* 34 (June 29, 1936), 310–11.
14 Quigley to Scully, Jan. 28, 1958, Legion of Decency, Pastoral Center, Archdiocese of Albany, Albany, N.Y. [hereafter as PCAA].
15 "Minutes of the Episcopal Committee on Motion Pictures," Nov. 12, 1957, box 56, AALA.
16 "National Legion of Decency Sermon Outline," Dec. 15, 1957, AS-33, CFO, 1939–58, Archdiocese of Milwaukee Archives, Milwaukee, Wisc.
17 Ibid.
18 Quoted in Skinner, *The Cross and the Cinema,* p. 133.
19 Vizzard related this to Breen, who relayed it to Quigley: Breen to Quigley, Feb. 21, 1957, box 1, MQ. Scully also was quoted by Vizzard (ibid.) as stating that "the interference of Martin Quigley" also made Little's job very difficult.
20 *Catholic Preview of Entertainment* 2 (Feb. 1958), 30.
21 Quigley to Scully, Jan. 21, 1958, PCAA.
22 "Minutes of the Thirty-Ninth Annual Meeting of the Bishops of the United States," Nov. 1957, NCCB–ECMP.
23 "Memo for the Files," June 6, 1955, *Cat on a Hot Tin Roof,* PCA.
24 Quoted in Gene D. Phillips, *The Films of Tennessee Williams,* p. 144.
25 Memo to Files, Feb. 13, 1958, *Cat on a Hot Tin Roof,* PCA.
26 *Time* 72 (Sept. 15, 1958), 92; *Nation* 187 (Oct. 11, 1958), 220.
27 Kenneth L. Geist, *Pictures Will Talk,* p. 292.
28 Tennessee Williams, *Suddenly Last Summer,* p. 77.
29 Ibid., p. 87.
30 *Newsweek* 75 (Jan. 11, 1960), 64.
31 Memo to Files, May 25, 1959, *Suddenly Last Summer,* PCA. My thanks to Professor Tom Poe for providing me with documentation on this film.
32 Shurlock to Spiegel, Oct. 30, 1959, *Suddenly Last Summer,* PCA.
33 There is nothing in the PCA file to indicate why the MPAA overruled Shurlock. Most likely everyone thought the taboo silly and that because there was no direct statement that Sebastian was homosexual it should be given a seal.
34 Little to Files, Dec. 1, 1959, *Suddenly Last Summer,* NLOD.
35 See Board of Consultors to Little, Nov. 21, 1959, *Suddenly Last Summer,* NLOD. I remind the reader that I have been asked not to reveal the names of these board members.

36 Ibid.
37 Fitzgerald to Little, Nov. 10, 1959, *Suddenly Last Summer*, NLOD; see *Our Sunday Visitor*, Apr. 10, 1960, clipping in *Suddenly Last Summer*, PCA.
38 Little to Hedda Hopper, Apr. 6, 1960, *Suddenly Last Summer*, NLOD.
39 *Commonweal* 71 (Jan. 1, 1960), 396.
40 *America* 102 (Jan. 9, 1960), 429.
41 *Tablet* 214 (May 21, 1960), 23.
42 *Time* 75 (Jan. 11, 1960), 64.
43 *New Yorker* 35 (Jan. 9, 1960), 75.
44 *New York Times*, Dec. 23, 1959, p. 22.
45 Quoted in Geist, *Pictures Will Talk*, p. 298.
46 Phillips, *Films of Tennessee Williams*, pp. 174–5.
47 *Variety*, Dec. 30, 1959, p. 7; see also Phillips, *Films of Tennessee Williams*, p. 192.
48 McNulty to Cardinal McIntyre, Nov. 24, 1959, box 56, AALA.
49 Ibid.
50 Quigley to Spellman, Dec. 3, 1959, box 1, MQ.
51 Vito Russo, *The Celluloid Closet*, p. 118.
52 Ibid., pp. 121–2.
53 Ibid., p. 116.
54 *Motion Picture Daily*, Apr. 19, 1962, clipping in *La Dolce Vita*, NLOD.
55 Little to Bishop McNulty, May 24, 1961, *La Dolce Vita*, NLOD.
56 See consultors' comments, *La Dolce Vita*, NLOD.
57 Ibid.
58 "Memorandum to Bishop McNulty," May 24, 1961, *La Dolce Vita*, NLOD.
59 Ibid.
60 Little to Spellman, May 1, 1961, *La Dolce Vita*, NLOD.
61 Little to Spellman, May 9, 1961, *La Dolce Vita*, NLOD.
62 Quigley to McNulty, May 5, 1961, box 2, MQ.
63 Quigley to McNulty, May 5 and May 17, 1961, box 2, MQ. Quigley sent two separate letters that repeated many of the same points.
64 Ibid.
65 Ibid.
66 McNulty to Quigley, May 17, 1961, box 2, MQ.
67 Little to McNulty, May 24, 1961, *La Dolce Vita*, NLOD.
68 See *Motion Picture Exhibitor* 66 (Oct. 18, 1961), 3.
69 *Albany Evangelist*, Oct. 5, 1961, clipping in *La Dolce Vita*, NLOD.
70 *Ave Maria* 93 (June 17, 1961), 17.
71 *Commonweal* 74 (May 26, 1961), 221.
72 *Catholic Standard*, July 14, 1961, clipping in *La Dolce Vita*, NLOD.
73 *Catholic Mind* 60 (Mar. 1962), 39.
74 *America* 105 (June 3, 1961), 411.
75 *Ave Maria* 94 (Aug. 26, 1961), 15.
76 Sullivan to Mrs. Harold Ainsworth, Nov. 28, 1961, *La Dolce Vita*, NLOD.
77 *Variety*, Jan. 10, 1962, p. 7.
78 Frank Walsh, *Sin and Censorship*, p. 146.
79 *Ave Maria* 101 (Jan. 9, 1965), 10.
80 *New York Times*, July 14, 1962, p. 23.
81 Vladimir Nabokov, *Lolita*, 4th ed. (Paris: Olympia Press, 1958), I, p. 160.

82 Ibid., I, p. 167.

83 Ibid., I, p. 175.

84 Ibid., I, pp. 177–8.

85 Ibid. II, pp. 35, 33.

86 Quigley to Shurlock, Feb. 2, 1961, box 3, MQ.

87 Shurlock to Files, Sept. 11, 1958, *Lolita*, PCA.

88 Shurlock to Files, Sept. 11, 1958, *Lolita*, PCA.

89 Leff and Simmons, *Dame in the Kimono*, p. 224.

90 Gene D. Phillips, *Stanley Kubrick: A Film Odyssey*, p. 86.

91 Shurlock to Quigley, Jan. 20, 1961, *Lolita*, PCA.

92 Quigley to Harris, Dec. 19, 1960, box 3, MQ.

93 Ibid.

94 Harris to Quigley, Jan. 2, 1961, box 3, MQ.

95 Shurlock to Quigley, Feb. 8, 1961, *Lolita*, PCA.

96 Quigley to Harris, Feb. 10, 1961, box 3, MQ.

97 Vizzard, *See No Evil*, p. 267.

98 Vladimir Nabokov, *Lolita: A Screenplay* (New York: McGraw–Hill, 1974), p. 110.

99 Quigley to Harris, May 25, 1961, box 3, MQ. It was in May 1961 that Quigley was battling with Bishop McNulty over *La Dolce Vita*.

100 Sullivan to Little, Sept. 1961, *Lolita*, NLOD.

101 Memo to Cardinal Spellman, Oct. 20, 1961, *Lolita*, NLOD.

102 Little to Cardinal Spellman, Oct. 11, 1961, *Lolita*, NLOD.

103 Little to David Stillman, Oct. 16, 1961, *Lolita*, NLOD.

104 Stillman to McNulty, Oct. 16, 1961, *Lolita*, NLOD.

105 Little to Spellman, Oct. 20, 1961, *Lolita*, NLOD.

106 Hyman to Little, Feb. 6, 1962, *Lolita*, NLOD.

107 Consultors' comments are found in *Lolita*, NLOD.

108 NLOD Press Release, Apr. 12, 1962, *Lolita*, NLOD.

109 *New York Herald Tribune*, July 15, 1962, pp. 22–3.

110 *Sign* 42 (August, 1962), 46.

111 *Commonweal* 76 (July 13, 1962), 401, and 77 (Nov. 16, 1962), 198.

112 *Our Sunday Visitor*, Aug. 18, 1962, clipping in *Lolita*, PCA.

113 *New Republic* 147 (July 2, 1962), 29.

114 *Variety*, June 13, 1962, p. 6.

115 *Motion Picture Herald*, June 20, 1962, p. 596.

116 *New York Herald Tribune*, July 15, 1962, pp. 22–3.

117 *Variety*, Aug. 29, 1962, p. 9, and Jan. 9, 1963, p. 13.

118 Gerard B. Donnelly, S.J., "The Bishops Rise against Hollywood," *America* 51 (May 26, 1934), 152. See also Gregory D. Black, *Hollywood Censored*, p. 167.

119 Walsh, *Sin and Censorship*, p. 310.

120 When the new pledge had first come up for a vote in 1959, the bishops had rejected it. It passed in 1963. Some dioceses kept the old pledge, most adopted the new, and a few did away with it altogether. For a negative reaction to the new pledge see William Mooring, "From the Hollywood Sets," *Extension* 58 (Nov. 1963), 30.

121 McNulty to Tanner, Oct. 12, 1961, box 31, NCWC. See also Alter to Tanner, Oct. 3, 1961, and Alter to Quigley, Oct. 3, 1961, both box 31, NCWC, as well as Quigley to Alter, Sept. 26, 1961, box 2, MQ.

7. The End of the Legion

1   "Minutes of the 44th Annual Meeting of the Bishops of the United States," Oct. 1962, NCCB.

2   See Sullivan to Little, July 11, 1961; Sullivan to Files, May 23, 1961; Little to Files, June 22, 1961, *Splendor in the Grass*, NLOD.

3   *Paterson Morning Call*, Oct. 31, 1961, clipping in *Splendor in the Grass*, NLOD.

4   Consultors' comments, *The Apartment*, NLOD.

5   *Saturday Review* 43 (June 11, 1960), 24.

6   Gordon to Little, Oct. 10, 1960, *Spartacus*, NLOD. The scenes have all been recently restored in a director's-cut version of the film, which is available on video.

7   William Gordon to Edward Muhl, Oct. 10, 1960, *Spartacus*, NLOD.

8   Sullivan to Louis Becker, Dec. 7, 1960, *Spartacus*, NLOD.

9   *Variety*, Jan. 4, 1961, p. 47, and Jan. 9, 1963, p. 13.

10 For a fascinating account of the problems Fast had in publishing the novel, see Howard Fast, *Being Red: A Memoir* (Boston: Houghton Mifflin, 1990), pp. 286–300.

11 Consultors' comments, *Spartacus*, NLOD.

12 J. J. O'Connor to Little, Oct. 26, 1960, *Spartacus*, NLOD.

13 Edward Quinn to McNulty, Nov. 26, 1960, and Sullivan to Quinn, Dec. 7, 1960, *Spartacus*, NLOD. That the Legion was an active supporter of the blacklist is confirmed in one other incident relative to *Spartacus*. Before the film opened in Kansas City, Missouri, a letter was sent to the Legion asking if it would be acceptable to arrange a private screening of the film as a fund raiser for Catholic charities in the city. The Legion response was firm: Sullivan wrote that the film would not be an appropriate choice because "the screen play for the film *Spartacus* was done by Mr. Dalton Trumbo who continues to be one of Hollywood's blacklisted writers. The American Legion at its recent National Convention once again censured this film for its employment of the said Mr. Trumbo." See Sullivan to Gordon, Nov. 2, 1960, *Spartacus*, NLOD.

14 *Variety*, Jan. 4, 1961, p. 47.

15 Sullivan to Files, July 11, 1962, *Boccaccio 70*, NLOD.

16 *Motion Picture Daily*, July 11, 1962, clipping in *Boccaccio 70*, NLOD

17 Hollis Alpert, *Fellini: A Life* (New York: Atheneum, 1986), p. 157.

18 Sullivan to Files, July 18, 1962, *Boccaccio 70*, NLOD.

19 Sullivan to Files, July 23, 1962, *Boccaccio 70*, NLOD.

20 Levine to Spellman, Aug. 8, 1962, *Boccaccio 70*, NLOD.

21 *Variety*, Sept. 9, 1962, p. 8, and Sept. 26, 1962, p. 8.

22 Ibid., Sept. 12, 1962, p. 11.

23 Memo to Diocesan Directors, Oct. 30, 1962, *Boccaccio 70*, NLOD.

24 Sullivan to the Files, Oct. 3, 1962, *Boccaccio 70*, NLOD.

25 *Tablet*, Nov. 10, 1962, clipping in *Boccaccio 70*, NLOD.

26 *Variety*, Oct. 3, 1962, p. 6.

27 "Minutes of the Forty-Fourth Annual Meeting of the Bishops of the United States," Oct. 1962, p. 47, NCCB.

28 Richard S. Randall, *Censorship of the Movies*, p. 208.

29 "Minutes of the Forty-Seventh Annual Meeting of the Bishops," pp. 60–5, NCCB–ECMP.

30 *America* 112 (June 26, 1965), 895.

31 For a full text of the code see the Appendix to the present volume.

32 Wallant's first novel, *The Human Season*, had a similar theme. For a discussion of Wallant see Dorothy S. Bilik, *Immigrant Survivors: Post Holocaust Consciousness in Recent Jewish Fiction* (Middletown, Conn.: Wesleyan University Press, 1981).

33 See *Time* 78 (Aug. 18, 1961), 75; *New Yorker* 37 (Aug. 19, 1961), 90; *Library Journal* 86 (Aug. 1961), 2686.

34 For an analysis of Lumet see Frank R. Cunningham, *Sidney Lumet: Film and Literary Vision* (Lexington, Ky.: University of Kentucky Press, 1991).

35 *Saturday Review* 48 (Apr. 3, 1965), 37.

36 See consultors' comments, *The Pawnbroker*, NLOD.

37 Little to Files, Mar. 8, 1965, *The Pawnbroker*, NLOD.

38 Landau to Little, Apr. 21, 1965, *The Pawnbroker*, NLOD. (Little's words are from a phone conversation, cited in Landau's letter.)

39 Little to Landau, May 10, 1965, *The Pawnbroker*, NLOD.

40 Little to Krol, Apr. 28, 1965, *The Pawnbroker*, NLOD.

41 Judy Stone, "What's Nude?" *Ramparts* 4 (Sept. 1965), 43–55, at p. 55.

42 *Variety*, Mar. 31, 1965, clipping in *The Pawnbroker*, NLOD.

43 Stone, "What's Nude?" p. 44.

44 *Cue* (Apr. 24, 1965), in clipping file *The Pawnbroker*, NLOD.

45 *Life* 58 (Apr. 2, 1965), 16.

46 *Film Daily*, Apr. 16, 1965, p. 3.

47 *New York Herald Tribune*, Apr. 21, 1965, clipping in *The Pawnbroker*, NLOD.

48 *New York Times,* Apr. 21, 1965, p. 21.

49 *Nation* 200 (May 10, 1965), 515.

50 *Time* 85 (Apr. 23, 1965), 103.

51 *Village Voice* 10 (July 15, 1965), 11.

52 *America* 112 (June 5, 1965), 838.

53 *Commonweal* 82 (May 14, 1965), 255.

54 *Sign* 45 (Aug. 1965), 54.

55 *Extension* 60 (July 1965), 33.

56 *Variety,* Sept. 15, 1965, p. 30.

57 *Christian Century* 82 (July 28, 1965), 942–3.

58 Pike to Landau, May 20, 1965, *The Pawnbroker*, NLOD.

59 Stone, "What's Nude?" p. 53.

60 Ibid.

61 "Who Is Immoral?" *Film Heritage* 1 (1966), 1.

62 Ibid.

63 *Variety*, May 5, 1965, p. 8, and Jan. 5, 1966, p. 36.

64 *Time* 88 (July 1, 1966), 78. For an extensive analysis of the film see Leonard J. Leff and Jerold L. Simmons, *Dame in the Kimono*, pp. 241–66.

65 Leonard Leff, "Who's Afraid of Virginia Woolf?" *Cinema Journal* 19 (1980), 42.

66 Ibid., pp. 44, 48.

67 Frank Walsh, *Sin and Censorship*, p. 321.

68 For an excellent account of the written reviews of the NCOMP consultors see J. D. Nicola, "Virginia Woolf: The Making of a Film Rating," *Ave Maria* 104

(Aug. 27, 1966), 7–11. The article reprints the comments of the consultors on the film.

69 Ibid. See also Leff, "Who's Afraid of Virginia Woolf?" pp. 49–50. The numbers add up to only eighty-five because some of the consultors did not file written reports; see *Who's Afraid of Virginia Woolf?*, NLOD.

70 For the a more complete reprinting of these comments see Nicola, "Virginia Woolf." NCOMP gave Nicola access to its files and permission to reprint the comments because their rating of A4 for the film set off a massive protest by conservative Catholics outraged by NCOMP's failure to condemn it.

71 See consultors' comments, *Virginia Woolf*, NLOD.

72 Leff, "Who's Afraid of Virginia Woolf?" p. 46.

73 Sullivan to Hyle, June 16, 1966, *Virginia Woolf*, NLOD.

8. Conclusion

1 *America* 113 (Aug. 21, 1965), 190.

2 Sullivan to Mrs. Jane Cosgrove, Feb. 16, 1966, *Darling*, NLOD.

3 Mrs. Van C. Newkirk to Little, Feb. 28, 1966, *Darling*, NLOD.

4 Sullivan to Mrs. Van C. Newkirk, Mar. 3, 1966, *Darling*, NLOD.

5 *Ave Maria* 102 (Nov. 27, 1965), 9–10; *Extension* 60 (Nov. 1965), 41; *Catholic World* 202 (Dec. 1965), 190–3; *Commonweal* 82 (Aug. 20, 1965), 598; *Sign* 45 (Nov. 1965), 62.

6 Leonard J. Leff and Jerold L. Simmons, *Dame in the Kimono*, p. 274.

7 Quoted in Frank Walsh, *Sin and Censorship*, p. 319. See also Mary L. Mc-Laughlin, "National Catholic Office for Motion Pictures," Ph.D. diss., p. 91. McLaughlin interviewed Little in January 1972.

8 *Catholic Free Press*, Feb. 11, 1972, clipping in *The Last Picture Show*, NLOD.

9 *The Messenger*, Mar. 10, 1972, clipping in *The Last Picture Show*, NLOD.

10 MPAA Press Release, June 2, 1971, box 2, National Legion of Decency Collection, Catholic University, Washington, D.C. For a history of the dispute over the ratings system see Sullivan to Most Rev. Joseph L. Bernardin, June 3, 1971, ibid.

11 Pauline Kael, *Reeling* (Boston: Little Brown, 1972), at p. 28.

12 *New York Times,* Jan. 28, 1973, II, p. 1.

13 Consultors' reviews, *Last Tango in Paris*, NLOD.

14 *Listener*, Mar. 22, 1973 in clipping file, *Last Tango in Paris*, NLOD.

15 *Commonweal* 98 (Mar. 9, 1973), 15.

16 *America* 231 (Feb. 24, 1973), 251.

17 *Newsweek* 81 (Mar. 5, 1973), 54.

18 For consultors' reactions see *Taxi Driver,* NLOD.

19 Walsh, *Sin and Censorship,* p. 323.

20 Ibid., p. 320.

21 Judy Stone, "What's Nude?" *Ramparts* 4 (Sept. 1965), 43–55, at p. 44.

22 *New York Times,* May 2, 1965, II, p. 1.

SELECTED BIBLIOGRAPHY

The bulk of research done for this book was in the archives listed below. The history of the Legion is told in great detail in the correspondence of the Legion and the film industry. The Legion story was also reported in thousands of articles in the Catholic press. The bibliography listed below is intended as a general guide for those interested in doing more reading on this topic.

Archives

AALA	Archival Center, Archdiocese of Los Angeles, Mission Hills, Calif.
AANY	Legion of Decency Files, Archives of the Pastoral Center, Catholic Diocese of Albany, Albany, N.Y.
CBDA	Cecil B. DeMille Archives, Harold B. Lee Library, Brigham Young University, Provo, Utah.
DS	David O. Selznick Papers, Harry Ransom Humanities Research Center, University of Texas–Austin, Austin, Tex.
HP	Will Hays Papers, Indiana State Historical Society, Indianapolis, Ind.
JB	Joseph Burstyn Papers, box H-208, Museum of Modern Art, New York, N.Y.
LP	Daniel Lord Papers, Jesuit Missouri Province Archives, St. Louis, Mo.
MQ	Martin Quigley Papers, Georgetown University, Washington, D.C.
NCCB–ECMP	U.S. [National] Catholic Conference [of Bishops] Archives, Episcopal Committee on Motion Pictures, Catholic University, Washington, D.C.
NCWC	National Catholic Welfare Conference Papers, Media/Motion Pictures, box 30, Catholic University, Washington, D.C.
NLOD	National Legion of Decency Papers, Catholic Archdiocese of New York, New York, N.Y.
PAHRC	Philadelphia Archdiocesan Historical Research Center, St. Charles, Borromeo Seminary, Overbrook, Pa.
PCA	Production Code Administration Files, Margaret Herrick Library, Academy of Motion Picture Arts and Sciences, Beverly Hills, Calif.
PCAA	Pastoral Center, Archdiocese of Albany, Albany, N.Y.
PP	Wilfrid Parsons Papers, Georgetown University, Washington, D.C.
TCF–USC	20th Century–Fox Collection, Doheny Library, University of Southern California–Los Angeles, Los Angeles, Calif.

Books

Addams, Jane. *The Spirit of Youth and the City Streets* (New York: Macmillan, 1909).

Balio, Tino, ed., *Grand Design: Hollywood as a Modern Business Enterprise, 1930–1939* (New York: Charles Scribner's Sons, 1993).

Basinger, Jeanine. *A Woman's View: How Hollywood Spoke to Women, 1930–1960* (New York: Alfred A. Knopf, 1993).

Behlmer, Rudy. *Behind the Scenes* (New York: Samuel French, 1990).

Black, Gregory D. *Hollywood Censored: Morality Codes, Catholics and the Movies* (New York: Cambridge University Press, 1994).

Blanshard, Paul. *American Freedom and Catholic Power* (Boston: Beacon Press, 1949).

Bondanella, Peter. *Italian Cinema: From Neorealism to the Present* (New York: Frederick Ungar, 1983).

Brownlow, Kevin. *Behind the Mask of Innocence* (New York: Knopf, 1990).

Byrnes, Timothy A. *Catholic Bishops in American Politics* (Princeton: Princeton University Press, 1991).

Carmen, Ira H. *Movies, Censorship and the Law* (Ann Arbor: University of Michigan Press, 1966).

Cooney, John. *The American Pope: The Life and Times of Francis Cardinal Spellman* (New York: Times Books, 1984).

Couvares, Francis G. *Movie Censorship and American Culture* (Washington, D.C.: Smithsonian Press, 1996).

Crosby, Donald F., S.J. *God, Church, and Flag: Senator Joseph R. McCarthy and the Catholic Church* (Chapel Hill, N.C.: University of North Carolina Press, 1987).

Curry, Ramona. *Too Much of a Good Thing: Mae West as Cultural Icon* (Minneapolis: University of Minnesota Press, 1996).

Cutler, John Henry. *Cardinal Cushing of Boston* (New York: Hawthorn Books, 1970).

deGrazia, Edward, and Roger Newman. *Banned Films: Movies, Censors and the First Amendment* (New York: R. R. Bowker, 1982).

Douglas, Susan. *Where the Girls Are: Growing Up Female with the Mass Media* (New York: Random House, 1994).

Drew, Bettina. *Nelson Algren: A Life on the Wild Side* (New York: G. P. Putman's Sons, 1989).

Facey, Paul W., S.J., *The Legion of Decency: A Sociological Analysis of the Emergence and Development of a Social Pressure Group* (New York: Arno Press, 1974).

Farber, Stephen. *The Movie Rating Game* (Washington, D.C.: Public Affairs Press, 1972).

Feldman, Charles M. *The National Board of Censorship of Motion Pictures, 1909–1922* (New York: Arno Press, 1977).

Fisher, James Terence. *The Catholic Counterculture in America, 1933–1962* (Chapel Hill, N.C.: University of North Carolina Press, 1989).

Forman, Henry James. *Our Movie Made Children* (New York: Macmillan, 1933).

Gabler, Neal. *An Empire of Their Own: How the Jews Invented Hollywood* (New York: Crown, 1988).

Gardiner, Harold C. *Catholic Viewpoint on Censorship* (Garden City, New York: Hanover House, 1958).

Gardiner, Harold C., and Moira Walsh. *Tenets for Movie Viewers* (Washington, D.C.: America Press, 1962).

Gardner, Gerald. *The Censorship Papers: Movie Censorship Letters from the Hays Office, 1934–1968* (New York: Dodd, Mead & Co., 1987).

Geist, Kenneth L. *Pictures Will Talk: The Life and Films of Joseph L. Mankiewicz* (New York: Da Capo Press, 1978).

Halsey, William. *The Survival of American Innocence: Catholicism in an Era of Disillusionment, 1920–1940* (Notre Dame: Notre Dame University Press, 1980).

Hays, Will. *The Memoirs of Will H. Hays* (Garden City, N.Y.: Doubleday, 1955).

Inglis, Ruth. *Freedom of the Movies: A Report on Self-Regulation* (Chicago: University of Chicago Press, 1947).

Izod, John. *Hollywood and the Box Office, 1895–1986* (New York: Columbia University Press, 1988).

Jacobs, Lea. *The Wages of Sin: Censorship and the Fallen Woman Film, 1928–1942* (Madison: University of Wisconsin Press, 1991).

Jones, James. *From Here To Eternity* (New York: Dell Publishing, 1951).

Jowett, Garth, Ian Jarvie, and Kathryn Fuller. *Children and the Movies: Media Influence and the Payne Fund Controversy* (New York: Cambridge University Press, 1996).

Jowett, Garth. *Film: The Democratic Art* (Boston: Little, Brown, 1976).

Kagan, Norman. *The Cinema of Stanley Kubrick* (New York: Holt, Rinehart & Winston, 1972).

Keyser, Les, and Barbara Keyser. *Hollywood and the Catholic Church: The Image of Roman Catholicism in the American Movies* (Chicago: Loyola University Press, 1984).

Leff, Leonard J., and Jerold L. Simmons. *The Dame in the Kimono: Hollywood, Censorship, & the Production Code from the 1920s to the 1960s* (New York: Grove Weidenfeld, 1990).

Leprohon, Pierre. *The Italian Cinema*, trans. Roger Greaves and Oliver Stallybrass (New York: Praeger Publishers, 1972).

Lord, Daniel. *Played By Ear* (Chicago: Loyola University Press, 1955).

McDonough, Peter. *Men Astutely Trained: A History of the Jesuits in the American Century* (New York: The Free Press, 1992).

Maland, Charles. *Chaplin and American Culture: The Evolution of a Star Image* (Princeton: Princeton University Press, 1989).

Marcus, Millicent. *Italian Film in the Light of Neorealism.* (Princeton: Princeton University Press, 1986).

Miller, Frank. *Censored Hollywood: Sex, Sin, & Violence on Screen* (Altanta: Turner Publishing, 1994).

Moley, Raymond. *The Hays Office* (New York: Bobbs–Merrill, 1945).

Murphy, Brenda. *Tennessee Williams and Elia Kazan: A Collaboration in the Theater* (New York: Cambridge University Press, 1992).

Murray, John Courtney, S.J. *We Hold These Truths: Catholic Reflections on the American Proposition* (Garden City, N.Y., Sheed & Ward, 1960).

Nash, Jay R., and Stanley R. Ross, eds. *The Motion Picture Guide* (Chicago: Cinebooks, 1985–7).

Nelson, Thomas A. *Kubrick: Inside A Film Artist's Maze* (Bloomington, Ind.: Indiana University Press, 1982).

O'Brien, David. *American Catholics and Social Reform* (New York: Oxford University Press, 1968).

Pauly, Thomas H. *An American Odyssey: Elia Kazan and American Culture* (Philadelphia: Temple University Press, 1983).

Peary, Gerald, ed., *Little Caesar* (Madison: University of Wisconsin Press, 1981).

Phillips, Gene D. *The Films of Tennessee Williams* (Philadelphia: Art Alliance Press, 1980).

Phillips, Gene D. *Stanley Kubrick: A Film Odyssey* (New York: Popular Library, 1975).

Pratley, Gerald. *The Cinema of Otto Preminger* (New York: A. S. Barnes, 1971).

Preminger, Otto. *Preminger: An Autobiography* (Garden City, New York: Doubleday, 1977).

Quigley, Martin. *Decency in Movies* (New York: Macmillan, 1937).

Randall, Richard S. *Censorship of the Movies* (Madison: University of Wisconsin Press, 1968).

Roffman, Peter, and Jim Purdy. *The Hollywood Social Problem Film: Madness, Despair, and Politics from the Depression to the Fifties* (Bloomington: Indiana University Press, 1981).

Rosen, Marjorie. *Popcorn Venus: Women, Movies and the American Dream.*(New York: Coward, McCann & Geohegan, 1973).

Russo, Vito. *The Celluloid Closet: Homosexuality in the Movies* (New York: Harper & Row, 1987).

Schatz, Thomas. *The Genius of the System: Hollywood Filmmaking in the Studio Era* (New York: Pantheon, 1988).

Schumach, Murray. *The Face on the Cutting Room Floor: The Story of Motion Picture and Television Censorship* (New York: William Morrow, 1964).

Skinner, James. *The Cross and the Cinema: The Legion of Decency and the National Catholic Office for Motion Pictures, 1933–1970* (Westport, Conn.: Praeger, 1993).

Sloan, Kay. *The Loud Silents: Origins of the Social Problem Film* (Chicago: University of Illinois Press, 1988).

Staiger, Janet. *Bad Women: Regulating Sexuality in Early American Cinema* (Minneapolis: University of Minnesota Press, 1995).

Thomas, Tony. *Howard Hughes in Hollywood* (Secaucus, N.J.: Citadel Press, 1985).

Vaughn, Stephen. *Ronald Reagan in Hollywood: Movies and Politics* (New York: Cambridge University Press, 1994).

Vizzard, Jack. *See No Evil: Life Inside a Hollywood Censor* (New York: Simon & Schuster, 1970).

Walsh, Frank, *Sin and Censorship: The Catholic Church and the Motion Picture Industry* (New Haven: Yale University Press, 1996).

Westin, Alan F. *The Miracle Case: The Supreme Court and the Movies.* InterUniversity Case Program No. 64 (Alabama: University of Alabama Press, 1961).

Williams, Tennessee. *Baby Doll* (London: Secker & Warburg, 1957).

Williams, Tennessee. *A Streetcar Named Desire* (New York: Dramatists Play Service, 1947).

Williams, Tennessee. *Suddenly Last Summer* (New York: New Directions, 1958).

Articles

Black, Gregory D., "Hollywood Censored: The Production Code Administration and the Hollywood Film Industry, 1930–1940," *Film History* 3 (1989), 167–89.

Black, Gregory D., "Movies, Politics and Censorship: The Production Code Administration and Political Censorship of Film Content," *Journal of Policy History* 3 (1991), 95–129.

Blanshard, Paul. "The Catholic Church as Censor," *Nation* 166 (May 1, 1948), 459–64.

Blanshard, Paul. "Roman Catholic Censorship," *Nation* 166 (May 8, 1948), 499–502.

Civardi, Luigi Msgr. "Motion Pictures as an Occasion of Sin," *Homiletic and Pastoral Review* 51 (Oct. 1950), 16–21.

Clancy, William P. "The Catholic as Philistine," *Commonweal* 53 (Mar. 16, 1951), 567–9.

Clancy, William P. "Freedom of the Screen," *Commonweal* 59 (Feb. 19, 1954), 500–2.

Corliss, Richard. "The Legion of Decency," *Film Comment* 4 (Summer 1969), 24–61.

Crowther, Bosley. "The Strange Case of 'The Miracle,'" *Atlantic* 187 (Apr. 1951), 35–9.

Dowling, Ellen. "The Derailment of 'A Streetcar Named Desire,'" *Literature/Film Quarterly* 9 (1981), 233–40.

"Duel in the Sun," *Life* 22 (Oct. 1947), 68–70.

Farrell, James T. "The Language of Hollywood," *Saturday Review of Literature* 27 (Aug. 5, 1944), 29–32.

Feldman, Harry. "'The Miracle' and the Constitution," *Sign* 30 (May 1951), 13–14.

Fitzgerald, John E. "What They Ask About The Legion of Decency," 89 *Ave Maria* (Jan. 3, 1959), 5–8.

Hayes, Paul J. "TeenAgers and Entertainment," *Catholic Preview of Entertainment* 5 (Mar. 1961), 18–23.

Kelly, Gerald, S.J., and John Ford, S.J. "The Legion of Decency," *Theological Studies* 18 (1957), 387–433.

Leff, Leonard, "A Test of American Film Censorship: *Who's Afraid of Virginia Woolf?*" in Peter Rollins, ed., *Hollywood as Historian* (Lexington: University Press of Kentucky, 1983), pp. 211–29.

Leff, Leonard, "The Breening of America," *PMLA* (May 1991), 432–5.

Little, Thomas Msgr. "The Modern Legion of Decency and Its Modern Outlook," *America* 113 (Dec. 11, 1965), 744–5.

MacMullan, Hugh. "Translating 'The Glass Menagerie' to Film," *Hollywood Quarterly* 5 (Fall 1950), 14–32.

McNulty, James A., D.D. "The Spirit of the Legion of Decency," 104 *America* (Mar. 11, 1961), 757–8.

Maltby, Richard. "The Genius of the Production Code," *Quarterly Review of Film & Video* 15 (Mar. 1994), 5–32.

Nicola, J. D. "New Look at the Legion of Decency," *Extension* 60 (Dec. 1965), 16–20.

Ryan, John. "Legion of Decency Under Fire," *Catholic Digest* 10 (Oct. 1946), 21–4.

Seldes, Gilbert. "Pressures and Pictures: I," *Nation* 172 (Feb. 3, 1951), 104–6.

Seldes, Gilbert. "Pressures and Pictures: II," *Nation* 172 (Feb. 10, 1951), 132–4.

Simmons, Jerold. "The Production Code under New Management: Geoffrey Shurlock, *The Bad Seed,* and *Tea and Sympathy*," *Journal of Popular Film and Television* 22 (Spring 1994), 3–10.

Skinner, James M. "The Tussle with Russell: *The Outlaw* as a Landmark in American Film Censorship," *North Dakota Quarterly* 46 (Winter 1981), 5–12.

Stone, Judy. "The Legion of Decency: What's Nude," *Ramparts* 4 (Sept. 1965), 43–55.

Vaughn, Stephen. "Financiers, Movie Producers, and the Church: Economic Origins of the Production Code," *Current Research in Film: Audiences, Economics, and the Law* 4 (1988), 211–17.

Vaughn, Stephen. "Morality and Entertainment: The Origins of the Motion Picture Production Code," *Journal of American History* 77 (June 1990), 39–65.

Walters, Fred. "The Supreme Court Ruling on *The Miracle* and *Pinky* Gives Censorship a Punch in the Blue Nose," *Theater Arts* 36 (Aug. 1952), 74–7.

Weber, Francis J. "The Legion of Decency," *America Ecclesiastical Review* 151 (Oct. 1964), 237–47.

"What's Happening to the Legion of Decency?" *Sign* 43 (Dec. 1963), 32–5, 74–7.

Whelan, Russell. "The Legion of Decency," *American Mercury* 60 (June 1945), 655–63.

Unpublished Materials

Linden, Kathryn Bertha. "The Film Censorship Struggle in the United States from 1926 to 1957, and the Social Values Involved," Ph.D. diss., School of Education, New York University, 1972.

Litzky, Leo. "Censorship of Motion Pictures in the United States: A History of Motion Picture Censorship and an Analysis of Its Most Important Aspects," Ph.D. diss., School of Education, New York University, 1947.

McLaughlin, Mary L. "A Study of the National Catholic Office for Motion Pictures," Ph.D. diss., Communication Arts, University of Wisconsin–Madison, 1974.

Phelen, John Martin, S.J. "The National Catholic Office for Motion Pictures: An Investigation of the Policy and Practice of Film Classifications," Ph.D. diss., Journalism, New York University, 1968.

Sargent, John Alan, "Self-Regulation: The Motion Picture Production Code, 1930–1961," Ph.D. diss., Speech/Theater, University of Michigan, 1963.

Turner, Jay. "Public Reaction to the Legion of Decency in the Public Press, 1934–1952." M.A. thesis, Mass Communications, University of Texas–Austin, 1984.

FILMOGRAPHY

Abbott and Costello Go to Mars, dir. Charles Lamont (Universal Intl., 1956)

Adventures of Tom Sawyer, The, dir. Norman Taurog (Selznick Intl. Pictures, 1938)

Advise and Consent, dir. Otto Preminger (Columbia/Alpha–Alpina, 1962)

African Queen, The, dir. John Huston (IFD/Romulus–Horizon, UK, 1951)

Alexander's Ragtime Band, dir. Henry King (20th C–Fox, 1938)

All My Sons, dir. Irving Reis (Universal, 1948)

All Quiet on the Western Front, dir. Lewis Milestone (Universal, 1930)

American in Paris, An, dir. Vincente Minnelli (MGM, 1951)

And God Created Woman (Et . . . Dieu créa la Femme), dir. Roger Vadim (Lena, UCIL/Cocinor, France, 1956)

Ann Vickers, dir. John Cromwell (RKO, 1933)

Anna Karenina, dir. Clarence Brown (MGM, 1935)

Apartment, The, dir. Billy Wilder (UA/Mirisch, 1960)

Arabian Knights, dir. John Rawlins (Universal, 1942)

Au Revoir les Enfants, dir. Louis Malle (Nouvelle Éditions de Films/MK2/Stella, 1987)

Babette's Feast, dir. Gabriel Axel (Panorama/Nordisk/Danish Film Institute, 1988)

Baby Doll, dir. Elia Kazan (WB, 1956)

Back Street, dir. Robert Stevenson (Universal, 1941)

Bad and the Beautiful, The, dir. Vincente Minnelli (MGM, 1952)

Barbary Coast, The, dir. Howard Hawks (Goldwyn, 1935)

Belle of the Nineties (orig. *It Ain't No Sin*), dir. Leo McCarey (Paramount, 1934)

Bells of St. Mary's, The, dir. Leo McCarey (RKO, 1945)

Ben-Hur, dir. William Wyler (MGM, 1959)

Best Years of Our Lives, dir. William Wyler (Goldwyn, 1946)

Bicycle Thief, The (Ladri di biciclette, a/k/a *Bicycle Thieves),* dir. Vittorio De Sica (PDS–ENIC, Italy, 1948)

Big Parade, The, dir. King Vidor (MGM, 1925)

Bill of Divorcement, A, dir. John Farrow (RKO, 1940)

Birth of a Nation, The, dir. D. W. Griffith (Epoch, 1915)

Bitter Rice (Riso amaro), dir. Giuseppe De Santis (Lux, Italy, 1949)

Black Narcissus, dir. Michael Powell (GFD/The Archers, 1946)

Blockade, dir. William Dieterle (UA, 1938)

Blonde Venus, dir. Josef von Sternberg (Paramount, 1932)

Blue Angel, The (Der blaue Engel), dir. Josef von Sternberg (UFA, Germany, 1930)

Boccaccio 70, dir. Federico Fellini ("Le tentazioni del dottor Antonio [The Temptation of Dr. Antonio]"), Luchino Visconti ("Il lavoro [The Job]"), Vittorio De Sica ("La riffa [The Raffle]") (20th C–Fox/CCC/Cineriz/Francinex/Gray Films, 1962)

Bombshell (a/k/a *Blonde Bombshell*), dir. Victor Fleming (MGM, 1933)

Bonnie and Clyde, dir. Arthur Penn (WB/Seven Arts/Tatira/Hiller, 1967)

Brave One, The, dir. Irving Rapper (King Brothers, 1956)

Bridge on the River Kwai, The, dir. David Lean (Columbia, 1957)

Buccaneer's Girl, dir. Frederick de Cordova (Universal Intl., 1949)

Bulldog Drummond Strikes Back, dir. Roy Del Ruth (UA/20th Century, 1934)

Caesar and Cleopatra, dir. Gabriel Pascal (Rank/Gabriel Pascal, UK, 1945)

Calabuch (a/k/a *The Rocket from Calabuch*), dir. Luis García Berlanga (Aguila/Constellaxione, 1956)

Cardinal, The, dir. Otto Preminger (Gamma, 1963)

Carnival in Flanders (La Kermesse heroïque), dir. Jacque Feyder (Tobis, 1935)

Carpetbaggers, The, dir. Edward Dmytryk (Paramount/Embassy, 1964)

Carnal Knowledge, dir. Mike Nichols (Avco Embassy/Icarus)

Casablanca, dir. Michael Curtiz (WB, 1942)

Cat Ballou, dir. Eliot Silverstein (Columbia, 1965)

Cat on a Hot Tin Roof, dir. Richard Brooks (MGM/Avon, 1958)

Cheaper by the Dozen, dir. Walter Lang (20th C–Fox, 1950)

Children's Hour, The, dir. William Wyler (UA/Mirisch, 1961)

City Streets, dir. Rouben Mamoulian (Paramount, 1931)

Clockwork Orange, A, dir. Stanley Kubrick (WB/Polaris, 1971)

Come Back, Little Sheba, dir. Daniel Mann (Paramount, 1952)

Confessions of a Nazi Spy, dir. Anatole Litvak (WB, 1939)

Conformist, The, dir. Bernardo Bertolucci (Mars/Marianne/Maran, 1970)

Coralie & Cie, dir. Alberto Cavalcanti (Films Jean Dehelly, France, 1933)

Corn Is Green, The, dir. Irving Rapper (WB, 1945)

Court Martial of Billy Mitchell, The, dir. Otto Preminger (United States Pictures, 1955)

Crossfire, dir. Edward Dmytryk (RKO, 1947)

Dancing Lady, dir. Robert Z. Leonard (MGM, 1933)

Darling, dir. John Schlesinger (Anglo–Amalgamated/Vic/Appia, UK, 1965)

Day in the Country, A (Une Partie de campagne), dir. Jean Renoir (Panthéon/Films de la Pléiade/Pierre Braunberger, France, 1936; U.S. release as part of *The Ways of Love*, 1950)

Dead End, dir. William Wyler (Goldwyn, 1936)

Deep Throat, dir. Gerry Damiano (Aquarius Releasing, 1973)

Design for Living, dir. Ernst Lubitsch (Paramount, 1933)

Desire, dir. Frank Borzage (Paramount, 1936)

Dr. Strangelove, or How I Learned to Stop Worrying and Love the Bomb, dir. Stanley Kubrick (Columbia/Stanley Kubrick, 1963)

Don't Go Near the Water, dir. Charles Walters (MGM/Avon, 1957)

Doorway to Hell, dir. Archie Mayo (WB, 1930)

Duck Soup, dir. Leo McCarey (Paramount, 1933)

Duel in the Sun, dir. King Vidor (Selznick Intl. Pictures, 1946)

Easy Rider, dir. Dennis Hopper (Columbia/Pando/Raybert, 1969)

Ecstasy (Extase), dir Gustav Machaty (Electra/Jewel, Czechoslovakia, 1932)

Everybody's Acting, dir. Marshall Neilan (Famous Players–Lasky, 1926)

Exodus, dir. Otto Preminger (UA/Carlyle/Alpha, 1960)

Farewell to Arms, A, dir. Frank Borzage (Paramount, 1932)

Finger Points, The, dir. John F. Dillon (First National, 1931)

Fireworks, dir. Kenneth Anger (Filmmakers Cooperative, 1947)

For Whom the Bell Tolls, dir. Sam Wood (Paramount, 1943)

Forever Amber, dir. Otto Preminger (20th C–Fox, 1947)

Frankenstein, dir. James Whale (Universal, 1931)

French Connection, The, dir. William Friedkin (20th C–Fox/Philip D'Antoni)

French Line, The, dir. Lloyd Bacon (RKO, 1954)

From Here to Eternity, dir. Fred Zinnemann (Columbia, 1953)

Front Page, dir. Lewis Milestone (Caddo, 1931)

Fury, dir. Fritz Lang (MGM, 1936)

Garden of Allah, The, dir. Richard Boleslawski (Selznick Intl. Pictures/UA 1936)

Garden of Eden, dir. Max Nosseck (Excelsior Pictures, 1957)

Gaslight, dir. Thorold Dickinson (British National, UK, 1939)

Gene Krupa Story, The, dir. Don Weis (Columbia, 1959)

Gentleman's Agreement, dir. Elia Kazan (20th C–Fox, 1947)

Germany, Year Zero (Germania, anno zero), dir. Roberto Rossellini (Union Générale Cinématographique/DEFA, France/Italy, 1947)

Glass Menagerie, The, dir. Irving Rapper (WB/Charles Feldman, 1950)

Godzilla, King of the Monsters (Gojira), dir. Inoshiro Honda (Toho, Japan, 1954)

Gone with the Wind, dir. Victor Fleming [George Cukor et al., uncredited] (MGM/Selznick Intl. Pictures, 1939)

Graduate, The, dir. Mike Nichols (UA/Embassy, 1967)

Grand Illusion (La Grande Illusion), dir. Jean Renoir (RAC, France, 1937)

Grapes of Wrath, The, dir. John Ford (20th C–Fox, 1940)

Greatest Show on Earth, The, dir. Cecil B. DeMille (Paramount/Cecil B. DeMille, 1952)

Guess Who's Coming to Dinner?, dir. Stanley Kramer (Columbia, 1967)

Gunfight at OK Corral, dir. John Sturges (Paramount, 1957)

Harder They Fall, The, dir. Mark Robson (Columbia, 1956)

Hell's Angels, dir. Howard Hughes (Caddo, 1930)

Hercules, dir. Pietro Francisci (Lux/Galatea, Italy, 1959)

High Noon, dir. Fred Zinnemann (Stanley Kramer, 1952)

Home of the Brave, dir. Mark Robeson (Stanley Kramer, 1949)

How Green Was My Valley, dir. John Ford (20th C–Fox, 1941)

Hunchback of Notre Dame, The, dir. William Dieterle (RKO, 1939)

I Married a Communist for the FBI, dir. Robert Stevenson (RKO, 1949)

Idiot's Delight, dir. Clarence Brown (MGM, 1939)

I'm No Angel, dir. Wesley Ruggles (Paramount, 1933)

Imitation of Life, dir. Douglas Sirk (Universal Intl., 1959)

Intruder in the Dust, dir. Clarence Brown (MGM, 1949)

It Can't Happen Here (MGM, unproduced)

It's a Wonderful Life, dir. Frank Capra (Liberty Films/RKO, 1946)

Joan of Arc, dir. Victor Fleming (RKO, 1948)

Jofroi, dir. Marcel Pagnol (Les Auteurs Associés, France, 1934; U.S. release as part of *The Ways of Love,* 1950)

Jules et Jim, dir. François Truffaut (Films du Carrosse/SEDIF, France, 1961)

Keys of the Kingdom, dir. John M. Stahl (20th C–Fox, 1944)

King Kong, dir. Merian C. Cooper and Ernest B. Schoedsack (RKO, 1933)

Kitty Foyle, dir. Sam Wood (RKO, 1940)

Klondike Annie, dir. Raoul Welsh (Paramount, 1936)

La Dolce Vita, dir. Federico Fellini (Riama/Pathé, Italy, 1960)

La Ronde, dir Max Ophuls (Sacha Gordine, 1950)

La Strada (a/k/a *The Road*), dir. Federico Fellini (Ponti/de Laurentiis, Italy, 1954)

Last Picture Show, The, dir. Peter Bogdanovich (Columbia, 1971)

Last Tango in Paris, dir. Bernardo Bertolucci (Les Artistes Associés/PEA/UA)

Laura, dir. Otto Preminger (20th C–Fox, 1944)

Le Messager, dir. Raymond Rouleau (Films Albatros, France, 1937)

Les Liaisons dangereuses, dir. Roger Vadim (Films Marceau, 1959)

Les Miserables, dir. Richard Boleslawski (20th Century, 1935)

Little Caesar, dir. Mervyn Le Roy (WB, 1930)

Lolita, dir. Stanley Kubrick (MGM/ Seven Arts, UK, 1962)

Long Day's Journey into Night, dir. Sidney Lumet (Ely Landau, 1961)

Longest Day, The, dir. Andrew Marton, Bernhard Wicki, and Ken Annakin (20th C–Fox, 1962)

Lost Boundaries, dir. Alfred Werker (Film Classics, 1949)

Lost Continent, dir. Michael Carreras (Hammer, UK, 1968)

M (*M, Mörder unter Uns*), dir. Fritz Lang (Nero Film, Germany, 1931); remake dir. Joseph Losey (Columbia, 1951)

Mademoiselles Ma Mère, dir. Henri Decoin (Regina Productions, France, 1937)

Man for All Seasons, A, dir. Fred Zinnemann (Columbia/Highland, 1966)

Man with the Golden Arm, The, dir. Otto Preminger (Otto Preminger, 1956)

Martin Luther, dir. Irving Pichel (Louis B. Rochemont/Lutheran Church Productions, 1953)

Mating Call, The, dir. James Cruze (Caddo, 1928)

Ménage Ultra Moderne (*Ultra Modern Couples*), dir. ? (Joinville Studios, France, 1932)

Merry Widow, The (a/k/a *The Lady Dances*), dir. Ernst Lubitsch (MGM, 1934)

Miracle, The (*Il miracolo*), dir. Roberto Rossellini (Tania Film, Italy, 1948; U.S. release as part of *The Ways of Love,* 1950)

Miracle on 34th Street, dir. George Seaton (20th C–Fox, 1947)

Mission to Moscow, dir. Michael Curtiz (WB, 1943)

Modern Times, dir. Charles Chaplin (Chaplin/United Artists, 1936)

Mom and Dad, dir. William Beaudine (Hygienic Productions, 1944)

Moon Is Blue, The, dir. Otto Preminger (Otto Preminger, 1953)

Morocco, dir. Josef von Sternberg (Paramount, 1930)

Mr. Cohen Takes a Walk, dir. William Beaudine (WB, 1935)

Murder in the Cathedral, dir. George Hollering (George Hollering, UK, 1951)

My Man Godfrey, dir. Henry Koster (Universal Intl., 1957)

My Son John, dir. Leo McCarey (Paramount, 1952)

Never on Sunday (Pote tin Kyriaki), dir. Jules Dassin (Lopert/Melinafilm, Greece, 1959)

Northwest Passage, dir. King Vidor (MGM, 1940)

Now, Voyager, dir. Irving Rapper (WB, 1942)

Of Human Bondage, dir. John Cromwell (RKO, 1934); remake dir. Henry Hathaway (MGM/Seven Arts, 1964)

On the Waterfront, dir. Elia Kazan (Columbia/Sam Spiegel, 1954)

Only Angels Have Wings, dir. Howard Hawks (Columbia, 1939)

Open City (Roma, città aperta, a/k/a Rome, Open City), dir. Roberto Rossellini (Minerva/Excelsa, 1945)

Our Daily Bread, dir. King Vidor (UA/King Vidor, 1934)

Outlaw, The, dir. Howard Hughes (Howard Hughes, 1943)

Paisan (Paisà), dir. Roberto Rossellini (Foreign Films Productions/OFI, Italy, 1946)

Paleface, The, dir. Norman Z. McLeod (Paramount, 1948)

Paths of Glory, The, dir. Stanley Kubrick (UA/Bryna, 1957)

Pawnbroker, The, dir. Sidney Lumet (Landau–Unger, 1965)

Peyton Place, dir. Mark Robson (20th C–Fox, 1957)

Pied Piper, The, dir. Irving Pichel (20th C–Fox, 1942)

Pinky, dir. Elia Kazan (20th C–Fox, 1949)

Place in the Sun, A, dir. George Stevens (Paramount/George Stevens, 1951)

Prince of Players, dir. Philip Dunne (20th C–Fox, 1955)

Psycho, dir. Alfred Hitchcock (Paramount/Shamley/Alfred Hitchcock, 1960)

Public Enemy, The, dir. William Wellman (WB, 1931)

Quiet Man, The, dir. John Ford (Republic/Argosy, 1952)

Racket, The, dir. Lewis Milestone (Caddo, 1928)

Rainmaker, The, dir. Joseph Anthony (Paramount/Hal Wallis, 1956)

Rebel without a Cause, dir. Nicholas Ray (WB, 1955)

Rebecca, dir. Alfred Hitchcock (Selznick Int'l. Pictures, 1940)

Red Menace, dir. R. G. Springsteen (Republic, 1949)

Red River, dir. Howard Hawks (UA/Monterey, 1948)

Robe, The, dir. Henry Koster (20th C–Fox, 1953)

Roman Holiday, dir. William Wyler (Paramount, 1953)

Rose scarlatte (a/k/a Twenty-Four Red Roses), dir. Vittorio De Sica (Amato–Era Film, 1940)

Rose Tatoo, The, dir Daniel Mann (Paramount, 1955)

Scarface: Shame of the Nation, dir. Howard Hawks (Caddo, 1932)

Search, The, dir. Fred Zinnemann (MGM/Praesens Film, 1948)
Secret Six, The, dir. George Hill (MGM, 1931)
Sex Kittens Go to College, dir. Albert Zugsmith (Allied Artists, 1960)
Shanghai Express, dir. Josef von Sternberg (Paramount, 1932)
Shining, The, dir. Stanley Kubrick (WB/Stanley Kubrick, UK, 1980)
Shoeshine (Sciuscià), dir. Vittorio de Sica (Paolo W. Tamburella, Italy, 1946)
Sign of the Cross, dir. Cecil B. DeMille (Paramount, 1932)
Since You Went Away, dir. John Cromwell (UA, 1944)
Singing in the Rain, dir. Gene Kelly and Stanley Donen (MGM, 1952)
Snake Pit, The, dir. Anatole Litvak (20th C–Fox, 1948)
Snows of Kilimanjaro, dir. Henry King (20th C–Fox, 1952)
Song of Bernadette, The, dir. Henry King (20th C–Fox, 1943)
Song of Russia, dir. Gregory Ratoff (MGM, 1943)
Spartacus, dir. Stanley Kubrick (Universal Intl./Bryna, 1960)
Splendor in the Grass, dir. Elia Kazan (WB/NBI, 1961)
Stalag 17, dir. Billy Wilder (Paramount, 1953)
Star Is Born, A, dir. William Wellman (Selznick Intl. Pictures, 1937)
Star Witness, dir. William Wellman (WB, 1931)
Storm Center, dir. Daniel Taradash (Columbia, 1956)
Stranger, The, dir. Orson Welles (International Pictures/RKO, 1946)
Streetcar Named Desire, A, dir. Elia Kazan (Charles K. Feldman, 1951)
Stromboli (Stromboli, terra di dio), dir. Roberto Rossellini (Be-Ro/RKO, Italy,
  1949)
Suddenly Last Summer, dir. Joseph L. Mankiewicz (Columbia, 1959)
Summertime, dir. David Lean (Lopert/London Films, 1955)
Susan Lenox: Her Fall and Rise, dir. Robert Z. Leonard (MGM, 1931)
Swiss Family Robinson, dir. Ken Annakin (Disney, UK, 1960)
Taxi Driver, dir. Martin Scorsese (Bill–Phillips, 1976)
Tea and Sympathy, dir. Vincente Minnelli (MGM, 1956)
Ten Commandments, The, dir. Cecil B. DeMille (Paramount/Famous Players–
  Lasky, 1923)
These Three, dir. William Wyler (Samuel Goldwyn, 1936)
They Won't Forget, dir. Mervyn Le Roy (WB, 1937)
Three Coins in the Fountain, dir. Jean Negulesco (20th C–Fox, 1954)
3:10 to Yuma, dir. Delmer Daves (Columbia, 1957)
Thirty Seconds over Tokyo, dir. Mervyn Le Roy (MGM, 1944)
This Thing Called Love, dir. Alexander Hall (Columbia, 1941)
Tobacco Road, dir. John Ford (20th C–Fox, 1941)
Tom Jones, dir. Tony Richardson (UA/Woodfall, 1963)
Tom Sawyer, dir. John Cromwell (Paramount, 1930)
Twelve Angry Men, dir. Sidney Lumet (UA/Orion–Nova, 1957)
Two Arabian Knights, dir. Lewis Milestone (Caddo, 1927)
Two-Faced Woman, dir. George Cukor (MGM, 1941)
2001: A Space Odyssey, Stanley Kubrick (MGM/Stanley Kubrick, 1968)
Umberto D, dir. Vittorio de Sica (Dear Films, Italy, 1952)
Viva Zapata!, dir. Elia Kazan (20th C–Fox, 1952)

Walking Dead, The, dir. Michael Curtiz (WB, 1936)

Ways of Love, The, comprising Renoir's *A Day in the Country*, Pagnol's *Jofroi*, and Rossellini's *The Miracle* (U.S. distrib. 1950)

We Live Again, dir. Rouben Mamoulian (Goldwyn, 1934)

West Side Story, dir. Robert Wise and Jerome Robbins (Mirisch/Seven Arts/Beta, 1961)

Who's Afraid of Virginia Woolf?, dir. Mike Nichols (WB, 1966)

Wife versus Secretary, dir. Clarence Brown (MGM, 1936)

Wild Bunch, The, dir. Sam Peckinpah (WB/Seven Arts, 1969)

Will Success Spoil Rock Hunter?, dir. Frank Tashlin (20th C–Fox, 1957)

Wilson, dir. Henry King (20th C–Fox, 1944)

Wizard of Oz, The, dir. Victor Fleming (MGM, 1939)

Yellow Sky, dir. William Wellman (20th C–Fox, 1948)

Young Mr. Lincoln, dir. John Ford (20th C–Fox, 1939)

INDEX